Sustainability and Cities

SUSTAINABILITY AND CITIES

Overcoming Automobile Dependence

Peter Newman • *Jeffrey Kenworthy*

ISLAND PRESS

Washington, D.C.   Covelo, California

Library of Congress Cataloging-in-Publication Data

Newman, Peter, Dr.
    Sustainability and cities : overcoming automobile dependence /
  Peter Newman and Jeffrey Kenworthy.
      p.   cm.
    Includes bibliographical references and index.
    ISBN 1–55963–660–2 (alk. paper)
    1. Urban transportation policy.   2. Urban transportation—
  Environmental aspects.   3. Sustainable development.   4. Land use,
  Urban.   5. Automobile—Environmental aspects.   I. Kenworthy,
  Jeffrey R., 1955–   . II. Title
    HE305.N483   1998   98–42239
    388.4—dc21   CIP

Printed on recycled, acid-free paper

Manufactured in the United States of America
10 9 8

For Sam and Nathanael

Contents

Preface

A meeting of environmentalists in early 1990 focused on the need for the future environmental agenda to address sustainability in cities. Significantly, the First International Ecocity Conference was held at Berkeley, California, where so much of the early environmental movement had started. Many of the participating long-term environmentalists expressed a new concern for the city; conference organizer Richard Register expressed it this way:

> While making small conscientious adjustments in our lives because we are disturbed by ecological degeneration of our planet, we have somehow failed to notice that the largest edifice made by human beings— the city—is radically out of sync with healthy life systems on earth, and is functioning in nearly complete disregard of its long-term sustenance.
>
> Many of us believe something is very right about our life in our cities. We seem to be a sociable species and cities serve this sociability ... now if only we can make cities fit gracefully into the world we share with all other natural creations.

Since that conference there has been a lot of activity by groups trying to demonstrate how ecological matters can be integral to a city, as well as substantial literature and many conferences on what constitutes a more ecological city. The process has now become a global one with the emergence of an international sustainability agenda and with every nation, region, and city trying to see how they can relate to this issue of simultaneously solving economic and social matters along with the ecological.

This book tries to show how sustainability must be an urban issue, that cities are a necessary focus for this global agenda. We place a particular emphasis on the need to address automobile dependence—that is, where cities assume the use of an automobile in their design, infrastructure, and operation. We are therefore rarely far away from this critical issue, whether we are addressing matters of energy, greenhouse gases and smog, or stormwater, sewage, and other greening issues.

Many books explore the problems associated with automobile dependence. We, however, are trying to show that the new sustainability agenda must focus on finding out how to overcome such intractable problems as automobile dependence. Thus we are constantly seeking to provide a hopeful message by showing how some cities and communities within cities are implementing this agenda.

The land use and urban form of cities are, as we show, fundamentally shaped by priorities in transportation. Those priorities are influenced by many economic, social, and political factors, but the essential character of a city's land use comes down to how it manages its transportation. With this as our major context, we try to show how all elements of the sustainability agenda for cities can be accommodated. But if attempts are made to address these issues without dealing with crucial underlying transportation issues, then we are largely just whistling in the wind.

Chapters 1 through 3 of this book define the concept of sustainability, show how this applies to cities and automobile dependence, and examine the extent of automobile dependence using a new survey of global cities that updates our previous study (Newman and Kenworthy, 1989a).

Chapter 4 presents a theory of how cities can overcome automobile dependence and provides a series of case studies showing the potential that is now being demonstrated around the globe. Chapter 5 examines how other sustainability issues having to do with water, waste, and greening can be managed simultaneously as we overcome automobile dependence.

Chapters 6 and 7 examine the process of professional praxis in cities in light of the new sustainability agenda as well as the kind of ethical base needed to ensure that we take this critical set of issues seriously.

Chapter 8 summarizes the book by answering the questions set out below.

Questions Posed by This Book

This book attempts to guide the process of developing more sustainable cities by trying to answer the following questions:

Chapter 1: What is sustainability? How does sustainability apply to cities? What are sustainability goals and indicators for a city? How does a city make a Sustainability Plan? How can Sustainability Plans help a city move forward? How does city size relate to sustainability?

Chapter 2: How are cities shaped? What is automobile dependence? How does sustainability relate to automobile dependence? How has sustainability been addressed in other eras of city development (Walking City and Transit City eras)? Can Auto City problems be solved by incremental changes (largely engineering) or do they require more fundamental urban system changes? What are the new economic forces confronting the Auto City? Are globalization and information technology leading to greater or less automobile dependence? What are the social views about automobile dependence and the continuing provision of Auto City infrastructure? What kinds of scenarios face Auto Cities in an era of oil depletion?

Chapter 3: What are the patterns of automobile dependence in global cities? How do transportation patterns relate to technology, infrastructure, economics, and urban form? What are the trends in automobile use, transit, and density? How do the direct and indirect economic costs of transportation vary in cities? What does this suggest about the future of Auto Cities?

Chapter 4: What are the myths about the inevitability of the Auto City? How can cities reduce their automobile dependence? Why is city planning so important to reducing automobile dependence? What is a future "Sustainable" City vision with reduced automobile dependence? How can this city be achieved in stages? What cities are already showing reduced automobile dependence?

Chapter 5: How do other aspects of sustainability, such as management of the water cycle, solid waste, urban agriculture, and greening, fit into the future "Sustainable" City concept? Why are local, community-scale options proving to be more sustainable? Is there a conflict between greener cities and lower-energy cities? Why is there conflict over density and transit in sustainability discussions, and can this be resolved? What is local urban ecology, where is it happening, and how does it relate to global urban sustainability?

Chapter 6: How has urban professional praxis been shaped by modernism and the Auto City? How is urban professional praxis now being challenged by post-modernism and sustainability? What is the organic city tradition? Can the organic city tradition be a guide for future professional praxis? What are some detailed guidelines for professional praxis in such areas as sustainability in new development, growth management, water-sensitive design, the new urbanism, economic impacts of urban options, physical planning targets, and better transit–land use integration?

Chapter 7: What are the ethical foundations for city sustainability from traditions of local ecology, human ecology, and urban ecology? What spiritual tradition do they come from? How can individuals and cities express these traditions today—in particular, how do they relate to the Auto City? What is the role of the community in groups such as churches and community artists? Is there hope for sustainability in our cities?

Motivations and Sources for This Book

The book has two major motivations that arise from the two complementary sources from which it comes: academic teaching and community involvement.

Academic Teaching

First, the book comes from our experience teaching courses on three continents: to master's students in city policy and undergraduate students in environmental science at our alma mater, Murdoch University in Perth, Australia; to undergraduate urban design students at the Royal Danish Academy of Fine Arts in Copenhagen; and to master's students in city planning at the University of Pennsylvania in Philadelphia. Thus it has origins in trying to make sense of the various approaches to cities and to sustainability in the academic world. But academia is only one aspect of life, and sustainability is not an issue discovered nor won in academia.

Involvement

This book also comes from our struggles at implementing sustainability in cities and from observing the struggles of others as they attempt to demonstrate what this new world is about. Thus it is influenced by our involvement in:

- *our local community,* in local politics in our home town of Fremantle, with issues such as saving the Fremantle railway and determining how to rebuild and extend it, stopping a major highway planned through the city and then implementing traffic calming, struggling with how to reverse the decline of our inner city and then how to guide it in more environmentally and socially acceptable paths when the revitalization occurred, and involvement in local greening projects, community arts projects and in local churches struggling with the spirituality of sustainability and the city;

- *our broader Australian community*, in similar issues across our continent involving local, state, and federal governments, particularly our involvement in efforts to try to stop major city freeways in each capital city, to develop a vision for Melbourne's transit system and a new approach to planning Australia's capital of Canberra, to design an urban village for the city of Newcastle, and to participate in the Australian Better Cities program, the Ecologically Sustainable Development process, and the *Australian State of the Environment Report;* and

- *our global community*, through invitations to help groups in cities worldwide that are struggling to redirect big road projects into more sustainable city building, through visits to communities that have won victories for sustainability in transportation, water, waste, and greening, to find out how they did it, and through consulting engagements and attendance at the many international meetings of agencies from the UN, OECD, APEC, and World Bank.

This book is therefore a combination of textbook and life story. We hope that it serves as both a source of learning and of inspiration on how to make a more sustainable city. Its inspiration will most likely come from the many communities around the world whose stories of hope in city sustainability we have tried to weave into our more academic analysis. To those groups we owe a debt of gratitude for the time they have given us and for the work they are doing. We are also indebted to the many urban professionals who helped us with data on their cities. We hope we have been able to do justice to both your challenges and your achievements.

This book has been emerging for twenty-five years, and the work on which it is based is ongoing. We accept any errors in these pages as ours and would also like to learn where it is missing the mark and to hear other stories of sustainability and cities.

Acknowledgments

This book has been many years in preparation. It has evolved out of the authors' long involvement in teaching, research, and community action at local, national, and international levels. As such, there are innumerable people along the way who deserve to be personally acknowledged, but only a few of whom we can list in this brief overview.

First, we would like to thank all the students in the many courses and lectures we have given, at home and around the world, who have provided beneficial feedback and inspiration and who have helped us refine some of the work in this book. In particular, Tom Gallagher, Mark Bachels, Jan Scheurer, and David Wake assisted with certain parts of the book.

Much of this book was written overseas on the authors' respective study leaves at the Royal Danish Academy of Fine Arts (Urban Design) in Copenhagen, the University of Pennsylvania (City and Regional Planning) in Philadelphia, the University of British Columbia (School of Community and Regional Planning) in Vancouver, and the University of Colorado (College of Architecture and Planning) in Boulder. The authors are grateful for the support and friendly, stimulating atmosphere provided by these institutions and in particular Professor Spenser Havlick, from the University of Colorado, whose commitment to sustainable cities is so inspirational.

The research in this book could never have been undertaken without the tireless support of hundreds of people in government departments and other institutions worldwide who have supplied data and other information for their particular cities. This help has been given in the face of increasing workloads and pressures, which seem to be a global phenomenon in every walk of life, and so we are truly thankful that people still find the time to help research efforts such as this one. We trust that the book in some way recompenses at least a few of those people by providing perspectives on the many vexing policy issues at the heart of urban planning and transportation with which they must grapple every day.

The authors have also been privileged to work with many dedicated community groups striving to create better urban environments, whether through trying to stop freeways, campaigning for better transit, or simply setting up community gardens. From all these people we have learned a great deal, and we hope that some of the case studies in this book reflect at least a little of their invaluable work. We also trust that the book will become a valuable resource and inspiration in furthering the indispensable role such groups play in fighting for more livable and sustainable urban environments. We thank you for your inspiration.

In addition to our more general acknowledgments, we cannot fail to thank a number of our colleagues at the Institute for Science and Technology Policy (ISTP) for their support: Peter Vintila, Laura Stocker, Ian Barns, John Phillimore, Dora Marinova, Michael Booth, Patsy Hallen, and Aidan Davidson. Our research students have been central in developing much of the data in this book as well as many of the fine graphics. First, we thank Felix Laube for a very large amount of the data collection on global cities and for his brilliant graphs of the resulting global cities data. We also acknowledge the work of Paul Barter, based in Kuala Lumpur, who was primarily responsible for the collection of data on Southeast Asian and East Asian cities, along with specific help from Chamlong Poboon on Bangkok data, Benedicto Guia, Jr., on Manila data, and Hu Gang on data for Beijing. We also want to thank Tamim Raad of the University of British Columbia's School of Community and Regional Planning for his assistance with developing the data on Canadian cities while on an internship at ISTP. Mike Mouritz developed a lot of the ideas on urban water systems with us while pursuing his Ph.D., and we appreciate the many long conversations with him about the nature of sustainability.

There are a number of other people we wish to thank for their contributions to the book. We wish to thank our publisher, Island Press, and in particular editor Heather Boyer, for keeping us on task and for obtaining a considerable number of peer reviews of the manuscript. These have been invaluable in helping to refine the contents of the book. In the final stages of manuscript preparation, Lena Eskilsson and Karin Book from Lund University in Sweden were invaluable assistants, and they were helped by Vanessa Karafilis and Jesse Vintila. Our secretaries, Susan Davidson, Rosalina Stone, and Sally Paulin, were always there to keep us going as we tried, not always successfully, to balance work and writing.

Finally, our families have lived with this project for as long as we have, and we are indebted to them for their patience and support.

Chapter 1

The Concept of Sustainability and Its Relationship to Cities

The Concept of Sustainability

Sustainable development, or *sustainability* for short, is easily understood at its most basic level. It means simply that in a global context any economic or social development should improve, not harm, the environment. This concept guides our book and, as is shown below, has developed from a global political process over the last three decades of the twentieth century into one that now touches every part of society.

Nevertheless, sustainability is one of the most diversely applied concepts among academics and professionals discussing the future. It has cut across all disciplines and professions and has developed many complexities.[1]

In whatever way sustainability is defined and analyzed, it is important to see that its roots did not come so much from academic discussion as from a global political process.

Sustainability and Global Politics

The first elements of sustainability emerged in the global arena at the 1972 UN Conference on the Human Environment in Stockholm. At this conference, 113 nations pledged to begin cleaning up the environment and, most importantly, to begin the process of tackling environmental issues on a global scale. The problems of air pollution, water pollution, and chemical contamination do not recognize borders. It was acknowledged, for example, that it is not possible for DDT or PCBs or radioactive materials to be released anywhere without it affecting everyone. Natural resource depletion was also discussed since awareness had grown that depletion of forests, groundwater, soils, and fishstocks has impact across national boundaries.

Concern about the global environment was very high. Evidence was presented at Stockholm that the scale of the human economy was now significant relative to the natural environment. For example, the flow of human energy (mostly in settlements) was now roughly equal to the flow of solar energy through ecosystems, with inevitable impacts from the wastes (Newman, 1974).

1

This sense of limits was not new for many nations. In the nineteenth century a similar sense of limits drove Americans to set aside the first national parks as they realized that their apparently limitless new frontier had reached the West Coast. George Marsh's book *Man and Nature: Or Physical Geography as Modified by Human Action*, first published in 1864, analyzed the environmental impacts of U.S. urban and rural development. One hundred years later this sense of limits had become a global phenomenon as the last frontier lands were being developed.

The effects of human activity on this biosphere were also beginning to impact human welfare negatively. The specter of Malthus was raised as a global phenomenon but focused on the rapidly growing areas of the Third World, where it was thought that much of the world's future growth and impact would occur (e.g., Ehrlich and Ehrlich, 1977).

This environmental sensitivity is, however, only one aspect of sustainability. The Third World was not so impressed by this new environmental globalism. The new agenda was rapidly turning to one of antigrowth as environmentalists saw the rapacious consumption of natural resources as inevitably linked to economic development. Third World nations saw the agenda as just another way to prevent them from attaining their development goals. The 1 billion people living in abject poverty, with not even enough food to eat, did seem to have some legitimate claim on more of the world's resources. Thus the UN established the World Commission on Environment and Development in 1983 to try to resolve this fundamental conflict. In 1987 the Commission published *Our Common Future*, or the Brundtland Report, which launched into common parlance the phrase *sustainable development*. This was then given form, as shown below, at the 1992 Earth Summit in Rio de Janeiro.

Sustainability was presented as an agenda to simultaneously solve the global environmental problem and to facilitate the economic development of the poor, particularly those in the Third World. Whereas in 1972 the environment had been placed on the global political agenda, in 1992 the environment was placed on the global economic agenda. Thus the principles of sustainability can be distilled into four broad policies that have since become the basis for much global action.

Principles of Global Sustainability

The following four principles are derived from the Brundtland Report and are the fundamental approaches to global sustainability that must apply simultaneously to any approach to the future.

1. *The elimination of poverty, especially in the Third World, is necessary not just on human grounds but as an environmental issue.*

The Brundtland Report presented evidence from around the globe that poverty is one factor degrading the environment because populations grow rapidly when they are based on subsistence agriculture or fishing or plant collection. In the past, the population of subsistence communities was controlled by high death rates, but the globalization of health care has meant that there is no way forward to a new equilibrium but to reduce birth rates. This seems only to occur sustainably when families want fewer children, not more, and in subsistence economies children are a source of wealth and security (United Nations, 1987).

Where economic and social development do not occur and populations continue growing, the environment inevitably suffers. This feeds back in a poverty cycle—for example, much of the Rwanda tragedy in the mid 1990s has been traced to this process (UN Centre for Human Settlements, 1997). Grassroots economic and social development (particularly women's rights) are necessary to break this cycle (United Nations, 1987). The alternative is a constant degradation of the "commons" as more forest is cleared, more soil is overgrazed, more fisheries are destocked (Hardin, 1968). Thus Third World economic and social development are precursors to global sustainability.

2. The First World must reduce its consumption of resources and production of wastes.

The average American (or Australian) consumes natural resources at a rate 50 times that of the average Indian, and the poorest groups in abject poverty across the world consume 500 times less. Raising the standard of living of the global poor from 1/500th to 1/50th would not be a huge extra strain on resources. The primary responsibility for reducing impact on global resources lies in the rich part of the world.

Such a goal cannot be achieved without economic and social change. For example, industry cannot continue with 1980s machinery; it must develop new technology for replacing CFCs, for using less energy, and for switching to new renewable fuels and more efficient materials. Such change requires economic and social development. Cities will not be less energy-intensive if they are frozen in their sprawling 1980s structures, and they can rebuild in more compact, transit-oriented forms only if they are growing economically and socially. Thus First World economic and social development are precursors to global sustainability, but they must be much less resource-intensive in the future.

3. Global cooperation on environmental issues is no longer a soft option.

Hazardous wastes, greenhouse gases, CFCs, and the loss of biological diversity are examples of environmental problems that will not be solved if some nations decide to hide from the necessary changes. The spread of international best practice on these issues is not a management fad, nor a conspiracy for world domination from certain industries or advanced nations—it is essential for the future of the world. Thus a global orientation is a precursor to understanding sustainability.

4. Change toward sustainability can occur only with community-based approaches that take local cultures seriously.

Most of the debate on sustainability has been through UN conferences and high-level international meetings. However, it is recognized that this can only create the right signals for change, it cannot force the kinds of changes discussed above. These will come only when local communities determine how to resolve their economic and environmental conflicts in ways that create simultaneous improvement of both. Thus an orientation to local cultures and community development is a precursor to implementing sustainability.

Academic discussions on the meaning of sustainability need to build from this base of four principles. The definition most people have excerpted from Brundtland is that "sustainable development is development that meets the needs of the present without compromising the ability of future generations to meet their own needs" (World Commission on Environment and Development, 1989, p. 43). Certainly the sustainability agenda is about future generations, but it is not trying to create some infinitely durable means of managing society so that it can be sustained indefinitely. This is particularly important when it comes to discussing sustainable cities, which can become a diversion into ideal city forms or the impossibility of creating eternal cities rather than more real world issues.

The concept of sustainability has emerged from a global political process that has tried to bring together, simultaneously, the most powerful needs of our time: (1) the need for economic development to overcome poverty; (2) the need for environmental protection of air, water, soil, and biodiversity, upon which we all ultimately depend; and (3) the need for social justice and cultural diversity to enable local communities to express their values in solving these issues. Thus in this book, when we refer to sustainability, we mean simply achievement of global environmental gains along with any economic or social development. This concept is pictured in Figure 1.1.

The sustainability movement is first and foremost a global movement that in

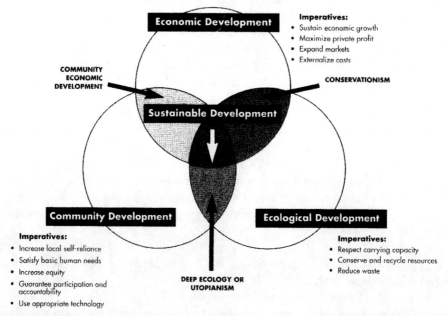

Figure 1.1. There are always three distinct development processes underway at the local level—economic development, community development, and ecological development. Each of these processes has its own distinct imperatives. *Source:* International Council on Local Environmental Initiatives (1996).

particular is forcing economists and environmentalists to find mutually beneficial solutions.

The sustainable development process has been proceeding at many different levels:

- In academic discussions—for example, how ecological economics can be defined and formulated (Daly and Cobb, 1989)
- In laboratories, industry, and management systems as they strive to be innovative within the new parameters of reduced resource use and less waste (e.g., the "clean production" agenda)
- Within governments at all levels and in community processes

These approaches are usually called "green economics," "green technology," "green planning," etc. When they are no longer called "green" but are accepted as normal, perhaps it will be possible to say the world is becoming more sustainable. However, sustainability is not likely to be a state that is reached, but one toward which the world must constantly strive. Sustainability is a vision and a process, not an end product.

Global Government Responses to Sustainability

Most countries began to respond to the Brundtland Report in the late 1980s. One of the first responses was Canada's establishment of a Round Table on the Environment and the Economy, which began mapping out what the new agenda meant. In Australia, the Ecologically Sustainable Development process was begun in 1990 involving government, industry, conservation groups, unions, social justice groups, and scientists. And in New Zealand, the Resource Management Law Reform process began its reexamination of all aspects of government from an environmental perspective. In the United States, a private-sector organization, the National Commission on the Environment, published a report in 1993 entitled *Choosing a Sustainable Future*, which states:

> The economy and the environment can no longer be seen as separate systems, independent of and even competing with each other. To the contrary, economic and environmental policies are symbiotic and must be molded to strengthen and reinforce each other. (p. 21)

The Clinton administration set up the President's Council on Sustainable Development in 1996 as the first U.S. government response to sustainability.

On a global level, after three years of preparatory meetings involving thousands of the world's scientists and administrators, the UN Conference on Environment and Development was convened in Rio de Janeiro in 1992. The "Earth Summit" drew together more heads of government than any other meeting in history, and its final resolutions were signed by 179 nations representing 98 percent of the world—about as global as is ever likely to be possible. The agreed-upon documents were: a statement on sustainability called the Rio Declaration, a 700-page action plan for sustainability called Agenda 21, a Convention on Climate Change, a Convention on Biological Diversity, and a Statement on Forests (Keating, 1993).

Documents are still working their way through governments, industries, and communities. International treaties are being developed each year to put some substance into the global sustainability agenda, including a CFC agreement and the late 1990s climate change agreements. In 1997 the "Rio plus five" Earth Summit was held in New York in order to report on how well nations were progressing on the sustainability agenda.[2]

At the local level, the sustainability agenda began to be taken seriously by more than 2,000 local governments that have implemented Local Agenda 21 Plans, or Sustainability Plans, since the 1992 Rio conference. The stories of hope are rich and diverse when examined at the grassroots level (e.g., Pathways to Sustainability Conference, 1997). The reason for this is that at the local level it is possible for government to more easily make the huge steps in integrating the economic, environmental, and social professions in order to make policy developments that are sustainable. Local governments are also closer to concerned people and more distant from the powerful single-issue lobbies such as the fossil fuel and road lobbies, which are so influential in shaping national priorities. (This is pursued further in Chapter 6.)

The local sustainability agenda and the global sustainability agenda are beginning to make more sense when the focus is shifted away from nation-states to cities and towns. This is the theme of our book, which is partly a plea to do more for sustainability, partly an attempt to help define how we can be more sustainable in our settlements, and partly a celebration of those cities and towns that are showing us what can be achieved.

Application of Sustainability Principles to Cities

The principles of sustainability outlined above can be applied to cities, though guidance on how this can be done was not made clear in Agenda 21 or the other Earth Summit documents. It is probably true to say that the major environmental battles of the past were fought outside cities, but that an awareness of the need to come back to cities is now universally recognized by environmentalists, governments, and industry. The Organization for Economic and Cultural Development (OECD), the European Community, and even the World Bank now have sustainable cities programs. In 1994 the Global Forum on Cities and Sustainable Development heard from fifty cities (Mitlin and Satterthwaite, 1994), and in 1996 the UN sponsored Habitat II, the Second United Nations Conference on Human Settlements, in Istanbul. At the "City Summit," nations reported on progress in achieving sustainability in their cities (UN Centre for Human Settlements, 1996).

Anders (1991), in a global review of the sustainable cities movement, pointed out that "The sustainable cities movement seems united in its perception that the state of the environment demands action and that cities are an appropriate forum in which to act" (p. 17). In fact, others such as Yanarella and Levine (1992) suggest that all sustainability initiatives should be centered around strategies for designing, redesigning, and building sustainable cities. In this global view they suggest that cities shape the world and that we will never begin the sustainability process unless we can relate it to cities.

The City as an Ecosystem

Throughout this century the city has been conceived by sociologists, planners, and engineers as a "bazaar, a seat of political chaos, an infernal machine, a circuit, and more hopefully, as a community, the human creation par excellence" (Brugmann and Hersh, 1991, cited in Roseland, 1998).

One of the strongest themes running through the literature on urban sustainability is that if we are to solve our problems we need to view the city as an ecosystem. As Tjallingii (1991) puts it:

> The city is [now] conceived as a dynamic and complex ecosystem. This is not a metaphor, but a concept of a real city. The social, economic and cultural systems cannot escape the rules of abiotic and biotic nature. Guidelines for action will have to be geared to these rules. (p. 7)

Like all ecosystems, the city is a system, having inputs of energy and materials. The main environmental problems (and economic costs) are related to the growth of these inputs and the inevitable increase in outputs. By looking at the city as a whole and by analyzing the pathways along which energy and materials (and pollution) move, it is possible to begin to conceive of management systems and technologies that allow for the reintegration of natural processes, increasing the efficiency of resource use, the recycling of wastes as valuable materials, and the conservation (and even production) of energy.

There may be ongoing academic debate about what constitutes sustainability or an ecosystem approach (Slocombe, 1993), but what is clear is that many strategies and programs around the world have begun to apply such notions to both new development and redevelopment of existing areas.

Sustainability Goals for Cities

How can a city define its goals in a way that is more sustainable? How do we take a systematic approach that begins to fulfill global and local sustainability agendas? The approach adopted here is based on the experience of the Human Settlements Panel in the Australian State of the Environment Reporting process (see Newman et al., 1996) and on the experience of creating a Sustainability Plan for Philadelphia with graduate students at the University of Pennsylvania in 1995 and 1997, as well as an awareness of the World Bank/UN Habitat project on developing sustainability indicators for cities (World Bank, 1994).

It is possible to define the goal of sustainability in a city as the reduction of the city's use of natural resources and production of wastes, while simultaneously improving its livability, so that it can better fit within the capacities of local, regional, and global ecosystems.

This is presented in Figure 1.2 in a model that is called the Extended Metabolism Model of Human Settlements. Metabolism is a biological systems way of looking at the resource inputs and waste outputs of settlements. The approach has been undertaken by a few academics over the past thirty years, though it has rarely, if ever, been used in policy development for city planning (Wolman,

1965; Boyden et al., 1981; Girardet, 1992). Figure 1.2 illustrates how this basic metabolism concept has been extended by us to include the dynamics of settlements and livability in these settlements.

In this model it is possible to specify the physical and biological basis of the city, as well as its human basis. The physical and biological processes of converting resources into useful products and wastes are like the human body's metabolic processes or those of an ecosystem. They are based on the laws of thermodynamics, which show that anything that comes into a biological system must pass through and that the amount of waste is therefore dependent on the amount of resources required. A balance sheet of inputs and outputs can be created. It also means that we can manage the wastes produced; but energy is needed to turn them into anything useful, and ultimately all materials will eventually end up as waste. For example, all carbon products will eventually end up as carbon dioxide, which cannot be recycled any further without enormous energy inputs that in themselves have associated wastes. This is the entropy factor in metabolism.

What this means is that the best way to ensure reductions in impact is to reduce resource inputs. This approach to resource management is implicitly understood by scientists but is not inherent in the approach of economists, who see

Figure 1.2. Extended Metabolism Model of Human Settlements.

only "open cycles" whenever human ingenuity and technology are applied to natural resources. A city, however, is a physical and biological system. Figure 1.3 and Table 1.1 apply the metabolism concept to Sydney.

The metabolic flows for Sydney in 1970 and 1990 are summarized in Table 1.1; they show that apart from a few air quality parameters, there has been an increase in per person resource inputs and waste outputs. The reduction in hydrocarbons is because they are more completely burned in modern automobile engines—but this just means that there's more carbon dioxide produced. If carbon dioxide is to be reduced, there must be more fundamental change.

The metabolism approach to cities is a purely biological view, but cities are much more than a mechanism for processing resources and producing wastes—they are about creating human opportunity. Thus Figure 1.2 shows that this basic metabolism concept has been extended to include livability in these settlements so that the economic and social aspects of sustainability are integrated with the environmental. This approach now becomes more of a human ecosystem approach, as suggested by Tjallingii and others above.

Livability is about the human need for social amenity, health, and well-being and includes both individual and community well-being. Livability is about the

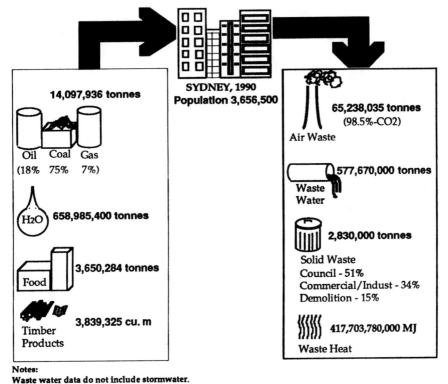

Notes:
Waste water data do not include stormwater.
Timber products and food data derived from national per capita data.

Figure 1.3. Resource inputs consumed and waste outputs discharged from Sydney, 1990. *Source:* Newman et al. (1996).

Table 1.1. Trends in Certain per Capita Material Flows in Sydney, 1970
and 1990

	Sydney 1970	Sydney 1990
Population	2,790,000	3,656,500
Resource Inputs		
Energy/Capita	88,589 MJ/capita	114,236 MJ/capita
Domestic	10%	9%
Commercial	11%	6%
Industrial	44%	47%
Transport	35%	38%
Food/Capita (intake)	0.23 tonnes/capita	0.22 tonnes/capita
Water/Capita	144 tonnes/capita	180 tonnes/capita
Domestic	36%	44%
Commercial	5%	9%
Industrial	20%	13%
Agricultural/Gardens	24%	16%
Miscellaneous	15%	18%
Waste Outputs		
Solid Waste/Capita	0.59 tonnes/capita	0.77 tonnes/capita
Sewage/Capita	108 tonnes/capita	128 tonnes/capita
Hazardous Waste/Capita	0.04 tonnes/capita	
Air Waste/Capita	7.6 tonnes/capita	9.3 tonnes/capita
CO_2	7.1 tonnes/capita	9.1 tonnes/capita
CO	204.9 kg/capita	177.8 kg/capita
SO_x	20.5 kg/capita	4.5 kg/capita
NO_x	19.8 kg/capita	18.1 kg/capita
HC_x	63.1 kg/capita	42.3 kg/capita
Particulates	30.6 kg/capita	4.7 kg/capita
TOTAL WASTE OUTPUTS	324 million tonnes	505 million tonnes

Source: Newman et al. (1996).

human environment, though it can never be separated from the natural environment. Thus sustainability for a city is not only about reducing metabolic flows
(resource inputs and waste outputs); it must also be about increasing human livability (social amenity, health, and well-being).

Livability indicators were produced for Sydney and other Australian settlements for the Australian State of the Environment Report (Newman et al., 1996)
but were only for the one year. Further studies can determine if these aspects of
sustainability are improving or not.

How a city goes about achieving an integrated approach to all aspects of
sustainability is the theme of this book. It is essential to understand the
dynamics of settlements as shown in Figure 1.2. Chapter 2 explores these dy-

namics by outlining how transportation, economic, and cultural priorities shape our cities.

Applications of the Extended Metabolism Model

The Extended Metabolism Model can be applied on many levels and to a wide range of human activities. For example:

- Industrial areas can examine their resource inputs and waste outputs while measuring their usual economic parameters and other matters, such as worker health and safety. These data can then be used to find mutually useful solutions, such as the recycling of one industry's waste as an important resource substitute for an adjacent industry. Industry in the Kalundborg area of Denmark has made an assessment of this kind (Tibbs, 1992). Ayers and Simons (1994) propose similar ideas for industrial areas with their "zero-emissions eco-industrial metabolism" concept.
- Households and neighborhoods can make assessments of their metabolic flows and livability and together make attempts to do better with both. Chapter 5 presents examples of this approach in which households and neighborhoods are taking the initiative to reduce resource use and waste production in actions that are being labeled "urban ecology."
- Urban demonstration projects can be assessed for their sustainability using the Extended Metabolism Model. For example, we were asked to evaluate the Australian Better Cities program, which consists of forty-five demonstrations of urban innovations. The approach adopted was to try to see the extent to which each project was reducing resource inputs, lowering waste outputs, and simultaneously improving the livability of the urban area (Diver, Newman, and Kenworthy, 1996). An urban demonstration project in Jakarta was evaluated in terms of sustainability using the Extended Metabolism Model (Arief, 1998).[3] Cities can even extend sustainability assessments to events such as the Olympic Games and all the facilities and infrastructure they require (see Box 1.1).
- Individual businesses can apply the Extended Metabolism Model and create a Sustainability Plan. The first business to do a "Sustainability Report" was Interface (Anderson, 1998), a large U.S. company that makes flooring. The company began the process in 1994 after the CEO had read Paul Hawken's *The Ecology of Commerce* and chose to follow a Swedish set of principles called Natural Step (Greyson, 1995).[4] Its process was similar to the metabolism model in that it examined resources ("what we take"), dynamics ("what we make"), and wastes ("what we waste"). It did not specify livability outcomes, though the report stressed that economic productivity improved as much from staff morale as from new technology. Four hundred separate sustainability initiatives were specified in the firm based on the work of eighteen different teams.
- City comparisons can be made using the Extended Metabolism Model. By comparing indicators for resource use, wastes, and livability in different cities, it is possible to identify those cities (or parts of cities) that have something to contribute to policy debates on sustainability. Much of this book is based on this approach, though few cities have made full assessments of their resources, wastes, and livability.

Box 1.1. Sustainability and Construction

The Sydney 2000 Olympics are described as the "Green Olympics" due to the Greenpeace award-winning design for the Olympic Village. In this Olympic Village there will be 100 percent renewable electricity (from rooftop PV and wind power), energy-efficient buildings, solar hot water, no PVC or rain forest timber, a rail service connection, a bicycle/pedestrian-oriented layout, and water and waste recycling systems (Bell et al., 1995). Karla Bell and Associates, who were closely involved in the design, have also designed a Swedish new town, Hammarby Sjostad, which was part of Stockholm's failed 2004 Olympics bid, but which will still be built as a "spearhead for ecological and environmentally friendly construction" (City of Stockholm, 1997).

The goals for reduced metabolic flows in the new town model are:

Energy
- 100% renewable-based electricity and heating.
- Energy use not to exceed 60 kwh/m^2 in 2005 and reducing to 50 kwh/m^2 by 2015.

Transport
- 80% commuting by nonautomobile means.
- 20% less traffic by 2005 and 40% less by 2015.
- 15% of vehicles using biofuels by 2005 and 25% by 2015.
- 100% of freight vehicles electric or low emission vehicles.

Material Flows
- 100% of solid waste recycled.
- 20% reduction in waste by 2005 and 40% by 2015.
- Water consumption reduced by 50% in 2005 and 60% by 2015.
- Sewage used for energy extraction and nutrients for farm soil.
- Stormwater used locally.

Building Materials
- No PVC or nonrecyclable materials to be used.
- No rain forest timbers to be used.
- New building materials only 50% of construction by 2005 and only 10% by 2015.
- No "sick-building" chemicals to be used in carpets and furniture glues.

Australian cities were studied using this approach and exhibited the broad trends shown in Box 1.2. Chapter 3 offers comparison data on a set of global cities, and other chapters review case studies on cities that are overcoming unsustainable policies.

Photo 1.1. Big cities like Sydney have lower per capita use of energy and lower per capita air emissions than other smaller cities in Australia but can reach air shed capacity limits sooner.

Box 1.2. Australian Settlements and Sustainability—Based on *Australian State of the Environment Report* (1996)

1. The larger the cities the more sustainable they are in terms of per capita use of resources (land, energy, water) and production of wastes (solid, liquid, gaseous) and in terms of livability indicators (income, education, housing, accessibility). The reason for this is explored in "City Size and Sustainability" below.

2. Larger cities are, however, more likely to reach capacity limits in terms of air sheds, watersheds, etc. For large cities to continue to grow, they must be even more innovative if they are to be sustainable.

3. In geographic cross-sections of Australian cities there is an increase in metabolic flows and declines in livability indicators from core to inner to middle to outer to fringe suburbs. This pattern is related to different urban development periods and most recently is related to reurbanization by more wealthy residents and firms. This rapid reurbanization of more central areas appears to be related to processes of economic change related to the new Information Age and will be examined further in many other sections of this book.

4. Ex-urban and coastal settlements are the least sustainable of all Australian development. They have large environmental impacts, high metabolic flows, and low livability on all indicators.

5. Remote Aboriginal settlements have low metabolic flows and low livability (especially in employment and health) but are the settlements where new small-scale eco-technologies are being tried.

Cities can apply this model on many levels, but above all, they must be able to measure how well they are doing overall in reducing their metabolic flows while improving human livability. Most cities will be able to point to a few innovations they are making in sustainability, but until they can make a full assessment of these matters, they will not be addressing the fundamentals of urban sustainability.

City Size and Sustainability

The evidence from Australian settlements in Box 1.2 shows that as cities get larger they become more efficient. This is not new in terms of quantitative studies, nor should it surprise us in theoretical terms. But it does. There are thus some important issues that must be discussed concerning city size and sustainability; these are only introduced here but are continued at various points throughout this book. These issues will be looked at from the perspective of economics and ecology.

The data on city size were clear in our original global cities study (Newman and Kenworthy, 1989a). This thirty-two-city survey showed the same pattern: transport energy use per capita generally declines as city size increases. Peter Naess from the Norwegian Building Research Institute wanted to investigate this phenomenon by eliminating the major variable of cultural difference that so clearly influences a survey of global cities. He chose twenty-two Scandinavian cities and found a very clear relationship between the size (as well as density) of the city and its per capita transport energy use.[5] The cities of Copenhagen, Oslo, and Stockholm were significantly lower in transport energy use per capita than were smaller provincial towns (Naess, 1993a and b, 1995).

For decades, urban economists have been pointing to the efficiency advantages of scale as well as of density (the two are generally linked). There have been many studies of cities that have found significant economic benefits arising from increased scale and density (Hoch, 1976, 1979; Sternlieb, 1973; Richardson, 1973). The benefits in terms of sustainability come from the same kind of economic efficiencies that are applied to environmental technologies—e.g., public transport systems become more efficient as cities grow; waste treatment and recycling systems become more efficient as cities grow (all other factors being equal).

There are economists such as Neutze (1977, 1978) who point to the diseconomies associated with size due to the growth in externalities. Others stress social problems that are said to increase with city size and density (Troy, 1996). The data on this question are usually very sparse, however, and the issue seems to be dominated by ideological stances (see Newman and Hogan, 1981, and subsequent discussions in Chapters 5 and 6). Fischer (1976) summarizes the elusive search for optimal city size in the following way:

> Most urban scholars seem convinced, to quote a British economist, that ". . . the search for an optimal city size is almost as idle as the quest for the philosophers' stone" (Richardson, 1973, p. 131). The en-

tire area of speculation is misconceived on several grounds. First, there are no substantial empirical findings pointing to city size at which any "good"—income or innovation or governmental efficiency—is maximized, or any "bad"—crime or pollution—is minimized. In fact, some data suggest that for economic purposes an optimal city size would be larger than any we now have. We have certainly not identified an optimum size for any social-psychological variable in this book. Even if such ideals could be found, they would probably not be the same for a wide variety of social products. The size that maximizes personal incomes would differ from that which maximizes artistic creativity, or that which minimizes pollution, and so on. And it would surely be a vain task to try to sum up all these various "goods" and "bads" into a single measure. (Fischer, 1976, p. 250)

In ecological terms, it should come as no revelation that as cities grow and become more complex and diverse, they begin to create more efficiencies. Ecosystems grow from simple systems with a few pioneering species to more mature ecosystems with diversity and interconnection. Thus, after a fire or flood or some other disturbance, a cleared piece of land will begin developing the structure of its ecosystem with an emphasis on rapid and simple growth. After a period it becomes more diverse and more efficient as it establishes a more complex network of interactions. As Table 1.2 shows, this succession process involves a series of changes that parallel the processes of urban development.

Critical to the process of succession becoming more efficient in its use of the

Table 1.2. Characteristics of Young and Mature Ecosystems and Their Application to Sustainable Development in Cities

Ecosystem Succession		Sustainable City Development	
Young Ecosystem	Mature Ecosystem	Young City	Mature City
Energy and Materials			
• High gross photosynthetic activity, low efficiency	• Reduced gross photosynthetic activity, high efficiency	• High energy, low efficiency	• Reduced energy, high efficiency
• Waste of nutrients	• Recycling of nutrients	• Waste of nutrients and materials	• Recycling of nutrients and materials
Economic Diversity			
• Producers mainly	• Balance of producers, consumers, decomposers, and integrative species	• Emphasis on producers, less on manufacturers, little on services	• Balance of producers, manufacturers, and services
• Few functional niches—generalists	• Many functional niches—specialists	• Low functional diversity	• High functional diversity

(continues)

Table 1.2. (*continued*)

Spatial Efficiency

• Low spatial efficiency—dispersed	• High spatial efficiency—compact	• Low spatial efficiency—dispersed	• High spatial efficiency—compact
• Low structural diversity—small lateral, little variety	• High structural diversity—small and large, lateral and vertical, large variety	• Low structural diversity—small, lateral, little variety	• High structural diversity—small and large, lateral and vertical, large variety

Information and Organization

• Low species and community diversity	• High species and community diversity	• Low community diversity	• High community diversity
• Low community organization—little interconnection	• High community organization—much interconnection	• Low community organization—few networks	• High community organization—many networks

Environmental Control

• Low environmental control—resource availability external to biotic system, climate unbuffered	• High environmental control—resource availability controlled within biotic system, climate buffered	• Weak protection from environmental perturbations—resources poorly managed, vulnerable to changes in the physical environment	• Strong protection from environmental perturbations—resources tightly managed, more able to buffer and cope with changes
• System instability	• System stability	• System instability	• System stability

Note: Young ecosystems pioneer newly cleared or burned sites and progressively develop into mature ecosystems.

natural environment is its increase in information. This is both the raw genetic information of its individual components and the complex interactions and networks that hold it together as a system.

All analogies from nature need to be carefully considered before they are taken as principles for human society—social Darwinism caused wars and the rise of such socially disastrous theories as the "master race." But the analogy of the ecosystem and its obvious application to the urban system at least shows us that it is quite understandable when human activity in cities seems to parallel natural activity.

Ecological patterns thus help us to see that big cities can be moving, like a maturing ecosystem, toward a more efficient use of resources and a higher level of information, organization, and environmental control.

Cities can, of course, choose not to become more efficient as they grow. Cultural forces discussed in this book can always be used to deny the opportunities created by scale and density of activity. The evidence suggests, however, that smaller cities find the process of achieving efficiency in economic and resource terms harder than larger cities.

The strong emotional appeal of "smallness" to our age is not, however, without its basis. E. F. Schumacher's book *Small Is Beautiful*, with its attack on modern gigantism, is discussed in Chapters 6 and 7. The message Schumacher created was that all technology needs to be at the appropriate scale of the community that it is meant to be serving. Chapter 6 discusses how community-scale technology is emerging as communities begin to assert their role—whether in villages in the Third World or in modern large cities.

The thrust of the New Urbanism and the "urban village" movement (see Chapters 4 and 6) is that communities need to be physically designed for and given infrastructure at the scale of the community. Vast suburbs can be given new coherence when focused around a subcenter.

The recognition of the need for a community scale does not deny the realities of efficiency associated with a big city. Community is the appropriate focus for infrastructure within big cities and small towns. To suggest that all big cities should be dispersed into smaller ones on social or environmental grounds is to deny some very major forces—both economic and ecological. And the evidence is that this would be counterproductive in terms of sustainability. However, ensuring that communities work within big cities is a major factor in achieving sustainability.

This is also the approach we have taken to growth management, of trying to bring order and focus into the megalopolis around community goals. This is not anti-city but, as is illustrated in the case study on Boulder in Chapter 4, is a part of asserting the importance of community and the need for environmental and economic responsibility within the city.

In the United States there has been a long-held belief in the value of small communities and small towns. The December 15, 1997, issue of *Time* magazine talked about a return to small towns, based on the move of some (generally wealthy) people to small towns after finding that even a move to suburbs from the city was not meeting their expectations. But this is not a statistically significant movement—nor can it be separated from the continuing problems of U.S. inner cities. As will be shown in Chapter 3, even the U.S. city is growing larger and is becoming denser, along with most other cities around the world.

The driving force behind the growth of cities is human opportunity. The diversity of opportunity in cities continues to be their main attraction around the world. We can try to thwart these opportunities by attempting to artificially constrain city size, as the former USSR tried to do (unsuccessfully) with Moscow. Or we can initiate experiments in de-urbanization such as those conducted by Pol Pot and Mao. Indeed, some environmental philosophy becomes very anti-urban and verges on suggesting this as a policy framework (see Trainer, 1985, 1995). The idea pursued in this book suggests that the human quest, the process of civilization, the development of human society, is all about the growth of cities.

There is no question that most cities are now heading in many wrong directions. They are not sustainable, as outlined further in Chapter 2. But to suggest that sustainability means the systematic dismantling of cities is neither realistic nor does it have an historical or theoretically sensible basis to it. The urban adventure needs to be grasped and pursued, not denied.

Cities must change, but the historic quest for human achievement through urban civilization will go on. The great challenge for our cities is that they must now take seriously the quest for sustainability. Cities can be more livable, more human, more healthy places, but they must learn how to do this by simultaneously using fewer natural resources, creating less waste, and thus impacting less on the natural world. How this can be done is the theme of this book.

Indicators of Sustainability in Cities

Cities around the world are now recognizing the need to pursue the sustainability agenda. To do so, they are seeking to define indicators of sustainability.

With the Extended Metabolism Model as the fundamental basis, it is possible to derive a set of practical goals or indicators for a sustainable city. Specific indicators are chosen on the basis of being feasible and measurable each year to guide a city as it attempts to create livable communities. Examples of such indicators are listed in Box 1.3. Each one requires further explanation and detail, but the basic idea can be seen. Improvements can no doubt be made on this list, which is a scaled-down version of the 150 indicators suggested by the World Bank and UN Center for Human Settlements (World Bank, 1994).

The problem with indicators (whether for guiding sustainability in cities or for managing a business) is that they are not always linked to a process that can lead to improvement in the indicator. If they are just for public relations purposes or individual motivation, they are not going to work very well. They need to be tied into policies and programs that can create some potential for improvement for the whole city. This book emphasizes the role of policies and programs for overcoming automobile dependence as the basis for creating more sustainable cities. It examines how this relates to many of the above indicators and the kinds of policies and programs that can simultaneously improve all the indicators.

Each city is, of course, best able to define the indicators that matter most to it. Seattle, for example, has defined twenty different indicators, including the diversity of the local economy, the number of pedestrian-friendly streets, the percentage of youth participants in community services, and the quantity of wild

Box 1.3. Annual Goals and Indicators for a Sustainable City

1. Energy and Air Quality
   - Reduce total energy use per capita
   - Decrease energy used per dollar of output from industry
   - Increase proportion of bridging fuels (natural gas) and renewable fuels (wind, solar, biofuels)
   - Reduce total quantity of air pollutants per capita
   - Reduce total greenhouse gases (e.g., Kyoto's goals of "demonstrable progress" by 2005 and 5 percent reductions by 2008-12 from 1990 levels and then further reductions annually)
   - Achieve zero days not meeting air-quality health standards
   - Reduce fleet average and new vehicle average fuel consumption

- Reduce number of vehicles failing emission standards
- Reduce number of households complaining of noise

2. Water, Materials, and Waste
   - Reduce total water use per capita
   - Achieve zero days not meeting drinking-water-quality standards
   - Increase proportion of sewage and industrial waste treated to reusable quality
   - Decrease amount of sewage and industrial waste discharged to streams or ocean
   - Reduce consumption of building materials per capita (including declining proportion of old-growth timber to plantation timber)
   - Reduce consumption of paper and packaging per capita
   - Decrease amount of solid waste (including increasing recycle rates for all components)
   - Increase amount of organic waste returned to soil and food production

3. Land, Green Spaces, and Biodiversity
   - Preserve agricultural land and natural landscape at the urban fringe
   - Increase amount of green space in local or regional parks per capita, particularly in "green belt" around city
   - Increase proportion of urban redevelopment to new development
   - Increase number of specially zoned transit-oriented locations
   - Increase density of population and employment in transit-oriented locations

4. Transportation
   - Reduce car use (VKT or VMT) per capita
   - Increase transit, walk/bike, and carpooling and decrease sole car use
   - Reduce average commute to and from work
   - Increase average speed of transit relative to cars
   - Increase service kilometers/miles of transit relative to road provisions
   - Increase cost recovery on transit from fares
   - Decrease parking spaces per 1,000 workers in central business district
   - Increase kilometers/miles of separated cycleways

5. Livability Human Amenities and Health
   - Decrease infant mortality per 1,000 births
   - Increase educational attainment (average years per adult)
   - Increase local leisure opportunities
   - Decrease transport fatalities per 1,000 population
   - Decrease crimes per 1,000 population
   - Decrease deaths from urban violence
   - Decrease proportion of substandard housing
   - Increase kilometers/miles of pedestrian-friendly streets (based on specific indicators) in city and subcenters
   - Increase proportion of city/suburbs with urban design guidelines to assist communities in redevelopment
   - Increase proportion of city allowing mixed-use, higher-density urban villages

salmon returning to urban streams (City of Seattle, 1993). Copenhagen has an indicator of the number of seats available for public use in its streets, squares, and parks since this seems to correlate to both enhanced economic vitality and reduced traffic (Gehl and Gemzøe, 1996). Adelaide has an indicator of the number of local frog species and the amount of rainwater reuse occurring in this water-sensitive urban region (City of Adelaide, 1997). The Hague's indicators include the number of storks breeding successfully, the installed wind-energy capacity, and the number of thirty-kilometer-per-hour residential zones in the city. It also has combined its environmental indices for water, noise, air, waste, soil, energy, nature, business, and mobility into one "environmental thermometer" that can give a visual representation of whether the city is improving or not (City of the Hague, 1995).

One of the indicators that has attracted significant interest as an overview of a city's environmental impact is the "ecological footprint," developed by Wackernagel and Rees (1996), who created a technique for measuring the impact of a city on the global ecosystem based on the metabolic flows of resources into wastes. They try to estimate the amount of land required to sustain the activities of a city. This includes the land to produce the food and fiber, to mine the resources, and to actually build the city, and it also includes the land needed to absorb the wastes. Energy is accounted for by considering the land required to absorb as biomass the carbon dioxide produced.

The calculations show that a typical North American requires four to five hectares of ecological footprint. If everyone on the planet had the same requirement, we would need three planets the size of the earth to live on.

This approach to sustainability graphically shows the extent of our problem in cities: we must reduce our ecological footprint. However, it is difficult to use this technique to bring all the impacts back into one land-based parameter. Also, energy dominates the calculation. The ecological footprint is therefore a bit artificial to use as a planning tool, but it can be a sustainability indicator guiding cities as they face up to the agenda of reducing metabolic inputs while improving livability.

Sustainability Plans

The implementation of sustainability tools is both an exciting and a frightening prospect for all cities. It is exciting because it gives us a clear task, a whole paradigm for organizing our cities, and yet it is rooted in local environments and responses, which means everyone can make a unique contribution. It is frightening because it is up to the present generation to reverse the trends of increasing natural resource usage that have been in place for at least this century and probably more.

Critical to implementation is the development of Sustainability Plans, or Local Agenda 21 Plans, as set out in Agenda 21:

> Each local authority should enter into a dialogue with its citizens, local organisations and private enterprises and adopt a 'local' Agenda 21. Local authorities should learn from citizens and local, civic, com-

munity, business, and industrial organisations the information needed for formulating the best strategies. This process will also increase household awareness of sustainable development issues. (Sitarz, 1994, p. 177)

The process can enable a city to define its indicators and assist in the process of change toward achieving them.

Although most nations have signed Agenda 21, the process of developing Sustainability Plans has been slow in some countries, particularly the United States and Australia (though Seattle was quick to develop a plan, and the state of New South Wales now requires LA21 Plans by all local authorities). In most of Scandinavia, annual Agenda 21 Plans, or Sustainability Plans, are required by law, and it is even common among local authorities in India.

Techniques for developing such plans have been outlined (International Council on Local Environmental Initiatives, 1996; Selman, 1996), and literature evaluating them is beginning to appear (Parenteau, 1994; Birch, 1994; Brugmann, 1994). Sustainability Plans require two central approaches: integrated planning and community participation. Both of these are familiar concepts, but the critical nature of the task means that we must undertake them with renewed commitment and creativity and, in particular, we must develop policies to reduce the metabolic flows in local areas. Such policy development then needs to be given priority in implementation.

Integrated Planning

A sustainable city must constantly learn how to merge its physical/environmental planning with its economic planning. This is essential not only for its environment but also for it to compete economically. Much more will be said in the rest of the book about how city economies are going to be competitive only if they offer a good environment in which to live and work—this is a postindustrial reality. As the British Transport Secretary said while announcing the one-third reduction in the UK road budget in 1995:

> We need to recognise that costs to the environment are real costs. There is no simple choice between an 'expensive' environmental protection option and a 'cheap' option of trying to ignore environmental impacts.
>
> A deteriorating environment, in the form of worsening air quality, degraded towns and cities and damaged landscapes would make the United Kingdom an unattractive location for investors and would cost us a great deal in economic terms as well as in our physical health and the quality of our lives. (*Daily Telegraph*, December 16, 1995)

Critical to how this integration of environmental and economic goals will be achieved in cities is how professionals will integrate their skills. This is a major theme of Chapter 6.[6]

The other economic imperative of sustainability is that economic competition is global today, and cities that are addressing the global sustainability agenda are going to be better able to compete in this new and expanding marketplace (Ohmae, 1990; Jacobs, 1984). Inward-looking cities that just try to sustain the narrow interests of those who would like to hide from global obligations will not be sustainable in the full sense of the word and are likely to decline economically. Many cities that tend to be isolationist or that try to deny the reality of global issues will miss out on new opportunities for innovation. The Japanese and Europeans are viewing sustainability as the next major global agenda for which they can provide the technology and services.

Indeed, it is our experience that cities that are innovative on sustainability are not always the major centers of commerce at the present time, but they are the ones that are looking to expand their horizons. Perhaps this is illustrating what Peter Hall has shown, that real innovation tends to come from the margins of a civilization, where people have greater freedom to be creative:

> The great innovative cities in history tend to emerge from the edge of the civilised world. They spring from egalitarian, self-reliant societies, at the moment of transition between a conservative, tradition-bound past and an open trade-oriented future. Their strength comes both from their traditions and from their new global horizons. (Hall, 1994)

For a city to ignore the sustainability agenda is not very clever. It only means that it will miss out on the innovation process that is rapidly developing—and the world will have to wait a bit longer for that city to catch up. In this book, particularly in Chapter 4, we try to highlight those cities that are setting the pace in terms of integrated environmental and economic planning for sustainability.

In addition to merging physical/environmental planning with economics, physical/environmental planning must also merge with social planning.

Improvement of the human environment should go hand in hand with improvement of a city's use of natural resources and reduction of wastes. Improving health is obviously part of the sustainability agenda, but other social goals can be more subtle in their relationship to sustainability. There is clear evidence, for example, that when you traffic-calm streets in commercial and shopping centers so that it is safer and friendlier for children, the elderly, and those with disabilities, you not only reduce fuel use and improve the local air, noise, and traffic disturbance, you also improve local business (Roberts, 1989a and b; 1000 Friends of Oregon, 1993). Human health can also improve due to greater opportunities for walking and cycling and more social contact among people.

Once basic needs are met, the next most important social goal for a city and its sustainability is the development of community. This is because the opposite of community—the withdrawal into private individualism, or privatism—is what feeds all the unsustainable trends we face. One of the observations made in recent years about sprawling, privatized cities is that they seem to be associated with the loss of community (Kunstler, 1993). Davis (1990) has typified Los Angeles as the "ecology of fear," a state brought about by withdrawal of the population into secured, guarded spaces.

There has been a new awareness of the importance of community for the economy of a city since the work of Robert Putnam, the Harvard professor of government who studied the role of civil society, or "civic community" as he called it, in creating wealth. Putnam found in a study of modern Italy that there were close relationships among the level of community activity, the effectiveness of government, and the strength of the economy (Putnam, 1993). These linkages contradict much economic rationalism, which views wealth as being largely due to free and unfettered markets. The new perspective views wealth as being related to networks: business networks, government networks, and community networks. Putnam found that wealth was related to the extent to which the community was engaged in public-spirited activity (choral societies, soccer clubs, etc.) based on a "social fabric of trust and co-operation." The importance of this message is that the generation of wealth cannot be viewed apart from such community-based social cohesion.

This book examines the processes of civil society and shows how privatism can be reversed through improving the local environment with urban streetscape projects, low-cost housing, community arts, and urban ecology projects such as recycling centers and community gardens. Projects that create a stronger sense of place also help to reduce car use and create a more inviting social atmosphere. Case studies of cities that have integrated environmental planning with social planning are presented in later chapters.

Community Participation

Sustainability is a global agenda, but as previously explained, its roots are in community processes. There are large sections of Agenda 21 devoted to how communities can become drawn into the implementation process.

This is a process in which it is essential—not merely advisable—to involve the public. At a time of transition from one paradigm to another, professionals in transportation, planning, and engineering have little to fall back on in their training. Some of the best books on sustainability have been written by nonprofessionals who have emerged from intense fights over freeways or some other expression of the old order (Jacobs, 1961; Engwicht, 1992). The process of how urban professional praxis should change to incorporate sustainability is outlined in Chapter 6.

Sustainability requires new approaches, most of which must be worked out by communities. As in other periods of great social change, the traditional disciplines must reexamine their solutions in light of the new set of values and goals being embraced by the community. Professionals need some humility in this process but are still essential participants in creating sustainable cities. Critical, therefore, to developing a direction on sustainability in any city is the need for successful community participation and partnership with urban professionals (Sarkissian and Walsh, 1996). Chapters 5, 6, and 7 attempt to show how this can be done as part of the urban sustainability process.

Conclusions

Sustainability has mostly been defined at the global and national level and only recently has begun to be applied to cities (Mitlan and Satterthwaite, 1994). The Extended Metabolism Model provides a way of integrating environmental considerations with the social and economic aspects of cities. The task of applying sustainability principles can seem rather overwhelming at the global level, but at the level of cities it becomes meaningful. With 50 percent of the world's population predicted to be in cities by the year 2000, cities are an obvious focus for the sustainability agenda, with enormous potential to generate change in how we use natural resources. This book tries to show some of the potential for promoting the sustainability agenda for cities from economic and social—as well as environmental—dimensions. The first step is to create a vision and then design a series of practical projects to work toward the sustainability goals laid out for a particular city.

The Extended Metabolism Model is an effective way for cities to try to create a holistic picture of their sustainability agenda. It enables urban managers to create sustainability indicators that together can give a sense of whether they are reducing or increasing their resource inputs and waste outputs and at the same time reducing or improving in livability. These indicators can be used to show cities how much they are contributing to global problems such as greenhouse gases and oil depletion, and to show local citizens how well they are managing sustainability issues that impact them directly. However, if a city concentrates on local issues only, it is likely to miss major components of the sustainability agenda as outlined above.

The sustainability agenda is a major global and local issue. Communities around the world are trying to determine how they can simultaneously reduce their impact on the earth while improving their quality of life. This is happening to a greater or lesser extent in all cities, and this book attempts to present the best and most innovative examples from around the world. We will try to show how the global and local can be managed together. In Chapters 2, 3, and 4, we emphasize the broad structural matters that relate to global and regional issues stemming from urban transportation and land use, particularly automobile dependence. In Chapter 5, we return to more of the local ecosystem issues. However, it is always obvious that the global and local must be integrated in this new sustainability agenda.

Notes

1. In an overview on sustainability, Pezzoli (1996) found ten categories of literature using the term and four principal spheres of concern:
   - Environmental context: holistic world views that integrate sociological imagination and biogeographical thinking
   - Legal and institutional: empowerment and community building, which bring localized knowledge and diversity into management and politics
   - Culture and civil society: incorporating ethics and moral philosophy into the technical and organizational aspects of society
   - Economy and technology: bringing production and consumption into harmony with the capacity of local and global ecosystems to perform in the long term

   This book uses all of these categories in applying sustainability to cities. The emphasis is on the last category concerning resources and ecosystem capacity; but there is always an awareness of the need for a more "holistic" environmental context, with Chapter 6 devoted directly to the "empowerment/community building" processes of cities and Chapter 7 focusing on the "ethical/moral philosophy" base for city sustainability.

2. For many environmentalists the "Rio plus five" summit was a dismal performance since so many issues seemed to be no closer to a solution. Nations seemed to be failing to deliver on so many fronts. However, a more perceptive view would be that significant progress had occurred at the global or international level and at the local community level between the Rio and New York summits, giving hope for a continuing global process.

   At the global level, the following landmarks had been achieved:

   • The Biodiversity Treaty, which emerged from the Rio Summit, took effect in 1993 and now requires all nations to keep better inventories of their biodiversity and ensure protection and sharing in profits from the world's life forms. This is now part of international law.

   • The Law of the Sea, which took forty years for agreement, is also now part of international law since the required number of nations finally agreed to it in 1993. It now means, for example, that fishing of migratory ocean species is regulated.

   • The Ozone Layer Treaty took the world's governments a mere ten years to develop and implement, so that 1996 saw the end of most global production of ozone-depleting chemicals.

   • In 1997 a new global treaty took effect, preventing the transport of hazardous wastes to developing countries.

   • In 1997 the Kyoto negotiations set targets on greenhouse gases that for the first time agreed on reductions.

   The global agenda in terms of international environmental treaties and laws is quietly and slowly changing how the world does business. There are now more than 200 such international agreements.

3. In a study of squatters living along the Ciliwung River in Jakarta, Arief (1998) surveyed the residents and compared them to residents of a nearby high-rise apartment block who had previously been squatters. The question was whether the shifting of squatters was "sustainable" in terms of the Extended Metabolism Model. The apartment dwellers were found to use a little less energy and water (as they had to pay for it), and their waste management was considerably better since the squatters put all waste directly in the river. In human terms, the apartment dwellers had improved incomes and employment (they were able to enter the formal economy) and maintained their accessibility and health; but in terms of all community parameters, the squatter development was far superior because the layout of the housing encouraged people to know and trust their neighbors. The lack of community orientation in the high-rise design questions the fundamentals of its development ethos and points to alternatives like the Kampung Improvement Scheme (Silas, 1993).

4. Natural Step is based on four principles that question whether any action will: (1) reduce use of finite mineral resources; (2) reduce use of long-lived synthetic products or molecules; (3) preserve or increase natural diversity and the capacity of ecocycles; and (4) reduce consumption of energy and other resources. The founder of Natural Step is Karl-Henrik Robert, a Swedish scientist, and his principles provide a way of approaching the physical and biological metabolism of any system. However, they do not bring out livability aspects, which seem to be necessary for a full approach to sustainability.

5. Larger cities in the United Kingdom were also found to have lower car use per capita (Smith, Whitelegg, and Williams, 1998). The role of density in reducing transportation energy use has been more well known. Density reduces transportation energy through several mechanisms: it shortens distances for all modes and makes transit, bicycling, and walking more viable as alternatives to the car; it also reduces the number of journeys, since when transit is used, many journeys are combined—for example, shopping on the way to or from the train. The data in Figure 3.3 show that gasoline consumption goes up by a factor of five between Manhattan and the outer New York suburbs as the density goes from 250 per hectare to 13 per hectare. See also Dunphy and Fisher (1996).

6. In Australia, the Better Cities program began to demonstrate the importance of this integrated planning process. It took professionals from water, transport, statutory planning, housing, and environment and facilitated a process of achieving a set of strategic, integrated goals for forty-five different areas across Australia. The process was often painful and challenging, but rarely were the results not something that everyone could see was contributing to sustainability as defined here. The program was dropped, however, so everyone in the higher levels of government went back to their isolated professions. Thus, integrated planning has not yet been grounded in professional praxis.

Chapter 2

The Problem of Automobile Dependence at the End of the Twentieth Century

What Shapes Cities?

If we are to address the application of sustainability to cities, we need to understand the forces that shape them. Only then can we begin to offer both local and global solutions with the potential to work. These forces are obviously very complex (Kostoff, 1991), but in this analysis three factors are considered to be the dominant forces that have shaped cities:

- *Transportation priorities*, in particular the extent of automobile infrastructure compared to transit
- *Economic priorities*, especially how new suburban infrastructure enables greenfield growth to occur rather than redevelopment and renewal of present urban areas
- *Cultural priorities*, particularly perspectives on urban space

As shown below, these factors are linked. Together they help us to understand how we have developed the cities we have and hence how we can begin to contemplate changing them into more sustainable forms.

Transportation Priorities

One characteristic people have shown that has been important in shaping the nature of our cities is that they do not like to commute, on average, more than half an hour to major urban destinations (see Manning, 1978; Pederson, 1980; Zahavi and Ryan, 1980; Neff, 1996). In the United Kingdom, a government study found that travel time for work trips had been stable for six centuries (Standing Advisory Committee on Trunk Road Assessment, 1994). Thus it is possible to see how this has caused three types of cities to develop as transportation technologies have evolved toward greater speed and freedom.

The Walking City

Between 10,000 and 7,000 years ago, the first cities were settled in the Middle East. From then until the middle of the nineteenth century, the form of cities everywhere was based on walking. Figure 2.1 shows the traditional Walking City characterized by high density (100 to 200 people per hectare), mixed land use, and narrow streets in an organic form that fits the landscape. In Walking Cities, destinations can be reached on foot in half an hour on average, and thus rarely are these cities more than 5 kilometers across (an average trip being 2.5 kilometers).

Many cities today have sections that retain historical walking characteristics—for example, the medieval core areas of many European cities. Much larger parts of Third World cities retain their high-density, mixed-land-use, walking characteristics.

The central parts of all American and Australian cities were once Walking Cities, but this characteristic has largely disappeared. Today, just a few historical neighborhoods retain this old form, including Society Hill in Philadelphia, the North End in Boston, the Rocks in Sydney, and the West End of Fremantle in Perth. For some who live in newer high-density neighborhoods in central parts of New York, San Francisco, Melbourne, or Sydney, it is possible to reach a majority of destinations by walking, but this is rare in U.S. or Australian cities.

It is feasible to re-create Walking City areas within modern cities. These "urban villages," such as the new suburban centers along Stockholm's rail system, or new district centers such as Arabella Park (Bogenhausen District Center) in Munich, are the focus of much design attention today. They are discussed later in this book.

The Transit City

From about the 1860s in Europe and the New World, the old Walking Cities began to collapse under the pressure of population and industry. A new city form developed that enabled the city to accommodate many more people at somewhat reduced densities while keeping to the half-hour average accessibility maxim. This was achieved through new transit technology. Cities pushed increasingly outward as the train (first steam and then electric) and tram or streetcar (first

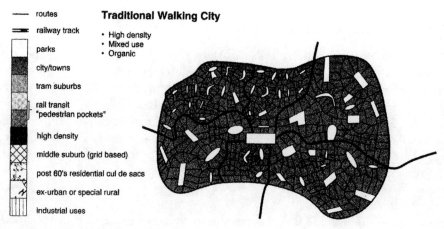

Figure 2.1 Traditional Walking City

Photo 2.1. Old Walking City centers like this one in Berne, Switzerland, work better environmentally, economically, and socially when given pedestrian-friendly characteristics.

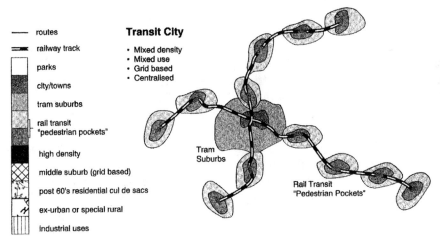

Figure 2.2. Transit City

horse-drawn, then steam, then electric) allowed faster travel to occur, creating the Transit City (Figure 2.2).

The trains generally created subcenters at railway stations that were small "cities" with walking-scale characteristics. Trams, on the other hand, created linear development that followed the routes in corridors or "main streets." In both cases, medium-density, mixed-use areas were formed at the rail nodes and along the tram routes.

Photo 2.2. Transit corridors like those in Stockholm enabled development to be contained and the forest to be part of the city.

The Transit City could now spread twenty to thirty kilometers based on these technologies, and where the rail lines met at the city center, very intense activity resulted. The overall density of Transit Cities was between 50 and 100 people per hectare.

Most U.S. and Australian cities were formed during the train and tram era and retain characteristics from this period (Davison, 1978; Spearitt, 1978; Warner, 1968). Even the planned new city of Canberra, Australia's capital, was designed by American Walter Burley-Griffin as a tram-based garden city, though later his original design was transmuted into a city based almost solely around automobiles. Melbourne and Philadelphia retain their tram-based linear developments in the inner suburbs, and even though the trams were removed in most other cities, the basic form can still be seen even in many parts of Los Angeles, which had one of the most extensive streetcar systems the world has ever seen. Railway station subcenters are still very clear in all U.S. and Australian cities, and both tram-based "main streets" and high-density station nodes are prevalent in cities such as Toronto (see case study in chapter 4) and New York.

As noted above, Los Angeles once had one of the most extensive and efficient transit systems in the world (Wachs and Crawford, 1991). In the 1930s the famous Pacific-Electric red trolleys (along with streetcar transit systems in forty-four other cities) were bought up by a consortium, National City Lines, composed of General Motors, Firestone Tyres, Mack Trucks, and Standard Oil—and closed down. The L.A. Freeway era was born in the wake of this decision. It was not, however, a community decision—it was a commercial one, and illegal at that. National City Lines was found to have broken antitrust laws and was fined

$5,000. However, this commercial decision basically ended the Transit City era in the United States, particularly once the Federal Highway System began in 1956.[1]

European cities have tended to retain their transit-oriented form and tram systems, though in recent decades they have begun to disperse around their main corridors based on automobile travel. There is a powerful planning movement today that is trying to reemphasize the importance of transit-oriented development (TOD). Often it is part of what is now known as the New Urbanism. Both are discussed in Chapter 4.

The Automobile City

Beginning before the Second World War, but really accelerating after it, the automobile, supplemented by the bus, progressively became the transportation technology that shaped the city, particularly in North America and Australia. It became possible to develop in any direction, first filling in between train lines and then going out as far as fifty kilometers for the average half-hour journey (Figure 2.3). The Auto City was born.

Low-density housing became more feasible, and as a reaction to the industrial city, town planners began separating residential and business centers by zoning. This also helped to increase journey distances. The city began to decentralize and disperse. Overall density of the Auto City decreased to between ten and twenty people per hectare.

With the availability of cars, it was not necessary for developers to provide more than basic power and water services since people could make the transportation linkages themselves. As this "ungluing" process set in, the phenomenon of automobile dependence became a feature of urban life. Use of an automobile became not so much a choice but a necessity in the Auto City. And as

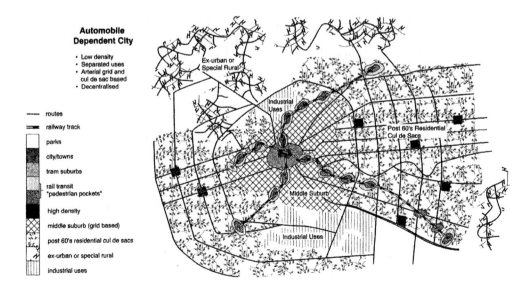

Figure 2.3. Automobile-dependent City

Photo 2.3. The Automobile City can spread in all directions, offering freedom over space and time. Los Angeles shows how such freedom is soon enslaved to the problems of automobile dependence.

automobile dependence became dominant, the Auto City began to lose much of its traditional community support processes.

Australian and North American cities have grown most of all in the automobile era. Cities such as Canberra and Phoenix have developed almost exclusively as Auto Cities; others, such as Denver, Houston, and Perth, are mostly Auto Cities. Now, after fifty years of automobile-based growth, such cities have spread almost to the limits of comfortable car commuting. Some cities are developing fast commuter trains that allow people to live up to eighty kilometers out of the city and still commute. But there is little else that people can reach easily in the rest of the city other than by car.

Many residents of the suburbs have known no other style of city. New suburbs beyond forty or fifty kilometers from the city center have an extra dimension of isolation from traditional urban functions. The level of automobile-based problems in such cities is growing rapidly. The next section of this chapter outlines these problems and then the book tries to show how such cities can begin to reverse their dispersed, car-dependent land use patterns.

Cities in the Third World have also grown dramatically in the post-1940s period, but most have not developed in the Auto City pattern, though many have automobile-dominated traffic systems. In general they have a more walking-and-transit-oriented urban form. There are exceptions such as Kuala Lumpur and Bangkok, which have large "footloose" residential areas many kilometers from the city center that have been formed and are accessed predominantly by car.

The reality of most cities today is that they contain some elements of all three city types, as distinguished by their different patterns of transportation and density. The data on New York, San Francisco, and Melbourne in Table 2.1 reveal that there are considerable variations in car use with density across these cities.

The good news in these data (and in data presented in Chapter 3) is that cities can choose to have a more sustainable transportation system if they choose to change their transportation priorities and start to reform their land use patterns. There are also diverse forces that are starting to reshape urban form away from the Auto City as its transportation and land use limits are being exceeded. These are discussed further under "Economic Priorities" and "Cultural Priorities."

Table 2.1. Variations in Car Use with Urban Density Across Cities, 1980 (as Reflected by Gasoline Use per Capita)

City	Core Suburbs (Walking-oriented)		Inner and Middle Suburbs (Transit-oriented)		Outer Suburbs (Automobile-oriented)	
	Gasoline use (GJ per person)	Urban density (persons per ha)	Gasoline use (GJ per person)	Urban density (persons per ha)	Gasoline use (GJ per person)	Urban density (persons per ha)
New York	11.9	251	20.1	107	59.6	13
San Francisco	17.5	128	33.3	57	58.4	8
Melbourne	13.2	32	20.3	20	26.9	10

Source: Newman and Kenworthy (1989a).
Notes:
   1. Core "suburbs" are those areas within a short distance of the city center. In the case of San Francisco, these are neighborhoods clustered around the central business district (CBD); in New York, it is New York County, also known as the Borough of Manhattan, and in Melbourne, core suburbs consist of the fifteen local government areas as of 1981 located, on average, about five kilometers from the CBD. They are always the densest neighborhoods in any city.
   Inner and middle suburbs are those areas of each city that were built to a large extent in the transit era prior to the Second World War and that retain more transit-oriented characteristics, such as medium population densities. In San Francisco, they consist of the City of San Francisco, and in New York, the whole City of New York area (counties of New York, Kings, Queens, Richmond, and Bronx). Melbourne's inner/middle suburbs consist of twenty local government areas as of 1981 that average fifteen kilometers in distance from the CBD.
   Outer suburbs are the remaining parts of the urban region outside the inner/middle suburbs and extending to the fringes of the built-up area. These areas were mostly built in the era of the automobile, after the Second World War.
   2. Urban density is the number of people per unit of urbanized land area. Urbanized land is land that is used for urban functions, including local open space, roads, industrial purposes, and so on, but not agricultural land, undeveloped urban land, regional-scale open space, or large water bodies.
   3. GJ is gigajoules or 10^9 joules. There are 0.0347 GJ in every liter of gasoline and 0.1313 GJ in every U.S. gallon of gasoline.
   4. Variations in gasoline use per capita between the two U.S. cities and the Australian city are partly due to the very much higher fuel use of American vehicles in 1980.

Economic Priorities

The transportation priorities of a city will obviously be a major factor in shaping a city. However, to build any transportation infrastructure still requires commitment of economic resources. History shows that in some cities the Auto City kind of urban form was resisted and a more compact, less car-oriented city was facilitated, at least for a large part of this century. This was primarily due to an economic priority overriding the priority for road-based infrastructure.

Historical Economic Forces

Frost (1991), an Australian economic historian, shows there were two distinct types of Western city in the nineteenth century and into the twentieth century: (1) the "traditional" high-density cities of Europe, east coast North America, and east coast Australia (London, Paris, Berlin, St. Petersburg, New York, Philadelphia, Chicago, Sydney) and the low-density "new frontier" towns of western and southern North America and Australia (Los Angeles, San Francisco, Seattle, Denver, Melbourne, Perth, and Adelaide).

The reason for this difference is not just the time of development, since new cities in these regions followed both patterns. Frost suggests that the major difference was the way the two types of cities used their capital. The "traditional" city directed a high proportion of its capital accumulation into industrial plant and had little left for urban infrastructure; hence housing was dense. The "new frontier" city directed a far higher proportion of its wealth into suburban infrastructure, thus enabling low density to be the major form of housing.

The differences in capital availability came from the different wealth base: the "traditional" city developed wealth from an industrial base for import substitution and innovation; the "new frontier" city developed wealth by servicing a large rural hinterland.

As Frost says:

> The enduring physical artifact of the great European grassland colonisation is in fact the New Urban Frontier. Its cities were the product of an era when resource endowments and market conditions permitted easy, almost effortless development. (1991, p. 163)

Since that period the two city types have largely merged, with most urban development based around low-density, expensive infrastructure. Frost goes on to argue that there is a powerful lesson in this historical analysis:

> For most of this century, economic growth has been sufficient to carry the level of investment required to provide most income groups with a detached house and a patch of suburban lawn. But the costs of sprawl are mounting. (p. 163)

This latter comment is the essence of our present sustainability problem. We are now faced with a simultaneous need to reduce environmental impacts while improving the economies of cities. New evidence is pointing more and more to the need to reduce spending on the Auto City kind of development if we are to achieve this dual objective. Some of this evidence will be presented later in this chapter and some in Chapter 3, where a comparison of the economies in thirty-seven global cities is made.

Future Economic Forces

There is growing evidence that the impact of the Information Age on cities is not necessarily one of dispersal, but could assist reconcentration of cities. Early notions about information technology first suggested that its impact on cities would be to create "community without propinquity" to disperse people into "non-place urban realms," or exurbs, where people only needed to telecommute (Webber, 1963, 1964, 1968). More recently, people have recognized that information technology has the ability to reform urban economies based on the simultaneous power to reduce some face-to-face interchanges (routine and follow-up communications) and the continuing and perhaps greater need for other face-to-face interchanges where creative interaction and sharing of skills are required (Castells, 1989; Castells and Hall, 1994). Hall (1997), after several years of being very equivocal on this, now states:

> The new world will largely depend, as the old world did, on human creativity; and creativity flourishes where people come together face-to-face. (p. 89)

Evidence in this book on the reurbanization or recentralization of cities shows that new commercial development is concentrating, but not just in the central business district (CBD) and inner areas but in a series of nodes. The forces that

Photo 2.4. The historic purpose of cities—to enable face-to-face interactions for economic and social ends—is a critical element for sustainability in cities today. Utrecht, like all Dutch cities, retains the quality of street-based "accidental interaction."

appear to be behind this are as old as the city: although we have the technological means to interact through computers and telephones, we still need personal contact as well. Thus businesses that are part of the new global Information Age need to interact with others that complement their skills. For example, professionals in architectural firms, engineering firms, graphic design firms, and computer firms all need to meet to plan business projects. Therefore professions with overlapping interests are clustering into nodes, with later additions of other services and even residences. Some nodes can be based on a dominant kind of industry, such as biotechnology; Willoughby (1994) calls this the development of "local millieux."

At the same time as there has been a pressing need for face-to-face interaction in the new global cities, there has been a shift away from smokestack industries in cities, particularly in central and inner-city areas. This shift has meant that it is much more attractive for people who need to meet regularly in central or inner-city areas to locate their housing there as well as their business. Thus nodes of information-oriented work mixed with housing and recreation services are becoming a feature of cities in the last part of the twentieth century (Winger, 1997; Newman, Kenworthy, and Laube, 1997).

These nodes can form in the inner city or in the suburbs; in Europe and Australia they are mostly in the inner cities, while in the United States they tend to be forming in "edge cities" away from their inner cities. Data in Chapter 3 show that this concentrating force is now of considerable significance in all global cities. The same process that has revived the inner city in Europe and Australia appears to be beginning in U.S. inner cities as well, with a lag due to the social problems there (see Chapter 3 and 4).

On the other hand, the new information technology can leave large dispersed suburban areas with little of this new economy or its services. This is likely to be a growing social policy issue for cities in the Information Age (Castells, 1989).

It is important, however, to see that late-twentieth-century urban economies are not necessarily working against sustainability. People still need each other and want the personal contacts that cities can provide for their economic functions. Information technology in the electronic age does not necessarily lead to dispersal and continued growth in automobile dependence. Indeed it is possible to see an emerging new alignment of globalization, information technology, and the reduction in automobile dependence. The Future City (see Chapter 4) is likely to have a series of nodal/information centers that can, if designed properly, be much more transit- and walking-oriented. This should be good news for sustainability in cities if this new economic force can be aligned with the global need to reduce metabolic flows in cities.

Cultural Priorities

All cities have been shaped by transportation technology priorities and economic priorities. To this analysis should be added cultural priorities—in particular, the urban perspective on space.

The New World cities of America and Australia are generally low-density and are located largely in places where land has not been considered as a constraint to development. For example, Australia is a large country with a small population by any comparison; thus when people came to Australia from Europe or Asia, the one resource that seemed virtually endless was space.

Urban development in Australia in each of the above-noted transportation phases was therefore under cultural pressure to provide as much space as possible. So density tended to be relatively low in each historical period. The density of Sydney in the nineteenth century was more than 100 people per hectare, which is ten times the density being built in new suburbs today; however, densities in European cities at the same time were about 150 to 200 per hectare (Newman and Hogan, 1981).

The culture of space was also fed by a strong anti-city, pro-rural tradition that came largely from England in the nineteenth century. This pastoral tradition was partly a reaction to the "dark satanic mills" and polluted air of the uncontrolled industrial cities of England. Poets and authors writing in this tradition expressed the idea to the English-speaking world that the more space built into a city, the healthier and more socially adapted its citizens would be (Williams, 1985). This gave an ethical basis to modern town planning—a reformist movement designed to create "healthier" and more "morally upright" urban residents by imposing density standards and segregating land uses (Boyer, 1983; Boyer 1978).

The academic basis for the imposition of low-density standards on new suburban development is, however, very shaky. We have analyzed the data on health and social problems apparently associated with density and find no such correlation (see Newman and Hogan, 1981). In fact, the evidence, if anything, points in the other direction (e.g., crime rates are generally higher in lower-density cities; see the section "Dispelling the Myths about Automobile Dependence" in Chapter 4).

Nevertheless, the imposition of spatial standards had a ready acceptance in the New World cities of America and Australia (King, 1978). The British Town and Country Planning Association has pushed its slogan "Nothing gained by overcrowding" for most of this century. Thus English-speaking cities have had a long cultural tradition of residents desiring as much space (private and public) as possible to be planned into their urban environments. For example, local authorities throughout the English-speaking world have placed a strong emphasis on ensuring large spaces between buildings and setbacks from the street for "health" reasons based on this ideology, rather than on the quality of urban design involved. This has meant that streets have been increasingly seen as space for cars rather than as community space.

The culture of low density was not the only urban tradition in the English-speaking world. There has always been a strong urban culture in London that has rejoiced in the human qualities of compact human scale and well-designed streets and streetscapes (Williams, 1985). The urban culture that London has fed continues to be one of the most lively and creative in the world.

This urban pro-density tradition can be seen in all the cities of Australia and America. Despite the availability of cars and trains that allowed escape to the suburbs, the economic pressures of suburbanization and the influences of anti-urban culture, there has remained a strong pro-urban tradition. The dense centers of all major American cities have had their cultural support base (e.g., Allen,

1980). Despite the dominant suburban culture of Australian cities, there has been between 20 percent and 50 percent of the population who much prefer to be urbanites (Australian Bureau of Statistics, 1981), and recent trends show that the trend back to the city is accelerating in Australian cities and is beginning again in U.S. cities (see Chapter 3).

Thus transportation technology, economic forces, and culture do not necessarily lead to the Auto City. Indeed, the process of globalization, which is impacting on all technology processes, has the potential to help create nodal subcenters with reduced automobile dependence and to replace increasing numbers of trips as routine interactions are replaced by electronic communication. Also, globalization, according to Naisbett (1994) and Ohmae (1990), is stimulating local cultures to become more important sources of meaning and interaction as it makes national borders less relevant. Thus cities and communities within cities can become more significant and fuel the process of creating more vital and livable cities. In addition, global youth culture is increasingly very urban rather than suburban, thus providing a cultural opportunity to challenge the assumption of car-dependent suburbs as the only future for our cities. As will be shown in Chapter 5, sustainability for our settlements requires that our cities become more urban and our countryside more rural. Thus, as with economic and technological trends, there are cultural trends that can be seen as positive for city sustainability.

Cultural forces are played out in a different way in Asian cities. They do not have a history of cultural resistance to density as does the English-speaking world and so have willingly and eagerly built their cities at increasing densities. The resulting urban form is generally higher in density than the urban form of most global cities (see Chapter 3). This form leads these cities to walking and transit. Some Asian cities, including Singapore, Hong Kong, and Beijing, have transportation patterns that reflect this. Despite having the density of Walking and Transit Cities, however, some Asian cities, such as Bangkok and Jakarta, have transportation policies that are totally automobile-oriented. These cities have developed automobile dependence of a different kind than that of the Auto City. They do not have transit options other than buses, which become stuck in increasing car traffic. Nonmotorized transportation is unattractive and dangerous in such a traffic environment. People become dependent on automobiles because there are no real options. Thus, although cultural choices have led to this kind of automobile dependence (mostly due to city policies favoring automobiles rather than quality rail-system options), it is a lot easier to overcome automobile dependence in these Asian cities because no changes to urban form are required.

Conclusions to Priorities Shaping Cities

Transportation technology, economics, and culture are instrumental in shaping cities. Figure 2.4 shows how the priorities in all three can lead either to automobile dependence or to overcoming it. For example:

- High priority for the automobile in a transportation system would mean a high priority for new roads and parking. New roads create great pressure for new suburban infrastructure at the fringe as the extra speed of travel enables greater distances to be traveled. Parking lots and roads take up considerable urban space that often replaces houses, and hence more housing is needed on the fringe. On the other hand, a lower priority for the automobile can mean less pressure for suburban infrastructure and less need to waste urban space.

- Low priority for transit (and walking) means that compact housing and other development that is built adjacent to stations also becomes a lower priority. As transit services decrease, there is a complementary lowering in value of urban

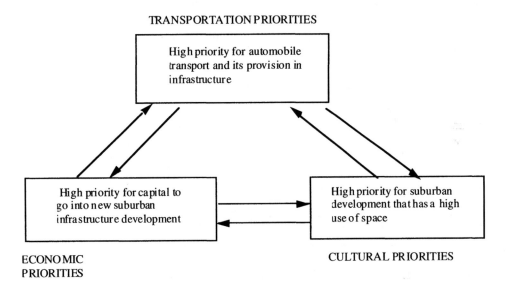

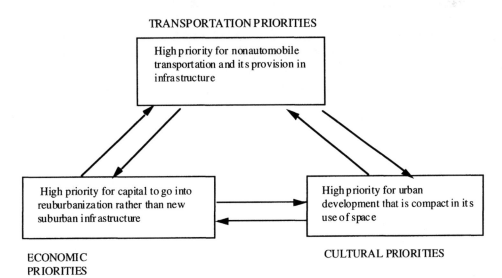

Figure 2.4. The interlinkage of transportation, economics, and cultural priorities in creating automobile-dependent cities (*top*). The interlinkage of transportation, economic, and cultural priorities in overcoming automobile dependence in cities (*bottom*).

development served by them. On the other hand, a reversal in these priorities can change development priorities since attractive transit systems facilitate walking-based urban villages around stations.

- High priority for the automobile creates traffic that requires large buffer zones and setbacks—that is, high use of space. Low priority for cars means less space for traffic is needed.
- High priority for capital investment in new suburban infrastructure creates low-density suburbs that are nonviable for transit, which in turn creates the need for high car priority. Low priority for suburban infrastructure capital links to low car priority. Such capital can then be used for economic and social development of cities.
- The priority for capital investment in new suburban infrastructure or redevelopment of the inner city is not just an economic decision but is based on cultural priorities about the spatial preferences for a city. It can now no longer be assumed that cultural priorities are automatically biased toward suburban rather than urban values.

Constraints on Automobile-dependent Cities

The 1890s was a decade of great change in the world's major cities. The Industrial Revolution had brought wealth, mobility, and diversity to urban citizens in ways that were impossible to dream about 100 years before. The old Walking Cities had been largely swept aside as trams and trains led new development patterns.

But with these changes had come great stresses and new challenges. Industry polluted the air and waterways. Workers were crammed into tenements, and streets were filled with uncollected garbage, animal waste, and kitchen water. Recession hit, and unemployment led to crime and vice of all kinds. A new century was coming, and for many it was a time of fear.

The writers and politicians of the day called out for reform. The visionaries of the 1890s dreamed of "Garden Cities," and there was a move to vegetarianism, Eastern religions, cooperatives, eco-villages, education for the unemployed, public playgrounds and parks, and public health (Boyer, 1978; Girouard, 1985).

Perhaps one of the most enduring social institutions to have developed during that period was town planning. This did not mean a set of regulations for controlling land (at that stage), but a set of visionary concepts for laying out cities in a more orderly way, for taking hold of the apparently overwhelming problems of cities and saying, "Let's change this for the better." And so largely town planners did (Hall, 1988).

Today, in the 1990s, we face a range of constraints on the auto cities of the world (see Box 2.1). Each individual problem is not a constraint that by itself would warrant us to make the comparison with the need for change that manifested in the 1890s. But together they may lead us to consider whether we are not moving toward a similar need for change to a whole new way of managing our cities.

Box 2.1 presents the constraints on automobile-dependent cities in terms of economic efficiency, environmental responsibility, social equity, and human livability—all part of the sustainability agenda for cities.

Box 2.1. Constraints on Automobile-dependent Cities

Economic Efficiency

- *Infrastructure costs.* There are excessive costs for new suburban infrastructure (usually subsidized) while older city infrastructure is underutilized.
- *Transportation costs.* The total costs of the car transportation system exceed transit system costs by 30 percent to 40 percent and are not paid for by users (see "Approaches to Constraints").
- *Time costs.* The more committed a city is to building its way out of congestion, the more it loses the battle to save travel time as people just travel farther. In all cities, no matter what their infrastructure, people take about thirty minutes for the journey-to-work. Thus infrastructure justified on the basis of time savings (the main rationale for big roads) is not providing this benefit but in general is time neutral.
- *Land waste.* The loss of land to parking and roads is greatly reducing the amount of productive land available.
- *Housing waste.* The mismatch of housing type and household need is increasing.

Environmental Responsibility

- *Oil vulnerability.* With global oil production peaking around 2005, there will be increasing vulnerability to oil shocks.
- *Greenhouse gases.* Pressures to reduce carbon dioxide will prompt leaders to turn to transportation for changes, since it is the fastest-growing user of fossil fuels.
- *Smog.* Clean air is fundamental to a city's health, yet car-based cities are regularly exceeding smog limits.
- *Sprawl impacts.* The loss of countryside on the urban fringe is proceeding at a rate of 0.4 ha or 1 acre per new household in Australian cities and higher in U.S. cities. Sprawling cities have higher quantities of asphalt for their cars (about eight parking spaces per car in the United States, as well as more roads per capita) and hence there is more stormwater pollution.
- *Traffic Impacts.* The noise, visual intrusion, community severance, road accidents (250,000 deaths per year globally), and parking blight caused by excessive traffic impacts cast doubt on the sense of a transportation system dominated by individual car use.

Social Equity

- *Inequities in being car-less.* More than half the population in automobile-dependent cities do not drive because they are too young, too old, too poor, disabled, or just unwilling and are thus transportation disadvantaged.
- *Inequities in location.* Residents in middle, outer, and fringe suburbs built in the era of the car are access-disadvantaged due to the lack of transit.

(continues)

> **Box 2.1. Continued**
>
> Human Livability
>
> - *Loss of community.* Community and neighborhood interactions are lessened by the loss of "accidental" or casual interaction that occurs in cities with pedestrian and transit systems.
> - *Loss of urban vitality.* The vitality and culture of the city is reduced as public spaces are dominated by cars rather than people.
> - *Loss of public safety.* The safety of the city is reduced as the public realm is lost to privatized urban life.

Approaches to Constraints

Each of the issues listed in Box 2.1 has a large following of technically oriented people who believe that through incremental, largely technological change, these constraints can be managed. However, they often produce solutions that worsen other problems. Equity problems, for example, can be eased by increasing car ownership and reducing fuel costs, but this increases economic, environmental, and livability problems. Minimizing traffic impacts with buffers and noise walls rather than modal shifts just increases the other automobile-based problems. Easing air pollution by designing highly efficient, low-emission vehicles can extend automobile dependence.

Such incremental changes are based on the assumption that the kind of city we now have is essentially adequate to meet future challenges. We don't believe it is.

In Box 2.2 we have presented each of the above constraints in terms of an in-

> **Box 2.2 Incremental and Urban Systems Approaches to the Constraints on the Auto City**
>
> | INCREMENTAL APPROACH | URBAN SYSTEMS APPROACH |
> |---|---|
> | *Economic Efficiency* | |
> | Infrastructure Costs | |
> | Infrastructure costs will be reduced by proper pricing and new technology, but will continue to be car-based. | Capital will still be wasted (even if it is private money) if development is low-density and scattered (car-dependent) rather than focused and transit-oriented. |

Transportation Costs

By pricing operations adequately there will be an efficient allocation of resources, and the more flexible the technology the better.

Pricing and flexibility are only one part of the equation since the urban system could become totally car-based with minimal transit; regulations and planning need to be redirected to ensure that the total system works as well as the separate parts, and this means fixed-rail systems that facilitate more concentrated land use.

Time Costs

Time loss is overcome by costing this into any proposed transportation projects.

Time loss cannot be addressed by transportation alone but needs land use changes that reduce the need to travel.

Land Waste

Land loss is not an issue since higher-value urban uses legitimately replace lower-value ones. Parking and road space can be more efficiently used, but the only question is to get the pricing correct.

Land loss is important in the longer term since good arable land and bush land are important resources. In a city with excessive parking and road space it is necessary to intervene and regulate such loss of urban space for social as well as economic reasons.

Housing Waste

The more efficient provision of housing requires more small-lot subdivisions and simple urban consolidation such as dual occupancy.

The housing mismatch requires fundamental change as well as the incremental changes suggested. It requires a revision of building bylaws and planning schemes based more on performance and design standards than density as well as facilitating larger-scale change, such as in urban villages.

(continues)

Box 2.2. Continued

Environmental Responsibility

Oil Vulnerability

The oil problem will be handled by a transition to using marginal oil and then alternative fuels and by a combination of the fuel price rising and new technology being developed for both fuels and vehicles. Behavior will adapt due to these changes, rather than any other social or urban systems change.

The oil problem requires a solution that is bigger than all the incremental approaches, although it will include elements of each. The most important part of an urban systems approach to this problem is to start providing more housing and employment location choices with less in-built transportation energy requirements and with inherently less-energy-intensive modes as their base.

Greenhouse Gases

Greenhouse gas reductions will occur when prices are more appropriate, and hence technologies will begin to adjust to less fossil fuel use. Regulations could hasten this.

Greenhouse gas reductions in transportation will be assisted by pricing changes, technological approaches, and changes in behavior. However, they will be more effective in concert with urban systems changes that begin to take the growth momentum out of greenhouse gas emissions by providing housing, employment, and transport options with inherently lower greenhouse gas generation rates.

Smog Pollution

Air pollution from transportation will be reduced by a combination of regulations, vehicle and fuel technology, and traffic management.

Reductions in smog pollution must come from a combination of incremental approaches, such as technological improvements to cars and engines and selected improvements in the traffic system; but unless action is taken to reduce annual growth in car travel, then these approaches will be running hard just to stand still.

Environmental Impacts from Suburban Sprawl

Impacts from suburban sprawl can be minimized by zoning to preserve sensitive areas and by some urban consolidation.

Incremental approaches are part of reducing the environmental impacts of sprawl but are not enough to fundamentally slow down the momentum of environmental degradation at the fringe; only bigger changes in the density and style of urban development in new and existing areas will be able to achieve this.

Local Traffic Impacts

Local traffic impacts can be ameliorated through schemes that redirect traffic away from sensitive areas using bypasses, techniques that mask traffic emissions and the presence of cars, pricing formulas that penalize car use, and/or market responses by individuals in shifting to a better environment. Ultimately, improved vehicle technology will significantly reduce traffic impacts.

The urban systems approach contends that there is a limit to how much the local effects of increasing car numbers and car use can be ameliorated through traffic management. Such management can be enduringly effective only in the context of decreasing, not increasing, car dependence. Reducing car dependence will be possible only through urban systems changes such as area-wide traffic calming, providing inherently less-car-dependent housing and employment arrangements, building new public transportation systems, and giving priority to nonauto modes.

Social Equity

Transportation and Locational Disadvantage

Incremental solutions to problems of transportation and locational disadvantage possess two key features: (1) they emphasize transportation rather than land use policy approaches; and (2) they favor private cars over public transportation.

The urban systems approach to transportation and locational disadvantage favors integrated land use and transport policy solutions that reduce the need for car travel and make transit more viable.

(continues)

Box 2.2. Continued

Human Livability
Loss of Community

Unplanned access is not an issue in transportation planning. The only kind of access that can be planned for, or is of any practical relevance in auto-dependent cities, is deliberate access, and this is, and will continue to be, more than 90 percent by car, with the remainder by public transportation. Walking and cycling do not figure at all in traditional computer-based land use transportation planning.

Public transportation should be viewed purely in terms of its economic effectiveness and ability to cater to a diminishing market of deliberate access trips.

Intangible benefits such as helping to enhance a sense of community through accidental interactions are of no real consequence.

The basic philosophies and practices of transportation planning need to change to recognize the crucial role played by walking and cycling (and particularly their future potential), as well as to consider the qualitative, more human aspects of access and transportation, such as opportunities for unplanned interactions, not just quantities of motorized traffic and the roads needed to cope with them.

An effective public transportation system well utilized by all sections of the community, not just the transportation disadvantaged, is not only important for planned access but also for its unplanned access and community-enhancing possibilities (e.g., through interactions among passengers and by drawing people through major activity centers along its route).

Loss of Urban Vitality

Overcoming social isolation is best left to the individual decisions and actions of families or formal urban institutions specializing in the problems of youth, the elderly, the disabled, and others.

Modern communications technology is making the need for face-to-face contact less and less relevant.

Many problems, such as the isolation of elderly people and youth, as well as issues such as juvenile car-related crimes, are at least partly rooted in the way we structure our cities around compulsory car use and an emphasis on private rather than public space.

Modern technologies will never replace the need for most face-to-face meetings and contacts, particularly for creative economic functions and recreation purposes.

Loss of Public Safety

The safety of the public realm is maintained by greater use of police.

Safety requires policing to be a partnership with communities, thus protecting and enhancing the public realm of our cities through healthy and humanly attractive spaces that encourage interactions, enabling crime to be reduced through "defensible space" and the strength of community values.

cremental approach to the problem or an urban systems approach that tries to address both the technological and urban form issues—that is, it extends to more of the underlying causes that shape automobile dependence. Under each approach a list of changes are noted as necessary to solve the problems. The total picture suggests that an incremental approach in our cities is not sufficient. Thus it is the challenge of sustainability to implement more fundamental system shifts that begin to move us away from the Auto City to a more sustainable Future City.

In the next section we discuss two of the most difficult global sustainability problems: oil depletion and the greenhouse effect. They raise serious questions about the direction of our urban society since cities (particularly automobile-dependent cities) are heavy oil users and greenhouse gas emitters. These issues are different from the types of pollution problems industrialized societies have addressed so well over the past decades. They are not environmental impacts that are subject to normal environmental assessment procedures. They raise the question of whether industrialized economies are facing a structural change similar to those associated with long-term economic changes often discussed as Kondratief cycles (Freeman, 1996; Linstone and Mitroff, 1994; Freeman and Perez 1998). These types of change are associated with substantial shifts in resources, the nature of technology, and the organization of society (see Table 2.2).

The school of economists known as "evolutionists" are grappling with this issue. Metcalfe (1990), for example, has suggested that normal orthodox economic analysis and thinking is based around assumptions of incremental change. The whole thrust of professional thinking is thus geared to analyzing problems in terms of gradual changes to technological artefacts. However, at certain periods the problems become more severe and point to a more significant structural change; technologies are adopted that are of a different kind entirely. They are changes that require more than artefact changes but social change that can facilitate the new technology. These changes, Metcalfe suggests, can only be understood in terms of an evolutionary model in which punctuated steps and phase changes occur, as well as incremental changes.

Commentators suggest that the new era involves information technology and more environmentally sensitive technology, together with associated social

Table 2.2. The Five "Long Waves" or Kondratiev Cycles

Wave	Time	Description and Main Industries	Key Factor	Business Paradigm
1.	1770s/80s–1830s/40s "Industrial Revolution" "Hard Times"	Early mechanization era. Textiles, potteries, canals.	Cotton and Iron	Capital-based local industries.
2.	1830s/40s–1880s/90s "Victorian prosperity" "Great Depression"	Steampower and railway era. Trains, steamships, machine tools . . .	Coal	Large firms.
3.	1880s/90s–1930s/40s "Belle Epoque" "Great Depression"	Electrical and heavy engineering era. Electricity, cable and wire, trams, radio . . .	Steel	Giant firms, monopoly, oligopoly.
4.	1930s/40s–1980s/90s Golden age of growth and Keynesian full employment "Structural adjustment" crisis and worse (?)	Fordist mass production era. Cars, trucks, tractors, aircraft, petrochemicals, fertilizers.	Oil	Multinational firms, subcontracting, hierarchical control.
5.	Late twentieth century "global recession" next wave of economic activity	Information technology (communication and control systems), environmental technology (renewables, recycling, zero emissions), and sustainable transportation.	Sustainability	Networking, systems, flexible specialization, "community" scale.

Source: Freeman and Perez (1988).

change (Freeman, 1996; Linstone and Mitroff, 1994; Freeman and Soele, 1997). Our assessment is that we are entering a phase change era in our cities as well. The responses needed to the problems associated with automobile dependence as highlighted by the issues listed above, are not the usual incremental changes to cars to make them more efficient, but are structural and involve new types of technology as well as new kinds of social organization.

Oil Depletion, Greenhouse Gases, and the Auto City

Perhaps the most significant reasons for cities to reassess the driving forces that shape their priorities and their urban form are the global constraints that are emerging. The environmental issues on the global front, such as oil depletion and greenhouse gases, are enough in themselves to warrant structural reassessment. But there is a growing awareness that the economic fundamentals are also skewed, and economic competitiveness is now fundamentally a global issue for cities. Because these global issues are the ones that have shaped the sustainability concept and continue to be a major force that drives it, we have chosen to highlight these matters. Thus we present the oil depletion and greenhouse issues below and, in the next section, the economics issue in further detail.

Oil Depletion

Oil is the fundamental resource of modern cities and civilization. It is the most concentrated of our energy forms (apart from nuclear power); it has been the most easily extracted, processed, and transported of all our fossil fuels; and we have become highly dependent on it for the majority of our transport needs. Moreover, we built our cities in the past fifty years as though cheap, easily available oil would last through the next fifty years in the same way it had in the past. It will not.

The global oil situation was first questioned by M. King Hubbert in the 1950s and 1960s and it was only when his predictions about U.S. oil production peaking in 1970 came true that his views were taken seriously (Hubbert, 1965). His scenarios for the world (Figure 2.5) suggested that global oil production would peak around the year 2000 or shortly thereafter.

The Hubbert projections have been confirmed by several major studies (e.g., Hall et al., 1986; Campbell, 1991; Campbell and Laherrère, 1995; Fleay, 1995). Campbell shows that between 1950 and 2050 we will have consumed 80 percent of the world's oil. This "golden age of oil," as he suggests, will begin to change quite dramatically as we face having to use less and less oil each year rather than more and more as we have done for most of this half-century. He concludes his comments by suggesting that:

> The world is indeed approaching the midpoint in the depletion of its oil resources: the epoch of increasing production is almost over, and the epoch of declining production is about to begin . . . Future generations will likely look back and see this inflection point as one of the great turning points in history. (pp. 51–2).

Increasing acceptance of oil's approaching production peak has occurred by bodies such as the International Energy Agency and even major oil companies

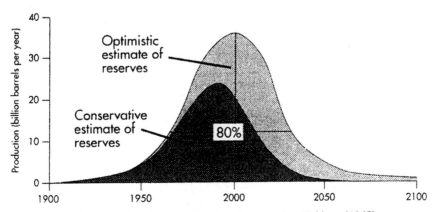

Figure 2.5. The cycle of world oil production. *Source:* After Hubbert (1965).

like BP and Shell (though they tend to push the production peak to between 2010 and 2020). What this means is that world oil will become less and less available and comparatively more expensive over the next major planning horizon—and yet many automobile-dependent cities continue to build suburbs and transportation infrastructure on a fifty-year scale as though nothing will be different.

Obviously, technological efficiency of automobiles will improve, though there are signs that thermodynamic limits mean that efficiency gains are becoming harder to achieve and a further doubling in efficiency after the past one is much more difficult. New fuels will be developed, but these will likely be a good deal more expensive than oil has been since their net energy efficiency is much lower. No other fuel option has anything like oil's energy profit ratio (the ratio of energy produced over energy used in its production): early production oil had EPRs of more than 100; offshore oil and late-production oil wells are more like 5 to 10; while alternative fuels such as oil shale and biomass are closer to 1 (Hall, Cleveland, and Kaufman, 1986).

Even with major breakthroughs in technology, which have not appeared in the decades since the first oil crisis in 1973, there are limits to how far technology can help if our cities continue to create the need for more and more car use.

The recent gains in fuel efficiency have meant that global oil consumption has remained relatively stable. However, U.S. cities in particular (as shown in Chapter 3) are continuing to expand rapidly in their car use and will be increasing their nation's dependence on imported oil. Already, 30 percent of the U.S. trade deficit is caused by imported oil (another 15 percent results from imported cars). At the same time, there is a rapid increase from very low levels of oil consumption by newly industrializing countries and from Eastern Europe.

Meanwhile, in the rural villages of the Third World there is a firewood crisis for cooking. Between 50 percent and 90 percent of energy use in Africa is fuel wood, with trees being stripped at nonsustainable rates (Davidson and Karekezi, 1993). In Sudan, between 1962 and 1980 wood fuel consumption contributed 92 percent of the deforestation of some 34,000 square kilometers (UN Centre for Human Settlements, 1997). There are many aspects to the sustainability strategy for this issue, but a small amount of kerosene for cooking would be a short-term major step in preventing further loss of trees in Africa. And the global sustainability agenda suggests that the moral case for a tiny increase in oil coming to rural Africa should have precedence over the continued sprawl of the rich world's Auto Cities.

Global oil reserves are often presented to suggest there is no real problem by saying we have about forty-five years of current use, though this is misleading as production follows a bell shape. Most importantly, all non-OPEC oil (including Alaska and the North Sea) has now peaked, and all of the world's thirty-seven biggest oil fields have also peaked. We are approaching the point at which world oil will peak by the early part of the next century, making cost increases a structural necessity (Walker and Kanaki, 1988).

Figure 2.6 presents the production cycle of world oil as it is envisioned by a series of oil experts.

This scenario by Campbell and Laherrère (1995) from Petroconsultants is part of a three-volume study of the world's oil assets based on detailed geophysi-

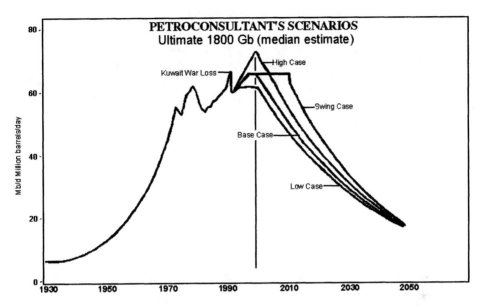

Figure 2.6. World oil production, 1930–2050. *Source*: Campbell and Laherrère (1995). *Notes*: Base Case: anticipated path; High Case: strong economic growth path; Swing Case: swing oil producers in Middle East decide to rationalize oil production; Low Case: weak economic growth path (some expensive oil is never developed).

cal data. These experts suggest that some countries overestimated their reserves in the past decade in order to increase their OPEC quotas and hence the production peak is looming much closer.

So the world's oil is running down. It is not "running out" in the popular conception whereby we suddenly have no oil; indeed, we are about halfway through the global oil well. But the global peak in oil production will reverberate through our cities.

The implications will be felt eventually, even if the world is able to maintain an orderly flow of oil from its major sources in the Middle East. But we are already only too aware of the problems of building dependence on the Middle East (where 66 percent of the world's oil reserves are located).[2]

The three global oil crises since 1973 were perhaps foretelling of how disruptions to oil flows can challenge the very core of city life and geopolitical stability. Stable oil prices in the 1990s led most commentators to cease worrying about the potential impacts if rapid oil price increases were to occur. However, it is not hard to imagine scenarios in which this could occur.[3]

Greenhouse Gases

It is now a political necessity to draw up strategies for reducing greenhouse gases. The 1997 Kyoto UN Climate Change Convention agreed that the developed nations of the world will reduce greenhouse gases by 5.2 percent over 1990 levels (the United States, 7 percent; Europe, 8 percent) before 2008–12; also, "demonstrable progress" must be evident by 2005. This is an historic global step for sustainability. After hundreds of years of increases, these climate-changing waste products of industrialism must now begin to diminish. Further reductions will follow since an expert group of climate scientists, the International Panel on Climate Change, has recognized that eventually just to stabilize carbon dioxide at present levels we will need to reduce emissions by 60 percent. The details of the problem have been assessed scientifically for decades, but the political will to act on reductions came when the 1995 UN Conference on Climate Change in Berlin recognized for the first time the evidence that human society had begun to change climate patterns.

There is now a debate over how far and how fast reductions can realistically go. Europe seems to be leading the way and is planning a carbon tax to facilitate energy conservation. There are also more than 180 cities involved in the International Council on Local Environmental Initiatives (ICLEI) program on Cities for Climate Protection Campaign. These cities represent 100 million people. Each city involved in the campaign is committed to reducing carbon dioxide by 20 percent by the year 2005 (the original Toronto target). At the Kyoto Climate Change Summit, ICLEI reported that the 180 cities had so far reduced carbon dioxide by more than 41 million tons and that in all cases the reductions were associated with a boost to the local economy through new jobs and greater efficiency (ICLEI, 1997). A similar network of cities in Europe (Energie Cités) is working on energy reduction strategies.

Substantial cuts in greenhouse gases are possible in all sectors. In nearly all reports, however, urban transportation is seen as the really difficult area in which to make reductions (United Nations Centre for Human Settlements, 1996; Organization for Economic and Cultural Development/European Community Ministers of Transport, 1996; McKenzie and Walsh, 1990). Why is this so? Despite three oil crises and considerable technological advances, few cities have reduced car use. Most cities show continued increases in per capita car use, particularly in the United States (see Chapter 3). With expansion so in-built, how difficult will it be to make reductions in transportation greenhouse gases, let alone stop the expansion?

We believe it will be impossible unless we shift the focus of activity to rebuilding Auto Cities.

New Economic Awareness of the Auto City

There has always been an awareness that elements of the Auto City, such as urban freeways, do environmental and social damage (with some confusion about freeways' role in increasing emissions and fuel use as discussed in Chapter 5). But this impact has been acceptably traded off by decision makers, who saw economic gains from the extra mobility. Now there are significant questions about the economic benefits to be gained, even if a government is able to allocate the enormous funds associated with freeways.

The accepted myth for most governments, at least in the English-speaking world, has been that transit systems are inherently a waste of money while road funding feeds the economy. The reality appears to be the opposite, at least in cities, as is shown below and in Chapter 3. Yet it appears that in most nations the acceptance of the myth of economic progress based on the Auto City has not come about from analysis or evaluation but merely from assertions, often dressed up in scientific form in the guise of a model—particularly in the United Kingdom, United States, and Australia.

In the United Kingdom, Oliver Tickell tried to find the economic basis of the government's "Roads for Prosperity" program (Tickell, 1993). He examined the direct employment impacts and the economic repercussions. He found "very poor value for money as a job creator" compared to other investments: £66,000–80,000 was needed to employ one person in road building compared to £30,000–50,000 for railways and £20,000–40,000 for building houses and just £9,000–18,000 for installing domestic insulation. "Roads are built by machines, not men" was the comment from employment secretary Lord Young.

Even with a poor record in employment, roads may still lead to prosperity through improving economic activity. Unfortunately, the economic repercussions, or flow-ons, are not so obvious either. Tickell examined the claim that congestion is costing UK businesses £15 billion a year (similar claims are made in the United States and in Australia). He found only "anecdotal" support for the claim, and the Department of Transport was "equally short on hard data to back up its view that prosperity follows where roads lead."

No part of Birmingham is more than 8 kilometers from a motorway, but as Tickell says, "If access by road is the key to economic prosperity, then Birmingham should be the wealthiest city in Britain. It is not."[4] The UK Department of Transport eventually recognized that "the effectiveness of transport policy in stimulating regional growth may be somewhat limited." This very guarded comment is not the conclusion of most "roads-based recovery" approaches that were standard fare from this department and most others like them around the world for the past forty years.

Whitelegg (1993) examined a number of major UK road-building projects (M58 and M62 in particular) that have failed to materialize economic benefits and concluded: "There is simply no evidence of the claimed link between access and employment or economic prosperity. The emperor has no clothes."

Whitelegg concluded that the factor that most attracts businesses to a locality in this postindustrial Information Age is "a high quality environment." He said:

> My advice to local authorities is to go for clean air, protected countryside and quiet residential areas. These are the assets that stimulate economic development. Unfortunately, too many authorities are providing the opposite: an area with terrific accessibility, but which is noisy, polluted and criss-crossed with motorways.

Whitelegg points out that areas such as Covent Garden in London or the city of York are thriving economically but have very poor road access. The same experience has been well known in Europe for some time. Roberts (1989b) found that those European cities that had slowed their road systems and not increased capacity had all benefited economically. Cities, says Roberts, must be "user friendly," and users in the end are pedestrians.

In Australia this link between controlling the automobile and economic success can now be seen in many cities. For example, the revival of Fremantle (see

Chapter 7) owes much to the stopping of major road proposals, because several roads had been planned that would have destroyed its unique heritage and character (see Newman, 1988b).

It is not hard to understand how improving the urban environment rather than building roads leads to a better economy. Road construction leads to dispersal of land uses and, together with the greater road capacity, facilitates a rapid growth in car use. The resulting congestion sets up a never-ending spiral in demand for road space. As Phil Goodwin of London University's Transport Studies Unit says, ". . . to try and build our way out of congestion is impossible, since the rate at which traffic levels are likely to increase will far outpace any realistic construction programme" (quoted in Tickell, 1993). But even before the limits to construction are met, the city will have experienced significant reductions in the quality of its urban environment, reductions that today translate directly into decreased economic performance.

The situation in Los Angeles illustrates this well. Los Angeles has the most extensive freeway system the world has ever seen, yet the city has huge traffic problems. Gobor (1993) suggests that the city faces serious social and economic problems as it adjusts to the middle-class flight from the city over the past decade due to its poor environment.

In this postindustrial era, the quality of a city's environment is critical to its success. As the OECD said in their Ecological City Project, "Cities that are pursuing innovations to improve their urban environment are among the most successful in the system of places making up the global economy" (OECD, 1996).

Photo 2.5. New laws in the United Kingdom prevent "big box" shopping centers and favor small "main street" shops wth housing above like the new Tesco Metro, which has no parking but provides a delivery service.

The role of transportation is crucial in this: an overemphasis on road building and an underemphasis on transit and the pedestrian environment can spin a city into a decline phase.

For the United Kingdom the next stage in this debate on how transport impacts on the economy was a new government approach defined as: a transport strategy that restrains traffic, reduces the need for travel, and provides high quality transport alternatives (Tickell, 1993). The new policy was announced in 1993 along with the abandonment of plans for most of the United Kingdom's controversial motorways. The paradigm seemed to be shifting. The next step was the set of regulations called PPG6, which gave guidance on how to reduce travel through land use changes, and PPG13, which banned the development of any further automobile-dependent shopping malls outside traditional centers.

This was followed by the Traffic Reduction Strategy Bill of 1997, which was the last legislation by the Major government and which requires all local authorities to develop strategies not on how to manage traffic (their traditional responsibility) but how to reduce traffic.[5]

Similar economic work to that in the United Kingdom has been going on in the United States, though the political outcomes have not been as obvious. In Boston a detailed assessment was made of the full costs of transportation in the city by urban area and by time of day, see Table 2.2.

The results of this study also include the following:

- A typical suburb-to-city commute costs $10.60 by car and $6.13 by rail.
- The government subsidy for drive-alone commuting into Boston is 43 percent higher than it is for rail commuting.
- Growth in roadway traffic pushes up the full costs per automobile passenger, while growth in transit ridership reduces full costs per transit rider.
- New commuting trips associated with development in the center of Boston cost about $2.30, only one-sixth as much as new commuting trips resulting from development in outer areas (about $13.00). Shopping trips likewise are about one-third as much.

Aschauer (1989) has calculated that for every $1 million invested in road funding, private-sector capital productivity increases 0.24 percent, and private sector total factor productivity increases by 0.27 percent. This study has been used everywhere by the road lobby (e.g., AAA, 1994). However, they rarely note Aschauer's later study on transit investment, in which he concludes: "Within the broad category of transportation spending, the evidence indicates that public transit spending carries more potential to stimulate long run economic growth than does highway spending" (Aschauer and Campbell, 1991).

Table 2.3. Costs (in cents per mile) of Travel in Central Boston

	Bike/Walk	Rail	Bus	Carpool	Solo Car
Peak	13–14c	29c	58c	41–43c	81–94c
Off Peak	13–14c	69c	$1.38	33–40c	79–91c

Source: Conservation Law Foundation (1994).

The major findings of Aschauer and Campbell's study were:

1. *Transit spending has more than twice the potential to improve worker productivity than does highway spending.* A ten-year, $100 billion increase in transit investment nationwide would yield improved worker output valued at $521 billion; a comparable expenditure on highways would yield $237 billion. Futhermore, the highest annual level of net benefits from such an increase in transit would be $15 billion in the year 2000; the highest annual level of net benefits for highway spending would be $7 billion, also in 2000. In the peak year, the productivity of each American worker would be increased by $185 from transit spending versus $87 from highway spending.
2. *Net economic benefits from transit expenditures occur sooner for the economy as a whole than do net benefits from highway expenditures.*

In addition to these critical assessments of road funding, there is a growing movement to more properly account for the total costs of transportation, especially in accounting for the external costs of private motor vehicles. Table 2.4 presents a summary of the studies we have collected, mostly from the Untied States, but also from Europe and Australia.

Our own calculations on a comparison of the total costs of transportation modes contradict the myth concerning transit's inherent economic problems. Table 2.5 shows how car, bus, and rail costs vary when their total costs are considered.

The costs in Table 2.5 do not take into consideration the added benefits due to land development that is inherently more concentrated around transit rather than road systems. There are some who do not accept that road developments lead to more dispersed cities, though the evidence is very suggestive of this in historical studies and in correlations of levels of road provision, levels of road use, and levels of urban dispersal, as well as urban concentration related to good transit levels (see Chapter 3, as well as Newman and Kenworthy, 1989a; Newman, Kenworthy, and Vintila, 1992; Naess, 1993a and b).

Table 2.4. External Costs of the Automobile, as Found by Various Studies

Country	External Cost per Car in $US per Year	Source
USA	$4,220	Ketcham and Komanoff (1992)
USA	$2,965	Litman (1992)
USA	$2,312	MacKenzie et al. (1992)
USA	$2,185–3,636	Moffet (1991)
USA	$3,647	Voorhees (1992)
Switzerland	$2,813	VCS (1991)
Germany	$3,376	UPI (1991)
Australia	$3,868	Laube and Lynch (1994)

Note: Costs are all external costs due to things such as automobile accidents, smog, noise, etc., not private costs.

Table 2.5. Capital, Operating, and External Costs of Rail, Bus, and Car Modes in Australian Cities (Cents per Passenger Kilometer, 1991)

Cost Item	Rail	Bus	Car
Capital and operating	27.06	21.51	26.65
Depots/car parking	negligible	1.09	3.42
Roads	—	negligible	8.89
Road maintenance	—	0.03	0.00
Fatalities	0.12	0.03	0.35
Injuries	0.00	0.00	0.11
Property damage	0.01	0.00	0.18
Air pollution	0.00	0.25	0.43
Noise pollution	0.00	0.20	0.08
TOTAL	27.19	23.11	40.11

Source: Modified from McGlynn and Andrews (1991).
Notes:

1. The data represent the costs for any additional passenger kilometers of travel added to the Australian urban transportation system.

2. The data are mostly Australia-wide averages for the five main Australian capital cities (excluding Canberra), based on information from the BTCE and Rail Industry Council adjusted by McGlynn and Andrews for inflation and other factors such as petrol tax and car insurance.

3. Capital and operating costs for urban rail show a range of 21.24 cents per passenger kilometer to 50.35 cents per passenger kilometer. The low figure is based on the incremental or marginal costs of adding new passengers to existing rail systems, while the high figure is for new light rail systems for which the incremental costs equal the average costs because entirely new systems must be built. The figure used here is based on 80 percent conventional rail and 20 percent light rail to recognize the increasing interest in light rail and prevalence of LRT proposals around Australia and the likelihood that at least some new rail systems in the near future will be light rail.

4. The bus data in McGlynn and Andrews show a figure of 18.17 cents per passenger kilometer for busways (in line with the Rail Industry Council's work). However, this cost dominates the bus data and seems excessively large. It has been eliminated here since busways are relatively uncommon in Australian cities compared to the great bulk of services that operate in normal traffic.

5. Air pollution and noise costs are based primarily on health impacts and are likely to be underestimated due to inadequate data in these areas. Also, there is the wider, and as yet mostly unquantified damage, from air and noise pollution (e.g., materials and crop damage from air pollution, psychological/social impacts of noise, and reduced real estate values due to traffic intrusion).

The first outlines of a theory showing how transit helps to slow urban dispersal and thus make the city more economically efficient or, on the other hand, how extensive road systems lead to dispersed cities that are not so economically efficient, have been suggested by Jacobs (1984) and Frost (1991), as noted earlier. They suggest that this is due to excessive commitment to suburban infrastructure, which is a significant opportunity cost and which involves many hid-

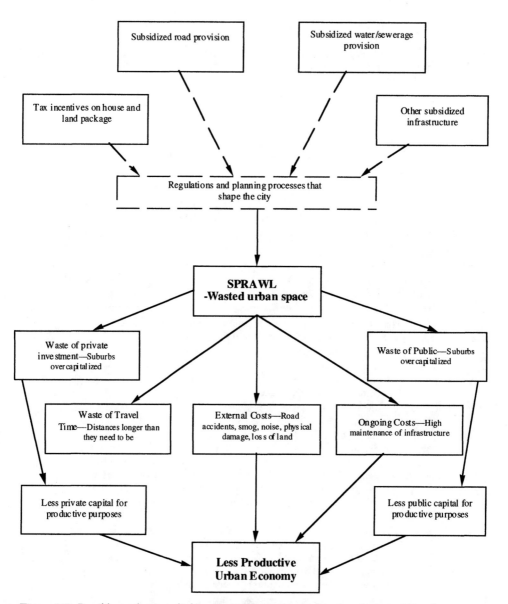

Figure 2.7. Possible mechanisms linking excessive provision of roads, urban sprawl, and economic problems.

den costs. We have summarized the possible mechanisms in Figure 2.7 and provide more data on this issue in Chapter 3, which shows how low-density cities have the highest total transportation costs as a proportion of their urban wealth.

The economic analysis in Figure 2.7 suggests that something fundamental has gone wrong with our approach to cities when we plan them around the automobile. It is quite simply the biggest part of the sustainability agenda for cities to reverse these patterns and achieve an approach that reduces the environmental and social impacts of excessive automobile usage while simultaneously improving the city's economy.

We are suggesting, therefore, that there needs to be a fundamental change that involves a different approach to the nature of the urban system.

The End of Auto Cities?

The automobile appeared to offer freedom in space and time—to live anywhere in a city and get quickly to all urban destinations regardless of location. The transportation engineering and planning models in the Auto City of this era simply had to predict the necessary infrastructure to provide for this new kind of freedom (Kenworthy, 1990). No land use planning was needed; housing and business could be placed virtually anywhere with individuals having the freedom to make the linkages themselves—as long as they had a car.

Unfortunately for the engineers and those who felt transportation utopia had arrived, it was never possible to truly achieve this freedom. Road and parking requirements became a bottomless pit that seemed to absorb any traffic solution and replace it with a new set of congestion constraints. The reality is that individual desires for mobility in a city where individualized locations are not subject to constraint will inevitably mean that traffic rises at superexponential rates.

The mechanism for this is now obvious: if it is possible to travel faster, then people just travel farther in their average half-hour work journey. So the city spreads and traffic grows. "Induced traffic" from new roads is now recognized by major transportation authorities (SACTRA, 1994), though most do so only grudgingly (Transportation Research Board, 1995). The literature nonetheless appears to be fairly conclusive on the matter (e.g., Goodwin, 1994).

The unfettered Auto City "dream" soon becomes a "nightmare" of traffic. The new sustainability agenda is a response to the demise of the thinking that allowed such a dream to be created. Thus it is now possible to imagine the end of the Auto City.

Fundamental to its demise is the limit that is now being experienced by most larger cities that have gone the way of the automobile: they cannot function well when (1) their land use pattern assumes all parts of the city are to be easily reached from everywhere else, and (2) the city spreads beyond forty to fifty kilometers (the half-hour limit when the best road-based solutions are working).

These circumstances lead to the ultimate Auto City where dependence on the automobile is almost complete (witness Detroit and Houston where fewer than 1 percent of total passenger kilometers are on public transportation; see Chapter 3). Such a city will rapidly fill with traffic at most times of the day, show severe environmental problems, be economically inefficient, and exhibit few signs of community. It is not globally or locally sustainable.

The problem of the car in cities is that the freedom and power it gives us come at a cost. It is easy to see some of the car-based environmental costs in polluted air, noisy environments, and acres of asphalt for parking and roads. But some problems such as urban sprawl, as discussed above, are also fundamentally due to an overemphasis on cars that facilitates dispersed, low-density suburbs.

Even stormwater pollution is found to be greater in car-based cities due to the higher amount of hard surface (Chapter 5). Now there are an increasing number of economic and social issues that are also being linked to excessive car use, due fundamentally to the way that freedom over space and time undermines community.

Thus the problem is seen to be not the automobile in itself but an overuse of and dependence on it. Excessive use of any product arises when we no longer exercise any conscious discretion but become addicted or develop a physical dependence problem. When cities are developing an automobile dependence problem they are usually aware of it, though there can also be an element of denial. Hart and Spivak (1993) have written a book, *The Elephant in the Bedroom: Automobile Dependence and Denial*, that suggests that many American cities have this problem. The twentieth-century problem of automobile dependence is, however, an urban sickness facing cities the world over—from Boston to Buenos Aires, and from Bangkok to Brisbane and to Budapest.

We define *automobile dependence* as a situation in which "a city develops on the assumption that automobile use will predominate so that it is given priority in infrastructure and in the form of urban development. Whereas automobile dependence was once assumed as a feature of the modern world, it is now being questioned in cities in all parts of the globe (UNCHS, 1996). Zuckerman (1992) says it is "The End of the Road."

The year 1993 saw the opening of the Century Freeway in Los Angeles, costing some US$200 million per kilometer to build. It appeared from commentary at the time that such structures had exhausted the political and financial will of citizens. Robert Reinhold concluded a story on the Century Freeway in the *New York Times* by saying, ". . . few cities will soon try again to build highways through their urban cores." Such a sentiment suggests that the end of the Auto City has arrived within the city that most gave substance to its expression. But freeway construction has not stopped in Los Angeles.

The Global Auto City Protest Movement

Throughout the world there is a powerful movement to end the building of freeways—that symbol of the Auto City.

An article in the *Economist* (February 19, 1994) describes how protesting about new roads in the United Kingdom at that time had become a "truly populist movement drawing supporters from all walks of life." The UK movement had over 900 anti-freeway groups with strong support from conservatives as well as environmental groups, their concerns were for the local countryside, the city's environment, and the global environment. The article explained how the Department of Transport had received 10,000 letters expressing opinions on the M25 proposal—only 8 were in favor. The *Economist* article concluded that "the pro-roads lobby, by contrast, draws upon a much narrower constituency—mostly road builders and car makers," and that the alternative of shifting public money from high-capacity roads into transit is almost universally accepted.

In the United States the movement to change priorities from road building to transit is very active. The Surface Transport Policy Project coordinates sus-

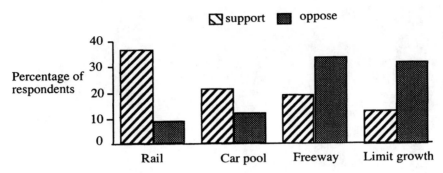

Figure 2.8. Californian support and opposition for options to solve traffic problems. *Source:* Franz (1989).

tainable transportation organizations across the country and was a major force behind the Intermodal Surface Transportation Efficiency Act (ISTEA), which provided U.S. cities with the option of changing their transportation priorities. In California, the home of the freeway, only 18 percent of the community believe that freeways help solve traffic problems, whereas 36 percent believe in transit (see Figure 2.8).

The U.S. mood is picked up powerfully by Jane Holtz Kay in a *Boston Globe* article entitled "The End of the Auto Age: Rebuilding a Way of Life Broken Down by the Highway Culture":

> Just because I gave up my car last winter doesn't mean I don't empathize with the poor motorist sliced and diced and driven to distraction by congestion. It's only that I feel for other things more: for the culture deprived of livability; for the ravaged landscape; for the environment bereft of clean air, fresh water, and a safe habitat; for the economy drained of viability, and for the Americans strangled by the seat-belt culture as surely as the Beltway chokes the landscape. (*Boston Globe*, October 30, 1994). See also Holtz Kay (1997).

Nevertheless, the political and bureaucratic procedures supporting the Auto City remain very powerful. It is not just an American phenomenon, though. In Norway a very revealing survey found a similar level of anti-freeway/pro-transit sentiment, and when asked whether they believed their politicians had correctly judged their feelings about private cars, people's responses were: yes 19 percent, no 53 percent, and don't know 18 percent (INRA Europe, 1991).

In Australia the tide is moving in this direction. In a survey of attitudes in Perth, the Community and Family Commission (1992) found a strong dislike for freeways, support for transit, and, interestingly, a powerful desire to try to create more diverse, village-style communities with close access to services. Across Australia there are many groups producing creative alternatives to large roads as well as opposing freeways. In Sydney various events, such as a Link-Up Conference, have brought together more than one hundred anti-freeway groups. These groups have all the energy, vision, and commitment of the early environmental movement.

Photo 2.6. Global anti-freeway movements are looking for alternatives to automobile dependence.

The one characteristic expressed by all these groups is cynicism about government involvement in creating Auto Cities: they tend to see government as their enemy, too closely allied to the road lobby and with virtually all government planners, engineers, and administrators facilitating the problem, not the solution. This movement is now calling for governments everywhere to act for the urban environment in the late 1990s as they did for the natural environment in the 1970s and 1980s and reexamine institutionalized practices that are still favoring the Auto City.

Institutionalized Automobile Dependence

The processes that seem to lead to the building of freeways despite strong popular feeling against them, can be set out in terms of the three factors shaping cities.

Transportation Priorities in Auto Cities

- The transportation system is demand-responsive rather than demand-management-oriented, particularly when it comes to the supply of roads and parking.
- The funding for road expansion is seen as economic, normal, and necessary, while rail expansion is generally seen as uneconomic, outdated, and unnecessary.
- The subsidy to automobiles is hidden, but for transit it is called a deficit and is fully public.
- Funding for road expansion generally comes from government grants; rail ex-

pansion is rarely as generous and requires special loans, private money, or special taxes.
- No secure funding to support bicycling or walking is available, or it is seen as too minor to worry about.
- Bus transit regulations in old and new areas are, in general, narrowly commercial and ensure that transit is marginalized and subsumed under the priority for car travel.
- Transportation agencies operate largely independently and often compete when they should be complementary.
- Transportation agencies and planning agencies operate independently most of the time; hence there is little likelihood of transit-oriented land use development.

Such practices and institutions generally mean that there will be priority given to the automobile system in Auto Cities.

Residential Development Priorities in Auto Cities
- Financial institutions are geared toward investment in new land development rather than new industry development, and tax laws facilitate this.
- Government planning resources are heavily committed to fringe development.
- Building bylaws and zoning regulations favor greenfield sites at low density.
- Financial institutions and the building industry are heavily committed to traditional kinds of housing in greenfield locations.
- Infrastructure subsidies heavily favor greenfield sites.
- Separate infrastructure agencies have budgets not subject to locational scrutiny since greenfield development is assumed to be part of the "normal" budget process, whereas large-scale redevelopment requires all new expenditure to be justified as "out of budget."
- There is a lack of strategic planning that incorporates and facilitates redevelopment, renewal, infill type of development through land packaging and other planning assistance, including coordinated infrastructure provision.
- The institutional framework is not oriented toward strategic planning that can integrate land use planning and transportation, especially public transit.

Such practices and institutions mean that Auto Cities continue to grow outward and apparently seem impossible to stop. Such developments are inevitably built around the automobile system with a few supporting buses.

Cultural Priorities in Terms of Urban Space in Auto Cities
- The advertising model of the "ideal home," presented as a separate, one-storey house to which all Auto City dwellers should aspire, is regulated into planning schemes; other options are seen as second-rate and are often regulated out.
- The economic, environmental, and social costs of high spatial priorities are

rarely if ever presented to Auto City dwellers or considered in town planning schemes.

- Wherever high-density development does occur, there is little attempt to facilitate environmental quality (in building styles and public spaces). The modernist architecture of high-density 1950s and 1960s development in Auto Cities did not do justice to traditional urban values for good urban design and gave "density" a very bad image.
- "Space" is equated with "health" in building bylaws and zoning, without regard for transportation implications, urban design, or isolation of people from one another.
- Country living is still seen by some city planners as a better environment morally and socially than a more urban environment; thus they facilitate exurban development, which is highly auto-dependent.
- A separate house with a large front- and backyard is seen as the only acceptable environment for children and any other options to provide for children are viewed with great suspicion.

Such practices and institutions mean that Auto Cities continue to sprawl and build in high car use.

Conclusions

The history of cities extends back some 7,000 to 10,000 years. For all but the last fifty years, land use and transportation have been closely connected; first in the dense, mixed-use Walking City, whose limited transportation options and travel speeds ensured that urban land use remained closely integrated, and later in the Transit City, with its fixed train and tram systems, which also ensured that development was closely tied to quite narrow transportation corridors. The advent of the automobile, however, and to a lesser extent the diesel bus, meant that for the first time in history, houses and businesses could be located almost anywhere, because personalized transportation could be used to join them together. Thus the transportation–land use connection was broken, and automobile dependence became established. But, as cities were to discover, this came at a great cost and is now seen as a fundamental cause of unsustainability in cities.

The cost involved building an almost open-ended supply of transportation infrastructure that was to cater to exponential growth in demand for travel. The process created huge impacts on the environment of cities, including the paving over of natural areas and farmland, air pollution from increasingly difficult-to-control motor vehicles, urban noise on a scale previously unthinkable, severance of communities, very large infrastructure costs (water, sewerage, roads, etc.), congestion costs, dependence on increasingly tenuous international supplies of oil, and a whole of array of unforeseen social costs, such as isolation, destruction of community, and degradation of the public realm. Excessive urban automobile travel is now also a focus of attention globally due to its contribution to greenhouse gases.

These combined environmental, economic, and social costs of automobile dependence are today forcing a widespread rethinking of the way cities are built. It demands that we consider how we can reconnect land use with transportation in order to reduce costly and destructive levels of automobile travel, and it demands that we reassess our transportation infrastructure priorities.

If the focus shifts to the Third World, those cities such as in China and India—in which transportation and land use are still tightly connected and which still have very low levels of auto ownership and high levels of walking, cycling, and public transportation—the realities of exponential increases in motorization raise serious questions. Could the world cope with a quadrupling in automotive use? Could these cities cope when cities such as Bangkok and Jakarta, which are the pacesetters for this new auto-focused world, indicate that automobile-based planning is a spectacular failure in such cities (see Chapter 3.)

Such local and global problems of automobile dependence are forcing a reassessment of the way cities are built and are regenerating a synergism that might be thought of as equal in strength to the power of the urban reform movements that gave birth to town planning during the Industrial Revolution. The kind of "modernist" thinking that produced the Auto City is now easily parodied as grandiose, with freeways seen as symbols of machismo and traditional car-based housing as bland, mass-produced suburbs. There is also considerable unease among the general public about the continuation of this kind of city building. But in this and many other areas of human endeavor, the postmodern world is still confused about whether any alternative future can exist. It is now clear that the economic basis for the continuance of the Auto City is shaky and that we must look for something more sustainable.

The evidence presented here suggests that the last days of the old paradigm are upon us. This is not to say that the old way does not have some momentum left or that the political battles are over (as shown in the long list of current automobile-dependent practices)—what it does mean is that the tide has turned.[6]

Notes

1. See *Taken for a Ride*, a 1996 video by independent filmmakers New Day Films.
2. Cheap oil from the Middle East leads to political risks, but a shift to oil from shale or tar sands has huge environmental risks. For example, Fleay (1998) has estimated that to replace global oil with oil shale and tar sands will require ten to fifteen times the land clearing that is presently associated with strip mining of coal.
3. Some of the social implications of oil dependence are discussed by Professor Kenneth Watt, from the University of California at Davis, who has developed a systems analysis view of how the reverberation of oil scarcity will course through our society and economy (see Watt, 1982). Below we have speculated on two contrasting scenarios for Auto Cities in an oil-constrained future:

SCENARIO A

The first response to the big oil crisis of 2007 was incredulity: "Surely the oil is being hidden away by big companies or foreign governments that want to make massive windfall profits. How can something as central to our way of life as this be allowed to reach such critical levels of depletion, without us all being aware of it?"

People in the sprawling city decided to sit it out. Holidays were taken rather than commuting. More telework was done from home. Little social and recreational activity occurred.

Fuel prices rose constantly for three months and then jumped considerably as local emergency supplies ran out. Fuel began to be supplied to local distributors on odd or even days. Emergency gasoline card holders were given fuel concessions due to their need for transportation, but the system soon collapsed as so many professions claimed to be essential and most were automobile-dependent. A black market in emergency gasoline cards led to them becoming worthless.

Transit usage improved but could not be increased to provide anything like the necessary levels of service. Besides, people didn't want transit. They had rejected that for decades and had grown up knowing only how to travel by car. They felt strange even trying to find out how buses operated in their area and couldn't believe things had gotten to the point where they would have to sit with others they didn't know or trust in a smelly bus.

City authorities organized carpools but couldn't find enough common ground to do anything more. "It will pass," they said. "The old order will return; just wait and see." Media discussions were dominated by those who were deflecting blame and seeing conspiracies everywhere.

Months turned into years and the situation did not improve. People started leaving the city. Businesses began closing, with shopping malls in the outer areas being hardest hit. Poverty crept into the formerly affluent automobile-dependent suburbs. Real estate prices dropped month after month. Houses began to be abandoned. Those remaining in the suburbs became more and more isolated. Fear dominated their lives. Fuel was saved for work trips, and everything else was done inside the house. Crime was rampant. Stealing gasoline became as common as stealing cars.

After fifteen years of continuing decline, the once great sprawling metropolis was reduced to a mere shell. The old city with its less-automobile-dependent form was still occupied, but the ravages of economic decline had so undermined the infrastructure and buildings that little hope for the future could be found.

Scenario B

The first response to the big oil crisis of 2007 was a series of local community-based meetings. How could the city begin to plan to accommodate what was almost certainly a significant change in their urban situation?

Huge interest was evoked. Many people found it difficult to see that fundamental hange would be needed, but most recognized that they should perhaps start to act as though it were.

Voluntary local carpools began to operate immediately, and everyone with an obvious emergency need for travel was given priority. Community buses grew from the carpools as people began to get to know one another better.

A transit plan for the city, complete with local linkages and cycleways, was drawn up and released for public comment. Immediate support was found, particularly when extra housing near stations was incorporated. The go-ahead to build the electric light rail spine was given in record time after a consortium of local businesses put up half the capital to build it.

Communities formed associations to provide more local social and recreational activities so that people did not need to travel so far. Community telecenters meant that people needed to travel less but could remain in close contact with others in the community, as well as doing global business. People began to meet neighbors they'd only briefly acknowledged before. Community life grew as pedestrian street activity increased. Coffee shops took over whole streets; artist workshops replaced parking lots, computer game arcades and public debating areas became features of all local centers.

After five years it was becoming clear that the fuel crisis was permanent. Electric cars and natural gas cars had taken over the new-car market, but the reduction in traffic was the biggest change. The new transit system was in place, and real estate values and housing had rapidly favored all new housing being transit-oriented as well as requiring much less heating and cooling. Concerns about density had been overcome by creative designs and the sheer desire of the community to get back together again.

After fifteen years there was hardly any discussion about the fuel crisis, but a few people reflected on how different the experience could have been.

4. You can go even further and see that Liverpool, the city-region of the United Kingdom with the most serious economic problems, is well served by roads.

5. One of the first results of pressure from local government professionals on how to do this was a study from Phil Goodwin showing that if road capacity is reduced, then up to 60 percent of the previous traffic just disappears (Hamer, 1998). The mechanisms for this are discussed in Chapter 4 under "Traffic Calming."

6. The Worldwatch Institute concluded its analysis on "Re-inventing Transport" in the following way: "All nations would benefit from an evaluation process that no longer prizes mobility above all. Given this much needed change in priorities, improved access could replace mobility as the benchmark of future progress in transport. Such a transformation will not happen quickly. But it may be hastened by people's growing sense that the long-standing preoccupation with automobiles has degraded our communities to such a degree—physically and otherwise—that our destinations are no longer places worth reaching. Eventually, societies may come to welcome a transport system in which access, not excess, is the predominant feature." (Lowe, 1994, p. 98)

Chapter 3

The Pattern of Automobile Dependence and Global Cities

Introduction

Urban sustainability can be examined quantitatively using the indicators presented in Chapter 1. This chapter examines a number of these quantitative indicators associated with transportation energy, land, and air quality, as well as some key livability indicators relating to transportation and wealth in a city. The aim here is not merely to list these indicators, but to attempt to understand the forces shaping the structure of different cities as outlined in Chapter 2. The extensive data in this chapter will thus be analyzed to draw conclusions on how sustainability can be pursued through the planning and development priorities of a city.

The data for the analysis below comes from two separate though overlapping sources. The tables in the text are taken from our updated global cities study, *Cities and Automobile Dependence: An International Sourcebook* (Newman and Kenworthy, 1989a). That study covered thirty-two cities in North America, Australia, Europe, and Asia and had extensive land use, transportation, and energy data for 1960, 1970, and 1980. The 1980 data were principally used in the analysis in that original work.

In the update of this work to 1990, the cities of West Berlin and Moscow have been excluded. West Berlin is no longer a valid urban area to analyze and the complexity of revising the original data for 1960, 1970 and 1980 to cover the whole Berlin area was considered impractical (gathering data now on East Berlin would be very difficult). Moscow was excluded after it was found that data collection had become virtually impossible in the administrative and economic climate after the breakup of the Soviet Union.[1]

The new data set, however, has been expanded to include sixteen new cities (three in the United States, one in Australia, six in Canada, and six in the developing Asian region), giving a total of forty-six cities. The data in the text here are a selection from that study (Kenworthy et al., 1999). Table 3.1 lists the cities involved in the international comparisons in this chapter.

The other data used in the international comparisons in this chapter are from a study we conducted for the World Bank and are contained in Appendix 1 along with the methodology used in collecting and processing the data. They consist of

Table 3.1. Cities in the International Comparisons of Transport and Land Use

U.S. Cities	Australian Cities	Canadian Cities	European Cities	High-income Asian Cities	Lower-income Asian Cities
Houston	Perth	Toronto	Hamburg	Tokyo	Seoul*
Phoenix	Brisbane	Vancouver*	Frankfurt	Hong Kong	Kuala Lumpur*
Detroit	Melbourne	Calgary*	Zurich	Singapore	Bangkok*
Denver	Adelaide	Edmonton*	Stockholm		Jakarta*
Los Angeles	Sydney	Montreal*	Brussels		Manila*
San Francisco	Canberra*	Winnipeg*	Paris		Surabaya*
Boston		Ottawa*	London		
Washington			Munich		
Chicago			Copenhagen		
New York			Vienna		
Portland*			Amsterdam		
Sacramento*					
San Diego*					

Note: The sixteen new cities in the sample are marked with an asterisk.

a subset of the above cities (thirty-seven cities in total, including Beijing, which is not part of broader international comparisons, but was required by the World Bank). The study for the World Bank has a range of different indicators of transportation efficiency in cities, particularly data related to the economics of urban transportation and environmental performance. These will be used in the discussion to expand on the analysis from the broader global cities study.

Transportation Energy Patterns

We begin with an overview of the patterns of urban transportation energy use, since the level of energy use in the transportation sector in a city is quite an effective barometer of its degree of automobile dependence.[2]

As can be seen in Table 3.2, there is an enormous range in per capita transportation energy use across the global sample of cities. The data show that U.S. cities use, on average, 64.3 gigajoules (GJ) of fuel per capita for urban transportation compared to 39.5 GJ per capita in Australian cities, 39.2 GJ in Canadian cities, 25.7 GJ in European cities, and 12.9 GJ in Asian cities. These data include both gasoline and diesel fuel used in private urban passenger and nonpassenger transportation and public transportation. The pattern of gasoline use per capita follows a similar pattern (55.8 GJ, 33.6 GJ, 30.9 GJ, 17.2 GJ, and 6.3 GJ per capita, respectively, for the regional groupings above).

These figures reflect an enormous variation in the degree to which cities in different regions are dependent upon diminishing conventional liquid fossil fuel resources. U.S. cities, for example, are some 5 times higher in their total per capita use of transportation energy than the Asian cities. Even compared with cities of a similar nature in Australia and Canada, U.S. cities are 1.6 times higher in their use of transportation energy. Compared to even wealthier European

Table 3.2. Transportation Energy Use per Capita in Global Cities, 1990

City	Private Transportation			Public Transportation			Total Transportation Energy (MJ)	Total Transportation Energy/ $ of GRP (MJ/$)
	Gasoline (MJ)	Diesel (MJ)	% Private of total	Diesel (MJ)	Electricity (MJ)	% Public of total		
Sacramento	65,351	10,998	100%	305	19	<1%	76,673	?
Houston	63,800	7,325	99%	499	0	1%	71,624	2.74
San Diego	61,004	5,689	99%	527	28	1%	67,248	?
Phoenix	59,832	4,507	100%	301	0	<1%	64,641	3.14
San Francisco	58,493	6,187	98%	935	275	2%	65,890	2.12
Portland	57,699	12,358	99%	614	27	1%	70,698	?
Denver	56,132	11,560	99%	594	0	1%	68,286	2.78
Los Angeles	55,246	6,279	99%	643	0	1%	62,167	2.50
Detroit	54,817	7,522	99%	405	0	1%	62,744	2.78
Boston	50,617	6,676	98%	845	252	2%	58,391	2.10
Washington	49,593	9,732	98%	753	376	2%	60,454	1.68
Chicago	46,498	8,355	98%	1,060	208	2%	56,121	2.16
New York	46,409	3,747	97%	975	494	3%	51,626	1.80
AMERICAN AVG.	55,807	7,764	99%	650	129	1%	64,351	2.38
Canberra	40,699	3,333	98%	962	0	2%	44,995	?
Perth	34,579	5,965	98%	851	0	2%	41,395	2.34
Brisbane	31,290	7,071	98%	632	284	2%	39,277	2.10
Melbourne	33,527	4,613	98%	411	338	2%	38,890	1.84
Adelaide	31,784	4,359	97%	953	6	3%	37,103	1.88
Sydney	29,491	4,481	97%	776	326	3%	35,074	1.63
AUSTRALIAN AVG.	33,562	4,970	98%	764	159	2%	39,456	1.96
Calgary	35,684	10,535	98%	808	106	2%	47,133	?
Winnipeg	32,018	6,358	97%	989	0	3%	39,366	?
Edmonton	31,848	11,116	98%	1027	69	2%	44,060	?
Vancouver	31,544	4,740	98%	743	184	2%	37,211	?
Toronto	30,746	1,058	95%	1,286	523	5%	33,613	1.49
Montreal	27,706	?	?	1,019	261	?	?	?
Ottawa	26,705	5,421	95%	1,526	0	5%	33,562	?
CANADIAN AVG.	30,893	6,538	97%	1,057	163	3%	39,173	?
Frankfurt	24,779	12,771	98%	243	499	2%	38,293	1.09
Brussels	21,080	6,297	95%	635	883	5%	28,895	0.96
Hamburg	20,344	15,463	98%	556	352	2%	36,716	1.21
Zurich	19,947	3,875	94%	609	813	6%	25,244	0.56
Stockholm	18,362	6,636	93%	1,06	751	7%	26,817	0.81
Vienna	14,990	4,387	94%	538	689	6%	20,603	0.74
Copenhagen	14,609	4,091	92%	1,313	372	8%	20,385	0.68
Paris	14,269	9,026	96%	323	946	4%	24,241	0.72
Munich	14,224	2,598	92%	210	1,166	8%	18,197	0.50

Amsterdam	13,915	5,096	96%	456	375	4%	19,843	0.79
London	12,884	9,140	94%	693	657	6%	23,374	1.05
EUROPEAN AVG.	17,218	7,216	95%	604	653	5%	25,692	0.83
Kuala Lumpur	11,643	7,600	96%	774	0	4%	20,017	4.92
Singapore	11,383	4,957	90%	1,608	131	10%	18,079	1.40
Tokyo	8,015	9,305	95%	212	711	5%	18,243	0.49
Bangkok	7,742	7,409	83%	3,026	0	17%	18,176	4.75
Seoul	5,293	2,604	82%	1,551	168	18%	9,615	1.62
Jakarta	4,787	3,845	95%	440	0	5%	9,072	6.02
Manila	2,896	2,734	77%	1,698	8	23%	7,335	6.67
Surabaya	2,633	2,684	95%	294	0	5%	5,611	7.73
Hong Kong	2,406	5,679	84%	1,217	310	16%	9,612	0.68
ASIAN AVG.	6,311	5,202	89%	1,202	148	11%	12,862	3.81

Note: The cities for which no energy per unit of GRP is available are those cities not included in the study for the World Bank and that therefore do not have the GRP data.

cities, U.S. cities use 2.5 times more transportation energy in keeping their urban passenger and goods movement systems operating.

The parameter of transportation energy per unit of wealth (i.e., MJ per dollar of GRP), also shown in Table 3.2, is an attempt to bring together both the environmental and economic aspects of energy use. Gross regional product (GRP) is the measure of all goods and services produced in the regional urban area of the particular city noted. The methodology for calculating this newly available parameter is set out in Appendix 1. Energy per unit of wealth thus brings together the two sides of the sustainability issue. Obviously on this very fundamental parameter there are some cities that are much more sustainable than others. For example, the U.S. cities consume an average of 2.4 MJ of transportation energy for every dollar of wealth they generate, ranging from a high of 3.1 MJ/$ in Phoenix to lows of 1.7 MJ/$ and 1.8 MJ/$ in Washington, D.C., and New York, respectively. Australian cities perform, on average, a little better than U.S. cities, with 2.0 MJ/$, while Toronto, the only Canadian region for which these data are available, uses only 1.5 MJ/$ in keeping its transportation system fueled. The European cities are even more fuel-efficient in relation to their urban economies, with just 0.8 MJ of energy expended per dollar of wealth produced.

The Asian cities present a mixed picture on this factor due to the huge disparities in wealth involved. While the wealthy Asian cities of Singapore, Tokyo, and Hong Kong expend a similar amount of energy per dollar as European cities (0.9 MJ/$) and are therefore low in an international context, the developing Asian cities with much lower incomes spend on average 5.3 MJ/$, or more than twice the level of transportation energy consumption relative to wealth as in U.S. cities. The demand for energy to run the transportation systems in these poorer cities appears to have a bigger impact on the local economy than in any of the other cities in the study.

The economic data on urban transportation are pursued in greater detail later in this chapter under "Car Use and Wealth." Before this we analyze the many fac-

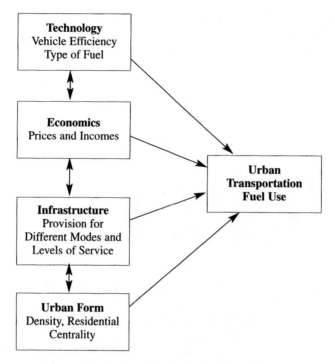

Figure 3.1. Interacting factors that explain differing levels of transportation fuel use in cities.

tors that can explain the variations in transportation energy use. As shown in Figure 3.1, the factors can be grouped into technology, economics, infrastructure, and urban form.

Fuel Types

The breakdown by fuel in Table 3.2 shows that gasoline is by far the biggest contributor to transportation energy use, but this is most marked in U.S. and Australian cities, where the automobile is more dominant and gasoline use constitutes some 86 percent of total transportation energy use and electricity constitutes only about 0.3 percent. In contrast, where cities become more public transportation–oriented, diesel and electricity become much more significant. In European cities, for example, gasoline use decreases to 67 percent of energy used in transportation, and in Asian cities it is 49 percent. Tokyo has 44 percent gasoline, 52 percent diesel, and 4 percent electricity, whereas Phoenix has 93 percent gasoline, 7 percent diesel, and no electricity.

The breakdown between private and public transportation shows an overwhelming proportion of transportation energy is consumed by private transportation in every city. Transit uses an average of only 1 percent of transportation energy in U.S. cities, 2 percent in Australian cities, 3 percent in Canadian cities, 5 percent in European cities, and 11 percent in Asian cities.

Average diesel consumption has a remarkably uniform pattern across the cities, though there is some variation within the sample for each regional grouping of cities: U.S. cities consume 8 GJ per capita; Australian cities, 5 GJ; Canadian cities, 7 GJ; European cities, 7 GJ; and Asian cities, 5 GJ. In other words, unlike gasoline use and indeed overall transportation energy use, there is no systematic pattern of variation in this factor. This would appear to highlight the similar dependence that most cities now have on the light van and truck for urban freight movement.[3]

The major difference among the cities is in the comparative use of gasoline and electricity. Gasoline-oriented cities are heavy energy users while cities with any significant level of electricity use in their transportation system are low energy users overall.[4]

These fuel use patterns are important for discussions about greenhouse gases: transportation-based carbon dioxide is an important issue in the post-Kyoto world. One of the immediate responses for cities is to try to reduce their use of coal. Although this is a generally positive policy to pursue, there is a twist to the greenhouse issue when cities are the focus, rather than just nations, as shown in the data here. Despite coal-based electricity being less fuel-efficient than gasoline (and being four times worse than gasoline in terms of carbon dioxide produced per MJ of transportation energy), it does not mean that cities with electric transportation are worse in energy use or greenhouse gases; in fact, the reverse is the case. This is primarily because of the nature of the technology and the effect of either the car or the train/tram on the city. This difference is fundamental to the concepts being presented in this chapter and in the book overall.

The fact that cities that do use a lot of electricity (even from coal) have lower energy use and carbon dioxide production is an important factor in the energy and greenhouse debate, in which coal is considered to be so much more damaging. If coal is used to provide electricity for an electric train or tram system, then the city overall uses less fuel and will produce lower greenhouse gases from the transportation sector. The mechanism for this appears to be land use changes, greater walking and cycling in transit-oriented environments, and the linking of a number of trip purposes when using transit. (This is examined in more detail later under "Transit Leverage.")

In addition, the advantages of electric-based public transportation become far greater in terms of greenhouse and other factors, such as smog and acid rain, when the source of power is renewable fuel. For example, Zurich, which uses Swiss hydropower, usually produces only 6 grams of carbon dioxide per MJ of electricity, whereas Melbourne, which uses very poor quality coal, produces 414 grams of carbon dioxide per MJ. This will become a more significant factor in the decades ahead as the Climate Change Convention agreements have to be implemented. The renewable-energy future will be one based on electricity, linking together the many dispersed ways of producing power from wind, the sun, biomass, garbage, and waves. A future based upon electric power will favor electric transit, perhaps supplemented by electric automobiles; but this must not be a one-for-one substitution of electric cars for gasoline cars because the need for energy conservation will require a substantial move toward electric transit–based cities. Further details on carbon dioxide are also provided under "Transportation Emissions" later in this chapter.

Technology-Vehicle Efficiency

Vehicle efficiency technology is often the first factor considered in discussions on fuel use. Obviously, the efficiency of vehicles must impact on fuel use, but how important is it in explaining the variations in urban fuel use? The data presented below show it is only a small factor in explaining the variation, if motor vehicles are the focus. But if we also consider public transit systems and their associated ridership, then we can begin to see some major variations.

For the 1980 data on cities we made a simple calculation to throw light on this issue. Table 3.3 adjusts the 1980 per capita gasoline use in the global cities for vehicle efficiency—that is, the table shows what the per capita gasoline use would be in other cities if all those cities had vehicles like those in the U.S. cities. Overall, the variation from U.S. cities to Asian cities in their gasoline use is reduced from a factor of ten to a factor of seven, and the variation from U.S. to European cities reduces from four times to three times. Thus this technological factor is a relevant parameter, but clearly it is not the dominant factor often described in energy conservation literature (LaBelle and Moses, 1982; Chandler, 1985; Wachs and Crawford, 1991). Other economic factors as well as planning factors need to be considered.

It should also be pointed out that the variation between U.S. cities and other cities in terms of fuel efficiency of vehicles has generally diminished between 1980 and 1990, as U.S. vehicle fleets have been downsizing. The 1990 average car fuel efficiencies based on actual 1990 fuel use are provided in Table 3.4 below. What appears to be clear by comparing Tables 3.3 and 3.4 is that all cities have improved their urban car fuel efficiencies. Whereas in 1980 the U.S. cities had cars that operated in city conditions with 1.28 times higher fuel use than the cars in the wealthy Asian cities (Singapore, Tokyo, and Hong

Table 3.3. Average 1980 Gasoline Use per Capita in Cities by Region to Account for Vehicle Efficiency (Relative to U.S. Vehicle Efficiencies, Using National Values and Adjusted for Average Speed in Cities)

	Unadjusted Gasoline Use per Capita (MJ)	Average Vehicle Efficiency (National Values) (liters per 100 km)	Adjusted for Average Speed in Cities (liters per 100 km)	Gasoline Use Per Capita U.S. Vehicle Efficiency (MJ)	
				National Values	Adjusted for Average Speed
American	58,541	15.35	19.33	58,541	58,541
Australian	29,829	12.50	15.33	33,446	37,612
Toronto	25,962	16.30	21.72	24,449	23,105
European	13,280	10.66	16.38	19,123	15,727
Asian	5,493	7.63	15.05	11,051	7,248

Notes:

1. Detailed data on vehicle efficiencies are contained in Newman and Kenworthy (1989a).

2. Adjustments for average speed are made by using $y = 1.0174x + 37.4291$, where y = fuel consumption in ml/km and x is the inverse of average speed in s/km and national fuel efficiencies are assumed to be at an average speed of 60 km/h.

Table 3.4. Fuel Efficiencies of Urban Cars in
Global Cities, 1990

Cities	Fuel Efficiency (MJ/km)	Fuel Efficiency (liters per 100 km)
American	5.03	14.50
Australian	5.11	14.73
Canadian	4.85	13.98
European	3.79	10.93
Wealthy Asian	4.93	14.21
Developing Asian	3.53	10.18

Kong), in 1990 the cars in U.S. cities operated at only 1.02 times higher fuel use than cars in those same cities.

Despite this flattening out in fuel efficiencies of the urban car fleets between U.S. and wealthy Asian cities, there still remains a very considerable difference in gasoline use per capita (U.S. cities are still 8 times higher than their wealthy Asian counterparts). Obviously, automobile technology cannot be the main factor in this considerable variation.

Likewise, in 1980, U.S. cities had 1.26 times higher fuel consumption in urban cars than Australian cities, but in 1990 the situation had changed so that U.S. cities are actually marginally more fuel-efficient in their urban cars than are Australian cities (1.02 times better, primarily due to Australia having one of the world's highest average ages for their car fleet and therefore lower penetration rates for new, more fuel-efficient cars; see note 9 in Chapter 4, which shows that the Australian car fleet has not improved its fuel efficiency for thirty-five years). Per capita gasoline use in U.S. cities, however, is still 1.7 times higher than in Australian cities.

Through the data that are available on all forty-six cities in this study, it is possible to develop an even more detailed picture of actual energy efficiencies by mode of urban transportation. These data measure energy efficiency in terms of MJ per passenger kilometer (i.e., including vehicle occupancy), as opposed to the technological efficiency of the mode as expressed in Tables 3.3 and 3.4. These data are summarized here in Table 3.5.

The data show that energy efficiency by car travel is at least less than half the efficiency of transit travel, or even worse when compared to urban rail systems (the only exception is U.S. city buses, which are comparatively inefficient compared to buses in other cities—see below). Urban car travel in North America (i.e., U.S. and Canadian cities) is 13 to 16 percent less fuel-efficient than car travel in Australian and wealthy Asian cities, 34 percent less efficient than car travel in European cities, and 66 percent less efficient than in newly developing Asian cities.

Table 3.5 shows that fuel efficiency of bus travel varies considerably by region and in comparison with other modes within that region. U.S. bus systems are similar in fuel efficiency to European urban car travel and are 19 percent *less* efficient than car travel in newly developing Asian cities. This is primarily because

Table 3.5. Modal Energy Efficiencies for Regional
Groupings of Cities, 1990

Cities	(MJ per passenger km)		
	Car	Bus	All Rail
American	3.52	2.52	0.74
Australian	3.12	1.64	1.12
Canadian	3.45	1.61	0.51
European	2.62	1.32	0.49
Wealthy Asian	3.03	0.84	0.16
Developing Asian	2.12	0.74	0.24

Notes:
1. Rail energy efficiency includes heavy rail, light rail, and trams where
relevant.

2. The data in Table 3.5 vary little from the data shown in Appendix 1
because they cover all forty-six cities in the study, whereas the data in
Appendix 1 from the study for the World Bank cover only thirty-seven
cities. Note also that Beijing is included in Appendix 1 data but is excluded from the above table to be consistent with averages for other parameters on the developing Asian cities used throughout the book (i.e.,
Beijing was included only in the study for the World Bank and is not one
of the forty-six cities).

of their low patronage levels, since buses throughout the world are not very different in technology. Bus systems in European cities and in places such as Sydney
and Toronto are about two to three times as efficient as in the U.S. cities. In
Asian cities bus travel is about three to four times as efficient as in U.S. cities,
with Beijing having an efficiency of 0.15 MJ per passenger kilometer, which is
seventeen times more efficient; bus loadings in peak hours in Chinese cities reach
twelve persons per square meter (Hu and Kenworthy, 1996). Such data show that
the gains in energy to be made from bus transport technology are dwarfed by the
possibilities offered through ridership improvements.

Rail modes (trains and trams) are by far the most energy-efficient motorized
transport technology in each regional grouping of cities. The only cities that are
exceptions to this are Perth and Adelaide, which in 1990 still had old diesel train
systems with low ridership (see Appendix 1). Perth has since electrified its rail
system and is now much more efficient (see Chapter 4 case study on Perth and
Newman, 1992). Apart from these two cities, the others show that rail travel is
between 2.5 and 5 times more energy-efficient than bus travel. Rail energy use
reaches a low of 0.06 MJ per passenger kilometer in Manila (0.07 in Beijing),
which is some 59 times more energy-efficient than car travel in the United
States. More typically, rail systems in European cities are 7 times more energy-
efficient than car travel in U.S. cities.

Electric rail technology tends to be more energy-efficient because of its speed
and capacity, which lead to higher ridership. Electric rail also has a demonstrated
capacity to induce higher-density development around stations due to its ability
to take large numbers of people to and from concentrated nodes of development
without harming the pedestrian qualities of an area. Furthermore, electric rail can

also be linked to renewable energy, which is a significant advantage as we enter the next century with its reduced oil production.

Not shown in Table 3.5 are the ferry systems that exist in a few of the cities (the averages are somewhat irrelevant because of the paucity of systems in each region). As shown in Appendix 1, however, ferries are remarkably inefficient in their use of fuel. The only possible exceptions are in Sydney, New York, and Bangkok, where small ferries and reasonable patronage seem to ensure a system roughly equivalent to the energy efficiency of buses. The efficiency of all other ferry systems is very poor, however. Hamburg has the least energy-efficient ferry system (9 times less efficient than their car system). Boston's ferries are 5 times less efficient than their cars, and even Hong Kong's ferries are 26 percent less efficient than their car system. Ferries in Hamburg have suffered from declining tourist patronage, which helps to explain their poorer energy efficiency.

Ferries, overall, are the least well exploited of urban public transport modes, and it might be expected that these figures could be significantly improved upon with research and wider planning commitment to better integrated urban ferry systems.

Table 3.6 summarizes modal energy efficiencies in the global sample of cities even further by showing the overall modal averages from all the global cities combined, but separating the rail modes into heavy and light rail, and dividing heavy rail into electric and diesel systems. It also shows the comparative loadings, or vehicle occupancies, which contribute significantly to the energy efficiency differences among the various modes.

Photo 3.1. Electric rail is the most energy-efficient motorized mode. European cities with good rail systems, such as the light rail systems in Bremen (*top*) and Hanover (*bottom*), have distinctly less automobile-dependent transportation patterns.

Table 3.6. Overall Modal Energy Efficiencies in the
Global Sample of Cities, 1990

Mode	MJ per Passenger Kilometer (average all cities)	Measured Average Vehicle Occupancy (average all cities)
Car	2.91	1.52
Bus	1.56	13.83
Heavy Rail (electric)	0.44	30.96
Heavy Rail (diesel)	1.44	27.97
Light Rail/Tram	0.79	29.73

Note: Rail mode occupancies are given on the basis of the average loading per
rail car, not per train. The average occupancy of cars is a twenty-four-hour figure.

These data reveal that urban car travel is, on average, nearly 2 times as en-
ergy-consumptive as average urban bus travel, 6.6 times more energy-intensive
than average urban electric train travel, and 3.7 times more than typical light rail
or tram system travel. Light rail and tram systems typically operate in environments requiring a lot more stopping and starting than heavy rail, with much
closer station spacings than heavy rail. So although their average loading is similar to heavy rail, their energy efficiency is a little poorer than electric heavy rail
but better than diesel heavy rail.

The data in Table 3.6 also show that diesel rail is only a little more fuel-efficient on average than an urban bus and that average train carriage occupancies
are roughly equal across the three rail types. Rail occupancies are on average
more than twice those of buses and about twenty times higher than cars. Overall,
these data reemphasize the importance of developing a good backbone of electric
rail in cities if energy conservation is to be enhanced. Those cities without such
systems are the ones with very high gasoline use.

Price and Income

The economics of transportation is dominated by considerations of price (especially gasoline prices) and income; these are considered to be among the major
determinants of travel demand and, in particular, significant determinants of the
level of car ownership and, through this, the level of car use.

Obviously the price of gasoline and how much disposable income people have
will be big factors in determining how residents of cities travel. When we examined the 1980 data on per capita transportation fuel patterns (Newman and
Kenworthy, 1989a), we made an analysis to adjust for price and income (as well
as fuel efficiency, as discussed above). The results showed that the extent of the
economic factors can be questioned. The data provided in Table 3.7, which
makes adjustments for price and income, indicate that these economic factors are
not able to explain the major variations in per capita gasoline use between the
cities. The effect of the economic adjustments in Table 3.7 is to give all cities
high U.S. incomes and low U.S. gasoline prices.

Table 3.7. Average Value for per Capita Gasoline Use in Cities by Region, 1980, Compared to Adjusted Values (for U.S. Gasoline Prices, Incomes and Vehicle Efficiency)

Cities	Actual Gasoline Use (MJ per capita)	Adjusted Gasoline Use for U.S. Gasoline Prices, Incomes, and Vehicle Efficiency (MJ per capita)		% Difference Between U.S. Gasoline Use and Adjusted Gasoline Use by Other Cities	
		Short-term Elasticities	Long-term Elasticities	Short-term Elasticities	Long-term Elasticities
American	58,541	58,541	58,541	—	—
Australian	29,829	38,488	43,680	51%	25%
Toronto	25,962	22,370	19,457	62%	67%
European	13,280	17,082	31,080	71%	47%
Asian	5,493	7,676	12,340	87%	79%
Average for non-U.S. cities	17,133	21,450	31,160	63%	47%

Sources: Pindyck (1979); Dahl (1982); Archibald and Gillingham (1981); Wheaton (1982).
Notes:

		Short Term	Long Term
1. Gasoline consumption elasticities used:	Gas price	−0.20	−1.0
	Incomes	+0.11	+0.6

2. As gasoline consumption elasticities include a component due to vehicle efficiency, it is necessary to subtract this when adjusting other cities for U.S. vehicle efficiencies; otherwise it would be accounted for twice.

		Short Term	Long Term
Vehicle efficiency elasticities used:	Gas price	+0.11	+1.0
	Incomes	−0.11	−1.0

3. Vehicle efficiencies used were national values in Table 3.3 adjusted for average speed in each city. In all cases, vehicle efficiencies in the long term became more than equivalent to U.S. levels and therefore the vehicle efficiency factor in the long term is canceled out.

Table 3.7 shows the expected gasoline consumption if U.S. incomes, gasoline prices, and car fuel efficiency were found in all the cities—that is, if these economic factors were the sole or primary factors, then all the cities should have the same gasoline use. They clearly do not. On average, the economic factors explain, at most about half the differences in gasoline use. It can be argued that these long-term elasticities are overestimates since they incorporate some degree of anticipated urban form change, but even they do not adequately explain the variations in gasoline use in the sample. What is suggested by these results is that a purely economic approach to transportation matters will be inadequate, and that matters of infrastructure and urban form have direct influence on transportation patterns.

Thus planners who provide the transportation infrastructure or who set out the physical plan of a city are directly and actively influencing transportation patterns, not just responding to economic factors.[5]

The same conclusion can be found by considering car ownership. Table 3.8 shows how car ownership varies, indicating higher values in U.S., Canadian, and Australian cities than in European and Asian cities, but there is a much larger variation in car usage per capita. Obviously, there are more people who do not need to use a car, or do not need to use a car as much, in European and Asian cities compared to U.S. and Australian cities.

Table 3.8 shows that mobility in the cities (the sum of car use and transit use per person) varies considerably but is not related to the wealth of the cities. Indeed, as shown later under "Car Use and Wealth," there appears to be a possible relationship between GRP and mobility when wealth levels are low, but as mobility rises there are fewer gains in terms of wealth, until there are possible negative impacts from the mobility. See Chapter 2 for a discussion of the suggested mechanism for this.

Thus the data suggest that there are simultaneous economic and environmental advantages from reducing mobility in automobile-dependent cities. Awareness of this relationship is not widespread. In *Scientific American's* special edition on transportation in October 1997, Schafer and Victor make the assertion that mobility will massively increase in the future based on the fact that as incomes rise, people travel more and faster. They predict an increase in global mobility of five times present levels. Such predictions bring to mind the endless growth in energy use predicted in the 1960s due to the same apparent link between GNP and energy. These predictions are now seen as quaint and out of touch since GNP and energy use have become decoupled due to the growth in energy efficiency over the past few decades. The same decoupling is likely to occur for mobility and wealth, and our data suggest it may well be occurring now. The sustainability agenda will show how wealth can be improved in cities by reducing mobility, thus increasing quality of life on both economic and environmental levels.

Table 3.8. Car Ownership and Usage and Their Relation to Transit and GRP in Global Cities by Region, 1990

Cities	Car Ownership per 1,000 People	Car Usage (pass. km/person)	Transit Usage (pass. km/person)	Total Travel (pass. km/person)	GRP per Capita ($US, 1990 per person)	Mobility per $1,000 of GRP
American	604	16,045	474	16,519	26,822	616
Australian	491	10,797	882	11,679	19,761	591
Canadian	524	9,290	998	10,288	22,572	408
European	392	6,601	1,895	8,496	31,721	268
Asian	109	2,806	2,587	5,393	9,018	598

Note: The Asian city data are averages of the wealthy and developing Asian cities combined. Canadian city GRP and mobility per $1,000 of GRP are for Toronto only (the only Canadian city for which GRP data were developed).

Infrastructure Priorities

Using other transportation modes is important not only because of a reduction in automobile use but also because it reduces unnecessary mobility in general. Thus it is important to address the variation in use of other modes and how this relates to the provision of infrastructure and services. Tables 3.9 and 3.10 present some variations in transportation patterns and, in particular, their relation to infrastructure provision in all the cities in the study.

Modal Splits

Transit

In the highly automobile-oriented U.S. cities at the top of the list in Tables 3.2 and 3.9, transit's role within the overall transportation system cannot get much smaller. For example, as a percentage of their total motorized passenger kilometers of travel, transit in Sacramento and Phoenix accounts for less than 1 percent of total passenger travel, while in Houston, San Diego, and Detroit it struggles to get above 1 percent. Even in Denver, where there is a strong policy to encourage bus usage due to photochemical smog, only 1.4 percent of total passenger travel is by public transportation. It is only in the U.S. cities with rail systems that any "significant" proportion of total transportation is by nonautomobile modes—e.g., Washington, D.C., 4.6 percent; San Francisco, 5.3 percent; Chicago, 5.4 percent; and New York, 10.8 percent. The proportion of total transit passenger kilometers per capita by trains in these cities is: Washington, D.C., 64 percent; San Francisco, 57 percent; Chicago, 67 percent; and New York, 76 percent.

Australian cities overall are a little less automobile-oriented than their U.S. counterparts, and Canadian cities are even less so. For example, while U.S. cities overall have only some 3 percent of total motorized travel on transit, Australian cities have 8 percent and Canadian cities average 10 percent. Sydney, with 16 percent public transportation use, is the least car-oriented Australian city, with a high proportion on rail (63 percent of transit passenger kilometers). Perth, on the other hand, is approaching U.S. city auto dependence, with only 4 percent of total travel on transit and only 18 percent of transit travel on rail (though this is changing; see Chapter 4). Within the group of Canadian cities, Toronto and Montreal stand out as being the least car-oriented. Metro Toronto in particular is significantly different from its North American neighbors, with 24 percent transit use, though usage is somewhat lower for the Greater Toronto Area (15 percent). The comparison with its nearest neighbor, Detroit, which has just 1.1 percent transit use, is quite stunning.

European cities, on average, have 23 percent of their total passenger transportation task accounted for by public transportation. This ranges from only 12 percent public transportation in Frankfurt to 32 percent in Vienna and 30 percent in Paris and London. In the European cities, 77 percent of all public transportation passenger kilometers are on trains, while Canadian cities have only 26

Table 3.9. Relative Performance and Provision for Transportation Modes in Global Cities, 1990

City	% of Total Passenger Km on Transit	% of Total Transit Passenger Km on Rail Modes	% Work Trips on Transit	% Work Trips by Walking and Cycling	Transit Service Level (vehicle km of service per person)	Road Supply (meters per person)	CBD Car Parking (spaces per 1,000 CBD jobs)	Average Speeds of Travel by Mode (km/h)		
								Car	Train	Bus
Sacramento	0.6	31.3	2.5	4.7	9.9	8.8	777	63.9	30.7	22.7
Houston	1.1	0.0	4.1	2.6	16.7	11.7	612	61.2	—	23.6
San Diego	1.4	27.0	3.4	5.8	23.7	5.5	688	55.7	35.0	26.7
Phoenix	0.8	0.0	2.1	4.2	9.9	9.6	906	51.5	—	24.5
San Francisco	5.3	56.6	14.5	5.5	49.3	4.6	137	44.3	43.3	20.1
Portland	1.9	18.4	5.8	3.9	27.2	10.6	403	49.7	31.5	26.0
Denver	1.4	0.0	4.4	4.3	21.2	7.6	606	58.1	—	24.2
Los Angeles	2.1	0.0	6.7	4.0	19.8	3.8	520	45.0	—	19.9
Detroit	1.1	0.0	2.6	2.0	14.0	6.0	706	56.3	—	22.5
Boston	3.5	75.7	14.7	7.4	36.0	6.7	285	52.3	32.6	20.1
Washington	4.6	64.1	15.1	4.5	37.3	5.2	253	42.4	39.4	19.3
Chicago	5.4	67.1	14.9	4.5	41.5	5.2	128	45.0	46.1	17.9
New York	10.8	76.0	26.6	6.7	62.8	4.6	60	38.3	39.0	18.8
AMERICAN AVG.	3.1	32.0	9.0	4.6	28.4	6.9	468	51.1	37.2	22.0
Canberra	5.6	0.0	10.0	6.0	67.9	8.8	842	49.5	—	34.5
Perth	4.3	17.9	9.7	4.1	47.0	10.7	631	45.0	34.0	24.6
Brisbane	7.4	65.7	14.5	5.1	55.1	8.2	322	50.1	44.0	28.7
Melbourne	7.9	79.7	15.9	4.7	49.9	7.7	337	45.1	28.6	21.0
Adelaide	4.9	21.1	11.5	5.4	46.4	8.0	580	46.4	26.3	22.1
Sydney	15.8	62.6	25.2	5.5	94.0	6.2	222	37.0	42.0	19.0
AUSTRALIAN AVG.	7.7	41.2	14.5	5.1	60.0	8.3	489	45.5	35.0	25.0
Calgary	6.5	42.0	16.5	5.3	49.7	4.9	522	47.1	32.0	24.6
Winnipeg	6.2	0.0	19.9	8.0	40.5	4.2	546	35.0	—	19.0
Edmonton	6.8	9.9	11.0	6.0	51.3	4.8	593	40.0	32.0	19.5

Vancouver	6.5	24.2	12.4	5.7	50.3	5.1	443	38.0	41.7	20.1
Toronto	23.6	55.1	30.1	5.3	98.4	2.6	176	35.0	30.9	20.3
Montreal	12.8	50.3	21.3	6.1	60.2	4.5	347	43.3	29.7	20.5
Ottawa	9.4	0.0	27.0	7.0	55.9	7.1	230	40.0	—	24.0
CANADIAN AVG.	10.2	25.9	19.7	6.2	58.0	4.7	408	39.8	33.3	21.1
Frankfurt	12.1	86.3	42.1	8.5	47.9	2.0	246	45.0	46.8	19.6
Brussels	17.3	76.4	35.3	19.1	62.7	2.1	314	37.9	31.8	19.1
Hamburg	15.3	73.5	38.1	12.5	71.0	2.6	177	30.0	37.3	22.0
Zurich	24.2	84.7	39.8	24.2	148.1	4.0	137	36.0	45.2	21.1
Stockholm	27.3	66.0	55.0	14.0	133.2	2.2	193	43.0	43.9	27.2
Vienna	31.6	81.8	43.9	11.9	72.6	1.8	186	27.5	26.5	19.1
Copenhagen	17.2	65.4	25.0	32.0	121.3	4.6	223	50.0	59.2	24.2
Paris	30.5	82.8	36.2	14.9	71.0	0.9	199	25.7	41.8	19.3
Munich	29.4	87.7	46.0	16.0	91.4	1.8	266	35.0	46.2	23.2
Amsterdam	14.0	71.2	25.0	35.0	60.3	2.6	354	35.0	25.0	16.3
London	29.9	74.2	40.0	14.0	138.4	2.0	?	30.2	48.3	19.0
EUROPEAN AVG.	22.6	77.3	38.8	18.4	92.5	2.4	230	35.9	41.1	20.9
Kuala Lumpur	20.0	0.3	25.5	16.9	49.7	1.5	297	29.4	—	16.3
Singapore	46.7	31.3	56.0	22.2	114.0	1.1	164	32.5	40.0	19.2
Tokyo	63.4	96.1	48.9	21.7	89.3	3.9	43	24.4	39.6	12.0
Bangkok	33.3	0.4	30.0	10.0	110.3	0.6	397	13.1	34.0	9.0
Seoul	54.0	35.7	59.6	19.8	113.9	0.8	49	24.0	39.8	18.8
Jakarta	46.1	2.9	36.3	22.3	54.5	0.5	?	23.6	35.6	14.6
Manila	66.7	6.2	54.2	17.8	257.9	0.6	27	25.5	37.5	15.4
Surabaya	26.1	0.0	21.0	23.5	62.2	0.3	?	27.0	—	17.5
Hong Kong	82.3	43.4	74.0	16.9	140.4	0.3	33	25.7	40.2	18.4
ASIAN AVG.	48.7	24.0	45.1	19.0	110.2	1.1	144	25.0	38.1	15.3

Source: Kenworthy et al. (1999).

Notes:
1. Train speeds include heavy rail, light rail, and trams, weighted by passenger kilometers per capita for each mode.
2. The percentage of total transit passenger kilometers on rail includes heavy rail, light rail, and trams.

Table 3.10. Annual Travel by Private and Public Transportation in Global Cities, 1990

City	Annual Travel in Private Passenger Cars (passenger km per capita)	Annual Travel in Public Transportation (passenger km per capita)	Total Annual Travel (passenger km per capita)
Sacramento	19,239	117	19,356
Houston	19,004	215	19,219
San Diego	18,757	259	19,016
Phoenix	15,903	124	16,026
San Francisco	16,229	899	17,129
Portland	14,665	286	14,951
Denver	13,515	199	13,714
Los Angeles	16,686	352	17,037
Detroit	15,846	171	16,018
Boston	17,373	627	18,000
Washington	16,214	774	16,988
Chicago	14,096	805	14,902
New York	11,062	1,334	12,396
AMERICAN AVERAGE	16,045	474	16,519
Canberra	11,195	660	11,855
Perth	12,029	544	12,573
Brisbane	11,188	900	12,088
Melbourne	9,782	844	10,626
Adelaide	11,173	572	11,745
Sydney	9,417	1,769	11,186
AUSTRALIAN AVERAGE	10,797	882	11,679
Calgary	11,078	775	11,852
Winnipeg	9,620	635	10,255
Edmonton	10,028	728	10,756
Vancouver	12,541	871	13,412
Toronto	7,027	2,173	9,200
Montreal	6,502	952	7,454
Ottawa	8,236	850	9,086
CANADIAN AVERAGE	9,290	998	10,288
Frankfurt	8,309	1,149	9,458
Brussels	6,809	1,428	8,237
Hamburg	7,592	1,375	8,967
Zurich	7,692	2,459	10,151
Stockholm	6,261	2,351	8,612
Vienna	5,272	2,430	7,702
Copenhagen	7,749	1,607	9,356
Paris	4,842	2,121	6,963
Munich	5,925	2,463	8,388
Amsterdam	6,522	1,061	7,583
London	5,644	2,405	8,049
EUROPEAN AVERAGE	6,601	1,895	8,496
Kuala Lumpur	6,299	1,577	7,875
Singapore	3,169	2,775	5,944
Tokyo	3,175	5,501	8,676
Bangkok	4,634	2,313	6,947
Seoul	2,464	2,890	5,354
Jakarta	1,546	1,323	2,869
Manila	1,281	2,568	3,849
Surabaya	1,568	555	2,123
Hong Kong	813	3,784	4,597
ASIAN AVERAGE	2,772	2,587	5,359

percent, U.S. cities have 32 percent, and Australian cities 41 percent. Asian cities overall have the least developed urban rail systems, with only 24 percent of transit on rail, though within this group Tokyo is a rail giant, with an incredible 96 percent of its transit on rail.

Nonmotorized Transportation

In terms of the importance of nonmotorized transportation, Table 3.9 shows that the U.S. cities have the least proportion of workers traveling by foot or bike to work (4.6 percent), followed closely by Australian (5.1 percent) and Canadian cities (6.2 percent). It is only in the European and Asian cities where nonmotorized transportation is featured strongly at about 19 percent of work trips, with the "cycling cities'" of Amsterdam and Copenhagen as high as 35 percent. It should be noted, however, that despite the Asian cities very high urban densities, they do not have commensurately strong nonmotorized traffic by comparison to European cities, though they are much higher than automobile-dependent U.S. and Australian cities.

This highlights an important policy issue: that whereas European cities have done much to encourage the return of walking and cycling through innovative pedestrianization, traffic-calming schemes, and other initiatives, walking and cycling are being squeezed out of Asian cities (especially developing Asian cities) through the increasingly hostile traffic and urban environments and lack of policy attention. Only in Japan and Singapore are major efforts being made to enhance conditions for these modes.

Photo 3.2. Groningen, the Netherlands, where one in three work trips is by bike.

Journey-to-work

The data in Table 3.9 also show specifically the role that transit plays in the journey-to-work, the period when road space is most constrained and the need for
managing travel demand is highest. The U.S. cities clearly score poorly in this
factor, with a meager 9 percent of work trips by transit. Australian cities fair a little better with 15 percent, and Canadian cities again are better with 20 percent
(more than double their U.S. neighbors); Perth is equivalent to an average U.S.
city in this factor, with only 10 percent of work trips by transit. Within these
groups the transit capitals are Sydney (25 percent), New York and Ottawa (27
percent), and Toronto (30 percent). Ottawa is a very centralized city with good
busways that attract high peak-period patronage, whereas the other cities are
strongly rail-based. At the low end of the spectrum, Phoenix, Sacramento, and
Detroit do not even reach a meager 3 percent of work trips on transit.

It is only in the European and Asian cities, where work travel is very strongly
transit-oriented, that transit becomes the dominant mode (39 percent to 45 percent of work trips, respectively). In Stockholm 55 percent of work travel is by
transit, primarily due to the exceptional integration of mixed-use subcenters
around rail stations (Cervero, 1995). Within the group of Asian cities,
Singapore, Seoul, and Hong Kong are very high in transit work travel (56 percent, 60 percent, and 74 percent, respectively), again due to the integration of
many work destinations into high-density centers over and around their mass
rapid transit stations.

Overall, it is interesting to note that in European cities only 43 percent of
work travel is by car, the rest being either by transit or foot and bicycle. In Asian
cities the figure is a mere 36 percent. In the United States, Australia, and
Canada, car travel to work in metropolitan areas averages between 74 percent
and 86 percent.

Travel Distances

Table 3.10 shows the annual per capita travel by private and public transportation that lies behind some of the data in Table 3.9. First, like the patterns already
discussed, it shows the U.S. cities leading the world by a long way in the absolute
amount of travel undertaken by private car. On average, U.S. urban residents
travel almost 1.5 times farther in cars than urban Australians and 1.7 times further than metropolitan residents in Canada. This is accentuated when compared
to urban Europeans and Asians: U.S. urban residents are respectively almost 2.5
and 6 times more mobile in cars.

The exact reverse of this pattern is true for transit. U.S. city dwellers travel a
meager 474 kilometers per capita via transit every year, while Australians travel
882, Canadians 998, Europeans 1,895, and Asians 2,587 kilometers per year.
However, the extra travel on transit in other cities does not bring them up to the
same level of overall travel found in U.S. cities.

For example, people in the Asian cities, the most transit-oriented of all the
cities, travel less than one-third as far in total as U.S. urban dwellers.
Furthermore, people in U.S. cities travel an average of nearly 9,500 kilometers
farther by car and about 1,400 kilometers fewer by public transportation than

people in European cities. Among other things, this suggests that urban travel distances are shorter in both Asia and Europe. In fact, work journey average distances are about 33 percent shorter in European cities, where the typical work trip averages about 10 kilometers, and 47 percent shorter in Asian cities (an average 8 kilometers), compared to 15 kilometers in U.S. cities and 13 kilometers in Australian cities.

As already shown with particular variables, all the comparisons presented so far from Tables 3.9 and 3.10 are even more striking when the Asian cities are examined. Overall in the Asian cities, almost 50 percent of all motorized travel is by transit, and when just the wealthier three (Singapore, Tokyo, and Hong Kong) are considered, the figure is even higher at 64 percent of all travel. What is even more striking is to realize that in the morning peak, less than 10 percent of workers in Hong Kong are traveling to work by private transport, 21 percent in Seoul, 22 percent in Singapore, and 29 percent in Tokyo.

Transit Leverage

These data support the notion of "transit leverage," or "transit multiplier" (Neff, 1996), which has been hinted at in the previous discussions on mobility and on fuel types. Calculations show that when transit replaces car travel, it does better than substitute 1 kilometer of car travel for 1 kilometer of transit. Neff suggests it could be anywhere from 8.6 to 12.0 kilometers of car travel that are replaced by 1 kilometer of transit based on US data. In our global cities data, it appears to be more like between 5 and 7 to 1, based on the relative decline in vehicle kilometers traveled per capita for every extra passenger kilometer traveled per capita on transit. The reasons for this multiplier effect include the following:

- If a good transit option becomes available, then people and businesses adjust by locating nearer to the line; thus transit shortens travel distances.
- People taking transit often combine several journeys in one—for example, picking up groceries on the way home from work, which in a car-based suburban setting would likely mean separate car trips.
- Households that switch to transit often give up one car and thus have less car use because the choice of using a car is less available.
- Transit users often find that the habit of walking or biking to stations flows into the rest of their lifestyle.

Transit leverage is extremely important as a concept when examining the future potential for travel pattern change. Most projections from transportation planners try to show how difficult it is to reduce car use significantly. The standard approach is to double the present amount of public transport use and subtract that from car use, thus showing only a few percent reduction for an assumed massive amount of investment (see, for example, Wachs and Crawford, 1991, and even the Danish government's scenarios for the future in Danish Energy Agency, 1995). However, the transit leverage concept means that by building new transit and attracting users, there is a flow-on of reduced mobility that is considerably more than the extra transit passenger kilometers. Understanding this requires a larger view of cities than is found in most engineering approaches (see Chapter 6). It suggests that by building new transit lines into automobile-dependent suburbs and creating urban villages around the new stations, a significant change in travel patterns could occur. This is the hope of the Future City concept as presented in Chapter 4.

Transit Service Levels

All the modal split and transportation patterns discussed so far are paralleled by the amount of transit service provided by the cities (measured in terms of service kilometers per person). Table 3.9 shows, for example, that transit service provision ranges on average from a low of 28 kilometers per person in the U.S. cities, through about 60 kilometers in the Australian and Canadian cities, up to between 90 and 110 kilometers in the European and Asian cities. However, this factor does not vary between cities to anywhere near the same extent as do the other transportation characteristics. Transit service per capita, for example, is nearly four times higher in Asian cities than in U.S. cities, but the proportion of total travel on transit in Asian cities is sixteen times higher. Obviously, the amount of transit service is not as critical as its quality if a city is to attract high transit usage. Buses that wander long distances around scattered suburbs to pick up passengers can rarely compete with the car, but rapid electric rail from one dense subcenter to another certainly can. These data are important in discussions of the viability of transit: increasing levels of service will no doubt improve patronage, but in automobile-dependent cities it is necessary to do a lot more than just improving services. There needs to be a holistic approach that incorporates urban form, the quality of service (including its speed; see below), and the selective supply of infrastructure for automobiles versus transit.

Road Supply and Parking

Table 3.9 includes data on how cities provide infrastructure for their automobile users in terms of road supply and central city parking. Here again, the automobile cities of the United States and Australia provide about three to four times as much road per capita as do European cities and nearly six to eight times as much as in Asian cities. The Canadian cities are not as strong in their provision of roads (i.e., 4.7 meters per person on average, compared to 6.9 meters in the U.S. cities and 8.3 meters in Australian cities). This is generally consistent with the other patterns already discussed showing Canadian cities to be somewhat less automobile-oriented than other Auto Cities. The Australian cities in general have the most roads per capita.

Central city parking does not have quite such a large variation across the city groupings. U.S. and Australian cities are very similar. Actually, the Australian cities are, on average, a little better provided with CBD parking than their U.S. counterparts (489 spaces per 1,000 jobs compared to 468). There is nevertheless a reasonable variation between the U.S./Australian cities and the other groups of cities. For example, they have twice as many spaces per 1,000 jobs as do European cities and more than three times the number provided by the Asian cities. Compared to the wealthier Asian cities, where the car is more controlled (only 80 spaces per 1,000 jobs on average), parking supply in the CBD is six times higher in U.S./Australian cities; in fact, Tokyo and Hong Kong provide 33 to 43

Photo 3.3. Central business district of Detroit. Detroit has one of the highest levels of parking provision in the world. Yet the supply of parking and the vitality of a city center seem to be almost inversely related.

spaces per 1,000 jobs. Bangkok and Kuala Lumpur have much higher parking provision (397 and 297 spaces, respectively), reflecting their greater commitment to the car among the Asian cities sampled.

The really outstanding cities in terms of central city parking space provision are Phoenix (906), Canberra (842), Sacramento (777), Detroit (706), San Diego (688), and Perth (631). When roads and CBD parking are considered together, the cities that appear to provide best for the car are Sacramento, Houston, Phoenix, Perth, and Canberra.

The parameter of roads per person is mostly a reflection of urban density, which is outlined in more detail below. However, CBD parking is a parameter that reflects much of a city's priority for the automobile. It is also a parameter that lends itself to direct and immediate impact on CBD traffic levels if cities want to go that way (e.g., Schoup, 1994). However, it will be an isolated and therefore politically difficult policy to implement if it is seen as the mechanism to try to change travel patterns beyond the city center.

Traffic and Transit Speeds and Travel Time

Table 3.9 details the speed of public and private transportation (car, train, and bus) in each of the cities. A very clear pattern distinguishing automobile-dominated cities from those with significant public transportation use (particularly rail) is revealed by how easy it is to travel by car and how the transit option competes in terms of speed. The data show the automobile-based cities to have average traffic speeds of 51 km/h (United States) and 46 km/h (Australia), and a reduction in the Canadian cities (40 km/h), consistent with all the other data. These speeds are relatively fast when compared with traffic speeds in European cities of 36 km/h and Asian cities of 25 km/h.

In terms of competition among modes, the bus-only cities of the United States, Australia, and Canada provide little incentive for car users to switch to transit. On average, transit speeds in these cities are 20 to 25 km/h.[6] Only the rail option can compete with cars since the average speed of urban trains in selected cities where rail systems are significant is close to that of cars (e.g., San Francisco, trains 43 km/h and cars 44 km/h; Chicago, trains 46 km/h and cars 45 km/h; Washington, D.C., trains 39 km/h and cars 42 km/h; New York, trains 39 km/h and cars 38 km/h). In Sydney train speeds exceed average car speeds by 5 km/h, as they do in Europe (average train speeds of 41 km/h and car speeds of 36 km/h). Train speeds in Asian cities are extremely competitive with cars (e.g., Singapore's trains are 8 km/h faster; Hong Kong's are 14 km/h faster; and Tokyo's and Seoul's trains are 16 km/h faster than average road traffic). Trains are also a lot faster in developing Asian cities where the services exist.

Tram speeds are generally much lower than train speeds and often lower than bus speeds, but that is because they usually act as distributors in central areas, linking to the major train stations (Vuchic, 1981), and typically operate with very high passenger loadings, especially compared with buses. New light rail systems have much higher speeds than trams (e.g., San Diego, 35 km/h; Portland, 32 km/h; and Sacramento, 31 km/h), but they are still slower than the older heavy rail systems in U.S. cities.

It is also interesting that the average speed of buses in U.S., Canadian, and European cities is a fairly stable 21–22 km/h. Australian cities are a little higher at 25 km/h, but this is only due to Canberra's unusual busways. Among the Canadian cities, Ottawa has busways, but these raise its average speed to only 24 km/h. These are remarkably constant figures, considering the enormous diversity in urban conditions in these cities. In the very much denser and congested Asian cities, bus speeds drop to 15 km/h. It would thus appear that, in general, bus-based public transportation systems seem to have an in-built limit on operating speed of no more than about 25 km/h, unless there are rather exceptional circumstances, and thus they cannot be considered genuine competitors in speed to the car in any city. Even in Canberra, average car speed is 15 km/h higher than that of the bus system and in Ottawa it is 16 km/h higher.

It could be concluded that any city seriously wishing to move toward sustainability by changing the private car/public transportation equilibrium in favor of public transportation, must move in the direction of electric-rail-based transit systems. Only in this way can a city begin to compete with the car in the most basic travel choice factor of all: relative speed. This is the kind of change occurring in many cities examined in Chapter 4 that have considered that a move toward a rail spine for their transit system provides the most promising means of boosting transit use and reducing car mobility. Busways are seen as a major boost for transit, but in our experience they are not as successful as rail options. In this respect, Table 3.11 gives some comparative data from the global cities study on Canadian cities compared to U.S. cities. The data show that:

Table 3.11. Comparison of Canadian Cities and U.S. Cities in Transport Trends and Density

		Ottawa	Calgary	Edmonton	Vancouver	Montreal	Toronto	United States
Urban Density/ha		31	21	30	21	34	42	14
Vehicle Usage (VKT/person)	1981	6,421	7,057	—	7,111	3,630	5,110	9,042
	1991	6,534	9,021	8,397	8,750	5,274	6,051	11,555
Transit Usage (trips/person) — Bus	1981	155	109	129	111	149	132	41
	1991	135	55	98	95	134	161	39
Rail	1981	—	12	11	0	79	160	16
	1991	—	40	11	19	88	189	24
Total	1981	155	120	140	114	228	292	57
	1991	135	94	109	117	221	350	63
Traffic Speed (km/h)	1981	42	43	—	—	40	—	44
	1991	40	47	40	38	43	35	51
Transit Speed (km/h) — Bus	1981	21	23	19	20	17	20	21
	1991	24	25	20	20	21	20	22
Rail	1981	—	32	32	—	29	36	41
	1991	—	32	32	42	30	35	38
Total	1981	21	24	20	25	23	26	26
	1991	24	28	21	25	25	26	28

Source: Kenworthy et al. (1997) and Kenworthy et al. (1999).

- Ottawa's bus system has declined, as have all other Canadian urban bus systems (except Toronto), though all rail systems grew.
- Only rail systems had speeds approaching traffic speeds.
- All Canadian cities do better than the U.S. city average (less car use and more transit use) and are significantly denser.

Average traffic speeds across the surveyed cities vary considerably, from Bangkok at 13 km/h to Sacramento at 64 km/h. However, most cities are in the 30 to 45 km/h range, with an average for the city region of 51 km/h for U.S. cities, 46 km/h for Australian cities, 40 km/h for Canadian cities, 36 km/h for European cities, and 25 km/h for Asian cities. There is a lot of debate about whether faster or slower speeds for traffic have the most benefit for sustainability. The history of this issue is presented in Box 3.1.

There is clearly less fuel use per capita in cities in Europe and Asia, with their low average traffic speeds, compared to the United States and Australia, with their high average traffic speeds (see Table 3.2). In essence, this means that although free-flowing traffic may improve individual vehicle efficiencies, the evidence suggests that it also causes overall fuel consumption increases due primar-

Box 3.1. Does Road Building Save Fuel and Emissions and Reduce Travel Time?

There is an ongoing debate that questions the standard approach to justifying new urban roads on the basis of their implied ability to save fuel and travel times and reduce emissions. The travel time savings are seen to be obvious since a new large road can reduce congestion, and therefore with faster speeds people will save time. This time is translated into economic savings at different rates according to the assumed value of travel time in a particular city (very often this is set at half the overall average hourly pay rate in the city).

The reduction in fuel and emissions is seen to be due to the increase in average speeds, which means vehicles can operate more efficiently. The rationale for this approach came out of the General Motors laboratories in the 1960s (see Newman and Kenworthy, 1984).

The alternative approach is to suggest that increasing travel speeds only increases the amount of travel (due to fixed travel-time budgets) and that the associated increase in traffic (called "induced traffic") will mean an overall increase in fuel and emissions.

We have analyzed this issue in several publications based on a critique of the literature (Newman and Kenworthy, 1984, 1988) and on a detailed case study of Perth (Kenworthy, Newman, and Lyons, 1992; Newman, Kenworthy and Lyons, 1992), which showed that there was an increase of more than 30 percent in travel as congestion was relieved.

The new data we now have confirms the overall perspective that road building does not save fuel or travel time or reduce emissions as set out above.

ily to greater private vehicle use. The evidence favors instead the policy of traffic calming, which attempts to slow traffic both as a means of managing local traffic impacts and facilitating modal shifts in cities.

Traffic calming deliberately sets out to provide for bicyclists and pedestrians on roads and to favor transit for longer distances. Many cities discussed in Chapter 4 are beginning to develop traffic calming as a policy for improved sustainability in both economic and environmental terms. There is also a growing awareness that the building of freeways is no longer consistent with urban sustainability, as outlined in Chapter 2 (see also Newman, 1996a).

The data from the study we undertook for the World Bank confirms this perspective through journey-to-work times in cities around the world. The travel time is remarkably consistent across all the different city types: Australian and North American cities average 26 minutes, European cities average 28 minutes, and Asian cities average 33 minutes. These differences hardly seem significant when compared to the massive difference in the use of cars and infrastructure for cars, especially when cars are facilitated and promoted on the basis that they are faster and save time.

The phenomenon is of course understood in relation to all the other studies that have also found a consistent travel-time budget, as discussed in Chapter 2. Depending on the transportation technology, the city adjusts its land use to accommodate the average half-hour travel maxim. People do not save time when a city builds in car travel infrastructure that enhances speed—they just travel farther.

In terms of both economic and environmental aspects of sustainability, it is

Photo 3.4. Chicago's freeways, like all large roads, were justified as a way to save time, but in reality they just increase distances traveled.

possible to question the implementation of large-scale capital projects that continue to provide ever faster means of car travel across cities. It appears that contrary to their justification in terms of travel time saved, all they do in the end is allow a city to disperse farther outward. People and jobs follow the new infrastructure and adjust to a new location with about a half-hour commuting time. This also explains why building high-speed roads does not save fuel or reduce emissions, as described above.

An advantage of higher-speed rail systems is that they compete with car systems, but they also have the potential to focus and concentrate development within a reasonable radius of stations, thus allowing travel on an inherently less environmentally damaging mode, as well as creating shorter local travel distances.

With strategic transportation and land use planning, it is possible to build infrastructure that favors transit, walking, and cycling and does not facilitate further urban sprawl. This would then provide greater efficiency in terms of fuel use and lower environmental externalities, as well as a more economic use of land. The economic use of time is likely to remain at about the same level, no matter what transportation policies are implemented.

At the very least, these data should mean that any further justification of large roads on the basis of time savings, fuel savings, and emissions reductions has no theoretical or quantitative reality to it.

Urban Form

Throughout the above discussion it was obvious that the urban form of the various groups of cities could not be neglected in any attempt to try to understand travel patterns and thus how cities can move toward sustainability. This section examines urban form by considering data on metropolitan-wide density and central city, inner-area, and outer-area density (see Table 3.12). Densities can be

Table 3.12. Intensity of Land Use in Global Cities, 1990

City	Metropolitan Density		Central City (CBD) Density		Inner-Area Density		Outer-Area Density	
	Population	Jobs	Population	Jobs	Population	Jobs	Population	Jobs
Sacramento	12.7	6.8	26.6	117.1	19.4	12.7	10.8	5.2
Houston	9.5	5.7	17.9	303.3	18.4	21.6	8.8	4.3
San Diego	13.1	7.0	27.2	128.0	32.1	19.6	10.9	5.5
Phoenix	10.5	5.1	16.6	89.7	16.4	31.1	10.4	4.7
San Francisco	16.0	8.5	111.1	744.3	59.8	48.3	13.6	6.3
Portland	11.7	8.5	34.0	371.0	23.7	23.5	9.9	6.3
Denver	12.8	8.7	16.7	175.9	16.3	14.5	11.7	6.8
Los Angeles	23.9	12.4	28.2	506.1	28.7	15.6	21.6	10.9
Detroit	12.8	6.1	16.5	256.9	28.6	10.9	10.5	5.4
Boston	12.0	7.1	71.2	297.7	43.1	34.1	9.8	5.2
Washington	13.7	9.5	27.3	688.5	38.1	45.1	12.0	7.0

Chicago	16.6	8.7	30.3	921.0	47.3	23.8	11.4	6.2
New York	19.2	11.0	226.6	989.1	91.5	52.4	12.6	7.2
AMERICAN AVG.	14.2	8.1	50.0	429.9	35.6	27.2	11.8	6.2
Canberra	9.5	5.0	4.3	160.9	8.6	13.4	9.8	3.4
Perth	10.6	4.4	9.5	131.5	16.3	15.9	9.8	2.7
Brisbane	9.8	4.0	11.8	528.6	20.3	20.7	8.9	2.5
Melbourne	14.9	5.9	27.1	530.6	27.2	43.0	14.4	4.3
Adelaide	11.8	5.1	10.2	408.1	18.7	26.0	11.3	3.6
Sydney	16.8	7.2	20.8	422.2	39.2	38.1	15.3	5.1
AUSTRALIAN AVG.	12.2	5.3	14.0	363.6	21.7	26.2	11.6	3.6
Calgary	20.8	12.1	33.6	290.9	22.7	23.8	20.2	8.3
Winnipeg	21.3	8.8	42.5	155.9	41.2	29.1	18.0	5.4
Edmonton	29.9	15.8	21.6	212.8	26.8	?	31.5	?
Vancouver	20.8	10.5	25.6	308.6	41.5	29.9	17.4	7.2
Toronto	41.5	23.2	51.1	927.0	60.0	44.3	35.4	16.3
Montreal	33.8	14.8	51.5	223.2	64.1	42.8	28.5	9.9
Ottawa	31.3	15.8	39.7	364.0	49.2	97.7	30.1	10.4
CANADIAN AVG.	28.5	14.4	37.9	354.6	43.6	44.6	25.9	9.6
Frankfurt	46.6	43.3	65.5	498.9	61.0	93.6	39.7	19.3
Brussels	74.9	46.8	50.3	470.5	91.0	82.5	62.7	19.8
Hamburg	39.8	23.6	29.9	331.7	85.7	95.1	33.6	13.9
Zurich	47.1	35.2	37.3	417.2	73.5	72.8	36.1	19.5
Stockholm	53.1	39.3	101.4	262.3	91.7	126.4	42.9	16.3
Vienna	68.3	37.4	60.4	378.4	128.6	110.4	56.5	23.0
Copenhagen	28.6	16.0	74.8	269.8	53.9	35.2	22.6	11.4
Paris	46.1	22.1	179.7	369.6	96.7	56.1	27.0	9.2
Munich	53.6	37.2	96.6	276.1	106.9	150.2	47.7	24.7
Amsterdam	48.8	22.2	93.2	98.0	89.3	43.1	29.7	12.4
London	42.3	23.6	63.0	423.7	78.1	63.8	33.2	13.3
EUROPEAN AVG.	49.9	31.5	77.5	345.1	86.9	84.5	39.3	16.6
Kuala Lumpur	58.7	22.4	123.1	178.5	68.8	35.7	53.7	15.7
Singapore	86.8	49.3	82.8	386.2	124.2	132.9	80.5	35.2
Tokyo	71.0	73.1	63.2	546.8	132.1	108.3	61.2	31.0
Bangkok	149.3	62.4	324.6	132.2	288.6	119.5	89.1	37.7
Seoul	244.8	101.6	203.7	579.5	298.8	209.7	235.7	83.6
Jakarta	170.8	58.8	235.1	203.5	266.7	135.2	138.0	32.6
Manila	198.0	67.7	444.8	226.5	372.4	111.4	138.2	25.5
Surabaya	176.9	77.9	360.2	355.6	265.1	?	144.9	?
Hong Kong	300.5	140.0	113.8	1,712.6	803.9	775.1	258.0	86.5
ASIAN AVG.	161.9	72.6	216.8	480.1	291.2	203.5	133.3	43.5

Notes:
1. The metropolitan job density in Frankfurt is high because Frankfurt in these data is only the City of Frankfurt, which has many jobs filled by residents of the surrounding larger urbanized areas. Data on the Frankfurt region as a whole is extremely difficult to assemble because of fragmented administrative arrangements.
2. The metropolitan job density in Tokyo is high relative to population density because the latter is for the entire Tokyo region, while the former is only for Tokyo-to, or the Tokyo Metropolis, as it is known. Tokyo is a highly centralized city for employment; thus job density in Tokyo-to is much higher than for the entire region. Employment data for the whole region could not be collected at the time.

measured only by clearly defining the area (see Appendix 1) and the land use to be included. Our definition of urban density is presented in Table 2.1.

Metropolitan Density

The main parameter describing the urban form of a city is its overall, or metropolitan density. Many studies have shown that the intensity of development in a city has a highly significant effect on travel distances and modal splits (Pushkarev and Zupan, 1977). However, there are continuing skeptics who do not take this seriously (Brindle, 1994).

The overall shape of the U.S. and Australian Auto City is of low density in residences and businesses, with European cities generally being three to four times denser. Canadian cities fill an interesting niche between the extreme low density of the U.S. and Australian cities and the medium density of the European cities. Their densities average about 28 persons per ha, or about double that of U.S. and Australian cities. Newer cities such as Houston, Phoenix, Perth, and Brisbane have densities about half that of older cities such as Chicago, New York, and Sydney. Toronto tends to be more like a European city in its overall urban form (41 persons per ha), though the data here refer just to the Municipality of Metropolitan Toronto (2.3 million) and not the Greater Toronto Area (4.2 million), which has a density of 26 persons per ha (though this is still high for an Auto City). The population density of the Greater Montreal Region (34 persons per ha) is also much higher than any metropolitan densities to be found in the United States or Australia. The Asian cities are even more extreme, with densities some twelve times those of the U.S. and Australian cities. Hong Kong is by far the highest-density metropolitan area in the sample and probably the highest-density city in the developed world.

Central City Density

Job Densities

One of the significant differences between the U.S., Australian, and Canadian auto-dependent cities and the more transportation-balanced European and Asian cities is that the former have central cities that have become areas of very high job concentration with generally few residents, while the latter have a much better balance between central city jobs and residences. It should be noted that the central city referred to here is the central business district (CBD), a tightly defined area at the heart of every metropolitan area.

The central city high-rise office block is a common sight in most cities, but it is a dominant characteristic of the Auto City and gives to U.S. cities, in particular, significantly higher average central city job densities than exist in Europe (430 compared to 345 jobs per ha). Some exceptional cases of the high-rise office block giving rise to high job densities in the CBD can be found in Washington, D.C., San Francisco, Chicago, and New York, where job densities range between 689 and 989 jobs per ha. (Toronto has 927 jobs per ha in its CBD, but it is an exception in the Canadian picture.)

In fact, the average job density profile of the U.S. city is extremely sharp, going from 430 jobs per ha in the central city to 27 per ha in the inner city and 6 per ha in the outer areas, compared with European cities, which have 345 jobs per ha, 85 per ha, and 17 per ha. Australian cities are almost as extreme as U.S. cities in the tailing-off of job densities toward the periphery of the city (364 jobs per ha in the central city, 26 in the inner area, and only 4 in the outer areas). Meanwhile, Canadian cities again fall between the U.S./Australian and the European characteristics (355 jobs per ha, 45 per ha and 10 per ha).

The average 1990 European CBD job density of 345 per ha is now not a lot smaller than that in Australia and is certainly similar to that in Canada. The higher central city job densities in European cities are being promoted through cities such as Frankfurt, Brussels, and London, which more than any of the others have adopted the U.S. model of high-rise office towers in the CBD. Other European cities achieve moderately high job densities through a compact mixture of five- to six-storey buildings with height restrictions preventing any further concentration of CBD employment.

Within the Asian sample there is a marked difference in CBD job densities between the more developed and the developing Asian cities. In Singapore, Tokyo, Hong Kong, and Seoul, job densities average a very high 806 per ha (almost double that of U.S. cities), while in the five developing Asian cities the figure is a very low 219 per ha. The difference appears to lie in the fact that the four wealthier Asian cities also have well-developed rapid rail systems capable of transporting huge numbers of commuters into tightly confined areas of job concentration with very little space demand (the cities of Washington, D.C., San Francisco, Chicago, New York, and Toronto, which have similar high job densities, also enjoy excellent rail systems). By contrast, the poorer Asian cities have major problems with traffic congestion and poor bus systems, which means that the high numbers of central city jobs have to spread out to maintain adequate accessibility (Barter and Kenworthy, 1997). Lack of space-efficient, high-capacity public transportation means that central city job densities cannot rise very high in these cities.

Population Densities

Unlike job densities, the residential density of the U.S. and Australian central cities is frequently very low. Out of the nineteen U.S. and Australian cities, fifteen have central city population densities of 30 persons per ha or less, going down as low as 4 to 10 persons per ha. The exceptions to this general picture (which give U.S. cities a relatively high average central city population density of 50 persons per ha) are New York, Boston, and San Francisco.

No Australian cities have high central city residential concentrations (the average is 14 persons per ha), though the situation between 1991, when these data were taken, and the present has improved significantly. All Australian cities are experiencing something of a boom in central city living. This is in response to the growing numbers of global city information jobs locating in the inner areas, as well as growing levels of road congestion, making location near the major job concentrations an attractive proposition (Newman, Kenworthy, and Laube, 1997).

The Canadian cities are, on the whole, comparatively healthy in their CBD populations. Only one is below 25 persons per ha, while four out of the seven are 40 per ha or more.

In contrast to the Auto Cities, European central cities average almost 80 persons per ha, and in the Asian cities, CBD population density averages some 217 persons per ha, ranging up to 445 per ha in Manila and 325 to 360 per ha in Bangkok and Surabaya. In general, though, the developed Asian cities have much lower density residential activities in their CBDs, though they are still high by international standards (116 per ha). By contrast, in the poorer Asian cities, CBD population density averages a very high 298 per ha. This means that there is a far greater opportunity to access CBD jobs by foot and bicycle in these cities.

With more subcenters that have substantial residential and job concentrations, there is the potential to reduce all travel needs and also to ensure that transit has its viable concentrations of activity across the city, not just in the central city.

Canberra is a good example of an Australian city planned to have subcenters with healthy job concentrations. The density of activity in its subcenters is too low, however, and residential development in particular is too limited; thus there is no obvious reduction in automobile travel. Part of the reason for this is that there is no rail system (Kenworthy and Newman, 1991). Much better examples can be found in Canadian cities, such as Toronto, and in European cities, such as Stockholm, which have had this kind of policy of subcenters based on rail systems firmly guiding their development since the 1950s.

Developed Asian cities and some Western cities, such as New York and Toronto, demonstrate very clearly the job concentration possibilities associated with well-developed, high-capacity rail systems. These cities tend to have much lower auto travel than cities with lower-density centers. This approach is discussed further in Chapter 4.

Inner City and Outer Area Density

The inner city by our definition (see Chapter 2) is the pre–World War II city area—that is, the area developed mostly before automobile-dependent town planning. In U.S. cities, these areas are often the old areas known as "the city"—for example, the City of New York, or City of Chicago, as opposed to the "suburbs," which are the areas outside that.

As well as the differences in overall density and central city density, there are clear differences in urban form between U.S./Australian cities and European/ Asian cities in terms of their inner cities and their outer areas. Again, Canadian cities fill a niche somewhere between these extremes.

The U.S./Australian inner city is between two and four times less dense than the inner city of European cities, and eight to thirteen times less than that in Asian cities. Canadian inner cities are half the density of European inner cities and seven times less dense than Asian cities.

However, the old inner cities of San Francisco, Washington, D.C., Boston, Chicago, Sydney, and particularly New York have higher inner-city densities, though only New York is really similar to European inner-city densities. In general, Canadian inner-city densities are mostly well above 40 persons per ha, except for Calgary and Edmonton. In the inner cities of younger U.S. and Australian cities, densities are generally less than 20 persons per ha or not really very different from their metropolitan densities. Canberra's inner city actually has a lower population density than its metropolitan area.

This confirms the generally accepted picture of older cities as having steeper population density gradients (Clark, 1982). Automobile-based planning is obviously responsible for such dispersion of activity in newer cities and urban areas.

In terms of Asian inner-city population densities, the more developed cities have average population densities of 340 persons per ha, while the developing cities have 252 per ha, both very high by international standards.

In order to reduce travel it is ideal to have job densities roughly similar in their pattern of distribution to population density. We have already seen how there was a huge disparity between population and jobs in U.S. central cities compared to European central cities. Inner-city job densities follow the same overall patterns of increasing density, from U.S./Australian cities (which are almost identical in this factor), through Canadian, European, and Asian cities. However, U.S. inner-city job density is significantly lower than its population density (24 percent), reflecting the more advanced dispersal of work in the United States away from the traditional population concentrations toward suburban locations. By contrast, Australian cities have somewhat higher inner-city job densities than population densities (21 percent), in Canada and Europe the two are more or less equal, and in Asia both are very high, with population densities some 30 percent higher than job densities in inner areas.

Nevertheless, inner-city job densities in developing Asian cities are much lower than those in developed Asian cities (100 jobs per ha compared to 307 per ha), reflecting again a need to spread the high numbers of jobs in their inner areas over a wider area to maintain accessibility through inferior, low-capacity buses operating on very limited, congested road systems. Rail systems predominantly service the very high density jobs in the inner areas of wealthier Asian cities.

The outer-area population densities of U.S. and Australian cities are amazingly uniform in all cases, with very low land use intensity (an average of 12 persons per ha in both groups of cities). The density of these outer suburbs is about the density of rural Java, raising questions as to whether such areas should even be classified as urban in any traditional sense. Certainly the exurban areas of modern auto-based cities are little different from rural areas.

Canadian outer-area population densities are double those of U.S./Australian cities, though they are often cast in the same mold by many commentators (Raad and Kenworthy, 1998). Casual observation of housing forms at the fringes of most Canadian cities reveals the reason for this consistent pattern of higher urban density: much smaller lot sizes and often generous scatterings of reasonably high quality, multifamily housing, which are not nearly as evident in the United States or Australia in such areas. This makes Canadian outer areas significantly easier to service with a reasonable transit service than their U.S. and Australian counterparts, though they are not ideal either.

The picture for job densities is similar to that for population, though in this case, Australian cities are lower again than U.S. cities (3.6 jobs per ha compared to 6.2). The outer areas of U.S. cities have been rapidly filling out in employment terms as almost totally auto-based "Edge Cities" with extensive office, commercial, and retail developments (Garreau, 1991). No comparable process of this scale is evident in Australian cities, though obviously jobs in the suburbs have been expanding.

Canadian outer-area job densities are some 1.5 times higher than those in U.S. cities, but in this case the density comes from much more focused suburban job centers, often linked to good transit (e.g., around Toronto's subway or on Vancouver's Skytrain).

The population density of European cities is marked by much more intensively utilized outer areas (39 persons per ha)—some 3.5 times more, on average, than in U.S. and Australian cities, but only 1.5 times higher than in Canadian cities. Thus even new urban areas planned in the era of the automobile are generally not nearly so dispersed in Europe as they are in U.S., Australian, or Canadian cities, though some new suburbs are. The outer areas within Metro Toronto are again more like a European city in their density; both Toronto and European cities appear to develop their density partly through a number of intensively utilized subcenters linked by rapid transit to the city center. Suburbs outside Metro Toronto are generally much lower in density, though even there they are denser than the outer areas of U.S./Australian cities (24 persons per ha compared to 12 per ha).

The Asian cities again distinguish themselves with extremely high population densities in their outer areas (133 persons per ha), with the developed Asian cities even higher (159 per ha compared to 113 per ha). The issue of transportation and managing the automobile in Asian cities, even in outer areas, is therefore not so much hinging on land use change as it is on investment in the appropriate modes of transportation; existing land use is still mostly transit-oriented but needs better transit systems. However, as roads continue to be built in these cities and little restriction of the automobile occurs, the form of new urban development is becoming more auto-oriented and therefore needs to be carefully considered and managed in future plans.

Job densities in outer areas of European and Asian cities follow patterns similar to population density, with very much higher densities than in U.S., Australian, or Canadian cities. In the Asian sample, only Kuala Lumpur has a lower job density than the European average (it is also the most auto-oriented of all the Asian cities).

Density and Transportation

Density patterns are obviously closely linked to transportation and therefore energy use. This link to the intensity of urban development is summarized in Figures 3.2 and 3.3, which show the variation in energy use in private passenger travel with density for the global cities in 1990 and gasoline use and density within the Tri-State New York region in 1980 to indicate how the same kind of variations in transportation exist across a metropolitan region. Similar relationships have been found in a study of twenty-two Nordic cities (Naess, 1993a and b) and within Paris (INRETS, 1995). In all cases there appears to be a critical point (about 20 to 30 persons per ha) below which automobile-dependent land use patterns appear to be an inherent characteristic of the city.

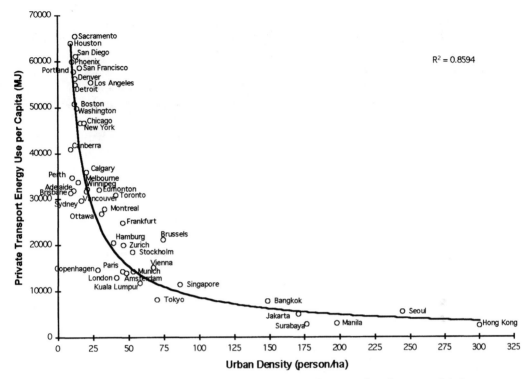

Figure 3.2. Energy use per capita in private passenger travel versus urban density in global cities, 1990.

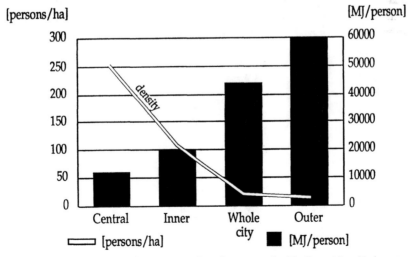

Figure 3.3. Gasoline use per capita versus urban density in the Tri-State New York region, 1980.

Brindle (1994) has suggested that it is wrong to try to graph two parameters that are both per capita because it will always guarantee a hyperbolic relationship. It is true that the shape will be a hyperbole, but there is no guarantee that there is a statistically significant link. However, there is clearly a strong statistical link in our data between transport energy use per capita and urban density. Evill (1995) shows that it is not spurious to do per capita correlations.

If, on the other hand, energy consumption is plotted versus urbanized land area, a straight line is achieved, which is highly statistically significant (Kenworthy et al., 1999). This has the policy implications of (a) preventing expansion of the existing urban area (growth management) and (b) increasing density within the existing urban area to reduce automobile dependence.

There is another implication of plotting transportation energy versus urban area—the fuel use and hence the emissions of a city can be predicted merely by knowing the urbanized land area. This is a potentially powerful tool for planners and modelers.

Thus there is support for increasing densities as an urban transportation energy conservation policy, as well as for overcoming so many of the other problems of automobile dependence. Density increases will be best achieved, however, if focused in nodes along corridors. This approach we have called "transit-oriented urban villages," which creates high-density nodes of mixed jobs, houses, and services linked to the rest of the city by good transit. Such an approach is becoming a new design orientation in many Auto Cities, as shown in Chapter 4.

As discussed in the history of cities in terms of their transportation patterns, there is a close link between transportation infrastructure priorities and density. Thus Figures 3.4 and 3.5 show this relationship between the relative priority for transit over roads versus urban density, and also for the proportion of workers walking and biking to work and urban density. The graphs show particularly strong correlations between the key urban form variable of urban density and the transportation characteristics of the metropolitan regions. The first graph, show-

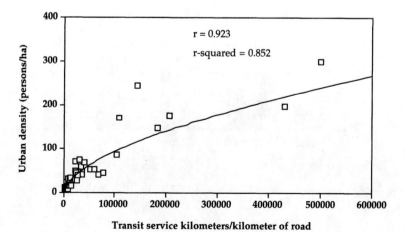

Figure 3.4. Relationship between relative priority for transit over roads and urban density in global cities, 1990.

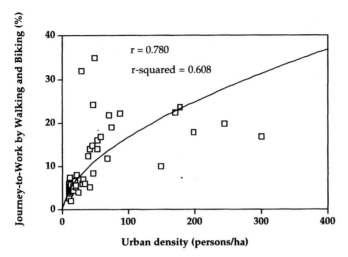

Figure 3.5. Relationship between urban density and workers walking and cycling to work in global cities, 1990.

ing a correlation coefficient (*r* value) of 0.923, is stronger than the second graph, which shows a value of 0.780 (though this is still very strong statistically).[7]

All these patterns seem to be influenced through journey distances. In the data on global cities, the length of travel to work follows very closely the density of a city, as would be expected:

- The low-density cities of North America and Australia average 14.7 kilometers and 12.6 kilometers, respectively (Toronto averages 11.2 kilometers and U.S. cities average 15.0 kilometers).
- The medium-density cities of Europe average 10.0 kilometers.
- The high-density cities of Asia average 7.9 kilometers.

There is a fair variation within each regional group, but these data help to explain the variations in transportation patterns. For example, European cities have less than half the car use of U.S. cities, not just because fewer people use cars, but because they travel shorter distances. If all the transit travel in European cities were transferred to cars, the cities would still have a total of only 8,500 passenger kilometers per person compared to the U.S. level of 16,500 passenger kilometers per person (i.e., half the total level of motorized mobility—see Table 3.10).[8]

The urban transportation and energy use patterns discussed in this chapter have been explained mostly in terms of a combination of land use and infrastructure patterns that either favor car use or favor transit, biking, and walking; lesser factors relating to vehicle fuel efficiencies, the price of fuel, and incomes have also been included. The next section looks at how the patterns in the different cities have been changing. Sustainability in cities (in this context) is about moving away from dependence on the car in a way that improves the environment and the economy of cities. Thus the process of updating our global cities study provided us with the first chance to see if cities had been able to respond to the 1980s agenda on sustainability.

Transportation and Land Use Trends

Trends will be examined in car use, journey-to-work distances, transit use, and density.

Car Use and Journey-to-work Distances

In 1989 we wrote an article in the *Journal of the American Planning Association* that summarized some of the above findings using 1980 data on cities (Newman and Kenworthy, 1989b). The next issue of the journal contained a strong reaction from Gordon and Richardson (1989) to our assessment that U.S. cities needed to change. In it they said the following:

> The idea of planners turning our lives upside down in pursuit of a singleminded goal is as horrible as it is alien. NK's world is the Kafkaesque nightmare that Hayek (1945) always dreaded, a world where consumers have no voice, relative prices have no role and planners are tyrants. . . . NK have written a very troubling paper. Their distortions are not innocent, because the uninformed may use them as ammunition to support expensive plans for central city revitalisation and rail transit projects or stringent land use controls in a futile attempt to enforce urban compactness. . . . Perhaps Newman and Kenworthy would be well advised to seek out another planet, preferably unpopulated, where they can build their compact cities from scratch with solar powered transit. (pp. 342, 344, 345)

Gordon and Richardson have also suggested that there is no need for so much concern about U.S. cities. They believe that the marketplace, quite independent of planning intervention, will adjust cities like Los Angeles so that car use will decrease automatically. The mechanism for this, it is claimed, is the dispersion of jobs to the suburbs, which follows the dispersion of housing and eventually adjusts travel patterns so that travel distances are shortened. They suggested that this process was well under way in Los Angeles (Gordon, Kumar, and Richardson, 1989; Gordon, Richardson, and Jun, 1991). The U.S. data that they suggested showed a stabilization in journey-to-work lengths came from two different surveys using different methodologies, so that deducing anything from these data is very hard (see Newman, Kenworthy and Vintila, 1995). They also found, to their apparent astonishment, that travel times in Los Angeles were stable at about half an hour!

Since then, various people have speculated as to whose model is right for reducing car use: NK's based on transit-oriented subcenters, or GR's based on dispersion of jobs and houses without subcenters or transit (e.g., Peter Hall, 1995, tends to come down on the side of GR). The two options are depicted in Figure 3.6.

The data are now available on a global basis to be able to answer the question. The trends in car use and journey-to-work trip lengths can be provided for the period 1980 to 1990 (when stabilization in both parameters was predicted by GR, at least for U.S. cities). Table 3.13 summarizes the data.

ALTERNATIVE CITY FORMS

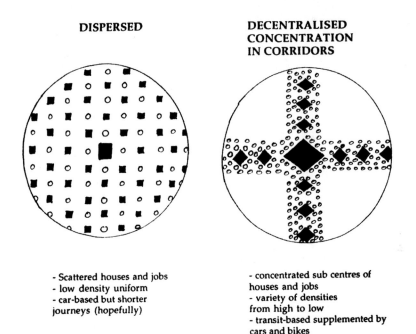

DISPERSED

DECENTRALISED
CONCENTRATION
IN CORRIDORS

- Scattered houses and jobs
- low density uniform
- car-based but shorter
  journeys (hopefully)

- concentrated sub centres of
  houses and jobs
- variety of densities
  from high to low
- transit-based supplemented by
  cars and bikes

Figure 3.6. Two model options for reducing car use in cities: (*left*) dispersion of jobs and population throughout a city, and (*right*) jobs and population in subcenters linked by transit along corridors.

Table 3.13 shows that the trend in the United States is to continue to grow substantially in car use and journey-to-work distances. The U.S. cities increased more than 2,000 kilometers per person in total car travel between 1980 and 1990. In fact, growth in car use in U.S. cities is still exponentially increasing, as can be seen for Los Angeles in the extra total VKT per capita every decade since 1960 (Figure 3.7). The nearest to the overall U.S. increase in car use was in European cities, but it wasn't even 1,000 kilometers per person extra, or less than half the U.S. increase. In Australian cities the increase was 742 kilometers, in Metro Toronto it was 781 kilometers, and in the wealthy Asian cities it was 564 kilometers per capita of extra car travel in the ten years from 1980 to 1990. Likewise, journey-to-work distance increases were highest in U.S. cities, where they expanded a full 2 kilometers over the decade when Gordon and Richardson said they would stabilize.

The growth in U.S. car use per capita, in the decade that it was anticipated to stabilize, is similar to the total level of car use per capita found in Tokyo and Singapore in 1990 or Paris and London in 1980. There is as yet no sign of stabilization in car use or travel distances in U.S. cities.

On the other hand, there has been an interesting slowdown in car use per capita growth in Australian cities (4.5 percent per year in the 1960s, 2.3 percent per year in the 1970s, and 1.2 percent per year in the 1980s). If projected, this

Table 3.13 Growth in Car Use per Capita and Journey-to-work Trip
Lengths in Global Cities, 1980–1990

Cities	Annual Car Use per Capita (km, 1980)	Annual Car Use per Capita (km, 1990)	Journey-to-work Length (km, 1980)	Journey-to-work Length (km, 1990)
American	8,806	10,870	13.0	15.0
Australian	5,794	6,536	12.0	12.6
Metro Toronto	4,238	5,019	10.5	11.2
European	3,526	4,519	8.1	10.0
Asian (Wealthy)	923	1,487	NA	NA

Note: Car use is the total annual distance traveled by cars (VKT) divided by the population of the urban region. The data in this table refer to cities in the World Bank study with fewer cities than in the other tables in this chapter, hence averages for the U.S. and Australian cities are slightly different. Journey-to-work trip length data are not available for Asian cities.

leads to zero growth in the 1990s, though it is still uncertain whether this will actually be achieved, as there has been a strong push from road organizations in Australian cities throughout the 1990s to build more freeways.

The Greater Toronto Area is similar with just 1.6 percent car use growth in the 1980s (873 kilometers of growth per capita), while Canadian cities overall (excluding Edmonton, for which 1981 VKT data are not available) experienced growth of 1,094 kilometers per capita.

The lower growth in car use in Australian cities, and to a lesser degree Canadian cities, compared to U.S. cities may be due to:[9]

- Reurbanization of older suburbs, which can lead to reduced travel; reurbanization in Australian cities is now more than 30 percent of all new residential development and up to 50 percent of all development, as noted in Chapter 1; it is also very strong in Canadian cities.

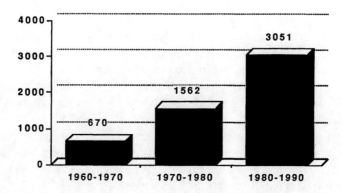

Figure 3.7. Increase in total per capita vehicle kilometers of travel in Los Angeles County, 1960–1990.

- Development of nodal subcenters in outer suburbs that also reduces the need for travel and makes transit more viable; signs of these emerging nodal/information subcenters are apparent in Australian cities and are very evident in Canadian cities, especially around rail stations (Kenworthy and Newman, 1994).
- More attractive and vital urban environments (especially in inner areas), which reduce the need for car journeys to avoid or "leapfrog" unsafe urban areas (as in U.S. cities) and which encourage people to engage more with their surroundings through greater walking and cycling (Davis, 1990).
- Less dispersion and development of highly car-dependent "Edge Cities," which have been characteristic of U.S. urban growth patterns, especially in the 1980s (Garreau, 1991).

The reurbanization of Australian cities is now occurring rapidly and (as suggested in chapter 2) could be a market process linked to the concentration of "global city" information-oriented jobs in the city and inner-area subcenters. The impact of the new information economy on city form may thus help to concentrate cities and reduce car dependence. However, reurbanization and more sustainable transportation practices occur only if the social conditions for facilitating them are in place.

The situation in U.S. cities is not the same as in Australian or Canadian cities. Despite strong environmental policies and economic rationale for reurbanization contained in legislation such as the Intermodal Surface Transportation Efficiency Act (ISTEA) and the Clean Air Act, there have been social barriers to reurbanization and sustainable transportation in U.S. cities due to the wide disparities in wealth and opportunities available in the inner city. Racial and crime issues continue to be major factors in these patterns of poverty.

If social policies in U.S. inner cities are not able to overcome these problems, then it is likely that future growth will continue to disperse U.S. cities. In such an event there is not likely to be much stabilization in car use or travel distances in U.S. cities by the year 2000. This is a clear example of how equity and culture are related to sustainability. There are signs of a change in this situation, however, with crime rates dropping in many U.S. inner cities, followed by an immediate process of rejuvenation and rebuilding of these areas. Such processes are discussed for Portland and Boston (but are also evident in New York and Chicago) in Chapter 4. There is also evidence of increased priority for spending on transit and other sustainable transportation modes (STPP, 1998). If the fledgling reurbanization process in U.S. cities grows and incorporates more sustainable transportation practices, then U.S. cities will reverse these patterns and move in a more sustainable direction.

The containment of growth in car dependence in U.S. cities is now a significant issue for global sustainability due to the quantities of oil this represents, the impact on the global economy through factors such as the U.S. trade deficit, and the need for global leadership on sustainability from the United States. The first hints of change are of considerable importance to global sustainability.

Transit Use

Charles Lave (1992), in an analysis of transportation trends, suggested that: "The desire for personal mobility seems to be unstoppable—it is perhaps the irresistible force . . . public transportation has lost the battle against the auto in the US . . . and it is losing it in Europe too . . . it is very, very hard to lure people out of automobiles and into transit" (p. 9). He continues that there is "no evidence in the literature" to support the view that this switch from cars to transit is possible. So is this dismal view correct? Is the automobile and thus the Auto City "irresistible" and is transit in a terminal state of decline everywhere? In a word, no! The data from most cities is quite positive, as shown in Figure 3.8

The data show that transit use in U.S. cities is still low, but the systems in most cities are growing again, even on a per capita basis. In fact, the trend in this sample of thirteen medium-to-large U.S. cities has been a growth in transit ridership from 48 trips per capita in 1970 to 63 per capita in 1990. Australian cities did decline from 118 trips per capita in 1971 to 93 per capita in 1981, but then stabilized at 92 per capita in 1991 and indeed may have started growing again in the 1990s (Kenworthy and Newman, 1993).

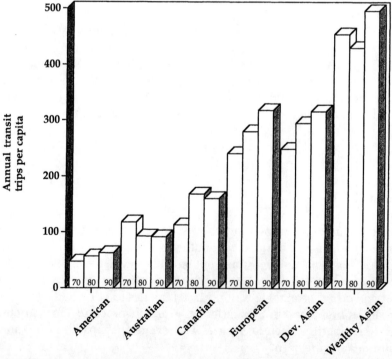

Figure 3.8. Trends in per capita transit use in the world's cities, 1970–1990. *Notes:* 1. All 1980 and 1990 data include all cities in the study except Bangkok in the developing Asian data (no 1980 data and also left out of 1990 picture). 2. 1970 data is sparser for some cities. Data for the U.S. and Australian cities are complete; Montreal is missing from the Canadian sample but is reasonably well estimated for this graph; Frankfurt is missing from the European cities but would be about average in 1970; Singapore is missing from the wealthy Asian cities; and in the developing Asian cities only Bangkok, Jakarta, and Kuala Lumpur are included in the 1970 picture (no data for any of the other cities).

Canadian cities had quite large increases in transit ridership from 1970 to 1980 (113 to 169 trips per capita) and then leveled off marginally as of 1991 at 161 trips per capita. There is evidence of a decline in transit in Canadian cities (especially Toronto) in the 1990s due to cuts in services [Canadian Urban Transit Association, (CUTA) 1997].

European cities have seen steady gains in transit ridership throughout the twenty-year period, from 241 trips per capita in 1970 to 318 per capita in 1990 (a 32 percent increase). The average transit trips per capita growth in European cities from 1970 to 1990 (77 trips per capita) is 22 percent higher than the total per capita transit use in U.S. cities in 1990.

In the wealthy Asian cities of Singapore, Hong Kong, and Tokyo, transit ridership is extremely high and grew between 1980 and 1990 from 430 to 496 trips per capita. The developing Asian cities also trended upward in transit ridership between 1980 and 1990 from 295 to 316 trips per capita (lower than their wealthier neighbors due to inferior bus-based transit systems, but still significant).

Indeed, by any accounts, Lave's dismal view of the future of transit is not borne out by the experience of many cities in this study.[10]

Such upward trends in transit need to be maintained in order to combat automobile dependence, and to achieve this is always a fight in any city. However, where transit growth does take place, it is a positive sign of sustainability, and some of the cities that have done best in transit growth are examined further in Chapter 4.

Density Trends

Table 3.14 shows the trends in activity intensity (the sum of jobs and population) for the full urban regions of thirty global cities for the 1960–1990 period.

For most cities the decades 1960–1970 and 1970–1980 have seen declines in activity intensity consistent with the role of the automobile in dispersing cities. For the last decade (1980–1990) of the data, however, the trend toward dispersal has slowed or stopped. There are only two cities that are clearly still declining overall in their activity intensity (London and Brussels). Fifteen cities have leveled off from their declines and are now steady. Thirteen have increased in the density of their activity. The trend could not be followed for the newly industrializing cities for which 1990 data alone have been obtained.

All the U.S. cities have increased in their activity density, apart from Detroit and Chicago, which held steady. This increased concentration has not been uniform, however: the concentration has been in the outer suburbs while the inner areas continued to decline, though not enough to lead to overall activity intensity declines as have occurred in previous decades. This is consistent with concentration around Edge Cities. The continued decline of U.S. inner cities seems to be related to the ongoing social problems there.

The Australian cities data show a stabilization of the decline from the previous decades, and since the main reurbanization process seems to have occurred in the 1990s, it is likely that the next decade will show an increase in activity density. Data from the 1996 census show increasing populations and jobs in all inner-city areas.

Table 3.14. Activity Intensity (Population and Job
Density Thirty Global Cities, 1960–1990

	1960	1970	1980	1990
U.S. Cities				
Boston	25	22	18	19
Chicago	34	29	26	25
Denver	28	21	20	21
Detroit	26	24	20	21
Houston	15	18	14	15
Los Angeles	32	35	35	36
New York	32	33	30	30
Phoenix	12	12	13	16
San Francisco	24	25	23	25
Washington	30	28	21	23
AVERAGE	26	25	22	23
Australian Cities				
Adelaide	—	20	18	17
Brisbane	28	—	14	14
Melbourne	28	25	23	21
Perth	21	17	15	15
Sydney	30	27	25	24
AVERAGE	27	22	19	18
Canadian City				
Toronto	52	60	59	65
European Cities				
Amsterdam	137	94	74	71
Brussels	167	148	133	122
Copenhagen	58	49	47	45
Frankfurt	151	135	97	90
Hamburg	106	89	66	64
London	101	95	89	66
Munich	92	106	91	91
Paris	101	91	70	68
Stockholm	100	95	89	92
Zurich	92	91	86	82
Vienna	140	127	111	106
AVERAGE	113	102	87	82
Asian Cities				
Hong Kong	—	478	403	440
Singapore	—	122	121	136
Tokyo	197	184	171	178
AVERAGE	—	260	232	251

The European city that shows the greatest reurbanization is Stockholm,
which increased in activity in its CBD, inner, and outer areas. It is particularly
worth noting that this trend is also associated with an absolute and per capita decline in car use across the whole city.

These trends are largely consistent with the postulated changes expected in the global city, and they again show that sustainability is not necessarily made more difficult by the emerging global information-oriented city. Indeed, it could signify the end of the automobile as the primary influence on urban form and the beginning of an era in which information technology is more dominant. Since these trends in urban form are only in their early phase, it is hard to distinguish on such a large scale; so more detailed internal studies would help to confirm that the process of concentrating, particularly around quality urban environments, is under way and that this is related to information processing.

For example, Cervero (1995) has shown how Stockholm has made its transition to an information-oriented city by stressing its transit corridors and subcenters. Gehl and Gemzøe (1996) have shown that Copenhagen has had a deliberate strategy for thirty years to build a competitive global city by continuously reducing car parking and creating more attractive public spaces in its central area. Monheim (1988) has shown that global businesses are attracted to pedestrian-oriented European urban environments that are very intensely active but are largely car-free. Roberts (1989b) found similar results for traffic-calmed areas in a study of six European cities. Linneman and Gyourko (1997) showed that in U.S. global cities big corporation headquarters are attracted to large central open space parks.

The processes of urban change that may be halting the apparently unstoppable sprawl of cities all appear to be related to the need for more face-to-face contact in quality urban environments. This need will be explored in subsequent chapters.

The next section brings together some data on the economic and environmental costs of automobile dependence in the thirty-seven global cities surveyed for the World Bank (data from Appendix 1). It aims to gain perspective on the commonly held belief that wealth is the primary determinant of automobile dependence and, in this sense, the automobile is seen as an "irresistible force" as wealth rises. The following data appear to debunk this position.

Car Use and Wealth

For many years there has been an implicit assumption among transportation planners, engineers, and economists that there is a close link between mobility and wealth (see Rainbow and Tan, 1993, and the "Price and Income" section above). This leaves very few policy options open to cities for managing growth in car use. However, as with Lave's negative assessment of transit, the data for such assertions tend to be national data and are rather selective.

Below we examine the link between mobility and wealth by comparing the per capita use of cars in thirty-seven global cities and seeing how this compares with their per capita city wealth (called gross regional product, or GRP). This is part of a study that we did for the World Bank and includes a number of other indicators of transportation economic performance with considerable significance for sustainability. These are therefore also examined to fill out the picture that is now developing—that mobility is not necessarily related to wealth.

The data on car use and wealth (in 1990 U.S. dollars) are given in Table 3.15 and also in Figure 3.9.

There is no obvious pattern to the data. Statistical analysis shows that only

Table 3.15. Car Use and Gross Regional Product per Capita for Thirty-seven Global Cities, 1990

Cities	Car Use per Capita (km)	GRP per Capita ($US, 1990)
Australian		
Perth	7,203	17,697
Adelaide	6,690	19,761
Brisbane	6,467	18,737
Melbourne	6,436	21,088
Sydney	5,885	21,520
AVERAGE	6,536	19,761
American		
Phoenix	11,608	20,555
Denver	10,011	24,533
Boston	10,280	27,783
Houston	13,016	26,155
Washington	11,182	35,882
San Francisco	11,933	31,143
Detroit	11,239	22,538
Chicago	9,525	26,038
Los Angeles	11,587	24,894
New York	8,317	28,703
AVERAGE	10,870	26,822
Canadian		
Toronto (Metro)	5,019	22,572
European		
Frankfurt	5,893	35,126
Amsterdam	3,977	25,211
Zurich	5,197	44,845
Brussels	4,864	30,087
Munich	4,202	36,255
Stockholm	4,638	33,235
Vienna	3,964	28,021
Hamburg	5,061	30,421
Copenhagen	4,558	29,900
London	3,892	22,215
Paris	3,459	33,609
AVERAGE	4,519	31,721
Wealthy Asian		
Singapore	1,864	12,939
Tokyo	2,103	36,953
Hong Kong	493	14,101
AVERAGE	1,487	21,331
Developing Asian		
Kuala Lumpur	4,032	4,066
Surabaya	1,064	726
Jakarta	1,112	1,508
Bangkok	2,664	3,826
Seoul	1,483	5,942
Beijing	351	1,323
Manila	573	1,099
AVERAGE	1,611	2,642

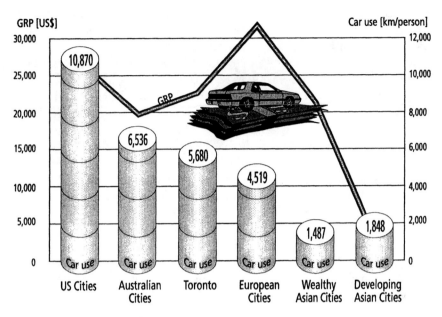

GRP [US$]

Car use [km/person]

Figure 3.9. Car use per capita (VKT) in 1990 and wealth (GRP per capita in 1990 U.S. dollars).

18 percent of the variance can be explained by a linear correlation. If a bell-shaped curve were fitted to the data, then 36 percent of the variance could be explained. This suggests that cities with high wealth (mostly European and wealthy Asian) are associated with lower mobility than those in the mid-wealth range (U.S. and Australian).

Some of the possible explanations for this can be pursued by examining the other indicators of transportation efficiency.

As already noted, North American and Australian cities have considerably higher car use per capita than would be expected just considering the level of economic activity or wealth, especially in comparison to the European and developed Asian cities.

The large U.S. cities in this sample have:

- 1.66 times higher car use than the major Australian cities but are only 1.36 times higher in GRP;
- 2.17 times higher car use than Metropolitan Toronto but are only 1.19 times higher in GRP;
- 2.41 times higher car use than the average European city but actually have only 0.85 the level of GRP per capita;
- 7.3 times higher car use than the wealthy Asian cities but have only 1.26 times the level of GRP.

Perhaps even more significant is the comparison between the developing Asian cities of Kuala Lumpur, Surabaya, Jakarta, Bangkok, Seoul, Beijing, and Manila and the three wealthy Asian cities of Tokyo, Singapore, and Hong Kong: the poorer cities have 108 percent as much car use but have an average GRP that is only 12 percent of that in the developed Asian cities. This is even more accentuated in the case of Kuala Lumpur, the most motorized developing Asian city. Kuala Lumpur has 2.7 times the average car use per capita of the wealthy Asian cities, yet only 19 percent of the per capita GRP.

The car use per capita figures in developing Asian cities in some cases include a reasonable amount of motorcycle use (motorcycle use is also included in other cities but is not as significant). However, this does not fundamentally affect the point being made here, which is that developing Asian cities, despite low levels of wealth compared to their more developed neighbors, are experiencing very much higher levels of private mobility. Within the United States, there is also a significant difference between cities that cannot be explained by simple economic factors alone. For example, New York (the lowest car-using U.S. city) has 36 percent less car use per capita than Houston (the highest car-using U.S. city) but is 10 percent higher in GRP.

The economic parameters discussed below provide some detail as to why there may be a negative link between economic performance in a city and high levels of mobility through automobiles. They confirm the picture presented in Chapter 2. The discussion covers direct economic costs, such as road expenditure, percentage of GRP spent on the journey-to-work, and transit cost recovery, as well as the indirect costs due to transport deaths and transportation emissions. Detailed data on these items can be found in Appendix 1.

Road Expenditure

Road expenditure per capita (Figure 3.10) follows the pattern of car use and car dependence in the sample of cities, though it does not display such extreme differences (U.S. cities spend $264 per capita each year, Australian cities, $142; Toronto, $150; European cities, $135; wealthy Asian cities, $88; and developing Asian cities, $39). There is a higher level of road maintenance in North American and Australian cities due to their greater length of roads per capita, but it is obvious that considerable road building is still occurring in these car-based cities. The sustainability agenda will require a change in these priorities in the future if car dependence is to be eased. It is apparent from the above data and the economic parameters below that such a change can also constitute a move toward lower transportation costs.

Road expenditure in European cities is relatively high since they also have many new areas on their peripheries where a more car-dependent urban form has been created. For example, Copenhagen suburbs and surrounding villages that have been developed into suburbs since the 1940s have densities of 25 and 21 persons per ha and have much greater car use than the old city, which has a density of 63 persons per ha. Such areas will also require reassessment in light of the sustainability agenda with a view to redirecting road funds to other modes as part of a strategic plan to reduce car dependence (see Newman et al., 1997).

In wealthy Asian cities, road expenditure per capita is one-third what it is in U.S. cities and 50 percent to 60 percent of what it is in Australian cities and Toronto. As shown below, it is also the lowest in relation to city wealth.

Road expenditure per capita in newly developing Asian cities appears to be comparatively small in absolute terms, though in Bangkok, Seoul, and Beijing, there is evidence of relatively heavy spending on roads compared to other cities

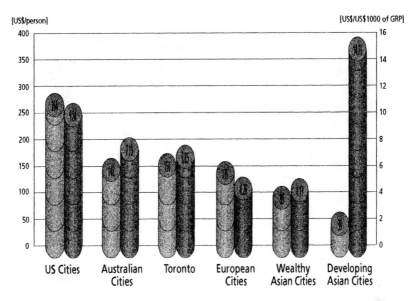

Figure 3.10. Road expenditure in global cities, 1990.

in this group ($61 to $72 compared with the average of $39). However, in terms of road expenditure per $1,000 dollars of GRP, or in other words, in relation to a city's capacity to pay, money spent on roads in these developing cities is high. The figures for all the cities are: $9.84 for the U.S. cities, $7.19 for Australian cities, $6.65 for Toronto, $4.26 for European cities, $4.13 for wealthy Asian cities, and $14.76 for developing Asian cities. This latter figure is 1.5 times higher than in U.S. cities, the next highest relative spender on roads. Bangkok is spending $18.56 per $1,000 of GRP or 1.9 times U.S. levels and Beijing is spending $46.11 or 4.7 times that in the U.S. cities.

Percentage of GRP Spent on the Journey-to-work

The percentage of GRP spent on commuting is very similar across all the global cities at about 6 percent (Figure 3.11). It is slightly higher in the United States at 6.9 percent and slightly lower in Europe at 5.4 percent. The developing Asian cities are higher with 7.4 percent of GRP spent on commuting due to their considerably lower GRPs and rapidly growing use of cars. Based on the data here, Manila and Surabaya seem to spend the most on getting to work (8.5 percent and 10 percent of GRP respectively).

It is not unexpected that most cities end up with about the same commitment of their resources to commuting. It appears to be related to the way commuting times adjust to about thirty minutes on average in all cities, independently of how they are provided with transportation infrastructure. Despite all the massive differences in transportation investment priorities and the large differences in transportation patterns in different types of cities, urban people everywhere put a very similar amount of their wealth into commuting. This at least suggests that cities have an opportunity to be strategic in how they invest in transportation.

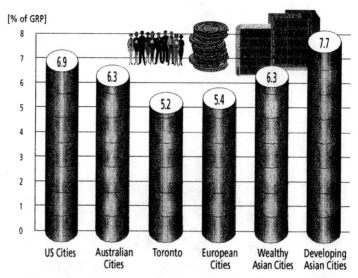

Figure 3.11. The proportion of city wealth spent on the journey-to-work in global cities, 1990.

In terms of sustainability this is a very hopeful sign. The sample of global cities shows that there are very similar levels of economic efficiency despite huge differences in car use. Thus transforming the transportation pattern of a city into one that is sustainable can be achieved without damaging overall economic performance (Serageldin and Barrett, 1993; World Bank, 1996).

Transit Cost Recovery

The indicator of transit cost recovery is one of the most emotionally debated issues of any area of public policy. This survey, which measures operating cost recovery, is one of the first to show a comparative set of data from the major cities of the world that has been compiled on as consistent a basis as possible. It shows that the percentage transit cost recovery follows very precisely the level of car dependence in the city (see Figure 3.12).

U.S. and Australian cities average a low 35 percent and 40 percent. Toronto stands out at 61 percent. The most bus-based, low-density, car-dependent cities of Perth, Phoenix, and Houston have a mere 28 percent and Denver only 19 percent cost recovery. In such cities, even if fares are set reasonably high, it is difficult to have a high cost recovery because of the inherently higher cost structures of such systems (e.g., high labor input per passenger kilometer, low occupancy per service unit, etc.).

European cities average 54 percent cost recovery, with a variation from 93 percent in London to 27 percent in Brussels. Such variations are not just reflections of inherent economic differences among systems, but are also the result of conscious political choices made by each city as to how much of their public transportation expenses they want to recover. London chooses to set high fares and recover almost all their costs (since the Thatcher years), while other cities, such as those in Germany and Belgium, choose to recover a lesser proportion in

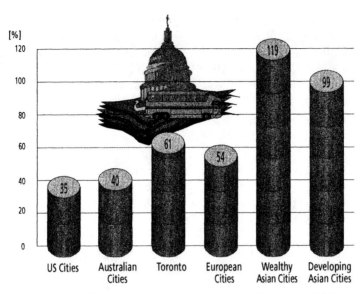

Figure 3.12. Transit operating cost recovery in global cities, 1990.

recognition of the fact that roads are also being subsidized. The case of Stockholm, with only 33 percent recovery, also reflects a social/political position on the role of transit in the community. Of course, having made a decision to recover a relatively high proportion of transit expenses, it is certainly easier to do so in a city environment that is physically supportive of high transit use and where the quality of transit services enables transit to compete with the car. Thus in London it is extremely expensive to use the underground, but it is still the best way to get around for many trips.

Asian cities have, on average, very high transit cost recovery at 105 percent, with the highest in Hong Kong (136 percent) and Kuala Lumpur (135 percent), and the lowest in Beijing, at 20 percent, due to its very low fares and high staffing levels. Chinese bus and trolley bus tickets are perhaps the cheapest in the world, the average rate in the early 1990s being less than U.S. 0.5 cent per passenger kilometer. This compares with public transportation prices (all modes) in other cities that range from a low of about U.S. 1.7 cents per passenger kilometer in Manila, through averages of about U.S. 6 to 9 cents per passenger kilometer in Australian, U.S., and European cities (Hu and Kenworthy, 1996).

The transit cost recovery debate tends to focus on how to reduce government costs. It often concludes that it would be much cheaper to provide only buses since these have lower capital and sometimes lower maintenance requirements. These data suggest that buses are effective in transit cost recovery only in situations where there are large numbers of captive users, as in newly developing Asian cities such as Manila. The more fundamental way to recover transit costs in developed cities is to influence the form of the city toward a more transit-oriented structure. The role of rail systems in influencing and facilitating this cannot be underestimated.

Traffic Deaths

In this section we examine the very real but nevertheless external costs of transportation due to traffic accidents. Many others have estimated what these costs
actually represent—for example, in the United States, the cost of road accidents
was estimated as US$150 billion in 1996 (*USA Today*, January 3–5, 1997). Here
we simply present the various patterns of traffic deaths in the different cities.
Deaths are gathered from all modes for 1990 but are negligible for rail systems and
thus are called traffic deaths rather than transportation deaths.

The data show that traffic deaths tend to follow both the degree of automobile dependence and the level of development of the traffic regulatory system
(Figure 3.13). In U.S. cities, despite their highly developed road systems, strictly
regulated traffic, and a population generally well educated in traffic safety issues,
traffic deaths are highest of all the regional groupings of cities (14.6 per 100,000
people). This seems to be due to the world's highest level of exposure of the population to auto traffic.

Traffic deaths then decline with decreasing car use, though not in a parallel
way, due presumably to the level of traffic regulation: Australian cities have 12.0
deaths per 100,000 people; Toronto, 6.5; European cities, 8.8; wealthy Asian
cities, 6.6; and developing Asian cities, 13.7 deaths per 100,000 people.

Thus, in developing cities such as Kuala Lumpur, which are motorizing at a
very rapid rate, with high levels of motorcycle ownership and use and a relatively
poorly developed traffic regulatory environment, traffic deaths are also very high
at 22.7 per 100,000 people. This is despite the fact that the absolute level of automobile dependence is still very low compared to U.S. and other developed
cities. Overall, the newly developing Asian cities have an average traffic death
rate of 13.7 per 100,000 which is a far worse record than their level of car use
would predict.[11]

Beijing, with 71 percent of total daily trips made by walking and cycling, also
has a comparatively low rate of traffic deaths compared to other cities, as do most

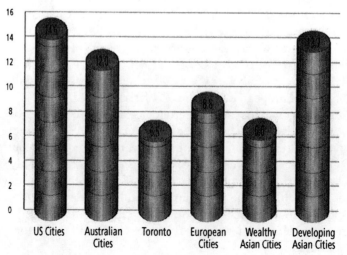

Figure 3.13. Traffic deaths in global cities per 100,000 people, 1990.

Chinese cities (6.1 deaths per 100,000). A study of seven large Chinese cities suggests a traffic death rate of 4.8 per 100,000 (Hu and Kenworthy, 1996). The situation in Chinese cities can, however, be expected to worsen, and perhaps begin to mirror the picture in the other rapidly motorizing Asian cities in this sample, as more and more traffic begins to mix with the high numbers of pedestrians and cyclists. This is especially true if little or nothing is done to slow down this rate of motorization or to plan for effective harmonization of motorized and nonmotorized transportation.

Overall, the data show how traffic deaths decline with car use though not to the same magnitude as the differences in car use; Australian cities have 18 percent fewer traffic deaths per 100,000 people but 40 percent less car use per capita than U.S. cities; European cities have 40 percent fewer deaths than U.S. cities but 59 percent less car use; and wealthy Asian cities have 55 percent fewer deaths but 86 percent less car use. As suggested above, there are therefore other factors at work that lend themselves to reducing traffic deaths; these include traffic engineering, management, and education. However, there are enormous resources and human energy poured into road safety when by far the biggest gains would be made by shifting to other modes and reducing the overall level of car use. This approach is rarely mentioned in road safety discussions.

There are some exceptional cities in terms of the patterns of traffic-related deaths:

- Metro Toronto, at 6.5 deaths per 100,000, has fewer than half the traffic fatalities found in U.S. cities, which suggests that a good transit system can have other flow-ons in terms of traffic safety (e.g., fewer teenagers need to drive). Metro Toronto's traffic death rate seems to be reasonably consistent with its other features (e.g., 24 percent of total travel is on transit, compared to only 3 percent in U.S. cities).
- Amsterdam, at 5.7, and Copenhagen, at 7.5 deaths per 100,000, have among the lowest rates in Europe and have among the highest rates of bicycle usage. This puts into perspective the perception that cycling is dangerous, perhaps indicating that the social patterns developed in a city to accommodate cyclists (such as giving priority to them at all intersections) can flow on to a generally safer road system. The case study on Copenhagen in Chapter 4 gives more detail on why that city has managed to reduce its traffic accident rates through an emphasis on bicycling and a "culture of respect" for all nonmotorized travelers.
- Tokyo and Hong Kong have among the best traffic safety records at 5.3 and 5.7 deaths per 100,000 due to their exceptional transit systems, which appear to be far more important in determining overall traffic safety levels than their congested major road systems.[12]

Transportation Emissions

This section examines the main greenhouse gas emissions (i.e., CO_2) and the main smog emissions (i.e., NO_x, SO_2, CO, VHC, and VP) that come from transportation in the different cities. These are a major external cost for urban economies.

Carbon Dioxide

Carbon dioxide is now a focus of international agreement on greenhouse gas reduction strategies, with all developed cities having to show how they are reducing CO_2. As discussed in Chapter 2, many documents have been presented on the issue at international forums, but invariably the area that is seen to be the least amenable to reduction is transportation CO_2 (OECD/ECMT, 1995; McKenzie and Walsh, 1990). The data here give some idea as to how progress can be made.

First, it is not just a matter of making technological improvements, as has already been shown. More fuel-efficient vehicles can just be used more, particularly if road conditions are improved to create freer-flowing traffic. An integrated transportation strategy is required that simultaneously improves technology, facilitates modal shifts, and reduces the need for travel. That this is possible without harming city economies is clear. The large variation in U.S. cities with respect to CO_2 generation rates shows some indication of this (total transportation CO_2 per capita varies from 3,778 kilograms per capita in the New York region up to 5,193 kilograms in Houston), but the fact that Toronto has 46 percent less CO_2 per capita than the average U.S. city suggests that its CO_2 generation rate in transportation can serve as a best-practice indicator in North American cities.

Toronto is providing transportation at a rate of 0.108 kilograms of CO_2 per dollar of GRP compared to 0.160 kilograms per dollar for U.S. cities (48 percent higher than in Toronto). Australian cities can do much better as well, with 0.141 kilograms of CO_2 per dollar of GRP. European and wealthy Asian cities may be approaching world best practice at 0.059 kilograms and 0.054 kilograms of CO_2 per dollar of GRP. The newly developing Asian cities at 0.317 kilograms of CO_2 per dollar of GRP need to do better, though their apparently high rate of CO_2 emissions per dollar of GRP is probably mostly due to their much lower wealth.

Figure 3.14 summarizes CO_2 emissions per capita for the global cities in 1990, showing the contribution from private and public passenger transportation. In all cases, CO_2 from transit is very small relative to that from automobiles.

Smog Emissions

The major automotive emissions of concern to health and regional air pollution, including photochemical smog precursors, presented in terms of NO_x, SO_2, CO, volatile hydrocarbons (VHC), and volatile particulates (VP), follow the same patterns as car use, with a few interesting exceptions (see Figure 3.15).

Australian cities are almost identical in per capita air pollutant emissions to U.S. cities, despite having 40 percent less car use per capita. This is presumably because the vehicle fleet is very old due to lower wealth, there are lax systems of vehicle inspections, and there are lower emissions standards on new vehicles than in the United States (see Newman et al., 1996).

Policy debates continue to emphasize traffic management as a solution to air pollutant emissions. Australian urban traffic congestion is probably among the lowest in the world, as suggested by the data in Table 3.9 on average speeds; this shows how minimal is the factor of smooth traffic flow in reducing emissions, compared to the sheer amount of vehicle use and the state of the vehicles them-

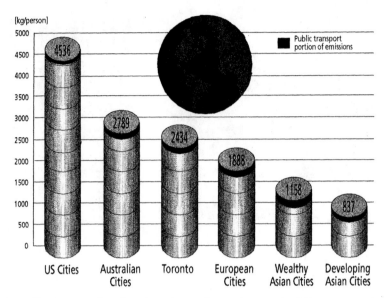

Figure 3.14. Per capita carbon dioxide emissions from private and public transportation in global cities, 1990.

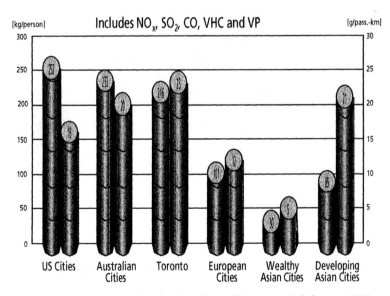

Figure 3.15. Per capita emissions of smog-related air pollutants in global cities, 1990.

Photo 3.5. Automobile domination in dense Asian cities such as Bangkok has created traffic and air quality problems second to none.

selves. U.S. cities have even higher average traffic speeds than do Australian cities, but with very high per capita transportation emissions, again emphasizing the futility of trying to tackle automotive air pollution through improvements in traffic flow.

Toronto is low in CO_2 due to its transit system and integrated land use (see Kenworthy and Newman, 1994), but it is only an average North American city in other emissions. This is probably again due to a vehicle factor, as its fleet is older and it has the least fuel-efficient cars in North America at 4.38 MJ/passenger kilometer, compared to an average of 3.51 MJ/passenger kilometer for the U.S. cities.

European city air pollutant emissions are, as expected, much lower in general than those in cities in North America and Australia, with 57% of the level of NO_x per capita in North American cities, 36 percent of the CO, 52 percent of the VHC, and 63 percent of the particulates.[13] SO_2 is 20 percent higher, however, due presumably to the higher amount of electricity (and hence coal) used in powering transit and the higher share of diesel fuel in the transportation system.

Asian cities for the most part have the lowest per capita air pollutant emissions. The exception is Bangkok, which, for its relatively low level of motor vehicle use, has very high volatile hydrocarbons: 23.2 kilograms per capita, similar to levels in U.S. and Australian cities with much higher vehicle use, and much higher than the European cities which produce 11.6 kilograms per capita. In addition, Bangkok has by far the highest level of particulates in the world: 9.1 kilograms per capita compared to a little over 1 kilogram per capita in most other cities.

Both these pollutants are linked to health problems. Volatile hydrocarbons are primarily from very inefficient, poorly maintained vehicles that are often idling for hours in traffic jams, with Bangkok being a global extreme in these problems. Particulates mainly come from poorly tuned diesel buses and trucks, as well as two-stroke motorcycles, and such vehicles are very common in Bangkok (they are also common in Jakarta and Surabaya, where particulate emissions are also comparatively high). It is not surprising that Bangkok traffic police wear gas masks and that there are increasing air pollution–related health problems in this city (see Kenworthy, 1995).

Proportion of City Wealth Spent on Transportation

A final parameter that in many ways brings together this perspective on automobile dependence is the percentage of GRP spent on transportation. This is the sum of all the direct costs attributable to private and public passenger transportation that is then expressed as a proportion of the city's wealth. It shows "how much" transportation-related goods and services are as a proportion of total goods and services in the city.

Figure 3.16 shows that those cities with the highest automobile dependence (Australian and U.S. cities) have the highest overall proportion of transportation costs. These proportions would rise even further if they incorporated external costs such as traffic deaths and smog, which are also higher in these car-dependent cities.

The cities (in the developed world) with the highest proportion of their wealth going into passenger transportation are Perth at 17 percent, Phoenix at 16 percent, and Adelaide, Detroit, and Denver at 15 percent.

The cities (in the developed world) with the least wealth going into transportation are the European and wealthy Asian cities (at 8 percent and 5 percent, respectively), with their stronger commitment to transit systems. The best North American and Australian cities—Toronto at 7 percent, New York at 10 percent,

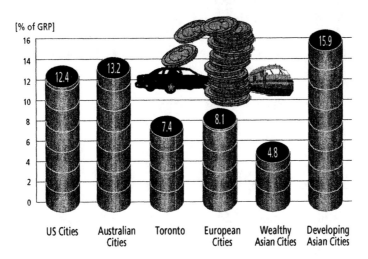

Figure 3.16. The proportion of city wealth spent on passenger transportation in global cities, 1990.

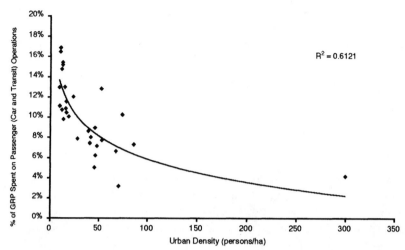

Figure 3.17. The total operating costs of passenger transportation versus urban density in developed cities, 1990.

and Sydney at 10 percent—also suggest that transit orientation is good for a city's economy.

The possible mechanism for this has been discussed in Chapter 2, where it is suggested that car dependence creates inefficiencies due to the extra land it consumes, the extra costs of infrastructure, and the direct and indirect costs of the automobile. Perhaps there is also a loss of investment associated with traffic-dominated urban environments (compared to quality pedestrian-friendly urban environments) and some opportunity costs due to loss of investment in productive industries instead of investment in unproductive suburb building.

Figure 3.17 demonstrates the significance of density in this relationship to city wealth. Dense cities have the lowest proportion of transportation costs and the sprawling car-dependent cities have the highest costs.

The cities that don't follow this trend are the developing Asian cities, which are not car-dependent but are car-dominated. These cities are pouring their productive financial and human capital into auto-related activity but are not showing much benefit from it. The transit-oriented model of the wealthy Asian cities, on the other hand, appears to represent world best practice on how to create wealth and not have car-dependence problems.

Conclusions

The patterns of transportation infrastructure and land use in cities around the world reveal automobile dependence to be a combination of high car use, high provision for automobiles, and scattered low-density land use.

It is now possible to conclude that these patterns of automobile dependence are not sustainable (as defined here) based on economic and environmental indicators.

1. There appears to be no obvious gain in economic efficiency from developing automobile dependence in cities, particularly as it is shown in U.S. and Australian cities. There is no relative gain in GRP per capita or in the percentage of GRP spent on commuting: trip times to work are roughly the same everywhere, transit cost recovery is much worse, and road expenditure is higher.

2. There are, on the other hand, significant external and environmental costs due to automobile dependence that have clear implications for sustainability. There are much higher levels of per capita transportation energy use and emissions generated, more urban land per capita, and more traffic deaths. As the global agenda is focussing increasingly on sustainability, there is an obvious need to address these differences by overcoming automobile dependence.

3. Trends in car use suggest that U.S. cities have continued to grow in automobile dependence up to 1990, but some reductions are appearing in Australian cities. The latter is an important trend that is consistent with the pattern of increasing density and focused land use. It suggests that the new information economy and reurbanization of cities may assist in the sustainability agenda. More recently, in the second half of the 1990s, U.S. cities have also begun to show some positive trends in the comeback of central- and inner-city areas both residentially and economically. This appears to have been due to a combination of factors, such as successful programs against crime resulting in major reductions in homicides and robbery in some cities, including Boston, New York, and Chicago, and a renewed appeal of central and inner areas for retired people tired of suburban inconveniences and professional people weary of long commutes on congested roads. It remains to be seen whether this can have any significant effect on auto dependence, which appears to have a long-term exponential trend upward in U.S. cities.

4. European and wealthy Asian cities appear to have transportation systems that are both the least costly and the least environmentally damaging. However, these cities will still need to do better in terms of car use, which is growing in all but a few cases.

5. Rapidly developing Asian cities have considerably less efficient and sustainable transportation systems than would be expected from their levels of wealth. The positive side, however, is that they still have strongly transit-oriented urban forms, which means that good electric rail systems and more provision for nonmotorized transportation have the potential to rapidly transform their transportation patterns into more sustainable ones.

6. Rail transit systems, compared to all other motorized transportation, appear to have the best energy efficiency and greatest ability to attract people out of cars. They are the most important factor in the recovery of transit operating costs; they seem to be the catalyst for compact subcenter development; and they make a major contribution to sustainability on all indicators. Moving cities toward sustainability in both economic and environmental terms would appear to involve good rail systems.

7. Nonmotorized transportation is highly significant in both economic and environmental indicators. Cities that implement plans for improving the contribution of nonmotorized transportation are likely to see immediate and long-term benefits.

From a global perspective on automobile dependence, this chapter has shown a mixture of hope and continuing concern when reviewing the comparative performance of cities. The hope reveals that the process of developing policies to overcome automobile dependence is worth pursuing.

Notes

1. We did have an experienced student located in the city, but even this on-site effort yielded very little useful information.

2. Transportation energy consumption not only gives an indication of the extent to which a city is using fossil fuels, especially oil, but is also an indicator of the quantity of air pollutants the city is producing (including smog and greenhouse gases). Other factors, such as the dominance of cars and the lack of transit, are also reflected in per capita transportation energy use. All of these other parameters can be measured, and in many cases we discuss them in this chapter; but the idea of highlighting transportation energy is to present first one of the most strategically important parameters for city sustainability.

3. This suggestion is somewhat confounded in the developing Asian cities, where there is a higher proportion of diesel fuel for passenger transportation.

4. Of course, the case of developing Asian cities again needs to be qualified. Even though they have not yet developed electric rapid transit systems, and therefore consume no electricity in transportation, they are also low energy users overall because their motorization and gasoline use are still very low in international terms.

5. Having asserted the importance of physical planning in this process of explaining urban patterns, we should also state that the economic parameters are significant. Kirwan (1992) has analyzed our data in terms of multivariate regressions and concluded that the price of fuel is the most significant variable in influencing travel patterns. He does admit, however, that there are strong factors influencing travel patterns that are part of the structure or physical form of the city. Obviously, pricing does influence travel and must be considered in any policy package designed to save transportation energy. We have begun a multivariate analysis on our new data using GRP as the wealth parameter, length of road as the infrastructure parameter, and density as the urban form parameter. It shows that density and road length are far more important in explaining vehicle kilometers traveled (VKT) than wealth; car ownership also follows the same pattern. This is discussed further, especially in Chapter 4.

6. Canberra is the only exception, at 34 km/h, due to its very low traffic density and high-speed services along bus lanes between subcenters.

7. The second graph is weaker because probably (1) there are some medium-density European cities that have done a lot to facilitate walking and cycling and have very high levels of use for these modes to work (Copenhagen and Amsterdam), and (2) there are some high-density Asian cities, such as Bangkok, that have atypically low walking and cycling to work for their density because of peculiar local conditions,

such as very hostile urban environmental conditions in Bangkok and difficult topography in Hong Kong.

8. It is also necessary to include nonwork journeys in this argument because they constitute about 70 percent of all travel, and they are far more local and thus shorter in denser, mixed-use cities than in dispersed, low-density cities. For example, in the Kanton (State) of Zurich, which is heavily urbanized, the percentage of work trips on foot and bicycle in 1989 was 26 percent, whereas shopping trips were 35 percent by foot and bicycle, and recreation trips were 33 percent (Statistische Berichte des Kantons Zürich, 1991).

9. The capital and variable cost of cars per kilometer in Australian cities is considerably higher than in U.S. cities (US$0.37 per kilometer compared to US$0.29, or 28 percent higher in Australia), which when combined with lower wealth (US$19,761 in Australia compared to US$26,822 in the United States) may also be contributing to lower increases in car use. However, these economic differences are less pronounced now than they were, so the other reasons above may be more fundamental.

10. Lave's analysis suffers from being based mainly on national data that are strongly influenced by factors such as air travel growth.

11. The apparent exceptions are Surabaya and Jakarta (7.8 and 4.5 deaths per 100,000, respectively). We are, however, suspicious of these low figures and suspect they are from police records (which always understate traffic deaths), whereas the other data are from health departments that use a standard WHO method for reporting causes of death (International Classification of Diseases, or ICD; see Appendix 1).

12. The parameter found in Appendix 1, "percentage traffic deaths of total deaths," follows the same pattern as discussed above except that the Asian cities are relatively higher. This may be due to their younger age structure and much lower homicide rate than in Western cities.

13. Two outliers that are hard to explain are Stockholm, which is much higher than average, and Vienna, which is much lower than average, but this is probably due to variability in the quality of data, as explained in the methodology (Appendix 1).

Chapter 4

A Vision of Reduced Automobile Dependence

Introduction

How did some cities become so automobile-dependent and not others? Aren't there other more fundamental causes than those discussed in Chapters 2 and 3? Answering this is a first step in exploring how automobile dependence can be eased and a more sustainable city created.

When we present our data on cities from Chapter 3 and make suggestions about how we should change, we find a range of questions directed to us from people who are concerned that we have not understood how really difficult it is to change a city. For them it is inevitable that their city is the way it is. They believe the number of barriers to altering cities makes the task impossible.

In Box 4.1, we list ten of the most common reasons that have been suggested to explain the phenomenon of automobile dependence, none of which, it will be argued, are sufficient in themselves. They are therefore called "myths about automobile dependence." They are the basis for addressing public policy and administration issues having to do with cities and cars since they concern the assumptions that are causing so many policy makers, practitioners, and activists to feel there is nothing they can do about automobile dependence. Once these are examined, it is possible to present a vision for reducing auto dependence as part of a wider plan for creating more sustainable cities. In order to show that such a vision is achievable, some case studies of innovative cities are presented later in the chapter.

Dispelling the Myths About Automobile Dependence

1. *Wealth.* Automobile dependence is an inevitable consequence of wealth. People will always buy cars and larger amounts of private urban space and thus alternative urban forms and transportation will inevitably die out as people get richer.

Box 4.1. 10 Myths About the Inevitability of Automobile Dependence

1. *Wealth.* Automobile dependence is an inevitable consequence of wealth. People will always buy cars and larger amounts of private urban space; thus alternative urban forms and transportation will inevitably die out as people get richer.

2. *Climate.* Automobile dependence is inevitably induced by warm climates, where people can enjoy low-density suburban lifestyles, whereas compact, transit-oriented cities are mostly in cold climates.

3. *Space.* Automobile dependence is inevitably part of countries that are very spacious, while those with little space have compact cities.

4. *Age.* Automobile dependence is an inevitable feature of modern life, and thus new cities, developed predominantly after 1945, express it more than old cities.

5. *Health and social problems.* Automobile dependence is inevitably created by the reaction to density and its health and social problems.

6. *Rural lifestyles.* Automobile dependence is inevitably created by the attraction of rural lifestyles in the suburbs with their associated promise of withdrawal from the evils of city lifestyles.

7. *Road lobby.* Automobile dependence is inevitably created by the powerful combination of road interests.

8. *Land developers.* Automobile dependence is inevitably created by the powerful interests of land speculators and developers and planning is powerless to stop them.

9. *Traffic engineering.* Automobile dependence is an inevitable outcome of the standard processes of transportation planning and traffic engineering.

10. *Town planning.* Automobile dependence is inevitably regulated into cities by local town planning.

Many urban commentators suggest there is an inevitable link between rising living standards and rising demands for private space and car use (e.g., Gomez-Ibañez, 1991). "As soon as people get enough money they will buy a car and move to the suburbs" is how the inevitability is generally expressed. Stopping these sprawling car-based cities is therefore like being the hapless King Canute.

Rising living standards obviously do impact on transportation and land use (Schafer and Victor, 1997). Historical analysis (as in Chapter 2) shows how cities have moved outward following trams and trains and then cars as people developed the economic means to take advantage of these technologies. Also, increasing incomes meant that people could afford to buy bigger homes and more spacious surroundings, which they appreciated for cultural reasons.

The link between living standards and a more car-based, low-density city is not automatic, however. In fact, the correlations are very weak (see "Price and Income" section of Chapter 3) and in more recent times are going in the opposite direction (see "Car Use and Wealth" in Chapter 3). Thus the future does not necessarily bring more automobile dependence. Technological determinism based on cars can be switched to transit if a quality service is available and the major road and freeway systems are operating close to capacity. Cultural choices vary, and the dream of space in the suburbs can be replaced for some with a dream of urban living, with its full range of amenities and cultural attractions. In addition to this, the economic processes that link wealth and urban form, as suggested above, are much more complex than conventional argument has considered.

The analysis by Frost (1991) outlined in Chapter 2 provides a detailed understanding of the link between wealth and urban form based on whether wealth is mostly reinvested in new suburban infrastructure or in industrial development. North American and Australian cities have mainly done the former and thus have developed low-density, car-based cities, while other cities have become more compact as they reinvested more in industrial innovation. Frost seriously questions whether any cities can continue to move in the direction that assumes growing wealth from our rural hinterlands is the basis of urban growth patterns.

Other urban researchers (reviewed in Newman and Kenworthy, 1989a) have shown how levels of car ownership and use are significantly lower in higher-density areas of cities at all levels of wealth (why use a car if you can walk or take transit more quickly and conveniently?).

Our global cities data, as outlined in Chapter 3, reveal a significant difference between U.S./Australian and European/Asian cities in their density and car use patterns—and yet European city incomes are higher. Indeed, many European cities have per capita incomes that are 20 percent to 50 percent higher than those in Australian and U.S. cities, yet they are four times as dense and two to three times less intensive in their car use.[1]

When we talk to European planners they are adamant that their urban policies are determined to minimize sprawl. Most European urban and transportation policy documents indicate a strong commitment to and belief in physical planning policies intended to contain sprawl and to provide effective alternatives to the car. There is a growing movement to "smart growth" planning in U.S. cities. These policies have taken a while to effect, but results are becoming more evident.

Perhaps some of the last European cities to tackle automobile dependence are those in the United Kingdom, but their new Planning Policy Guidance (PPG) 13 favors reurbanization and reducing the need to travel. It even bans new "out of town" shopping centers. This came in response to the decay of their cities under Thatcherism policies designed to encourage car use. These policies were reversed under pressure from the 900 anti-motorway groups and the business owners in traditional centers whose trade was dying. As the Royal Commission on Environmental Pollution put it: "There has been a significant shift in thinking away from what Lady Thatcher once called the 'great car economy'" (1994). In the United Kingdom, policy no longer assumes that greater wealth means greater use of cars and more sprawl. Mobility and wealth have become decoupled as the quest for the sustainability agenda has become more and more mainstream.

There are now many examples of wealthy cities in which densities have increased (as shown in the data in Chapter 3, as well as in many new urban villages) and in which transit and walking/cycling have grown at the expense of car travel (see later in this chapter). These changes have not occurred because incomes have been reduced. They have often occurred because of the cultural attraction of market processes that appear to favor compact urban nodes in the new information-based city, or through more intense urban environments, or simply because of different planning priorities (e.g., transit preferred over highways).

Finally, it is worth remembering that the most expensive places to live in all U.S. cities are in their high-density downtowns, such as in New York (Manhattan), Boston (Beacon Hill), Philadelphia (Society Hill), San Francisco (Nob Hill or Mission Bay), and so on. There appears to have been a long-term market in the United States for areas that favor dense, walking-based urbanity, and increasingly there is a shift in the suburban market to nodes that are more city-like.[2]

2. *Climate.* Automobile dependence is inevitably induced by warm climates where people can enjoy low-density suburban lifestyles, whereas compact transit-oriented cities are mostly in cold climates.

The argument generally goes like this: a warm, low-rainfall climate means people spend time outdoors, travel more, and have large private blocks of land for their houses so they can enjoy gardening, barbecues, and swimming in private pools and can give their children extra space for sports and games. In relation to Perth, one early 1980s transportation study proudly proclaimed: Our climate promotes the 'quarter-acre' and 'fifth-acre' block: we seek space for garages and gardens, pools and patios, barbecues and boats" (Director General of Transport, 1982, p. 65). Conversely, the argument is that in cold climates, snow and ice motivate people to take transit rather than drive a car on dangerous roads and that people don't mind living in compact, apartment settings because the outdoors is so unattractive.[3]

Our global cities study of thirty-two cities found there was no correlation between gasoline consumption (a key indicator of automobile dependence) and average annual temperature, or between urban density and average annual temperature.

This at least suggests that there is nothing about hot weather, as such, that induces travel or sprawling cities. Conversely, there appears to be nothing about cold climates that induces people to drive little and cram together in apartments. Certainly, indoor activities can be just as attractive in hot weather as in cold weather. The positive effect of climate on certain outdoor activities, such as gardening and games, is not limited to hotter climates, particularly considering the popularity of winter sports.

The use of transit seems also to be related to more than just climate. All our data show that it depends on how fast transit is relative to cars, how frequently it comes, and how easy it is to access.

If we go beyond the scope of the global cities study, it is easy to find cities that are not cold and yet have a high-density urban form with good transit and much more use of nonmotorized transportation. In Europe there are Athens, Barcelona, Madrid, and Rome. In the Middle East there are Istanbul, Cairo, Jerusalem, and Tehran, with many Middle Eastern cities continuing to build in a compact way to create microclimates with shade, orientation of buildings, and public spaces to optimize cool breezes. In South and Central America almost every big city has a hot climate—Mexico City, São Paulo, Rio de Janeiro, Lima, Buenos Aires—and all are compact and high density. In the United States there is Honolulu, which features some very-high-density areas such as Waikiki, and there is the dense, compact city center of old San Francisco. In Asia, all cities are densely populated regardless of the climatic conditions.

On the other hand, many cold northern cities are low density and car-oriented. Detroit and Denver have few supposed car-enhancing climate features for much of the year, but they are totally dominated by the automobile and extensive, low-density suburban land use.

If low-density planning and high car use are encouraged in a city, this is probably for deeper reasons than lifestyle induced by the climate.

3. *Space*. Automobile dependence is inevitably part of countries that are very spacious, while those with little space have compact cities.[4]

A number of points can be raised about such assertions. Other countries with "plenty of space" have not developed sprawling cities along the lines of those in Australia and North America with densities of about ten to twenty people per hectare.

Central and South America have vast areas of rural land similar to the United States and Australia, but their cities are all high density (Buenos Aires, 80 per ha; Salvador, 90 per ha; Santiago, 144 per ha; Lima, 171 per ha; Caracas, 175 per ha; and Mexico City, 224 per ha). Russia has no shortage of land, but its cities are very efficient users of space (Moscow, 139 per ha, and St. Petersburg, 85 per ha).

Sweden has vast expanses of rural land, mostly forest, but the few cities are, for the most part, highly compact with little wasted space. Sweden has a long tradition of planning urban services in an equitable and efficient manner. Stockholm has no "need" to concentrate its land use because of lack of space, but its planners believe that a good city has: (1) a railway station within 500 to 900 meters (i.e., a short walking or cycling distance) of most housing; (2) train service without a timetable, (i.e., a frequency of twelve minutes or less); and (3) people living not more than thirty minutes from the city center. These policies ensure a compact urban form based around a fast electric train service, with housing and other land uses concentrated around stations.[5]

If a nation has "plenty of space," it does not automatically lead to a low-density urban form where land use is highly inefficient, although this perception in the United States and Australia appears to play some role in facilitating or at least justifying the low-density city. Frontier land views of space (cowboy cities) can be rationalized in a frontier economy. Now we all live in a planetary economy, with a global sustainability agenda and those cities not addressing the global agenda (including sustainability) may well go the way of the cowboy.

4. *Age*. Automobile dependence is an inevitable feature of modern life, and thus new cities developed predominantly after 1945 express it more than old cities.

A city's age does affect its spatial and transportation traditions. Cities founded before the middle of the nineteenth century were built around walking, then transit spread the city out, and finally the car allowed even lower densities. However, many modern cities have been built with a walking-based or transit-based urban form around which they continue to develop. Asian cities, including modern Tokyo, Seoul, and Hong Kong, are high-density walking and transit cities with tiny levels of car use compared to U.S. and Australian cities. European cities mostly maintain their medium-density, transit-oriented land use in much of the new development that has been added to them in the age of the car's dominance.

The sprawling, low-density city is essentially a U.S. and Australian phenomenon—one taken to the extreme in old railway-based cities such as Detroit and Los Angeles, which were rebuilt into totally car-based cities. It is now being recognized that such fully motorized cities cannot function efficiently, and hence rail systems are making a comeback in most Californian cities, along with a growing trend toward reintegrating development into high-density, mixed-use patterns around stations.

Canadians have perhaps gone furthest in beginning to change from car-based sprawl to more compact, modern rail–based cities, having adopted a deliberate policy on this in the early 1970s (see case study on Toronto and Vancouver).

Although a city's age is important in its spatial traditions, it is not an inflexible determinant.

5. *Health and social problems.* Automobile dependence is inevitably created by the reaction to density and its health and social problems.

While recognizing the economic and environmental problems associated with automobile dependence, some urban commentators suggest that the primary motivation behind low-density cities is one of health and social amenities. They draw on a long tradition that "density is bad for you."

The spread of disease was always thought to be through the air (via "miasma"), and lowering densities was seen as a way to improve health through a "wholesome supply of good air." This justification for the garden suburb continued even after a century of medical evidence showed that sewerage and sanitary facilities were the key factors in the promotion of good health. Even though such high-density cities as Hong Kong and Singapore have extremely high health rates, some planners and academics still talk about the need for plenty of space for good health.

Social "ill health" (crime, delinquency, suicide, drug addiction) has also been linked to higher density, yet there is no consistent evidence to support this. We analyzed crime rates and density (Newman and Kenworthy, 1989a) and found that the data showing how low density reduces crime (as is so often stated) are very difficult to find. Poverty is the biggest correlate with crime, especially if there are extremes of wealth nearby (Knox, 1982). But this occurs at all densities. Indeed, crime seems to be higher in low-density cities in the United States (Newman and Kenworthy, 1989a). International data tend to suggest that European crime rates are lower than in the United States and Australia, and Asian city crime rates are even lower than in Europe (Fischer, 1976).

Obviously, sociocultural factors dominate the causes behind these data, but the evidence goes against the belief that increased density leads inevitably to increased crime. There is also a larger body of literature suggesting that higher density, that is designed to create "defensible space" for neighborhoods, may suppress some forms of crime, probably because of the "eyes on the street" phenomenon (Jacobs, 1961; Newman, 1972; Gehl, 1987; Sherlock, 1991; and the New Urbanist writers—see Chapter 6). Other literature shows the importance of community empowerment in easing crime (Herbert, 1982; Rosenbaum, 1986), and this process requires sufficient density for neighborhoods to become communities.

At the very least, the data suggest that there is no inherent relationship between higher density and crime and that the common fear about increased densities leading to increases in violent crime is unfounded.

The one main study by Schmitt in 1966 that suggested a relationship between density and social disorder is widely quoted, but Schmitt's 1978 paper in which he reexamined the data and no longer found the correlation, is rarely quoted. Australian sociologist Paul Wilson suggests that "rhetoric about the effects of high rise living must rank as one of the major hoaxes imposed by social scientists on an unsuspecting public." (Wilson, 1976, pp. 45–46)

Not only has urban sociology shown this particular anti-density bias, but other social sciences reflect it as well. Psychologists in Anglo-Saxon countries have studied rats in cages, students crammed into rooms, and people walking in crowded city streets and concluded that density is bad for us. Major critiques of these studies have shown that either their results cannot be reproduced, are meaningless (rat studies), or do not consistently show problems with density (Fischer, 1976; Baldassare, 1979; Guskaynak and LeCompte, 1977). For example, crowding sometimes produces positive effects in behavioral studies and not the expected negative ones. The classic studies of New Yorkers avoiding mugged victims in the street was attributed to the density of people, but when repeated in Dutch cities, similar behavior was not observed, indeed the opposite occurred (Korte, 1976). Despite such studies, the belief in the negative impact of density remains very strong. Yeung (1977) concludes that many of the studies on density were dominated by "half truths based on ethnocentric perspectives" (p. 594), suggesting that we have wanted to find negative aspects of density. Baldassare (1979) suggests that "In a sense crowding became the non-social explanation of the society's social problems" (pp. 6–7).

In contrast to the anti-density tradition there is another that has emphasized the positive human benefits of increasing densities. Freedman (1975) developed a crowding model that tries to make sense out of the conflicting evidence from empirical studies, while also recognizing the adaptability of humans. He suggests that "crowding is not generally negative and it does intensify human reactions to other people." It stimulates human interaction, which means the human effects of density are up to us. Higher density produces negative effects if we design it that way, but we can also make higher density into something beneficial.

This is why we can find examples of high-density areas with problems, and then identify examples where the opposite is true (studies summarized in Newman and Hogan, 1981). For example, Conway and Adams (1977), in a study of identical apartment buildings, found one had a high level of social disturbance while the other did not; the difference was attributed to better management. Others have studied the role of individuals or collectives of residents who were the catalyst for social cohesiveness and stimulation as part of a high-density complex.

The growing literature on crime reduction through urban design mentioned before is based on the need for human scale at the street level, with diversity and as much activity as possible (e.g., Gehl, 1994). The data are suggesting that if communities want to create livable areas, then it is essential that they are brought together. Minimizing crime and creating healthy cities is not a crude process of simply reducing densities. It is essential to do creative town planning right down to the neighborhood design scale and to enable communities to have a greater sense of their own destiny.

6. *Rural lifestyles*. Automobile dependence is inevitably created by the attraction of rural lifestyles in the suburbs, with their associated promise of withdrawal from the evils of city lifestyles.

Cities with low densities and a great commitment to the private car usually have an Anglo-Saxon tradition, and attempts to increase urban densities in Anglo-Saxon countries in the latter part of the twentieth century have been met with strong opposition from the urban community. The reactions have been so emotional as to suggest that more than just environmental or economic factors are involved, and that such reactions probably lie deep in cultural attitudes.

Literature of an anti-urban character frequently has an Anglo-Saxon source, suggesting such writers are afraid of increasing densities because they have little of a pro-urban tradition. British cultural traditions have been ambiguous about the city. Many artists and intellectuals from Anglo-Saxon origins have not believed the city is a force for good, a place where culture can grow and all that is best in the human spirit can thrive. Many English, American, and Australian artists and writers have idealized rural places, and their literary heroes are from the countryside, the prairie, and the bush. Cities, in this view, serve only to corrupt the purifying aspects of country life.

This idyllic view of rural life is called "pastoralism" and asserts that the country provides solitude, innocence, and happiness. The tradition has been seen as the answer to human yearnings right through the twentieth century and has its expression in arcadian philosophy, and to some extent it has been continued in the ecology literature of today. It reached its zenith in the works of such nineteenth-century authors as George Eliot, Thomas Hardy, and D. H. Lawrence in England and Banjo Patterson and Henry Lawson in Australia. In the United States the tradition is based around authors such as Thomas Jefferson, Ralph Waldo Emerson, Henry Thoreau, Nathaniel Hawthorne, Herman Melville, and Henry James.

The pastoral tradition has not led to a return to village life; instead it has helped create the rationale for the suburban lifestyle. The pastoral anti-urban tradition appears to have been grafted into Anglo-Saxon cities by people with-

Photo 4.1. "Far from the madding crowd" is Thomas Hardy's cottage, providing inspiration for English pastoral literature's anti-urban ideas.

drawing behind their private suburban walls to escape the negative impacts of city living.

The rationale for this kind of living has been developed through town planning theorists such as Frank Lloyd Wright, through organizations such as the Town and Country Planning Association with its motto of "nothing gained by overcrowding," and through the rural images promoted for each new fringe suburb by the real estate industry.

However, each new spacious "rural" kind of suburb is soon surrounded and engulfed by more suburbs, and the appeal of rural life is never quite what the real estate brochures promised. Indeed, most of the problems of the city seem to follow, and distances are so large that automobile dependence is endemic.

European and Asian traditions are much less anti-urban and have always maintained strong commitments to cities, where people can meet in the street and in public spaces, and where green space can be a public facility rather than a large private space; thus automobile dependence is not facilitated from these cultures.

Many social scientists have also criticized the romantic approach to rural life with its negative approach to cities. They instead have asserted that the city, particularly the high-density city, can be a positive force for culture and human experience, just as rural life can be a source of deprivation, and that the rural/urban dichotomy has directed attention away from more fundamental sources of social disorder and loss of innocence (Ellul, 1970). That is, the city need not be a source of human alienation and environmental disaster, but can in fact be the opposite. As Howarth (1976) says ". . . it is impossible to describe a natural element for man, in contrast to which city life may be considered unnatural" (p. 300).

Thus there is an opposing tradition that stresses the positive aspects of dense cities and tends to have an anti-suburban rather than anti-urban thrust. In this tradition there is much more hope for, and attraction to, the mixed, dense neighborhoods of old cities, with their variety and history. Writings in this tradition can be found in the midst of the more dominant anti-urban literature in Anglo-Saxon cities (Williams, 1985; Mumford, 1938; Kunstler, 1993). The writings of Jane Jacobs have provided a strong urban voice along these lines for town planners since the early 1960s. Gratz (1989) and others have followed in this organic city tradition, and today, youth culture in particular is far more celebratory about urbanism. In many cities, artists are among the pioneers that help in the revitalization of older urban areas, and the reurbanization process described in this book is being driven by younger professionals.

The power of the anti-city myths cannot be underestimated as a continuing force in creating automobile dependence, but it is not an inevitable process. The task for this generation of artists, writers, urban politicians, developers, and managers is to help facilitate some of the enthusiasm for urban life if the processes of anti-urban development are to be reversed. The evidence that such a reversal is possible is clear in virtually every Anglo-Saxon city, though those described later and in Chapter 7 show it more than others.

7. *Road lobby.* Automobile dependence is inevitably created by the powerful combination of road interests.

The politics of transportation is dominated by an acrimonious conflict between road and rail lobbies. The most controversial story of this sort concerns the road lobby that dismantled the urban electric rail systems in U.S. cities. In the 1930s a holding company, National City Lines, which was made up of interests from the oil, tire, and car industries, bought the private electric streetcar systems in forty-five U.S. cities and then closed them down (Klein and Olson, 1996). According to Snell, the reasons for this were clear: "one subway car or electric rail car can take the place of from 50 to 100 automobiles" (Snell, 1974). In 1949 a grand jury ultimately convicted General Motors, Standard Oil of California, Mac Trucks, Phillips Petroleum, and Firestone Tires on a criminal indictment of antitrust conspiracy, but the damage had been done. Los Angeles was the worst affected, with 280 million passengers a year being pushed into buses and cars. Within a few decades there were 4 million cars in Los Angeles, and the era of automobile-dependent U.S. cities had begun.[6]

Similar lobbies exist in all countries (Hamer, 1987), but not all are as successful as in the United States. The political power of the road lobby everywhere is strong but not overwhelming; governments are accountable to the wider public as well as to the lobbyists. The influence of strong private-industry lobbies for the automobile in many European and Asian countries has been minimized by equally powerful lobbies for transit. Data show that transit support and funding can be given a high priority, and recent trends in transit demonstrate that it can influence the future direction of our cities. The political appeal of new and upgraded rail systems in conjunction with urban villages can be a powerful force in reshaping automobile-dependent cities, just as road lobbies previously shaped them.

8. *Land developers*. Automobile dependence is inevitably created by the powerful interests of land speculators and developers, and there is little that planning can do to stop them.

In the same way that transportation politics can determine transportation priorities and hence urban land use, it is possible to examine land politics and see how it determines urban land use and thus transportation patterns.

Capitalism is based on the accumulation of wealth and its investment into physical assets that produce further wealth. Cities appear to have been built in cycles, with most construction related to the level of capital accumulation. Suburbanization is explained as the need to invest capital in both the land and the transportation systems to service it (Harvey, 1973; Walker, 1978). Most suburbanization follows economic booms, and when the economy contracts, so the city turns back on itself rather than expanding on its fringe.

North American and Australian Auto Cities have been analyzed to show how suburban land has been developed in response to capital accumulation (Cox, 1978; Sandercock, 1975; Badcock, 1984). In these cases urban planning is seen as having little power to direct urban growth for public purposes; private capital just maximizes private gain wherever it likes.

But not all capitalist cities have optimized private gain in an automobile-dependent way. European cities, in particular, have generally managed to create a far less auto-dependent kind of urban growth. Developers still make money, but their capital is used to help solve the problems that we are considering in this book, rather than exacerbating them.

The statement is often made that developers in the United States and Australia would not put up with this kind of socialistic control over their development "rights." We are not so sure that the systems in Europe and the United States/Australia are that different.

The land development system in U.S. cities and Australian cities is still under planning control. The process has many built-in subsidies that favor capital to invest in land on the urban fringe, as discussed in Chapter 2. Primarily, the building of large roads from federal grants opens up land that normally would not be worth developing. Then local government offers a range of incentives to have the development come to them rather than to other areas. Both of these processes are market interventions. In other places they would be described as socialism.

Then the developers take the large set of regulations that have grown over years of suburb building and dutifully carry them out in their development—again it is a process controlled by planning. Undoubtedly the process of achieving less-automobile-dependent cities is helped if there is a city-wide planning agency that is deliberately attempting to minimize sprawl. However, a city-wide planning agency can also facilitate car-dependent sprawl.

In the late 1990s there are developers in the United States and Australia who want to make money, yet want to do it in a more socially and ecologically responsible way. They do not want to extend the Auto City any further. Such developers are putting their capital into reurbanization, transit-oriented development, and New Urbanism development. For them, the planning process in the United States and Australia is hopelessly socialistic, full of inappropriate subsidies and out-of-date regulations. The revitalization of inner cities in Australia, the New Urbanism suburbs in the United States, the transit-based development in Portland, Washington, D.C., and Atlanta are all forging new, more sustainable ways of physical planning. Some of this is given direction by public agencies, but frequently the new alternatives are coming from private sector sources who are pioneering ways to create more sustainable settlements in a public planning milieu dominated by out-of-date, automobile-dependent assumptions. Chapter 6 explores how more sustainable public planning can be further facilitated, but much is already happening without this being the driving force.

Planning is always going to be needed to guide the development process. To steer development away from automobile dependence does not require draconian planning intervention—that is often already there. It just requires a new professional praxis that can facilitate different kinds of development, particularly reurbanization and urban villages. Investors can still make money, but the process can help to build in sustainability, not automobile dependence.

9. *Traffic engineering*. Automobile dependence is an inevitable outcome of the standard processes of transportation planning and traffic engineering.

The most important of the technical procedures in transportation planning is the land use/transportation modeling process that emerged in the mid-1950s as a distinct area of expertise. The purpose of these studies was to plan for anticipated growth in population, jobs, and traffic flows as far ahead as twenty years, so as to ensure an equilibrium between the supply of transportation facilities and demand for travel as it arises out of land use.

The concept of the "grand transportation study" was embraced with enormous enthusiasm, with virtually every developed city at some point between 1955 and 1975 undertaking at least one major transportation study. It was part of what a city had to do to be "modern." The 1950s and early 1960s were a very optimistic and prosperous period characterized by booming car ownership and the political expectation, at least in the United States and Australia, that the car would be the future of urban transportation. Thus, right from the outset, land use/transportation studies tended to be strongly associated with planning for roads and cars rather than a balance of transportation modes, and most of the U.S. and Australian land use/transportation studies pioneered the building of elaborate highway and freeway systems.

Transit, especially rail, was glossed over and almost eliminated from cities such as Detroit, Phoenix, and Houston. Most forecasting was based on private transportation growth and land use patterns based around this. Once such land use is in place, the only transit that can service it is an inefficient bus service; thus the conclusion is inevitably reached that a massive increase in road funding is needed to provide the "grand plan" needs.

Most major cities that built extensive freeways then found that this process spread out land use and generated more and more traffic, until very soon after completion the freeways were already badly congested.

The obvious response to the failure of freeways to cope with traffic congestion is to suggest that still more roads are urgently needed. The new roads are then justified again on technical grounds in terms of time, fuel, and other perceived savings to the community from eliminating the congestion. This sets in motion a vicious circle or self-fulfilling prophecy of congestion, road building, sprawl, congestion, and more road building. Automobile dependence is inevitable in such traffic engineering.

Awareness of this phenomenon, called induced or generated traffic, is now much more common in the literature. In fact, traffic is now being referred to not as a liquid that flows where it is directed, but as a gas that expands to fill all available space (Litman, 1998).[7]

An alternative to this kind of road planning treadmill has developed: namely, comprehensive land use/transportation planning that develops alternative transportation systems and different land use patterns aimed at minimizing unnecessary movement. The comprehensive plan is a much more community-based project that invites a city to envision its future and then seeks to find the appropriate infrastructure. This process requires a much more creative role from planners and engineers, who must provide the land use and transportation mix most able to meet the complex needs of the community. Other models are now available, such as LUTRAQ from Portland, which allows all options, including new transit systems, to be tested rather than just road options (1000 Friends of Oregon, 1997a and 1997b). There is also clear evidence that if road capacity is removed, then a high proportion of traffic just disappears; this "traffic evaporation" or "traffic degeneration" also provides another tool for cities struggling with how to manage their future.[8]

Urban planners and the general public are now in a key position to assert their roles in the development of cities. New goals and objectives can be defined in the transportation/land use modeling process based on balancing the roles of various transportation modes and minimizing total travel in the urban system. The need to revitalize city centers and to protect neighborhoods threatened by traffic means that the technical road planner using 1960s models cannot be the sole determinant of decision making.

Pressure from the community has meant that traffic calming is now on the agenda in virtually every developed city and many in the developing world. This concept has been a major focus for many traffic engineers in European cities for twenty years, but is now a central issue for engineers and planners in every Auto City.

Technical planning tools and the politics that seems to go with them will always play a role in the area of transportation planning, but there is no reason why these should favor roads and suburban sprawl to the exclusion of other transportation modes and more compact patterns of development. As shown later in this chapter, many cities are demonstrating how a new balance can be found.

10. *Town planning*. Automobile dependence is inevitably regulated into cities by local town planning.

Low-density suburbs around the world are often very similar in form as well as function. They can frequently be traced to a similar set of urban codes that have been developed and have become known as "town planning" regulations. Such heavily automobile-dependent suburbs, if left to a process of standardized mass production, will inevitably create more and more of the problems described earlier. This kind of planning is also facilitated when "town planning" is considered to be what occurs at the local subdivision level and no overall strategic direction for the city or its region is ever created.

Strategic planning is now a much more developed process, however, especially where a city-wide government or coordinated set of governments can provide a plan for an entire city. In such planning there are strategic networks of transportation, strategic land use that complements this, and comprehensive processes and incentives to encourage the plan's implementation. In the United States such plans are required as part of the Transportation Efficiency Act (TEA-21).

Nevertheless, the problem of how to implement detailed planning at the local level that is not automobile-dependent is still not solved. The regulations on setbacks, road widths and design, densities, and mix all favor the suburban model we see in nearly every new suburb. Developers who want to change this find the process very hard. This is the one area of inevitability that still seems to be true. The few new suburbs that have broken the mold have not yet been absorbed into professional praxis. Thus we turn our attention to this issue in Chapter 6.

Approaches to Reducing Automobile Dependence

Three general approaches are taken to managing our dependence on the automobile: technological improvements, economic instruments, and planning mechanisms.

Automobile Technological Improvements: Cleaning Up the Car

Many of the problems outlined earlier in Chapter 2 are amenable to some technological improvements. For example, much of the investment in improving urban air quality in the world has been in reducing car emissions. U.S. approaches to the problems associated with the automobile have concentrated on the technology (e.g., Altshuler et al., 1979, 1984; MacKenzie, 1994). Civilizing the car through technological advances is part of the solution, but increasingly this has been seen as insufficient as the sheer volume of cars overwhelms cities.

Despite doubling in fuel efficiency of new cars between 1973 and 1988, the United States increased oil consumption by 20 percent and by 1995 was 35 percent dependent on oil imports. As discussed, heavy oil dependence is a significant threat to the sustainability of many cities as we move to the end of the "golden century of oil" (Campbell, 1991). And now we must face up to planning for reduced greenhouse gases, which in a time of continuing urban population growth and the need for the very poor to be given some chance to develop does not seem possible to achieve by technology alone.

Furthermore, better technologies do not deal with the sheer space consumption of cars. It has been estimated, for example, that for every car added to a U.S. city, about eight parking spaces are required (Hart, 1990). This will be the same for electric vehicles as for gas guzzlers, except that parking spaces may be a little smaller.

Engineers must do their part for sustainability, but the problem with overemphasizing this solution is that so little attention is directed to the myriad other auto-related problems (Sperling, 1995).

The problem with technological solutions is that they invariably forget the Jevons Principle. This principle was first enunciated in 1865 by the economist Jevons, who predicted that making coal burning more efficient would lead to more coal use as the efficiencies would lead to more economic uses of coal. In transportation, sustainability will remain elusive if new superefficient motor vehicles are used merely to travel more. It really should be no surprise that people use cars more when they are made more efficient. From this perspective such efficiency only feeds the bigger problem of automobile dependence and as discussed in Chapter 2 it is only an "incremental" approach rather than an "urban systems" approach.

Economic Instruments: Getting the Prices Right

Policy makers everywhere are attempting to reduce car use and dependence by ensuring that users pay properly for such use (Kageson, 1993; Moffet, 1991; OECD/ECMT, 1995). As outlined in Chapter 2, many studies in different parts of the world have found that the subsidy provided to the car is about US$3,000 to 4,000 per vehicle per year for roads, parking, health costs, pollution costs, and so on. From this perspective it is clear that the "car is on welfare." Even people as involved in the industry as an ex-vice-president of General Motors have recognized that car users do not pay their way (Johnson, 1994).

It is good economics to ensure that people pay for these costs, but it is very difficult politics. While an essential part of any long-term strategy, charging for the use of all roads is not easily introduced and will have immediate social and equity impacts. In an automobile-dependent city, many people and firms cannot see any option other than to pay more, thus causing inflation and hardship. So, in general, charging for the full cost of the car is rarely on the political agenda.

Sustainability cannot wait for brave politicians. Those advocating that the car pay its way need to adopt a more appealing and positive strategy. Other travel choices must be provided, along with a phasing in of true costs. Singapore is a good example of a handful of places that have simultaneously introduced severe economic restrictions on car ownership and use, while dramatically improving transit and, more recently, ensuring good walking environments.

The Scandinavian countries are also doing more about pricing vehicle usage more effectively, but they, too, have other options to offer people who drive and who may be induced by prices to change their patterns of behavior (OECD/ECMT, 1995).

The problem with commentators such as Elmer Johnson and other U.S. economists is that they are yet to offer anything else to go with their increased pricing solution, which is therefore easily interpreted to mean "get the poor people off our roads." With no other options provided, the increased costs of driving can only be punitive and regressive. It sometimes appears as if they are suggesting their economic option just so they can be seen as addressing the issue. But perhaps they know that it will never be implemented and hence car dependence will continue. On the other hand, they may simply be presenting the toughest pricing approach because they know of no other policy options. This policy vacuum, due to the inherent inadequacies of technological and pricing solutions, has begun to be filled by those advocating planning mechanisms.[9]

Planning Mechanisms: Reducing the Need for Cars

Despite widespread cynicism that you cannot control the car, there is a growing awareness of the need for non-automobile-dependent planning (Newman, Kenworthy, and Vintila, 1995). The rest of this chapter is based primarily on the key approaches for planning a more sustainable city with inherently reduced automobile dependence.

As will be seen in the case studies and planning principles in this chapter, there are many cities implementing plans to reduce automobile dependence. They are not usually labeled by any generic planning philosophy, although they invariably use "sustainability" in the titles of their plans. However, in the United States, the "New Urbanism" has become the concept around which a lot of new urban planning to reduce automobile dependence has developed.

New Urbanism is a movement that incorporates the need to expose car-dependent assumptions in town planning rules and fashions; it orients instead around a transit system and attempts to create walking environments through denser, more mixed land use, houses fronting streets with garages behind, and other design qualities (Katz, 1994; Calthorpe, 1993; Duany and Plater-Zyberk, 1991). These developments have a long way to go since nearly all examples of New Urbanism in the United States have been on the urban fringe and have no transit option. They are often criticized because their idealism does not match their outcomes. But New Urbanism is rediscovering how planning and design can better incorporate less automobile-dependent land use, particularly in the layout of streets and the orientation of buildings to the street, as well as in density and mix of activities. There is little doubt that if transit systems are built and reurbanization on a large scale emerges, then it will be New Urbanism guidelines and practices that will be used to create less car-dependent options in U.S. cities. Even on the urban fringe, New Urbanist developments that are denser and incorporate mixed land use (with a focused town center) can significantly reduce car use compared to normal, scattered suburbia. This occurs because the journey-to-work is only about 30 percent of daily travel in most cities; so that if local services can be provided, then local trips can replace many cross-city trips.

The political imperative to overcome the negative aspects of automobile dependence as a part of the sustainability agenda is now appearing in all cities, including those in the developing world (Laquian, 1993). The OECD, the European Community, the UN, and the World Bank have all begun to recognize this and are stressing how transportation funding needs to be more critically evaluated (Kreimer et al., 1993; Serageldin and Barrett, 1993). This is particularly poignant in the developing countries' cities, where traffic problems are so obvious. But in a globally connected world the reduction of auto dependence (and its associated energy use, greenhouse gases, and air pollution) is also a focus of international agreements in which the major responsibility is on the developed world to take the lead. As already discussed, the developed world is where the majority of automobile dependence can be found, and where (particularly in the United States) the largest growth in absolute terms is still occurring.

There is little hope for achieving sustainability in cities without a renewed belief in the value of city planning and urban design. But planning professionals must earn new respect by showing that they can understand not only how cities work but how to create new market-oriented solutions, how to involve people in the new agenda, and how to implement policies that truly lead to sustainability. This requires, first, a vision of how the overall city can be shaped to produce lower resource flows and higher livability by reducing automobile dependence, and, second, a professional praxis and community process showing how to do it. This chapter and Chapter 5 help to set the vision, and Chapters 6 and 7 suggest some of the "how to do it."

Techniques for Overcoming Automobile Dependence

Five policies will be discussed that form the basis of overcoming automobile dependence:

1. Traffic calming—to slow auto traffic and create more urban, humane environments better suited to other transportation modes.
2. Quality transit, bicycling, and walking—to provide genuine options to the car.
3. Urban villages—to create multinodal centers with mixed, dense land use that reduce the need to travel and that are linked to good transit.
4. Growth management—to prevent urban sprawl and redirect development into urban villages.
5. Taxing transportation better—to cover external costs and to use the revenues to help build a sustainable city based on the previous policies.

Each of these policies is explored individually before we tie them together into a vision of a more sustainable "Future City."

Traffic Calming

Traffic calming (from the German *Verkehrsberuhigung*) is the process of slowing down traffic so that the street environment is safer and more conducive to pedes-

Photo 4.2. Traffic calming like this in Hamburg has narrowed roads (four lanes to two lanes) and created pedestrian havens and a greener environment. The elderly person and the cyclist are safe, and the car, truck, and bus still have access.

trians, cyclists, shoppers, and residential life. Traffic calming is best done by physically altering the street environment through different road textures; changing the geometry of the road through chicanes (also known as S-shaped diverters), neck-downs (also known as chokers), speed plateaus and bumps, and other traffic engineering devices; introducing new street furniture designed to create a more human, safe environment; and planting attractive landscaping. Together, these changes make drivers slow down by causing them to see less open black-top and to perceive the road as a space that is to be shared with pedestrians, cyclists, and transit vehicles. Through the avenues of trees and street gardens that accompany good traffic-calming schemes, urban wildlife habitats and corridors through cities can be created and soft surfaces can be increased so there is less stormwater pollution. Traffic calming has the potential not only to lessen the direct negative impacts of road traffic but to foster urban environments that are more human and interactive, more beautiful, and more economically successful due to the greater social vitality possible in a city's public spaces.

It is not known exactly where or when the concept of traffic calming originated, but the German term is believed to have first been used in German federal government reports in the early 1970s. The late John Roberts of Transport and Environment Studies (see TEST, 1989) in London was the first to translate the word into English and to bring the concept to the attention of transportation planners in other parts of the world. The idea of traffic calming, however, has its roots in earlier movements to protect city environments from the worst excesses of the automobile. This reached a watershed in the early 1960s with the publica-

tion of the major report entitled "Traffic in Towns," by Colin Buchanan
(Minister of Transport, 1963). Although the British approach was
to create more calmed city centers and protected residential precincts, the
Buchanan report was used mostly to build large ring roads and bypasses that
helped create automobile dependence. The report was used to justify major road
proposals in Australian and North American cities as well. However, the
European approach is based more on the organic integrity of the urban street and
this approach is now gaining currency in the United Kingdom (SACTRA, 1994;
Department of Environment, 1994).

Traffic calming emerged in Europe in the late 1960s from a number of sources:
the Dutch *woonerf* or "living yard," created streets that had one shared surface
with much planting to slow speeding traffic through inner-city streets and the
original pedestrianization schemes in cities such as central Copenhagen (Gehl
and Gemzøe, 1996). Traffic calming gained rapid growth and acceptance in
Europe in the 1980s through the successful action of many environmental groups
trying to curtail the impacts of the automobile on European cities. More detail
on the evolution of traffic calming can be found in Hass-Klau (1990a), Tolley
(1990), and Newman and Kenworthy (1991).

Traffic calming's major objectives are to:

- reduce the severity and number of accidents in urban areas;
- reduce local air and noise pollution and vehicle fuel consumption;
- improve the urban street environment for non-car-users;
- reduce the car's dominance on roads by reclaiming road space for living space;
- reduce the barrier effects of motor traffic on pedestrian and cycle movement;
  and
- enhance local economic activity by creating a better environment for people.

With these broad objectives, traffic calming can also be of benefit to urban
regeneration, housing renovation schemes, and city beautification programs (e.g.,
Freiburg, in southern Germany). These assist more deeply in reducing automobile dependence by bringing urban activity back to areas of the city that are
inherently less dependent on the automobile (i.e., denser central and inner areas
of cities built more around transit and nonmotorized modes). Traffic calming in
Germany was in fact pioneered and promoted much more aggressively by the
housing and urban development ministries than by the transportation ministry.
This was primarily because of the positive impact traffic calming can have on the
character and environmental quality of neighborhoods, making them much more
desirable urban redevelopment and residential areas, while a significant number
of transportation planners viewed traffic-calming changes with suspicion (Hass-
Klau, 1990a).

Techniques of Traffic Calming and Their Implementation

Traffic calming was originally restricted mainly to improving residential streets,
and this is still a major focus. Traffic calming seeks to alter road layout and design
without actually totally rebuilding a street system. It does this through a whole
suite of possible techniques such as narrowed entries to streets, plantings of trees
with strong vertical elements, variable street surfaces, speed restricting devices,

and visual barriers that encourages cautious driving (see Box 4.2). These are now well documented and illustrated in many detailed publications (e.g., City of Frankfurt, 1990; Pharoah, 1990; Tolley, 1990; Toyota Motor Corporation, 1990; Hass-Klau, 1990c; Federal Office of Road Safety). However, it has been recog-

Box 4.2. Traffic Calming Techniques

Traffic calming is achieved by a variety of methods including:

- Provision of street planting on reclaimed road space in the form of low gardens, shrubs, and tall trees. Trees with strong vertical elements also reduce the optical width and help to slow traffic. It is particularly important in any traffic-calming scheme to also green the environment.
- Widened sidewalks and the provision of segregated cycleways in each direction.
- Narrowed driving lanes (e.g., down to 3 to 3.25 meters).
- Provision of light rail occupying up to half the existing road space (e.g., Grenoble and Zurich).
- Planted central islands limiting long forward views and chicanes that convert straight streets into winding s-shapes through small landscaped protrusions in the road.
- Provision of angle parking (this also has the effect of better separating the widened pedestrian facility and cycleway from traffic).
- Conversion of traffic lanes to *woonerf*-style service and access roads, as in some Dutch cities.

Traffic calming in central cities and subcenters also involves:

- Pedestrianization of key activity center streets and squares.
- Provision of facilities for pedestrians, including quality paving, seats, and shade or cover areas (for the particular climate).

Other features of traffic calming on busy roads include:

- Strong entry statements, including well-designed signs to alert motorists to the type of roadway modifications ahead, repeated rumble strips (i.e., street surfaces roughened or cobbled) to signal approach of traffic-calmed sections, and pronounced narrowed entry points at the beginning and end of a traffic-calmed strip.
- Reduced-width pedestrian crossing points at regular intervals marked by a change in street surface and a particularly strong use of trees at crossing points.
- Planters, bollards, and other street furniture to strengthen the visual perception of the area as being not just for movement of traffic.
- Speed bumps and plateaus and other devices that restrict vehicle speed particularly near pedestrian crossing points, but that do not adversely affect the operation of larger vehicles such as buses.

Photo 4.3. Arterial roads like these in Copenhagen can be traffic-calmed to enable safe access while ensuring that traffic still flows.

nized that to be really effective and to not just shift traffic problems from one area to another, traffic calming must be applied more on an area-wide basis (Hass-Klau, 1990b), which means involving arterial or main roads.

There are now many examples of traffic calming on through roads and in other busy areas throughout Europe (e.g., Frankfurt, Hamburg, Nürnberg, Berlin, and Copenhagen). Denmark has a nationwide program of traffic calming on main roads called Environmentally Adapted Through Roads (Danish Road Data Laboratory, 1987, 1988).

The approach to traffic calming has to be somewhat different on main roads because of the volumes of traffic involved, although there is overlap in the basic techniques used. In busier areas where there is a need to better balance the needs of motor vehicles with the needs of pedestrians and cyclists, the main goal is to be able to reclaim road space for other uses by reducing the speed of traffic and its impact. In most cases roads are simply reduced from six to four traffic lanes, or from four to two lanes, through critical areas of a city. The potential benefits of traffic calming on main roads is summarized by Hajdu (1988) in his description of the transformation of a 1.3-kilometer main route in the inner area of Hanover, Germany:

> The city changed that road from an overloaded artery to a thorough-fare with a series of streetscapes, some with narrowed carriageways. The changes included footpaths containing trees, others fully pedestrianized with fountains, outdoor cafes, and a weekly market. The city resurfaced adjacent residential streets and limited access to residents' cars. (p. 328)

In some cases the reductions in road space are accompanied by significant improvements to transit such as new rail links (e.g., Nürnberg), and in others no major changes are made but incremental improvements are implemented. Road capacity is not necessarily reduced because the loss of lanes is offset by slower speeds that reduce vehicle headways and enable more vehicles to pass. Similarly, parking supply is not necessarily reduced and in some cases may be increased nominally. Often, parallel parking on two sides of a road is converted to angle parking on alternate sides separated by landscaped strips.

The implementation of traffic calming, however, is not just a technical process but a wide-ranging community process whereby local residents can have a strong input into identifying the problems and helping to find the solutions. It has been repeatedly shown that consultation with and involvement of the community are essential to the widespread acceptance of traffic-calming schemes. In fact, an important aspect of traffic calming is the way it has been able to provide a focal point for mobilizing and galvanizing many communities around the world into developing and fighting for a vision of a more sustainable and socially acceptable solution to the problem of traffic in urban environments (e.g., Tolley, 1990).

Effects of Traffic-calming Schemes

Many of the major traffic-calming schemes in Europe have been formally sponsored by national and local governments as demonstration projects, and one of the aims has been to test the effects of the traffic-calming schemes on key environmental indicators and safety factors. Much of the available evidence about the effects of traffic-calming schemes comes from before-and-after studies of these projects.

The following is a brief summary of the general effects of traffic-calming schemes, along with some specific examples:

Reduced Accidents. Accidents, particularly the severity of accidents, are generally significantly reduced with traffic calming because speed is the most critical factor in road accidents—particularly regarding the risk of serious injury and the danger to pedestrians and cyclists. In Berlin, for example, an area-wide scheme resulted in the reductions shown in Table 4.1.

Most other schemes report similar kinds of data, such as in Heidelberg, which experienced average accident reductions of 31 percent and a 44 percent reduction for casualties after thirty-kilometer-per-hour residential speed limits were introduced along with selected physical traffic-calming measures (Hass-Klau, 1990c). Area-wide schemes in the Netherlands have reduced accidents involving injury by 50 percent in residential areas and 20 percent overall (measured per million vehicle kilometers) and no increase in accidents has occurred in surrounding areas (Hass-Klau, 1986).

The Center for Livable Communities, in their *Livable Places Update* for March 1998, summarized some of the best U.S. examples of traffic calming, and in relation to accidents, found the following:

- The City of Seattle, where traffic-calming projects have been carried out for

Table 4.1 Accident Reductions in Berlin Moabit
Using Comparable Before and After Periods

Type of Traffic	Accident Measure	Percent Reduction
All traffic	Fatal accidents	−57
	Serious accidents	−45
	Slight accidents	−40
	Accident costs	−16
Nonmotorized	Pedestrians	−43
	Cyclists	−16
	Children	−66

Source: Reported in Pharoah and Russell (1989).

twenty years, surveyed the results of 119 completed projects and found an
overwhelming 94 percent reduction in accidents.

- In Portland, Oregon, 70 traffic circles and 300 speed bumps have been introduced and the number of reported accidents decreased by 50 percent.
- A 1997 study of U.S. street typology and accidents by Swift and Associates
  showed that as street width increases, accidents per mile per year increase
  exponentially. The safest residential street (curb to curb) turned out to be 24
  feet (7.2 meters). Present U.S. street regulations require 36 feet, primarily for
  access by fire vehicles, though the study found that fire vehicles can access 24-
  foot-wide roads when required. New Urbanism design guidelines are for 24-
  foot roads.

Noise Reduced. Traffic calming generally results in a reduction in vehicle noise.
Pharoah and Russell (1989) report that noise changes result from five factors:
changes in traffic volume and composition, changes in carriageway layout,
changes in carriageway surface, changes in vehicle speed, and changes in driving
style.

Air Pollution Benefits. Research in central Europe shows that in built-up areas, the
higher the vehicle speed the more will be the proportion of acceleration, deceleration, and braking, and this increases air pollution. By contrast, traffic-calming
schemes in some German residential areas have shown that idle times are
reduced by 15 percent, gear changing by 12 percent, brake use by 14 percent, and
fuel use by 12 percent (Hass-Klau, 1990a).

Evidence of the air pollution benefits of a slower, calmer style of driving
comes from detailed work in Buxtehude, a German demonstration project (population 33,000). Table 4.2 shows the changes in the different types of emissions
with a reduction of speed from fifty kilometers per hour to thirty kilometers per
hour under two types of driving. In both aggressive and calm driving, emissions
are reduced at the thirty kilometers per hour, though the calm driving has a generally greater reduction and fuel use is lower.

It is also worth noting that even in instances when individual vehicles may
experience an increase in fuel use and emissions (e.g., drivers do indulge in more

Table 4.2. Changes in Vehicle Emissions and Fuel
Use from 50 km/h to 30 km/h

	Driving Style	
	Second Gear, Aggressive	Third Gear, Calm
Carbon monoxide	−17%	−13%
Hydrocarbons	−10%	−22%
Nitrogen oxides	−32%	−48%
Fuel consumption	+ 7%	−7%

Source: Reported in Pharoah and Russell (1989) from German research.

acceleration, braking, and greater use of second gear), this may not result in an overall increase in local pollution and fuel use if the traffic-calming scheme has also resulted in lower traffic volumes.

Enhanced Pedestrian and Street Activity. Traffic calming seeks to make the public environment safer and more attractive, so it is to be expected that traffic calming will result in a greater level of pedestrian and cycling activity in the area affected. In general, it can be expected that the results will be more noticeable in busier areas with a mix of land uses and the potential for people to make good use of reclaimed areas, such as for outdoor cafes and markets, childrens' facilities, etc.

Some formal measurements of the benefits are available from a summary of European experience by Pharoah and Russell (1989), such as in Berlin's federal demonstration project, where nonmotorized traffic on a wide range of streets in the scheme increased by between 27 percent and 114 percent; in Vinderup, a village in Denmark, where the main through route was traffic-calmed and outdoor activities increased by up to 47 percent; and in Copenhagen, where traffic calming has led to immediate increases of pedestrian activity of between 20 percent to 40 percent and, in the long term, where central area activity is now 80 percent pedestrian and 14 percent by bike (Gehl and Gemzøe, 1996). Where traffic calming reduces road capacity there is an overall decrease in traffic (Goodwin, 1997) and therefore better conditions are created for pedestrians.

Traffic calming also tends to increase the area used by pedestrians and cyclists and the extent to which streets are crossed by these users, since the severance effects of traffic are reduced. Pedestrians and cyclists tend not to confine themselves purely to walkways, but rather they extend their territory to the roadway in some instances.

Reduced Crime Rates. Appleyard (1981) showed that visiting among neighbors decreases when traffic increases, and when neighboring ceases and people stop watching out for one another, then criminal activity can occur. The *Livable Places Update* (March 1998) overview on traffic calming quotes a Harvard University study that showed violent crimes in communities where residents willingly worked together were as much as 40 percent lower than in neighborhoods where such relationships were not as strong. Race and income were not factors in people's willingness to take part in such community activity. An example of a place

Photo 4.4. Groningen, the Netherlands. Creating pedestrian spaces for a less traffic-dominated city makes sense for a more socially just city but is also of benefit to local businesses.

where crime rates diminished after traffic calming is Weinland Park in Columbus, Ohio.

Positive Economic Implications. As pointed out in the objectives of traffic calming, economic revitalization of an area is an explicit aim in some schemes. A study by TEST (1989) attempted to confirm the hypothesis that "A good physical environment is a good economic environment" and examined ten European cities in detail. Roberts (1988, p. 141) sums up the work by saying: ". . . the message is simple: there is a strong likelihood that traffic restraint in all its forms, and environmental improvement, and a healthy economy, are causally related."

The basis of this finding would appear to involve at least the following factors:

- People like to come to humanly attractive, green cities.
- Businesses like to locate in areas with a high quality urban environment.
- Car access is not banned, but it is not facilitated to the point of dominating everything else.
- Other modes are generally facilitated.

Hass-Klau (1993) shows conclusively that pedestrianization and traffic calming both have positive effects on the economic performance of an area; the more aggressive is the traffic calming, the more pronounced is the positive economic effect.

In the United States, a West Palm Beach, Florida, neighborhood was economically depressed and bisected by fast-moving traffic. A traffic-calming scheme slowed the traffic through road narrowing and construction of speed bumps, traffic circles, and pedestrian islands. Then the city raised intersections, made sidewalks level with the street, and added a fountain, benches, and an amphitheater for "block parties." The development spurred new private investment and the cost of commercial space rapidly moved from five dollars per square foot to twenty-five dollars per square foot (Center for Livable Communities, 1998). Similar case studies are given in the U.K. Friends of the Earth (1998) publication.

Traffic Calming: A Broader Approach

Traffic calming can be viewed as a broader transportation planning philosophy and not merely as a series of physical changes to roads (Hass-Klau, 1990a). Traffic calming in this broader sense is aimed at reducing total dependence on the automobile and promoting a more self-sufficient community with a transportation system more oriented to pedestrian, cycle, and transit use.

These broader objectives can be summarized as follows:

- A reduction of average motor vehicle speeds to discourage long-distance road travel in urban areas and promotion of a more compact urban form; traffic calming of main roads is included in this approach.
- Specific land use policies that better integrate transit and land development; the policies are directed at reducing the number, length, and need for motor vehicle trips.
- Strong promotion of walking, cycling, and transit.
- Restrictive measures against private traffic, including parking restrictions, limited major road building, and the direction of funds into transit and nonmotorized modes, as well as taxation policies on fuels and cars, including policies on company cars and road pricing.
- A shift in transportation planning philosophy from a traffic-generation approach of seeking to predict future traffic levels and the roads and parking needed to cope with them, to a traffic-dissolving approach of setting limits on motor vehicle growth and ensuring that transportation/land use policies and practices are aimed at minimizing the need for more motor vehicle facilities.

A good example of a broader traffic-calming policy in action is the Dutch national policy from 1982 that openly promotes transit, walking, and cycling. It states that:

> Henceforth other functions will be given priority over motor traffic [and] the car's dominance should be diminished by deliberately increasing travel times, by creating a less dense network of main roads, and by reducing speeds. (Ministry of Transport and Public Works, 1982)

Quality Transit Development, Bicycle Planning, and Pedestrian Strategies

This is an integrated strategy to promote sustainable transportation modes, but each mode will be considered separately.

Transit

There are always experts who see transit as a waste of money (e.g., Pickrell, 1990; Lave, 1992; Gordon and Richardson, 1989). However, there are few of the general public who do not see the critical role of quality transit systems in cities, even if they are not transit users themselves. Even conservatives in the United States are recognizing that transit should be improved in their cities. For example, Weyrich and Lind (1996) of the Free Congress Foundation state in their publication *Conservatives and Mass Transit: Is It Time for a New Look?*:

> The dominance of the automobile is not a free market outcome, but the result of massive government intervention on behalf of the automobile. That intervention came at the expense of privately owned, privately funded, tax paying public transit systems. . . . A growing conservative constituency does use mass transit, when transit is high quality. . . . Mass transit can serve some important conservative goals, including economic development, moving people off welfare and into productive employment, and strengthening feelings of community. (pp. 3, 4)

This new awareness, crossing former political divides, that it makes economic sense for a greater transit role in cities is due to the kind of analyses now available that show the following:

- Transit investment has double the economic benefit to a city than does highway investment (see Chapter 2).
- Transit can enable a city to use market forces to increase densities near stations, where most services are located, thus creating more efficient subcenters and minimizing sprawl (Cervero, 1992a).
- Transit enables a city to be more corridor-oriented, making it is easier to provide infrastructure (Whitelegg, 1993).
- Transit enhances the overall economic efficiency of a city; denser cities with less car use and more transit use spend a lower proportion of their gross regional product or wealth on passenger transportation (see Chapter 3).

But perhaps the strongest appeal of transit-oriented planning today is that it offers genuine, high-profile solutions to the environmental and social problems of the automobile dependent city.

The sustainability agenda demands transit, especially the development of rail systems that are competitive with the car in passenger appeal and speed. This is not only because energy use, emissions, noise, and other problems associated with the automobile can be dramatically reduced with competitive electric rail systems that attract car users, but also because so much more can be done with the urban space generated by rail's low land demands. For example, a double-track light rail system occupies fifty times less urban space than the highways and parking needed for cars. As Trancik (1986) shows, this can mean the renewal of much "lost space" in automobile-dependent cities, as most new rail, especially surface light rail projects, are accompanied by urban design programs that dramatically upgrade urban streetscapes.

Light Rail. Many cities are now finding that the best means to provide a quality transit spine for a city is with light rail. In fact, light rail's mix of environmental friendliness, high quality, and comparatively low cost has meant hundreds of cities, both large and small, in Europe, North America, Australia, and other nations, have joined the light rail revolution in recent years (Bayliss, 1989).

.The important characteristics of light rail in terms of the broad sustainability agenda are that it is:

- *Electric*, and therefore part of a future based on renewable energy.
- *Fast, quiet, and does not generate local emissions*, so it can compete with the car while fitting into the existing urban fabric along narrow alignments, including being completely compatible with people on foot in pedestrianized city centers.
- *Flexible*, since it can operate on present streets, negotiating roundabouts and turning at right angles, or it can run on its own dedicated right-of-way at speeds up to about 100 kilometers per hour, depending on its design.
- *Adaptable*, since its passenger-carrying capacity can be increased with multiple-unit trains (where the operating environment permits) and vehicles can be designed for dual power sources (AC power for use on existing heavy rail freight lines, then switching to DC power for on-street operation, as in Karlsruhe, Germany).
- *Competitive with the car in image and functionality*. Many new light rail systems are sleek and aerodynamic and operate as low-floor systems, allowing easy access for wheelchairs, strollers, shopping carts, and elderly people.
- *Compatible with bikes*. Many light rail systems are designed to carry bikes, which extends the transit catchment area and effectiveness.
- *Cheap*, in comparison to heavy rail or any highway option. This assumes that the light rail system is not underground or elevated, which are both more expensive options and can make accessibility to stations a problem (though, in some circumstances, underground or elevated systems are the only solutions and can have the advantage of offering speeds that are more competitive with the car in heavily built-up areas);
- *Attractive to development*. Light rail stations can act as magnets for urban development seeking a dependable transit service that enhances the appeal and livability of a local area. Light rail can thus help cities achieve the kind of nodal, concentrated form of development needed to foster less-auto-dependent environments that are more compatible with the emerging Information Age city.
- *Able to help green the city*. Many cities are building their light rail systems by simply reclaiming two traffic lanes for the light rail alignment and grassing the entire track bed (e.g., in Freiburg and Zurich). Thus light rail can help meet other parts of the sustainability agenda, such as creating more soft surfaces in cities (as discussed in Chapter 5) and reducing the urban heat island.

Improving Transit: The Bus/Light Rail Debate. Despite light rail's advantages and its rapid adoption in many cities around the world, a major and sometimes bitter debate frequently occurs in auto-oriented, bus-only cities contemplating the use

Photo 4.5. The light rail system in Grenoble (*top*) has enabled the city to create a more attractive place for local investment. The route of light rail through suburbs can be a chance to create urban parkland corridors, as in Karlsruhe, Germany (*bottom*).

of light rail technology for the first time. This debate turns on whether a better bus system (achieved through busways), or a rail system, is the best, most cost-effective way to improve transit.

On the bus side, it is argued that buses are more appropriate for the less dense, less centralized urban form of Auto Cities, have more flexibility to cater to passenger needs in low-density environments, and are much cheaper. Part of this argument is that people do not like to transfer between modes, which is what often needs to happen in low-density settings if people are to use a new light rail system (or any rail system). The argument is essentially that, for a much lower investment, buses can achieve similar improvements in travel time and thus can be just as successful, if not more successful, than a light rail system.

But is this simple analysis really how competition between transit and the automobile works, and is it equal to the task of winning the wider sustainability argument and helping to build a more sustainable city?

The answer would appear to be no. Cities that have taken out old tram systems have found that the replacement bus services experience a big decline in patronage, and many cities that have attempted to win car users with busways have failed. Even Ottawa, the most extensive busway city in the Western world, has had declining transit use since it opted for busways. In San Diego the data show that many people have left their cars to use the new LRT system, something that the previous bus system was unable to do despite busways, and something that most Californians thought could never happen. In the northern corridor, where a line-haul busway service operates and park-and-ride facilities are provided, the utilization rates are about 50 percent that of the park-and-ride stations on the LRT lines. Mills (1989) states that:

> one-third of the people who ride our system each day come to it in their cars and park at the lots at our stations . . . surveys further show that most of those people, when asked how they would get to work if the light rail line did not exist, say they would drive the rest of the way. (p. 5)

The reality is that there are many factors that influence people's choice of transportation. However, these rarely figure in the transportation planner's models when it is predicted that a busway will be able to attract as many or more passengers as a new rail line. This is why there are now so many places around the world where new rail lines outperform the buses they replace (e.g., see case study on Perth later in this chapter), and are far more successful in patronage than any standard models are able to predict.

These other factors that favor rail over buses include:

- Greater comfort and convenience (both vehicles and stations/stops), particularly because passengers are more likely to get a seat on light rail; availability of a seat substantially decreases the cost that passengers attach to travel time (Algers, Hansen, and Tegner, 1975).
- Better schedule reliability (Jessiman and Kocur, 1975).
- Reliable transfers between modes—a number of authors show that modal transfers are nowhere near the negative factor they have been made out to be,

especially rail-to-rail or bus-to-rail, though bus-to-bus is not viewed favorably because of frequently poor reliability (Algers, Hansen, and Tegner, 1975; Vuchic, 1981). People appear relatively happy to make a transfer that enables them to take advantage of what they see as a superior mode.

- Greater inherent passenger appeal of the vehicles and stops, including width of aisles, smoothness, odor (diesel fumes and particulates are now seen to be a health issue: Hamer, 1997; Pearce, 1997), engine noise, all-weather reliability and weather protection at stops, and other environmental factors (Tennyson, 1985).
- The "Sparks Effect"—increased passenger appeal of an electric system over a diesel system, observed in all new rail electric systems. This is due to a combination of factors but includes the inherently faster acceleration and deceleration of the electric drive system in electric trains. The sparks effect is so consistently found that it is frequently built into passenger estimates at about 20 percent over other transit patronage.
- Route understandability of light rail versus buses; light rail has tracks and overhead wires that clearly indicate where it goes and station stops that are generally far more obvious than bus stops.
- The permanence of light rail lines versus the flexibility of buses. Vuchic (1989) states that:

  a strong image and identity of rail transit caused by the simplicity of its services and permanence of its lines, represents a major element of passenger convenience. The strong recognition contributes greatly to the large passenger attracting ability of rail transit.

- Attraction of real estate development that can significantly alter the medium- to long-term picture of patronage potential and financial performance of transit (Henry, 1989). Paaswell and Berechman (1982) explain it this way:

  Buses take people to where activities are and can follow the movement of activities over a wide geographic pattern. On a rapid transit line, there is a more active land use/transportation relationship. Large numbers of people are concentrated at specific spots, and activities become linked to the stops. Transit induces changes in station areas that often would not occur if no transit were there.

One of the key reasons why transit is seen by developers as offering excellent land use opportunities is that it "conserves the use of prime real estate for greater commercial and economic activity, rather than for the storage of automobiles" (Elms, 1989, p. 113).

The induced land use effects of new rail systems are especially important but unfortunately". . . professionally accepted ridership forecasting processes typically do not take them into account" (Henry, 1989, p. 175). Busways and their associated bus stations tend to have a stigma attached to them in the minds of the development community. The factors that most discourage residential and commercial development around bus stations are insufficient speed and service, poorly understood routes and service, and the image of a bus station as being noisy, polluted, or with other environmental problems (Henry, 1989). A bus system is also perceived as representing a lower level of public commitment to transit and one whose permanence is not guaranteed because of the ease with which services can be altered or rerouted (Austin Department of Planning and Growth Management, 1986).

The better potential of light rail to attract development also provides the possibility for governments to participate in joint development and value capture

Photo 4.6. The new urban village (Tiergarten) in Zurich is on a light rail line offering chances to create a less car-dominated environment with innovative water management in the central open space (*top*). Electric bus in Oxford provides local connections (*bottom*).

opportunities (e.g., see Keefer, 1985; Cervero, Hall, and Landis, 1992). These mechanisms are capable of yielding up-front capital contributions from the private sector for stations and other infrastructure, and ongoing nonfare revenue from leasing of air rights, property rents, station connection fees, and other methods, as well as returning to the public purse some of the windfall gains that can accrue to the private sector from public investment in transit, such as the rezoning of adjacent land to higher-value land uses.

The essential attractiveness of joint development and value capture opportunities is in their potential to provide a win-win situation. The benefits can work three ways:

- The transit authority/government gains in shared capital costs of new transit projects, additional nonfare operating revenue from leased lands, and a more efficient transit operation with a higher fare-box recovery ratio, especially higher off-peak and reverse direction patronage in peaks through high-density centers along the lines. Local governments benefit from a higher tax base and revitalization of the local area, including more local job opportunities.
- The developer/land owner gets a much higher value use from the land through density bonuses and rezoning advantages, easy accessibility for the development's work force from all over the city, and a guaranteed, captive clientele for businesses located around the station.
- The community gains in cheaper, quicker access to a wider range of employment opportunities, services, and housing, much better standards of urban and environmental design around stations and vital focal points for convenient urban facilities for the local population. Far greater choice becomes possible for those with and without cars.

The Role of Buses. The importance of buses in a quality transit system should not be diminished by the above analysis, which stresses the importance of a fixed rail spine. Buses have three significant roles: (1) as an inferior solution before a rail spine is built, to fulfill the same line-haul function; (2) as a local distributor for flexible linkage systems to the line-haul route; and (3)as an effective local service in areas of lower demand where there is little possibility or need for rail service.

Cities that are preparing to reduce automobile dependence must create a transit spine down each urban corridor and enable the planning system to focus around key nodes along it. Although buses will not do this as well as trains, a well-developed bus service operating like a rail system, with direct and rapid services, will be a lot better than nothing, or than a bus service that is not developed with rail operating characteristics. In Perth a "circle route" was developed to directly link several nodes of activity with fifteen-minute service and limited stops. The success of the service was immediate, with more than 4,000 passengers a day (the highest patronage of a bus route in Perth), suggesting that a "circle rail line" should be planned for the next phase.

A second key role for buses is to link neighborhoods into the line-haul routes. These can be community buses for particular groups or normal service buses. The use of low-floor, accessible buses is occurring globally to enable people with disabilities to more easily use buses, but they are appreciated by everyone (Vintila,

1996). Buses can also use new technology to introduce an element of demand-responsiveness since buses can now be tracked by global positioning satellites (GPS) so that electronic calls from bus stops can signal where and when the demand is required.

New technology, low floors, and smaller, large-picture-window buses are proving to be attractive in local areas as a friendly, flexible service. Some of these buses are electric. In many local areas, the likelihood of developing a rail service to provide for transportation needs is remote. It is important in such areas to ensure that the bus service is developed with a high level of community input to ensure its effectiveness. In many instances it is also necessary to exploit creative funding arrangements, such as partnerships between a local council and the regional transit provider (e.g., the new Hop, Skip, and Jump bus services in Boulder, Colorado, which have been a major success).

But urban areas still need cross-city connections that can bring people from these services to a line-haul rail system. Together, the flexible bus and the fast rail can compete effectively with the car.

Other Factors in Improving Transit. Better transit systems are not just a matter of choosing the right transit technology for the right situation.[10] Much more is involved (see Appendix 6), such as:

1. *Operation and service delivery issues*, including (a) the reliability of timetables, (b) the timing of connections between buses and trains, (c) service frequencies, especially in the off-peak, (d) whether buses are operated as a spider-web between major centers on a reliable, rhythmic, time-pulse transfer system, or whether they follow radial routes where passengers have to go through the city center to change directions, (e) availability of special night services and other factors.

2. *Station, and bus stop environs*, including their cleanliness, weather protection, accessibility, security, lighting, and general facilities such as telephones and trash cans.

3. *The quality, comfort, age, and security of transit vehicles*, including whether they are kept free from graffiti and vandalism, whether they are air-conditioned, whether security systems are in place, and so on.

4. *The priority given to transit in traffic management policies*, including whether buses, trams, and light rail vehicles are provided with protected rights-of-way and afforded full priority at traffic signals through a "green wave."

5. *Passenger information, marketing, and public education*, including whether timetables, maps, and other information are provided at every stop, or whether the passenger is left to guess when the next service will arrive and where it will go, and whether the system is actively marketed and sold through innovative advertising campaigns and marketing strategies such as specialized destination maps for different trip purposes (entertainment, restaurants, etc.) as in Zurich.

6. *Ticketing systems*, including whether they are integrated between operators and modes and whether they are geared to establishing committed customers by way of three-, six- or twelve-month passes, or whether they are

geared to the noncommitted, one-off cash fare rider. Vast differences can be noted in the performance of transit systems under these different strategies (Laube, 1997). It is also possible to develop innovations such as one suggested by Professor Anthony Perl (1998, personal communication), whereby a city provides a "gold card" for its transit system that also includes a proportion of cheap taxi rides for those times or destinations when and where transit services are poor, or for emergencies. Such a "gold card" could have a range of other privileges negotiated by the transit authority, as airlines do, and membership in a car-sharing club (for weekend or holiday trips outside the city), as is occurring in Europe. This would then provide the basis for car-free suburbs, which without the need for parking and heavy road requirements, would be far easier to design as human-scale villages with ecological features.[11]

7. *Overall management and planning strategies,* including whether responsibility for the planning and service standards of the system is under a dedicated government authority, such as the *verkehrsverbund* in Germany and Switzerland, or is more fragmented and subject to the decisions of various private and government operators, and thus unintegrated and unreliable. This does not mean the services have to be operated by a government system, just that a system of regulations enables a truly integrated and reliable system to be provided.

Collectively, such issues have a great bearing on whether transit is perceived by the community as a service that can be depended upon. A transit system must be designed for everyone at a high standard, not just the captive riders or poorer members of the community. Such a system ought to be something of which the city can be proud. If all these factors are well taken care of, and urban development is well integrated with the transit system, then a city will generally experience relatively high transit ridership, even if it is very wealthy and can afford high car ownership (e.g., Zurich).

Cities moving toward this kind of commitment to their transit systems will be reducing their car dependence and building greater sustainability into their transportation systems.

Biking and Walking

The sustainability agenda and its associated city planning based on reducing automobile dependence, must also incorporate walking and biking. Today, some cities, particularly in the West, are pedestrianizing their old walking cores and building new walking-scale urban villages as people discover the joys of attractive pedestrian areas. Many cities are also developing cycleways (even veloways for fast cyclists along rail reserves) and other cycle infrastructure, such as dedicated traffic signals for bikes and bike storage systems, though probably none as well as Dutch and Danish cities (see case study on Copenhagen later in this chapter). The transit catchment area and range of transit services are also being extended by the effective integration of bikes with rail and bus systems, both through bicycle parking areas and on-board facilities.

On the negative side, cities in the developing world with high-density, mixed

Photo 4.7. Hanover bike parking. Bicycle infrastructure creates opportunities to find "lost space" in cities.

land uses and a tradition of nonmotorized mode use are mostly experiencing a diminishing role for walking and bicycling (Kenworthy et al., 1995; Poboon and Kenworthy, 1997). This is apparent even in Chinese cities, where nonmotorized transportation can still cover up to 80 percent of total daily trips but where transportation priorities are sadly moving toward provision for extensive growth in automobile use (Smith, 1997).

There are a number of reasons for this. The first is simply policy neglect. Nonmotorized modes are seen to be backward, not a symbol of economic progress, whereas the car is a symbol of success and, along with motorbikes, is being increasingly accommodated in infrastructure investment and other policy areas. Motorized vehicles are consequently increasing at a very rapid rate in such environments, which are ill-equipped to deal with them because sufficient road space does not exist in the tight, compact, urban fabric that characterizes cities in the developing world. Computerized transportation planning methodologies, based primarily on cars and imported from the West, also completely ignore the existence of nonmotorized transportation, which is even more untenable in developing cities than it is in developed cities.

The conditions for cyclists, pedestrians, and other nonmotorized transportation users are consequently deteriorating rapidly in developing cities. Roads are becoming more dangerous and full of fumes and noise. Increasingly there is a lack of space to accommodate the modest demands of nonmotorized traffic as roads are widened and districts are severed by parking lots and major new highways. Shade for pedestrians and cyclists in many tropical Asian cities is also disappearing under similar pressure.

One of the key conclusions concerning bicycle and pedestrian infrastructure is that cities that develop nonmotorized transportation infrastructure learn quickly that it is hard to build it compatibly with Auto City infrastructure and essential to build it with quality transit systems. The two go together since it is rarely possible to live in a twentieth-century city where you can walk or bike to everything. But it is entirely feasible to manage short local trips on foot or bike and longer cross-city trips by transit. At each end of the transit trip people are required to be pedestrians or cyclists, and thus the integration of these modes into transit is essential.

All cities, therefore, regardless of their economic status, need to protect and enhance these most sustainable of all transportation modes. This can be done through selective pedestrianization and traffic-calming schemes, as well as through traffic management strategies that limit private transportation and transit improvements that foster nonmotorized modes for basic access. Land use planning that is compact and mixed in character will also help to enhance the role of walking and cycling. The capital and operating costs of nonmotorized mode infrastructure are also very modest when compared to road budgets, so there seems little justifiable impediment to improving these modes in all cities.

Higher Densities and Mixed Land Use in Urban Villages

Bernick and Cervero (1997) show that density is by far the biggest factor in determining the level of transit use in a city, but that mixed land use adds the extra component of encouraging walking. Thus a renewed emphasis on these qualities can make a city more sustainable—that is, more efficient, equitable, and livable. It is important, however, that any attempts to increase densities and mixed land use be part of a coherent design strategy that we have called an urban village.

Before specifically discussing different aspects of the critical density issue, it is important to establish two points: (1) the rationale that most major planning authorities in developed countries, especially those in auto-dependent cities, now see for higher densities and more mixed land uses and (2) exactly what we mean by the term "urban village."

Density emerged as a major determinant of automobile use in all the data in Chapter 3. This has been found before in other studies (for example, Pushkarev and Zupan, 1977). A recent study on U.S. cities confirmed the exponential relationship between transit ridership and density (both employment density and residential density). The elasticity for residential density and ridership was 0.592; that is, for every 10 percent increase in density there is a 6 percent increase in ridership [Transit Cooperative Research Program (TRCP), 1995].

Perhaps of most significance for overcoming automobile dependence is the work of Holtzclaw (1994). He found in a study of twenty-eight California communities that the VKT per household fell by one-quarter as densities doubled, and by only 8 percent if transit service levels were doubled. Bernick and Cervero (1997) conclude that "the biggest benefits come from going from very low to moderate densities, say from an average of 4 units per acre to 10 to 15 units per acre—that is, from a setting with quarter-acre estates to one with a mix of small-lot single-family homes and duplexes/triplexes" (p. 83).

As well as reasonable densities it is important to have a mix of activities in urban development. Bernick and Cervero (1997) summarize numerous studies that show reduced VKT, higher transit ridership, and more walking when land uses are mixed rather than uniform. They say: "The transportation benefits of mixed land uses can be significant but are not always obvious. Settings with a mixture of land uses can encourage people to walk or ride to various destinations instead of driving. Having shops and restaurants connected to a nearby suburban job center with a nicely landscaped pathway likely means more people will walk to these destinations during, say, lunch time. It might also mean some who otherwise would have driven to work now ride transit instead because they don't need a car to be mobile in the midday" (p. 85).

The importance of how density and mixed use is incorporated into the design of any urban development, is critical to how well it is received. Our approach is to use an urban village concept.

An urban village approach to urban development recognizes the need to bring more community values into new and redeveloping parts of every area of the city; it tries to bring greater walkability in the tradition of Walking City settlements that goes back thousands of years. Box 4.3 provides a summary statement of the characteristics of an urban village. Urban villages can perhaps best be understood by simply describing the key characteristics that constitute their coherent design strategy. These characteristics have been distilled from our examination of some of the best examples in Europe and North America of this kind of transit-oriented development (Newman and Kenworthy, 1992).

Such urban villages are not necessary for everyone in an Auto City, but the increasing number of such developments suggests there is a market; in a macro perspective, the growth of urban villages provides an opportunity for an increasing number of urban residents to live a less car-dependent lifestyle. Furthermore, it makes rail transit extensions viable and hence surrounding lower density areas can be provided not only with a subcenter for local services, but a transit system linked to the rest of the city. Increased densities are an essential feature of the core in an urban village; however, increasing density is a major problem in auto cities because of perceived threats to the existing quality of life in suburbs. It is important therefore to discuss the density issue in some detail and to see how it might be approached more positively in auto cities.

The Density Issue

There are increasing numbers of architects and planners who say positive things about density. For example, David Sucher (1995) in *City Comforts: How to Build an Urban Village* says: ". . . density is simply a by-product of people trying to be at the same interesting spot" (p. 171).

However, the reaction against higher-density housing, the most basic requirement of an urban village, is often because it is seen by local communities as a way of imposing poor-quality apartments on low-density residential areas in an ad hoc attempt at better utilizing vacant, derelict, or underutilized urban land, without

Box 4.3 Key Characteristics of Urban Villages

- High-density land uses, especially at the center, so that everything within the "village" is within walking and cycling distance.
- Mixed land use, with offices, shops, businesses, and community facilities integrated into residential development so that there is more local activity.
- A heavy rail or light rail station near the core.
- Considerable landscaping, including gardens on top of buildings and on balconies and attractive gardens in public spaces.
- A mix of public, private, and cooperative housing with an emphasis wherever possible on families and thus large internal dwelling spaces and spacious community areas.
- Extensive provision for children, such as playgrounds and other safe, creative kinds of play space in good view of dwellings.
- Recreational opportunities, such as sporting facilities (swimming pool, tennis courts, indoor sports, etc.).
- Community facilities, such as schools, libraries, child care centers, senior centers, recreation centers, and in some cases small urban farms. If these facilities are not within the village, they are always nearby.
- Special areas for secure storage of equipment such as boats or other recreational gear to allow for those who may like the community focus of such high-density development but need a little extra space.
- Pedestrian and cycle links with parking facilities placed underground where possible and traffic calming on peripheral roads. The aim is a traffic-free, people-oriented environment, not one designed around the space demands of surface parking lots.
- Public spaces with strong design features (water, street furniture, sculptures, playgrounds).
- A high degree of self-sufficiency in the community to meet local needs, but with good rail and bus links to the wider city for employment, higher education, and so on.

any thought to the effect on surrounding single-family housing. There are, of course, many examples of poorly conceived development of this type that justify people's fears, but there are also very many fine examples of high-quality reurbanization projects that put such fears and objections to rest. The difference is usually based on whether design guidelines are utilized that insist on developments being aesthetically consistent with the surrounding areas and having attractive, friendly street frontages rather than units featuring garages and high walls or a large modernist apartment block with a vast asphalt parking lot.

Our approach is that the positive qualities of density (and mixed land use), such as reduced travel and better transit options, are less likely to occur, or to be as effective in magnitude, unless development is designed to bring transportation and land use together in a very coordinated and consciously planned way. That is, to build Transit City or Walking City characteristics, planners must do a lot better than just scattering increases in density across a cityscape.

Town planning and the development industry need to work together to find centers and corridors to define as urban villages throughout the modern car-based cities we have constructed. A lot of reurbanization has already occurred in Australian inner cities, and the focus could perhaps now shift to middle and outer suburb locations for such nodes and corridors. Urban villages are needed across all parts of U.S. cities, especially in abandoned inner-city locations.

Many cities, such as Vancouver, are finding that this approach of selective, nodal densification also helps to gain community acceptance of higher densities, because it focuses redevelopment at a number of confined points and along corridors, rather than spreading its effects across the entire landscape. The land that is redeveloped in this way also often needs upgrading (e.g., rundown industrial sites), such that the redevelopment, if well designed, can be seen as a positive contribution to the local area (Gallin, 1996).

The urban village is primarily human in scale because walking (or cycling) is the best way to get anywhere. Car use obviously has to be restricted in such environments through pedestrianization, parking controls, and traffic calming, and it is critical to link urban villages together, preferably with electric transit, so that people can gain access to those needs that cannot be met at a local level. However, the hardest battle in Auto Cities seems to be over density, where often the smallest increases are feared.

There are valid and invalid reasons why people fear density, as alluded to above. The valid reasons are that many cities in the developed world haven't completed much successful, organic, high-density design (the 1960s apartment buildings in many North American and Australian cities are about as organic and attractive as plastic flowers) and some (mainly big, public, high-rise housing projects in the United States) have been so bad that they have eventually been torn down. But there are also, as outlined below, some wonderful examples of good high-density design to be found in these cities that can be a guide for the future.

For example, in Canada, the West End of Vancouver and many parts of Toronto and Montreal are living examples of organic, high-density, walking environments. In the United States, the Brooklyn "brownstones" areas and San Francisco "painted ladies" neighborhoods are testament to high-density elegance, human scale, and urbanity. In Australia, Fremantle and Subiaco (in Perth), much of inner Melbourne, and Balmain, Glebe, and Paddington (in Sydney) show that we once knew how to live graciously and efficiently in cities at much higher densities. New developments that use the qualities of these areas are generally the ones that are successful economically and have community support. There are often government programs seeking to do just that (e.g., the Australian federal government's Better Cities program of urban villages).

The invalid reasons for fearing density are those outlined above that suggest it is something inherently harmful or alien to the human spirit. One faction of the nineteenth-century town planning movement (primarily in England) identified all the environmental and social ills of industrial cities as being associated with density. They thus put all their effort into designing new low-density "gar-

Photo 4.8. False Creek in Vancouver (*top*) and the Dutch New Town of Almere (*bottom*) are both examples of urban villages where pedestrians (especially children) have greater freedom.

den suburbs" and low-density New Towns, which were, in fact, not in keeping with Ebenezer Howard's original Garden City vision. They gained some positive environmental features, such as the green "commons," and the original garden suburbs in London were close to railway stations and somewhat denser than their more automobile-based descendants. What they lost, however, was the human scale, as too little remained accessible by walking.

Drawing its basic inspiration from the original Garden City movement, Milton Keynes, outside London is typical of the later, car-based totally planned "Garden City" New Town, with low-density, strictly zoned areas that are set in a sea of heavily watered, grassed open space. The result is a town where few people ever seem to be visible, with the carefully designed walkways and cycle paths almost unused, while the roads and parking areas are full. Milton Keynes has been studied in comparison with a Dutch New Town called Almere, typical of a European tradition of building at a density that enables walking and cycling to be the central transportation modes (Roberts, 1991). The data are compared in Table 4.3.

Although both cities claim to be influenced by the Garden City tradition, only Almere has anything like the density recommended by Ebenezer Howard

Table 4.3. Comparison of Two Small New Towns, Milton Keynes (England) and Almere (Netherlands), in Travel and Land Use Characteristics

	Milton Keynes	Almere
Modal split		
Car	59%	35%
Transit	17%	17%
Bicycle	6%	28%
Walk	18%	20%
Average travel distance	7.2 kilometers	6.9 kilometers (much less for nonwork)
Percentage of trips under 3 kilometers	45%	85%
Density (dwellings/ha)	20	35–40
Description	Form scattered, separated use	organic, mixed use
Percentage who see a car as "essential"	70%	50%
Percentage of households with children under 12 years who are always supervised outside home	52%	16%
Percentage of households with children under twelve who are never supervised outside home	8%	48%

Source: Roberts (1991).

100 years ago. The British Town Planning profession (after Howard) believed they could have a green city without the higher densities needed for convenient pedestrian qualities—they were wrong, and the differences in Table 4.3 show it quite clearly. The rather sad differences in the freedom of children are particularly marked.

The "nothing gained by overcrowding"/abhorrence of density tradition was exported to all Anglo-Saxon cities by the Town Planning profession (King, 1978). It is rarely questioned, even though the evidence of problems associated with density has been shown to be false (see myths earlier in this chapter and Newman and Hogan, 1981).

Canberra is Australia's greatest contribution to the "nothing gained by overcrowding" tradition. The city is very green in the mechanistic, formal sense, since it has a great amount of green space, but a large part of it is along and between segments of its extensive road network and so is not particularly usable on a casual basis. The density of the city, at nine people per hectare, is about as low as it is possible to build a settlement and still call it a city. As a result, it is Australia's second-most-car-dependent city (behind Perth), despite its smallness (300,000 people compared to 1.2 million for Perth) and heavy commitment to the planning of ostensibly self-sufficient subcenters and neighborhoods (Newman and Kenworthy, 1991). Its suburban sprawl now extends more than thirty kilometers, and its need for new freeways is as endemic as in Los Angeles.

Tranter (1993) found that children in Canberra were largely unable to move around with any freedom, despite the city having relatively low crime rates. The sheer distances and car dependence have created a culture of chauffeuring; and now most children are even driven to school because the "traffic is so bad" and parents "fear for the safety of their children."

Cities clearly need to become more creative about densities. Urban villages can be developed where children are free to run around in attractive, traffic-free space, where people can live conveniently in communities that meet most of their needs without a car. People need to become involved in designing, building, landscaping, and filling such urban villages with all kinds of urban activity. This is the approach adopted by Jan Gehl in his studies of how to make central cities more human (Gehl and Gemzøe, 1996), and it tends to be the approach of the New Urbanists, though few examples yet approach the necessary densities. The technology for dense, solar-oriented, ecological urban villages is available to assist this process (see Chapter 5 and Woodroffe, 1994), and town planning can ensure that it occurs in an equitable, aesthetic, and sustainable way.

Examples of Urban Villages

In order to demonstrate that cities can become more creative about densities and that the urban village approach works, the following provides a brief overview of some good examples of urban villages in Munich, Stockholm, Vancouver, and Portland.

Arabella Park, Munich Arabella Park, or the Bogenhausen District Center, is a major subcenter in Munich and is an excellent example of the concept of an urban village, both in the intensity and mixture of the activities and in the

Photo 4.9. Arabella Park, a working urban village in Munich (*top*) and Ultimo, a planned urban village in Sydney (*bottom*).

extremely high quality of urban design and human-scale, traffic-free, and traffic-calmed public spaces in which the development is set. There is a particularly strong emphasis on landscaping and general greening of the environment. The whole development is based around an underground rapid transit station located in the center's Market Square, and a complex of eight- to ten-storey offices is sited adjacent to the station. The development is approximately five kilometers from Marienplatz in the heart of Munich's pedestrianized core. Arabella Park has excellent accessibility to other parts of the city via Munich's newest and most attractive U-Bahn line, which is an important selling point of the center.

Arabella Park consists of homes for 10,000 residents in rental and owner-occupied apartments, employment for 18,000 workers, and 2,000 hotel rooms. The result is a fine-grained, lively mixture of land uses including offices, shops, restaurants, hospitals, movie theaters, nightclubs, an adult evening school, a city library, post office, swimming pool, recreation center and sports facilities, as well as a multitude of peripheral facilities and service companies.

In the public spaces of Arabella Park there is much social interaction, with people of all ages on foot and bike making use of the greened boulevards and market areas to talk and relax. Some of the urban design elements, such as small areas of running water and sculptures, provide useful focal points for activity. There is also a steady stream of businesspeople walking through the area. The number of parents and grandparents with children on bikes and playing in the public areas is particularly striking.

The office sections of the development are set on a mix of traffic-free areas and small roads on the periphery. There are attractive bicycle storage facilities and paths for people with bikes or strollers.

Zamila Park, Munich Not all urban villages are of the size or diversity of Arabella Park, which is a genuine subcenter. Others, such as Zamila Park in Munich, are more residential in character, with some mix of land uses.

Zamila Park is located on Munich's S-Bahn system and is a short walk from a rail station. It is a nineteen-hectare site that contains a mix of 1,300 dwellings of different types (ranging from two-storey homes and units with private gardens up to six-storey quality apartment buildings), 50,000 square meters of office space, and a center within walking or bicycling distance of all dwellings (the center contains facilities such as restaurants, food shops, newsstands, a laundromat, etc.). There is also a large lake area on one side of the development and a good complex of sporting facilities a short walk from all dwellings.

The emphasis in the design is on traffic-free or traffic-calmed public areas, including quiet inner courtyards, pedestrian and bicycle spines, and parklike green areas that link the development together into a contiguous whole. There is minimal penetration of roads and traffic onto the site, and parking is underground and along a few traffic-calmed streets. Dwellings of different styles and colors add a large amount of visual variety to the project and avoid any sense of a monolithic environment. The public spaces within the area are characterized by children playing and parents and adolescents strolling or sitting on the seats provided. There is a noticeable amount of interaction between balconies and the public spaces. The number of families living in the development is clear from the amount of children's play equipment visible in the yards of many dwellings, the formal playgrounds built into the development, and the number of small bikes parked in courtyards.

It appears from observation that a sense of privacy and ownership over private territory is maintained but that this does not limit the opportunities for interaction if residents decide that is what they want, and play opportunities for children are many. By building in opportunities for sociability in well-designed, inviting public areas, it appears that the likelihood of isolation, and probably crime, would be considerably reduced in Zamila Park.

Stockholm's Satellite Centers   It has long been policy in Stockholm to focus urban development around stations on the rapid transit system. One of the first and best-known examples of this was the development of Vällingby in the 1950s. Since then, numerous other satellite centers have been added, including Kista, Akalla, Tensta, Rinkeby, and Skärholmen. The centers are strung together like pearls on a necklace along the railway system (tunnelbana) and are all of a high density, particularly around the station core. All these subcenters show the characteristics of urban villages, though some are predominantly residential while others are highly mixed centers. The general physical planning principles in Stockholm on which these centers are based can be summarized as follows (Stockholms Stadsbyggnadskontor, 1972):

- Locate workplaces close to houses.
- Minimize distances from houses to shops.
- Concentrate service functions in easily accessible areas and make premises easily convertible to meet new service needs as times change.
- Create housing variety with two-storey dwellings with good ground contact; four to six storeys around courtyards, and ten to thirteen storeys near stations.
- Urban environment to have rich variations in form and color.
- Multifamily housing to be no more than 500 meters from a station.
- Single-family housing to be no more than 300 meters from a bus stop (or station).
- A bus-rail interchange to be available in all communities.
- Centers to be linked and permeated by a coherent network of foot and bicycle facilities separated from roads with the convenience of seniors and people with disabilities in mind.

Stockholm's centers are compact and walking scale, with a rich array of facilities clustered together within a relatively small area. In Kista, for example, the rail system delivers passengers directly into an enclosed large shopping mall, which opens onto a car-free town center surrounded by community facilities, shops, and housing; and the excellent network of footpaths and cycleways feeding into the town center makes these modes the easiest and most convenient way to move around. The shopping center forms a bridge between the rail station and predominantly residential development on one side of the railway and the commercial/office development and high-tech businesses on the other side. Kista is Stockholm's "Silicon Valley."

The total separation of motorized and nonmotorized traffic in Stockholm's centers together with traffic-free town squares and well-integrated community spaces, such as children play areas, help make the environment human-scale, despite its being high density. Stockholm's centers are also well endowed with open space networks woven throughout the housing areas, and a comprehensive network of natural open spaces (lakes, forests, fields, etc.) are in direct contact with each center.

While there is an emphasis on local self-sufficiency within Stockholm's subcenters, the broader need for good transit connections to the rest of the city is seen as being paramount. It is recognized that the smaller satellite centers cannot contain all the diversity of typical central city functions and that people will always want to travel beyond their local centers for a range of needs. There is an assumption in Stockholm that feeder buses and the rail system, rather than cars, will be used as a major way of getting to Stockholm's core and other areas of the city during peak and off-peak periods. (See also Case Study 3 later in this chapter.)

Vancouver, British Columbia   There are examples of urban-village-style developments in Canada and the United States, but Vancouver has a few of particular note.

New Westminster: Since the introduction of Skytrain to Vancouver in 1986, a lot of development has clustered near some of the stations. This is particularly noticeable at New Westminster, which was the end station on the line prior to its extension a few years after opening. At this site, twenty-two kilometers from downtown Vancouver, there is a mixed commercial, office, residential, and public market development along the Fraser River within a short walk of the station. The new housing is extensive and ranges from quality high-rise towers, to three- to four-storey condominium-style developments, to townhouses. The housing consists of a mix of individual housing cooperatives and private market housing. The public environment in which the housing is set is of a high standard of urban design, including an extensive, landscaped, garden boardwalk along the riverfront onto which some of the housing units face. The area is maintained as a public park. There are also some community facilities, such as tennis courts.

The public market, which is in a multilevel building, has a wide range of goods and services under one roof and is within walking distance of much of the housing. It also has a direct link to the Skytrain station. The market provides something of a focal point for the center, with entertainment and somewhat more human appeal than most suburban shopping centers. The new compact, mixed-use development that has been spurred on by the rail system, in combination with the older center of New Westminster, means the area has achieved new vitality and attraction.

Metrotown: Approximately fifteen kilometers along the Skytrain line from downtown there is major new mixed-use development connected via a raised pedestrian concourse directly to the Metrotown station. Metrotown is a strong, mixed-use nodal development that has greatly strengthened its town center status in response to the added accessibility offered by Skytrain since 1986. Some of the uses within the center include a major hotel, office towers, department store, cinema complex, apartments, and a variety of shops. Although not as attractively designed as New Westminster, the Metrotown center is tightly ringed by a variety of medium- to high-density housing that maximizes walking and cycling access both to the station and center. There are also cycleway connections and a large bus-rail interchange that facilitates cross-city movement on buses to a variety of destinations. In 1996, Metrotown contained 18,000 residents (an urban density of sixty people per hectare) and 20,000 jobs within a 298-hectare area (a total activity intensity of 128 per hectare), making it a significant subcenter.

There are numerous other stations along the Skytrain line that have progressively integrated a mix of high-density residential and commercial development within a few hundred meters of the trains. Vancouver is gradually starting to reshape itself into a more transit-oriented metropolis through this very visible process of quality high-density nodal development (see the Vancouver case study later in this chapter for a further discussion of this process).

False Creek: Not on Skytrain, but linked to frequent trolley bus services, False Creek is a major inner-city housing area set on the waterfront opposite downtown Vancouver. This very compact site, begun in the 1970s, is presently home to about 10,000 people and is being actively extended. False Creek provides an excellent example of how to build a high-density urban village in the context of extensive and beautifully designed open space together with adjacent mixed land uses such as markets, hotels, cultural activities, a community center, shops, and restaurants (located at Granville Island). The extensive open spaces and children's play areas are traffic-free, since road access is from the rear of the development via a two-lane road and parking is mostly under the buildings at the rear. The False Creek urban village looks onto and runs along the waterfront opposite the central city area, and water forms an important part in the design of the open spaces.

There is an enormous variety in housing forms and styles, including townhouses, terraced units, and medium-rise apartments, many of which are early cooperative housing ventures facilitated through the Canadian Mortgage and Housing Corporation. False Creek is linked by a generous, meandering boulevard for pedestrians and cyclists along which there are some local shops and facilities built into the housing areas.

In many ways False Creek is something of a model in terms of planning and urban design that demonstrates how to combine the elements of urbanity, convenience, beauty and spaciousness into a dynamic and exciting urban environment. This is all the more important because it has been achieved in a relatively high-car-owning metropolitan area.[12]

The success of False Creek is confirmed by the ongoing extensions to the area on vacant land used for the 1986 Expo. The approach here, as in the early development, is to ensure that the public areas of the new high-density housing complexes are a positive addition to the city that can be used by all residents. They consist of parks, gardens, boulevards, cycle facilities, seating and viewing areas on the water, and so on, and are linked in a continuous way with other parts of the city so that movement by pedestrians and cyclists can occur with minimum interruption. This extensive public infrastructure is critical to the success of such high-density environments. In the new extensions of False Creek, urban densities will reach more than 800 persons per hectare, testament to the desirability of the location and the high quality of the public environment.

River Place, Portland, Oregon   This development is located in downtown Portland, overlooking the Willamette River, and consists of a complex of up to five-storey attractive apartments, small shops and businesses, and a hotel built in the same style as the housing units. The apartments are set amidst gardens, and the shops are located under apartments on a pedestrian and cyclist boulevard overlooking the river. River Place is part of Portland's planning commitment to encourage greater residential development in the central city area. It shows what can be achieved in terms of good-quality, compact housing in an urbane, well-designed total environment on a very constrained site (which once served partly as a parking lot).

These examples of urban villages are, of course, not exhaustive. There are sections of many other cities that could have been described. Many parts of Toronto have been built on urban village principles; San Francisco is developing an increasing number of urban-village-style developments around BART; and Washington, D.C., has reshaped parts of the city in the past two decades around a new rail service with high-density urban villages. Most Canadian cities, including Calgary and Edmonton, are actively pursuing the development of urban villages around their rail systems with varying degrees of success, and Melbourne has an excellent "Urban Villages" program sponsored by a number of government bodies (Energy Victoria et al. 1996).

Photo 4.10. River Place in Portland, Oregon, is a successful mixed-use area built when the Mt. Hood Freeway was dropped.

These examples show the extent to which automobile dependence can begin to be substantially altered by a commitment to higher densities and mixed land use based around transit.

Mixed Land Use

One of the obvious differences between premodern cities and Auto Cities is the degree of mixed land use. Old cities, particularly the inner areas of many cities that were built around streetcar systems (e.g., inner Philadelphia, San Francisco, and Sydney), and even late-nineteenth-century transit suburbs, have highly mixed land uses. The result of this fine-grained, diverse urban fabric is that auto travel is kept to a minimum through shorter distances that reduce the need to travel by all modes and that favor nonauto modes. Short distances mean greater opportunities for walking and cycling as well as for transit; there are simply more activities accessible within a small radius so that it is feasible to walk or ride a bike, or even to conveniently hop a few stops on a bus or train. Different trip purposes, such as shopping, work, and personal business, can also be strung together into a single trip in areas of mixed land use, often by just combining transit and foot travel. In zoned suburban areas these same trips would require separate, multiple car trips, adding up to many vehicle kilometers of travel.

Holtzclaw (1990) and Neff (1996) have quantified the travel advantages of such trip-linking in mixed-use, dense environments by showing that there is a "transit leverage" or "transit substitution" effect at work, whereby one kilometer traveled on transit can replace up to ten kilometers of car travel, depending on conditions (the average appears to be about five kilometers). Part of the mechanism for this appears to be the "hidden" nonmotorized mode use that occurs in transit-oriented, mixed-use environments.

The distinct influence of mixed land use on reducing automobile use has also been identified by authors such as Cervero (1995) and Holtzclaw (1994) through careful analyses of automobile and transit use in neighborhoods with mixed land uses versus those with zoned, separated land uses.

Despite the obvious advantages of mixed land use in terms of travel efficiency, for the past fifty years town planning has been "unmixing" cities by the use of rigid zoning that separates single uses into each differently zoned part of the city's town plan. The rationale is part of functional separation that is essentially a part of modernism. It makes sense to prevent pollution from industry getting to residential or other areas but that is now largely unnecessary since controlling industrial impacts is always best achieved by simple health regulations or through environmental control, and most new employment in the cities of the late twentieth century is information-oriented, rather than industrial.

Nodes of Mixed Land Use in the Information Age City

As discussed in several parts of this book, the city of the late twentieth century is no longer an Industrial Age city but is moving rapidly to express the Information Age. We can understand urban planners in the Industrial Age producing cities based on the dominant functionalism paradigm of the era: cities were zoned into clear, simple categories of residential activity in one area, work in another, shopping in yet another. This was necessary to separate out smoky, smelly industries, but functional separation was also how industrial thinking operated.

Thus it also meant the Industrial City separated people into clear functions: men worked full time, women worked at home, and children worked not at all. And it tended to create zones of social exclusion based on racial and socioeconomic classes.

All of this is not relevant or acceptable in an Information Age City. The world of information is not only postindustrial, it is largely postmodern, with a distinct blurring of all exclusive categories and functions: home/work, city/suburb, full-time/part-time employment, male/female employment—all become blurred. There is an important role in ensuring categories overlap where formerly there were different, exclusive roles; this is known in some circles as "fuzzy logic" and is a feature of postmodern integrated systems thinking (see Chapter 6).

Figure 4.1 illustrates the differences between the kind of urban outputs from

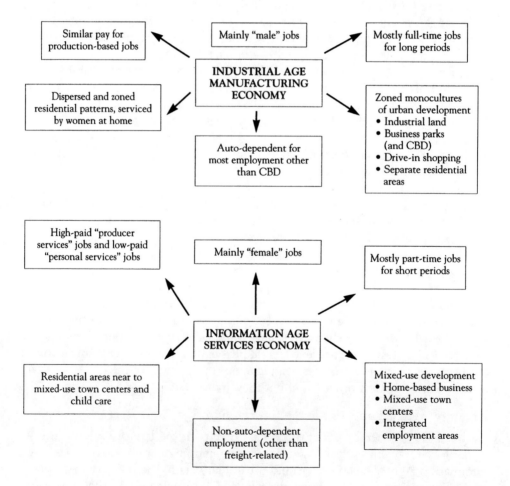

Figure 4.1. Outputs from Industrial Age and Information Age in terms of employment and urban development. Based on Kemp (1998).

the Industrial Age and the Information Age, based on Kemp (1998). In the Information Age City, there is a clearly important role for planning to enable nodes of mixed land use to emerge.

There is another critical role for the emerging nodal/activity centers or urban villages, based on quality, pedestrian-oriented urban spaces: this is where not only community processes are promoted through the "accidental interaction" of people in public areas, but where the various professions can meet for face-to-face contact in creative, information-oriented enterprise and job creation.

Almere was discussed earlier as an example of an urban village that is dense and mixed in its land use. The data on Milton Keynes and Almere (Table 4.3) show the difference between functional separation and mixed use: one has been rigidly zoned, and the other is more organic and mixed, with most local services within a short walk (80 percent of trips are less than three kilometers). It should be emphasized that the residents of Almere prefer their kind of neighborhood because they recognize the freedom it creates due to reduced travel needs and car-free street qualities.

The difference between the two types of urban development will continue to diverge. The information superhighway means that more and more information or service-oriented work can be done in local urban villages. Although there are often social problems associated with the greater isolation of solely home-based work, the reality is that more and more home-based businesses are starting and most town planning schemes rarely account for them. The era of greater integration in our cities is here, and the sustainability agenda makes it even more necessary for planning to achieve mixed use.

One of the features of New Urbanism is an attempt to reintroduce a greater proportion of mixed use into urban development. Sometimes this appears to be for purely aesthetic reasons (perhaps representing the new paradigm's need for diversity rather than functional uniformity), but as the following extract from a New Urbanist primer shows, the push for denser, mixed-use areas is a response to the double goal of environmental improvement and economic enhancement. The ideal New Urbanism development is described as having:

> . . . fine-grained, mixed use town and neighbourhood centres, and normally should have higher resident and employment densities than conventional suburban development. Because of its good accessibility, amenity and capacity to accommodate a diverse range of buildings whose uses may compatibly change over time, the urban structure of the New Urbanism provides a physical framework that facilitates employment generation in the emerging post-industrial economy of small business, home-based business and part-time multiple employment (Morris and Kaufman, 1996).

Mixed Use Through the Dutch A, B, C System

Although the majority of employment is in information-oriented services in the postindustrial city, there is still a considerable amount of production in the city that generally is not compatible with the emerging mixed-use subcenters since they have very different transportation requirements. Production areas invariably

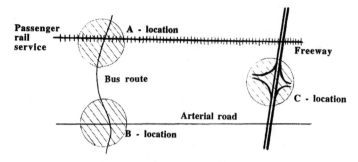

Figure 4.2. A, B, or C locations depending on transportation infrastructure.

need some kind of road access for trucks. Information-based areas need a more pedestrian-oriented environment linked by good transit.

It is important to try to match the different land use requirements with their transportation system requirements. Such a process is the Dutch A, B, C system sometimes called "the right business in the right place" (Department of Planning, Housing, and Environment, 1995). The system has been adopted by the United Kingdom as the basis of its Planning Policy Guidance 13 (Department of Environment, 1994).

The system allocates A, B, or C locations to businesses:

- The A locations require good transit (people-based activity sites, such as offices, hospitals, educational facilities, shops, and recreation facilities).
- The B locations have a mix of accessibility requirements.
- The C locations require good freight access (warehousing, industrial production, etc.).

The city is then given different accessibility profiles depending on whether it is more like an A, B, or C location (Figure 4.2). The plan is not only to try to match business to the most appropriate transportation system, but to help create development plans that (1) facilitate business relocation, and (2) build up the transit or road system to better service the businesses with transportation (e.g., goals for transit in A locations are to become more than 80 percent of all motorized trips in and to the area).

This system can enable a city to become less automobile-dependent while ensuring that its goods production and distribution are more efficient. In the Netherlands and the United Kingdom, local authorities use the system as a guide rather than as a statutory plan.

Growth Management

Underlying much of the approach to city sustainability in this book is the notion that the Auto City has become extraordinarily wasteful in land. This has obvious environmental impacts but also, as shown here, has impacts on the economy. Greater efficiency in the provision of infrastructure occurs linearly with density increases, and most civil engineering texts provide such advice (Macklin, 1977).

Some urban economists argue, however, that social costs may rise or that a few infrastructure items may need to increase in complexity due to densities over certain levels and advise strongly against such density increases (Troy, 1996). Our data confirm a growing problem with urban sprawl (see Chapters 2 and 3), and the private sector is increasingly concerned (Bank of America, 1994).

There are a variety of approaches to growth management that are summarized in Appendix 2. The solution proposed here is the "urban concentration" option—that is, to channel growth into the reurbanization of urban villages and to put severe curbs on growth at the fringe by the use of a green belt or urban growth boundary.

In Box 4.4 the guidelines for establishing a green belt for growth management planning are summarized (after Wake, 1997), and a more detailed set of tools for establishing and maintaining a green belt are provided in Appendix 2.

The only kind of growth that ought to be countenanced outside the green belt or growth boundary should be where development needs to occur around a particular resource or attraction and the possibility exists for a good transit connection. In that case, the nature of the development should be clustered and given a deliberate focal point for providing services and community activity. The dispersal of single homes or rural ranchettes based on an exurban location but a semi-urban existence should be resisted; they are the basis of unsustainable automobile dependence.

Growth management in its fully developed form is not widely practiced, especially in Auto Cities, though many cities have some element of control over

---

Box 4.4. Greenbelts for Growth Management: Planning Guidelines

Make green belt boundaries defensible.

- The land included in a green belt should be valued for its intrinsic nature, current use, or strategic role.
- The green belt should protect significant landscapes and land uses, such as natural habitat, agricultural land, water catchments, forests, recreation areas, and rural landscapes.
- The green belt should be delineated to shape and contain urban growth so that it sets an urban boundary consistent with regional growth goals.

Integrate a green belt with other strategies to manage urban growth.

- A green belt by itself is inadequate to contain and shape a city's growth.
- To be effective, a number of strategies are needed to manage growth. These could include reurbanization initiatives, such as minimum densities or urban village developments; policies to develop satellite towns or encourage growth in regional locations; or changes in population policy to influence regional population growth.

(continues)

Box 4.4. Continued

Manage rural land use.

- A green belt can provide a framework for managing rural land uses.
- Prohibition of urban development on green belt land is important but must be supplemented with other measures.
- A range of tools could be used to regulate development and encourage appropriate land uses to meet conservation and development aims, including conservation reserves and landscape protection zones, land stewardship programs, taxation incentives, limits on rural-residential development, and limiting urban service provision (sewerage, etc.) to urban areas.

Take a regional approach to managing growth.

- Managing growth in a local area may simply divert impacts elsewhere and could be ineffective in the long term.
- To shape urban form and influence urban and rural land use, growth management efforts need to extend across the metropolitan region and maybe beyond.
- A regional vision and growth management framework is needed to provide consensus and cooperation among authorities and communities and to integrate strategies to manage growth effectively.

Ensure long-term, proactive planning.

- A green belt should be planned as a long-term or permanent designation.
- A green belt can be an integral part of a regional growth management effort.
- Growth management and strategic planning should have a horizon of thirty to fifty years and should be proactive, looking to anticipate and manage change in population, urban growth pressures, and land use.

Build public support and political commitment.

- Public and political support is necessary to establish and retain a green belt and to shape a city's growth.
- Public involvement in the strategic planning process is important. Citizens, interest groups, and political representatives should be involved in discussing, developing, and reviewing regional growth goals and strategies.
- The green belt should be promoted and used as a public asset, part of the regional commons that sustains urban and rural communities.

Source: Based on Wake (1997).

sprawl (see Richmond [1994] and the Smart Growth Network in the entire issue of *On The Ground*, vol. 2, no. 2, 1996). The best examples (e.g., Boulder, Colorado) are given in the case studies presented later in this chapter, though even Tennessee has now adopted the American Planning Association's "Growing Smart" guidelines. Commenting on this, Peirce (1998) says, "revulsion with sprawl, a desire for strengthened neighbourhoods and communities, is mounting across America."

Taxing Transportation Better

As already discussed, there are many reasons why economic approaches to managing traffic problems are not very politically acceptable, especially in the Auto City. However, a start needs to be made, and thus in this section some of the options are reviewed for taxing transportation better. In particular, the whole process of developing a more sustainable city requires the provision of infrastructure and services for nonautomobile transportation modes and for redevelopment of urban villages. This requires funding, and the source of such funding can be from the proper taxing of the Auto City based on its full costs.

Congestion pricing is the latest panacea suggested by the transportation world, not only for reducing congestion, but also for improving sustainability (see *Economist*, December 6, 1997; OECD/ECMT, 1996). Suggestions are increasingly moving to the use of "smart cards" that charge drivers according to the level of traffic congestion. In this way drivers are expected to drive less, use transit, drive when congestion is less, and hence reduce stop-start driving with its fuel and emissions problems.

However, Neale (1995) suggests that there is no guarantee that congestion pricing will simultaneously improve congestion and sustainability. He suggests it is entirely predictable that motorists will:

- drive exactly as they always have if the congestion charge is covered by their firms (e.g., a majority of London's peak-hour commuters have company cars and perks);
- drive more if the congestion charge is used to build more roads rather than providing more transit alternatives;
- drive more as they shift to "rat running" through suburban streets to avoid congestion-priced streets; and
- drive more as they shift shopping, recreation, and even work destinations to suburban locations that are not being charged.

Congestion pricing could thus be used to undermine policies designed to reduce the need to travel; they could undermine the revitalization and reurbanization of the inner city, and they could have significant impacts on equity (pushing the poor into even more car-dependent situations as people with wealth choose the less expensive options).

Fuel taxes, on the other hand, can more directly and equitably be used to shift patterns in transportation, but they depend mostly on the way they are used: to build more roads or to provide other options. The key is to provide a feedback process whereby local communities can decide how best to use their transportation funds from the fuel tax. This ought to be part of an integrated land use and transportation approach with clear goals that each year achieve a more sustainable city. Citizens will respond to a tax that progressively demonstrates this.

The development of a more coherent user-pays approach to urban transportation is necessary. This cannot, however, be used to merely divert more funds into road building. Unfortunately this was how New Zealand planned their congestion-pricing system (called Road Reform)—through increased fuel taxes but reduced local authority rates, with an overall effect of putting more (most) taxes into roads. If implemented, this plan would have meant less coverage of external costs and, together with the loss of any democratic control over street improvements or transit, would have resulted in an even less sustainable city. The New Zealand government dropped the proposal under widespread community pressure.

The main components of a more user-pays, commercial transportation system that improves urban sustainability are:

- An increase in fuel taxes to cover the full external costs of transportation (the United Kingdom is committed to a 5 percent per annum real increase in fuel costs into the foreseeable future; OECD/ECMT, 1996).
- A channeling of funds into innovative sustainable transportation projects that reduce automobile dependence; this process should be through an agency that can draw in private sector involvement through joint development and value capture and must involve communities where a system of prioritizing enables reductions in motoring to be developed through city plans.
- Giving local authorities the right to tax congestion and use it for better public transit; innovative ways of doing this may emerge,
- An increase in neighborhood responsibility for local streets to use them for purposes other than the flow of traffic.
- Encouragement of the contracting out of the maintenance and operation of road works and transit systems, but within a tight regulatory system to ensure that the common good is maintained.

A range of economic penalties for overcoming automobile dependence is emerging in cities around the world. Some of the best approaches are included in the case studies later in this chapter. Nevertheless, this policy area is very weak in most Auto Cities and is likely to rely on simple fuel taxes for some time.

The Future "Sustainable" City

This section suggests how the Auto City needs to change to become the future "Sustainable" City in which automobile dependence is overcome. Sustainability as outlined un this book, is always going to be something for which a city strives.

The key characteristics of how land use patterns need to be changed in a highly automobile-dependent city so they become more sustainable and less auto-dependent are expressed in Figure 4.3. The text reviews the four steps required to transform such a city from an Auto City to a "Sustainable" City.

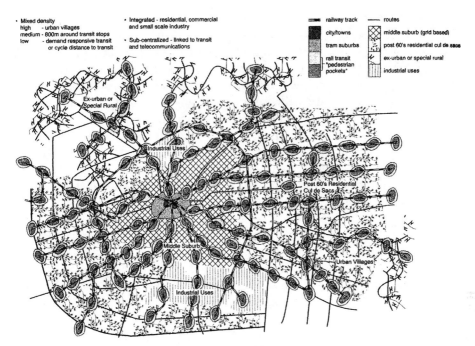

Figure 4.3. A conceptual plan for the "Future" Nodal/Information City.

Step 1 in creating a more sustainable city is to revitalize the inner city.

In the inner city there are already transit-oriented and walking-oriented characteristics, as well as dense, mixed land uses with urban design conducive to face-to-face activity. Here it is possible to reach destinations with short trips and without a car and to create walkable communities. In reurbanizing such areas, a city is extending the opportunities for people to live non-automobile-dependent lifestyles.

Reurbanization of essentially abandoned inner-city areas has occurred in many cities around the world. Invariably, such successful revitalization is closely associated with community processes that have developed a new vision for an area; it is thus associated with strategies such as historic building and streetscape preservation, street festivals and other community arts events, low-income housing to retain a mix of incomes, and investment in new businesses by innovative entrepreneurs. Finding the right spark for regeneration of some areas often requires great creativity and commitment by urban managers, but it always involves significant community input.

Although there are now strong market forces pushing the reurbanization process, little hope for regenerating the inner city will be found if there is an atmosphere of fear on the streets produced by crime, or if the schools in the area are not adequate. These problems have been the major cause of "white flight" in U.S. inner cities, followed by the "black flight" of middle-class African Americans. Reducing this atmosphere of fear is essential before urban regeneration can occur (see Chapter 7).

One of the most important policies for generating investment, creating a better environment, and promoting a more lively community in the inner city is
traffic calming and pedestrianization with reduced parking. This process can help
to begin the kind of upgrading of an area that reverses the sense of decline, since
it gives people who live and work in the area a more hopeful approach to their
own neighborhoods. If traffic calming and street improvements are imposed on a
demoralized community, they will achieve little, but once a community has a new
sense of its regeneration potential, then improving the public environment can
be the signal for broader revitalization processes. The most obvious places to initiate traffic calming are where the most intensive urban activity exists. Here
there is the greatest need to manage the automobile. The process will always be
political since motorists don't like any impedance, but it is critical if any area is
to gain a new lease on life. For this reason there is no choice but to make traffic
calming a community process to reclaim the city's streets. It is also necessary to
make traffic calming area-wide and to make it a part of a general approach to
reducing travel and shifting to other modes.

Regeneration will proceed only if people begin to invest in houses and businesses in the area. This process can occur quite rapidly once it starts, but such
market approaches require the necessary social infrastructure for an area to be
considered safe for investment (see Chapter 7 and Newman, 1986). Once the
inner city is regenerating, a city can then begin to take its "inner city" qualities
to the suburbs. These can include traffic calming of neighborhoods, but must also
include a process of beginning to provide subcenters that have "inner city" characteristics, linking them with good transit.

*Step 2 in creating a more sustainable city is to focus development around the present rail
system.*

If an Auto City has a rail system, it is quite possible that it has done nothing
to facilitate the market for higher-density, mixed-use development around its station areas wherever they are—in the CBD, inner city, or outer suburbs. This is a
common failing in Auto Cities, where zoning, inappropriate government land
uses, and lack of creativity are often preventing such development. Cervero
(1992a) and Bernick and Cervero (1996) have shown that good rail transit will
create such markets, but they can also be stymied by the planning system.

Joint development between public and private interests is the best way to
optimize the use of land within a short walk of stations. Park-and-ride areas are
not a good use of station environments and were deliberately prohibited by BC
Transit in Vancouver, Burnaby, and New Westminster in order to maximize
development potential. Park-and-rides do not promote better land use and can
be dangerous environments for transit patrons at night. They can, however, be
converted to urban villages later, so they may be an interim solution as a transit
system is developing. Bike-and-ride facilities are more compatible with stations;
they mean that the radius of those who can easily reach the train extends from
800 meters on foot to 5 kilometers, and yet bicycle facilities do not interfere with
the basically pedestrian qualities of the station precinct. There is also usually
space for a bus interchange point at a station; if bus timetables are integrated with
rail services and feed in from both sides of a corridor, it is possible to provide

cross-suburb transit. This extra activity makes it even more important that the station subcenter or urban village offer an attractive walking environment with mixed uses.

Bernick and Cervero (1996) have presented examples from around the world of such transit villages, including a growing list in the United States. Calthorpe (1990) drew up guidelines for transit-oriented design and has provided a number of examples (Calthorpe, 1993), together with other New Urbanists (Katz, 1994).

In California there is a set of initiatives that establishes the legal basis of transit-oriented development: the Transit Village Development Act of 1994 establishes all land within a quarter-mile of rail transit stations as transit-village development districts if applied for by a local authority. The area is then given the powers of a redevelopment agency and staffed to facilitate its transition into a mixed-use, high-density, pedestrian-scale urban environment. The district has first priority for funding from state and federal innovative transportation-land use programs. The bill came in response to growing transit investment in California and is aimed at ensuring that there is a better link between transit and land use on systems such as BART, which has large park-and-ride areas around many of its stations.

As mentioned previously, Melbourne has drawn up a plan, called the Urban Villages Project, in which more than 500 significantly underdeveloped sites located adjacent to tram stops and rail stations have been given special status for redevelopment. The local community is involved in creating plans to upgrade the areas. Calculations showed that development in such areas would save up to 40 percent of energy/greenhouse emissions from transportation and household uses (denser developments use less heating and require less transportation). Urban village redevelopment would be less expensive to build and would create opportunities for the local community through the shops, jobs, child-care facilities, etc., that would be built there (Energy Victoria et al., 1996). Perhaps of greatest significance, up to twenty-five years of potential greenfields urban growth in Melbourne could be accommodated on such sites. This approach provides the basis, therefore, of stopping urban sprawl.

Step 3 in creating a more sustainable city is to discourage further urban sprawl.

Stopping sprawl requires a simultaneous process of changing the investment in highways that take people out of the city to greenfield sites, and changing zoning processes to protect rural land on the urban fringe. Both steps are necessary. It is almost impossible to stop new sprawl through zoning alone if high-speed roads are still being built. They are like a loaded gun pointed at rural land in their vicinity. At the same time, people need to know the strategic goals for a city and to have them expressed in zoning ordinances. The goal of managing growth at the urban fringe can become acceptable to people if it is seen to be both a goal of sustainability and to be a market-based process.

A summary of approaches to urban growth management is presented in Appendix 2.

The market for development of land in the inner city and around transit stations needs to be under way if the third step of stopping sprawl is to be managed. Cities such as Vancouver and Portland, with active growth management greenbelt strategies, could not hope to achieve their goals without a program of reurbanization around transit stations. The same is the case in European cities.

Step 4 in creating a more sustainable city is to extend the transit system into poorly served suburbs, including cross-suburban and orbital rail lines, and to build new urban villages around them.

As shown in Figure 4.3, there are large areas of suburban development with no real transit service in most Auto Cities. It is possible (particularly with joint development) to build state-of-the-art electric rail transit systems into these areas at reasonable cost—but, as a rule, only if it can involve land development at stations to help pay for it. In this way, not only is it possible to develop the transit service, but it also becomes more feasible to create the subcenters or urban villages that these residential-only suburbs generally lack. It ensures that many more local services can be provided, and it becomes possible to reach other cross-city destinations by good transit directly from the subcenter, eliminating the need for a car.

This four-step process is the basis for reclaiming the Auto City. It means that the many low-density suburbs in existence do not have to be rebuilt but can be given a less automobile-dependent form or structure. They all would have a nearby urban village as their focal point. They would, however, also need to be laced with bike facilities and could be provided with other state-of-the-art local transit, such as demand-responsive minibuses for local services. Traffic calming would also play a key role in making such areas safer, more human in scale, and suitable for walking and cycling.

If such transit-based subcenters are built around or adjacent to current suburban shopping malls, then they can slowly begin to reclaim the acres of asphalt parking lots as they begin to diminish the need for car access.[13] There are few examples of this kind of development so far, but they are beginning to happen. One has occurred in Mountain View, California, where a 1960s shopping mall has been replaced by a transit-oriented, mixed-use urban village (Center for Livable Communities, 1996). An even more impressive example has been built in Addison Circle in Dallas, Texas, where a classic American "Edge City" surrounded by parking lots, freeways, and collector roads has been transformed into a new town center with "a finely woven grid of narrow streets, with pedestrian-friendly sidewalks and public seating areas, shaded by trees." The Addison Circle Master Plan provides for buildings oriented to the street, ten acres of pocket parks, outdoor spaces for public events, and a mix of housing forms in a four-storey configuration around semiprivate courtyards. The redevelopment will include a new light rail station by 2005 (Center for Livable Communities, 1997).

In the United States there are attempts to implement such concepts by groups other than the New Urbanists. A U.S. Department of Transportation publication called *The New Suburb* (Rabinowitz et al., 1991) outlines thirty-four innovative designs from recent U.S. developments and a number from an international design competition (Beimborn et al., 1991) promoting transit corridor developments. Critical to all the designs is that, not only are they dense and mixed to allow pedestrian activity (and to be viable for transit), they are also rediscovering the virtues of narrow streets, where people enjoy walking and where buildings are organically linked. The cul-de-sac housing form, where buildings do not relate to the street or to one another, and the large, undifferentiated open spaces typical of high-rise housing developments, have little place in New Urbanist design. Nor have they had much favor in European urban design (Gehl, 1987).

Others have tried to introduce the principles through planned unit developments, or PUDs (Kaufmann, 1991). Mostly, these new developments (designed to reduce car dependence) are known as transit-oriented developments, or TODs.

The role of subcenters with a strong commitment to information-oriented services is universally recognized to be a feature of the future "Sustainable" City (Castells, 1989; Brotchie et al., 1995). However, not all cities are moving to link these nodal/information centers with good transit systems or to traffic-calm them so that they are pedestrian-friendly. Very few cities are as committed as Stockholm and other Nordic cities to using the new technological imperatives to help create or maintain a connected city of communities. Rather they are using these new technologies to maintain a disconnected city of individual households, as in Auto Cities (Cervero, 1992).

Conclusions to Future "Sustainable" City Transformation

The change from the Auto City to the future "Sustainable" City can be seen in the summary table of characteristics of the four city types set out in Box 4.5.

The "Sustainable" City can be seen as incorporating a combination of changing characteristics. All of them, however, can be made part of the sustainability agenda and thus help to create the kind of city described in this chapter. These forces include:

- *Transportation priorities.* A key to all sustainability in cities is the balanced provision of all transportation modes with a link to land uses through, in particular, the building of transit-based, walking-oriented urban villages. This means that sprawl can be curbed. It does not mean that all the low-density car-based suburbs must somehow be bulldozed. With local, viable subcenters nearby, it is possible to create greater self-sufficiency with local services reached by walking, biking, or a short car ride. Directly reaching more distant places in the rest of the city will be made much easier through a good transit service linking the subcenters together. This is primarily an issue of public policy in cities, and the data presented in Chapter 3 show that it will benefit a city economically, socially, and environmentally if it were to be more balanced in its transportation priorities.

- *The global economy.* The new information/services-oriented cities are globally competitive if they are good urban environments in which to live and work. This is primarily an issue of where the marketplace is taking cities, though public policy also has a role to play. The evidence from cities in Australia and from the global cities data presented earlier is that the global, information-oriented city is likely to concentrate into central areas and nodal subcenters. These favor the provision of transit and quality walking environments—that is, the "Sustainable" City. Some similar data have been found in U.S. cities by

Box 4.5 Characteristics of Four City Types

	Traditional Premodern Walking City	Industrial Transit City	Modern Automobile City	Postmodern Future "Sustainable" City
Economy (and Technology)	Small household industries (local and small regional economy)	Larger industries, concentrated in parts of cities (national and regional economy)	Large-scale industries in zoned areas across the city (national and regional economy)	Information- and services-oriented; remaining heavy industries mostly in eco-parks or in small rural towns (global economy)
Social Organization	Person-to-person, community-based	Bigger cities losing person-to-person contact but still community-oriented in rail-based suburbs	Individualistic and isolated	Local, community-based, but globally linked
Transportation	Walking (and cycling later)	Streetcars and trains (also walking and cycling)	Cars (almost exclusively)	Walking and cycling (local), transit (across city), cars (supplementary), air (for global)
Urban Form	Walking City: small, dense, mixed, organic	Transit City: medium-density suburbs, dense, mixed center, corridors with green wedges	Auto City: high-rise CBD, low-density suburban sprawl zoned to further separate functions	"Sustainable" City: local urban villages (high-density mixed) linked across city by transit; medium- and low-density areas around villages; no more sprawl
Environment				
Resource use	Low	Medium	High	Low to medium
Wastes	Low	Medium	High	Low to medium
Nature orientation	Close to rural areas (dependent)	Some connection through green wedges	Little nature orientation (independent)	Close to nature (see Chapter 5)

Lucy and Phillips (1995), who conclude their paper on "Why Some Suburbs Thrive" by saying the communities that are flourishing are:

> . . . those communities that have encouraged public transportation and a mixture of residential, commercial and industrial development; have higher enough density to nourish pedestrian life; and—most important—have maintained a sense of place. (p. 21)

- *The spatial values of the community.* Individuals can try to optimize their own private space and not worry about other spatial values, but there is an awareness now that this individualism has destroyed community in cities; thus the "communitarian" movement has begun to reclaim urban public spaces. Chapters 5, 6, and 7 will show how important this movement is in making more sustainable local communities. The concept of urban ecology is outlined in Chapter 5 and is used to reveal how in some places communities are taking control of and reducing local metabolic flows.
- *The environmental movement.* The global environmental movement is now firmly involved in the future of cities, and although there are disputes about what is meant by a "greener" city (discussed in Chapter 5), there is considerable support for the kind of "Sustainable" City strategy described above. Environmentally, the city becomes low in resource use and low in waste outputs, as well as enjoying improved livability. One of the keys to this is the move to more community-scale technologies that can be used to provide water, waste, and energy services in local areas, including intensive community gardens to reorient cities more toward nature. This discussion is pursued further in Chapter 5 as well as in some of the case studies that follow.

Case Studies in Overcoming Automobile Dependence

In this section a series of case studies are provided that outline how some cities are beginning to move toward greater sustainability by reducing their dependence on the automobile. A summary table of techniques is used in each case to show the extent to which cities have used a variety of approaches, or just a few, in tackling auto dependence.

Case Study 1: Singapore and Hong Kong Success Stories and Their Implications for Developing Cities

Both Singapore (population of 2,705,115 in 1990) and Hong Kong (population of 5,522,281 in 1991) have remarkably successful transit systems and very low car usage, as shown in Chapter 3. Hong Kong's increase in per capita car use between 1981 and 1991 was only 146 kilometers (compared to 2,584 kilometers in Los Angeles), and its transit use increased by 104 trips per capita. Singapore had similar success.

Singapore and Hong Kong face the dilemma of the automobile but are opt-

Photo 4.11. The dense land use around a successful rail system is the secret to the efficient
operation of Singapore.

ing to provide more for transit than for the car. In order to achieve this, they have
introduced a range of strategies, summarized in Table 4.4.

The first strategy, city-wide planning, is given a very high priority (Wang and
Yeh, 1993). The transit system in both cities is fixed, rapid, and comfortable
(electric rail) and is also flexible and local (standard buses and minibuses). In the
case of Hong Kong, ferries also form a small, though important, part of the transit system. This is supplemented in both cities by high levels of nonmotorized
transportation (mainly walking) in the dense, mixed-use settings where the main
component of many trips is a vertical trip in an elevator. Cycling plays a very
minor role in Hong Kong for topographical reasons and is presently small in
Singapore, though major efforts are being made to increase it through cycling
facilities such as bicycle parking areas at rapid transit stations and the development of shaded cycleways.

Central to the success of the Singapore/Hong Kong model is high-density
urban development that is closely integrated around the transit system.
Singapore's basic urban structure plan shows a series of radial and circumferential
mass transit and light rail lines with major and minor subcenter nodes developed
at high densities around the intersection of all these lines (Kenworthy et al.,
1994).

The success of both Singapore and Hong Kong in integrating development
around their respective rail systems can be easily seen from Tables 4.5 and 4.6,
which show high percentages of the city's total activities lying within walking
distance of stations and the ease with which stations are reached either on foot
or by transit.

Table 4.4. Singapore and Hong Kong's Strategies for Overcoming Automobile Dependence

Traffic Calming	Favoring Alternate Modes	Economic Penalties	Non-auto-dependent Land Uses
Very low levels of road space to start with and limited amount of new road building to cater to private cars. Limited use of pedestrianization and formal traffic-calming schemes. Increasing pedestrian orientation in central area through wide sidewalks, etc.	Heavy investment in mass rapid transit systems. Priority to buses through bus-only lanes, bus-only streets, and bus-only turns. Buses favored as surface access to central city through traffic-restriction zone (Singapore). Heavy parking restrictions. Effective integration between trains and buses. Development of circumferential rail transit services as well as radial services.	High cost of car ownership and use through high taxes on cars and fuel and certificates of entitlement to purchase cars in Singapore. High parking charges.	City-wide planning totally based around the integration of high-density, mixed-use nodes at rail stations on the rapid transit system. Increasing orientation toward pedestrians and cyclists for local access to nodal centers and to transit. Land use planning totally predicated on encouraging nonauto modes.

The densities associated with these exceptional levels of transit and nonmotorized travel are generally regarded as being excessive by Americans and Australians. They are acceptable in Asian environments, particularly when they are associated with good planning that results in high levels of health and other quality-of-life indicators (Newman, 1993). Nor are these densities unheard of in some parts of North American cities, such as in central Toronto or Vancouver's West End and False Creek areas, and they are not generally as high as densities in Manhattan.

The story of Singapore's successful transit system is not without its battles, nor is it without the support of other highly successful policies aimed at restraining car use. The advice from the World Bank and some American consultants in the 1970s was that it would be wrong to invest in an expensive, high-profile, fixed-rail facility; all that was needed was to upgrade their buses. However, Singapore

Table 4.5. Integration of Land Use with Transit in Hong Kong

Descriptor	% of Population/Passengers
Percentage of Hong Kong population living within a mass transit railway (MTR) catchment area—a walking distance of 500 meters from any MTR station.	50.0%
Percentage of passengers who walk to and from MTR stations	69.4%
Percentage of passengers who walk either to or from an MTR station, requiring feeder service at only one end	28.3%
Percentage of passengers who require a feeder service at both ends of an MTR journey	2.3%
TOTAL	100.0%

Source: Donald (1993).

officials and the United Nations Development Program chose to go ahead with their rail system because they realized that buses alone do not offer a competitive service to the car and they would not be able to implement their transit-oriented city plan without a high-capacity rail service linking their subcenters both to the city center and across the city in a series of circumferential rings (Wardlaw, 1998).

Buses, it was realized, would not have the capacity to service such dense concentrations of activities without severe congestion problems, and bus station environments would of necessity be much larger, dirtier, and noisier places than electric train stations. Such environments would be unattractive places for the

Table 4.6. Integration of Land Use with Transit in Singapore

Descriptor	% of Population/Passengers
Percentage of Singapore population living within walking distance of MRT station	30.0%
Percentage of Singapore population living within 1 kilometer of the line	50.0%
Percentage of all businesses and industrial areas located near stations	40.0%
Percentage of passengers who walk to and from MRT stations	65.0%
Percentage of passengers who transfer to or from buses at MRT stations	35.0%
TOTAL	100.0%

Source: Letter from Singapore MRT Ltd, July 5, 1994, quoting Transit Link figures, and introduction to "The MRT Story" (Singapore: MRT Corporation, 1988).

density of the envisioned development and the resulting intense pedestrian flows, as well as being physically harder to integrate than an underground or elevated rail station. Singapore's MRT service and integrated bus system has been highly successful in both economic and environmental terms since it opened in 1987. In 1990 the overall transit system in Singapore achieved a 15 percent operating profit.

Some of the groundwork for transit's success, as well as its ongoing achievements in Singapore, are due to Singapore's famous area licensing scheme (ALS), introduced in 1975 to reduce morning peak commuting into the CBD, and its long history of steep vehicle taxes, including the more recent certificate of entitlement (COE) system, which requires would-be car owners to bid for the right to buy a vehicle. The price of a COE varies continuously, but in early 1994 it was as high as US$47,000, on top of the car purchase price (*Straits Times*, December 17, 1993).

The ALS has been attributed with many benefits, such as reducing the percentage of commuters driving to the CBD from 56 percent in 1975 to 23 percent in 1983 and increasing the bus mode split from 33 percent to 69 percent. The traffic flow improvements achieved by this simple revenue-producing scheme would have required $1.5 billion in road investment. Finally, car ownership models based on wealth were suggesting Singapore should have had more than 300,000 vehicles in 1982, whereas it had only 184,000 (OECD, 1988).

Not surprisingly, the ALS has been physically expanded and its times of operation extended to an all-day scheme (7:30 A.M. to 6:30 P.M.). Through the COE system and other vehicle taxes, as well as the ALS, the Singaporean government has been progressively tightening the screws on car ownership in response to the pressures from growing wealth, but it has also been expanding the opportunities for transit and nonmotorized mode use through continually expanding the MRT system and more recently by providing for bikes and pedestrians.

For example, separated bikeways are part of the planning of New Towns to facilitate access to MRT stations and commercial areas within the towns. Bikeways are also planned for many roads. Pedestrian malls and precincts, transit malls, promenades, and galleries consisting of covered streets with hosts of shops, restaurants, and cafes are occurring in the central area. Extensive greening of the city to moderate the harsh climate is an important part of pedestrian and bike plans (Urban Redevelopment Authority, 1991, p. 39).

Hong Kong also has a story to tell with respect to developing an effective transit system, integrating development, and restraining the automobile.

The intense pressure on available land in Hong Kong due to topographical constraints, and the potential for overwhelming congestion if the private car were to be unrestrained, has meant that Hong Kong's physical planning principles have always been strongly based on the need to create supercompact nodes of strongly mixed development in which people can access most local needs within a short walk. Now these nodes are mostly linked together by the MTR system so that longer trips do not require a car or a congested bus trip.

Coupled with effective land use–transit integration, Hong Kong's traffic management is directed not at facilitating car use by creating quantum leaps in road capacity, but at optimizing the existing road system. The success so far is evidenced by the fact that average traffic speed rose from twenty kilometers per hour in 1979 to twenty-four kilometers per hour in 1988 and again to twenty-six kilometers per hour in 1991 (Kam, 1993). Hong Kong has achieved such results through the following:

- Computerized area traffic control (ATC).
- Transit priority measures: bus-only lanes, bus-only streets, bus-only turns, etc.
- No requirements for developers to provide parking in the core urban area according to the size of buildings, in recognition of good accessibility by transit and on foot.
- Relatively high costs for car ownership and use, which help keep a lid on rising ownership.

Many cities in the developing world are rapidly modernizing, with significant growth in car ownership, and have put most of their transportation capital into new roads and parking. These cities include Bangkok, Manila, Jakarta, and now the Chinese cities. Bangkok, for example, with a gross regional product per capita of only US$3,826 in 1990, already had 199 cars per 1,000 people, whereas Hong Kong, with nearly four times the wealth (US$14,101), had only 43 cars per 1,000 people, or one-fifth the car ownership rate.

Rapidly developing cities that have not put in place any physical or economic restraints on traffic, have not built high-quality transit systems, and have not protected their traditional forms of nonmotorized mobility from the onslaught and dangers of motorized traffic, now have huge traffic problems as well as associated environmental and social problems (Poboon, 1997; Poboon and Kenworthy, 1997). For them there is the obvious solution: to implement transit systems in conjunction with restraints on car ownership and use on the model of Hong Kong or Singapore, and to begin recommitting themselves to traditional forms of nonmotorized mobility that are so effective in dense, mixed-use settings with short travel distances for many trips. The high density, and in many cases preexisting linear form of development in many Third World cities, is more than adequate to justify the construction of high-capacity transit systems.

Many proposals and plans for rail transit systems exist in these cities, which have huge fleets of often very dilapidated buses and other smaller collective modes such as tuk-tuks, jeepneys, and a variety of minibuses. Although essential for local transit services, these modes cannot cope with passenger demand and cannot compete in speed terms in the constrained, traffic-dominated streets. As incomes and consumer expectations rise in developing cities, these inferior modes of transit cannot compete with the car (or indeed motorcycles) in terms of comfort or general passenger appeal. Many residents are thus immediately lost to private transportation for a majority of trips as soon as they can afford to change over, whereas a competitive transit system reduces the need to make this transition to private transportation.

New rail transit systems (usually associated with funding from both private and public sources) therefore offer the only true rapid transit option across the city. Based on the models of Singapore and Hong Kong, the results of implementing rail systems in the rapidly motorizing cities of the Third World (preferably in conjunction with some physical and economic disincentives to car own-

Photo 4.12. Hong Kong's integration of land use and transit make it one of the least car-dependent cities in the world.

ership and use) are likely to be spectacularly successful, particularly because their land use is already transit-oriented (Poboon, 1997). It is important, however, to also address the rapidly declining and increasingly hostile conditions for pedestrians and cyclists in developing cities because, as shown in the case of Singapore and Hong Kong (Tables 4.5 and 4.6), most transit trips in dense environments involve pedestrian access at least at one end.

The key problem for transit systems in developing cities seems to be the lack of a politically powerful and well-coordinated city planning system that could approve and implement the building of quality, fixed-transit infrastructure. The participation of the public in city planning is also essential, particularly when a city becomes stuck in an inappropriate Western paradigm, as, for example, has Bangkok (Kingsley, 1993). An important part of the solution is thus to more adequately express community values through the planning system and to cease importing outdated and discredited Western planning techniques, such as traditional four-stage land use–transportation models that generate self-fulfilling prophecies of roads and congestion in endless cycles and that do not even consider that nonmotorized modes exist in such environments (Poboon and Kenworthy, 1995; Kenworthy, 1995).

The solutions are on the doorstep of developing cities and involve a three-pronged attack along the lines of Singapore and Hong Kong: (1) commitment to building up quality transit, preferably rail, (2) some preparedness to introduce parallel physical and economic restraints on private transportation that support the investment in transit, and (3) investment in relatively inexpensive improvements in the environment for pedestrians and cyclists.

Photo 4.13. The planned integration of the city of Curitiba around its public transportation system stands as a beacon for low-cost urban sustainability.

Case Study 2: Curitiba, the Low-Capital Transit Model

The problem for most cities, whether in developing countries or not, is how to minimize the capital cost of transit while providing sufficient investment to make it a viable alternative to rapid motorization. Curitiba, Brazil (population of 1,894,000 in 1990), is a city that has shown how to do this by channeling investment of scarce urban resources into a coherent, city-wide transit service that is closely integrated with land use policy and other social policy in the city (Rabinovitch, 1992). Table 4.7 provides a summary of Curitiba's strategies for reducing automobile dependence.

The transit system that has been developed over the last twenty years began with the use of express buses on exclusive busways on axes radiating out from the city center. These proved much cheaper and less disruptive to install than conventional metro or light railway systems. Over the years, these axes have been further developed, and urban growth has been encouraged along them. There are five main axes, each with a "trinary" road system. The central road has two exclusive bus lanes in the center for express buses and is flanked by two local roads. On each side of this central road, one block away, are high-capacity, free-flowing, one-way roads—one for traffic flowing into the city, the other for traffic flowing out of the city. In the areas adjacent to each axis, land use legislation has encouraged high-density residential development, along with services and commerce. The express buses running along these axes are served by interdistrict buses and conventional feeder buses with connections between different buses organized in a series of bus terminals.

Table 4.7 Curitiba's Strategies for Overcoming Automobile Dependence

Traffic Calming	Favoring Alternate Modes	Economic Penalties	Non-auto-dependent Land Uses
Pedestrianized central area. Traffic arteries converted to tree-lined boulevards for walking.	Very high priority given to well-organized, three-tiered, integrated bus system providing radial and circumferential travel. Express buses on bus-only lanes and all buses interconnected through a series of bus terminals. Complete integration of ticketing on all buses. Special floor-level loading tubes to increase operational efficiency.	Heavily subsidized bus fares.	Bus system highly integrated, with high-density, mixed-use nodes along the main express bus axes. Land use planning heavily oriented toward producing minimal in-built auto dependence in new development.

The central city areas have been pedestrianized and historic buildings protected from redevelopment as a result of the reduced pressure from cars and the balanced development of subcenters along the transit system. Several main thoroughfares have been closed to traffic and converted into tree-lined walkways. One important complementary action was the municipal government's acquisition of land along or close to the new transportation axes, prior to their construction. This allowed the government to organize high-density housing programs close to the transportation axes; in all, some 17,000 lower-income families were located close to these points.

As of 1992, there were 53 kilometers of express lines, 294 kilometers of feeder lines, and 167 kilometers of interdistrict lines. Buses are color-coded: the express buses are red, interdistrict buses are green, and the conventional (feeder) buses are yellow. There is full integration between express buses, interdistrict buses, and conventional (feeder) buses. There is a large bus terminal at the end of each of the five express busways where people can transfer to interdistrict or feeder buses. One single fare is valid for all buses. Along each express route, smaller bus terminals are located approximately every 1,400 meters and are equipped with newspaper stands, public telephones, and post office facilities. Here passengers arrive on feeder buses and transfer to the express buses. These new stations (with platforms at the same height as bus floors) cut boarding and deboarding times; a rapid bus system with "boarding tubes" can take twice as many passengers per hour. They also take three times as many passengers per hour when compared to a conventional bus operating in a normal street. The boarding tubes also eliminate the need for a crew on the bus to collect fares, which frees up space for more passengers.

Curitiba's transit system is used by more than 1.3 million passengers each day. Twenty-eight percent of express bus users previously traveled in their cars. This has meant savings of up to 25 percent of fuel consumption city-wide. Curitiba's transit system is a major reason for the city having one of the lowest levels of ambient air pollution in Brazil. Three other aspects of Curitiba's transportation policy are also worth noting:

1. It has one of the lowest accident rates per vehicle in the country.
2. There are considerable savings for inhabitants in expenditure on transportation. On average, residents spend only about 10 percent of their income on transportation, which is relatively low for Brazil.
3. Social policies have been integrated with the system through the insistence on low-cost fares across the city and access to the system for those with disabilities (wheelchairs can enter the bus directly once in the bus boarding tube, and old buses are used to provide special services for the heavily disabled). In addition, innovative, mobile, computer-education programs are provided in old buses in poor areas of the city.

The next phase of Curitiba's growth is to develop higher-capacity rail services along the main axes, which can now be done as the city develops based on its original low-cost buses.

Case Study 3: Zurich, Copenhagen, Stockholm, and Freiburg—European Transit-oriented Planning at Its Best

Zurich (population of 1,166,039 in 1990), Copenhagen (population of 1,711,254 in 1990), Stockholm (population of 1,641,669 in 1990), and Freiburg (population of 178,343 in 1990) are examples of European cities that have made concerted efforts to contain automobile dependence while improving the quality of life of their citizens. Many other cities, including Munich and Amsterdam, could easily qualify for worthwhile case studies, but these four have been chosen because they offer particularly striking lessons.

Zurich

The data presented in Chapter 3 have already shown that Zurich has had a spectacular increase in its transit patronage and managed to contain its growth in car

Photo 4.14. Minibus connecting to trolley bus and light rail gives a highly integrated transit system in Zurich.

use. Figure 4.4 shows the rapid rise in transit use and Figure 4.5 shows the steady car use in comparison to Stuttgart, a European city without the same priorities as Zurich. The changes in Zurich have occurred despite substantial growth in per capita incomes.

How has Zurich managed to channel its wealth into such positive city-building processes rather than the city-destroying processes of dispersal, pollution, and community disturbance associated with automobile dependence? Zurich's overall strategy for overcoming automobile dependence is summarized in Table 4.8.

In the 1970s Zurich had to make decisions about its trams. Why not build an expensive underground metro and leave the streets for cars? Instead of bowing to the car lobby, the community demanded that the city expand its old tram system and upgrade the services so that citizens rarely had to wait more than six minutes and that trams and buses be given absolute priority right-of-way at traffic signals.

"Suddenly trams became popular in Zurich. We found it impossible to attack the use of the tram . . . People simply won't accept it," says planning consultant Willi Husler. As trams became fashionable, public attention was directed to other amenities—pedestrian malls and outdoor cafes, which were allowed to take up road space and parking lots. The strategy, says Husler, was "to point out other, better possibilities of use. That way we can fight a guerrilla war against the car and win" (Husler, 1990). What appeared to happen was that people began to respond to the attractions of the public realm and made private sacrifices to be part of that.

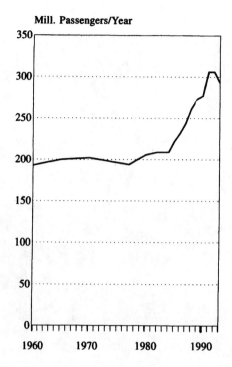

Figure 4.4. Zurich city public transport (VBZ), passenger trends 1960–1993. *Source*: Stadt Zurich and Verkehrbetrich Zurich. *Note*: Does not include S-Bahn trips.

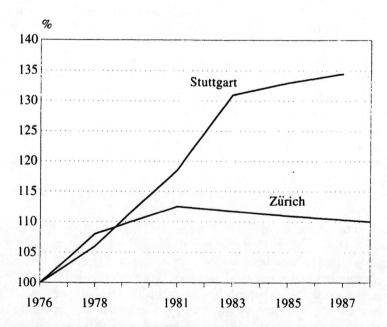

Figure 4.5. Trends in motorized road traffic in Zurich and Stuttgart, 1976–1988. *Source*: Pfeifle, M. (1988). Kordonzahlung—ein Hilfsmittel zu Aussagen über die Verkehrsentwicklung? *straasenverkehrstechnik*, H2; Stadt Zürich, *Statische Jarbücher*.

Table 4.8. Zurich's Strategies for Overcoming Automobile Dependence

Traffic Calming	Favoring Alternate Modes	Economic Penalties	Non-auto-dependent Land Uses
Regional traffic calming.	Expansion of the light rail and heavy rail systems and bike/pedestrian lanes.	Usual European fuel tax and registration.	Containment of growth.
Extensive thirty-kilometer-per-hour zones.		No congestion pricing.	Transit-directed growth.
Development of selected transit malls and pedestrian zones.	Carefully timed coordination among all services and modes.	High parking fees.	New urban villages around the rail system.
Reclamation of traffic lanes for light rail.	Professional marketing and passenger information campaigns.		Some mixed use.
Enforcement of car restraint.	No extra road capacity and a cap on parking.		
	Rainbow Pass for transit system.		

In the 1980s Zurich continued to dramatically improve its transit offerings. An S-Bahn system was fully developed and coordinated with other transit modes. Many lines use new high-quality double-decker train sets. Large shopping centers under transit authority control have been developed under and around major stations. Throughout the Zurich region there are also fine examples of the way the land use planning process and development industry have responded to the dramatic improvements and coordination of transit services. It is now possible to find many urban villages integrated tightly around the S-Bahn system (e.g., Tiergarten, an urban village built in a disused quarry in Zurich's inner area on the Uetliberg line).

In addition, the very effective transit services were brought to the attention of the public in dramatic and appealing ways through effective marketing and high-quality information systems. An anecdotal policy in Zurich is that you should never be able to take a photo in the street in Zurich without capturing the distinctive signs that are the trademark of the transit system. Special-purpose transit system maps were introduced to show people how to get to restaurants, sport facilities, cultural attractions, and so on using the transit system.

Environmental Travel Cards, or Rainbow Passes, were introduced to appeal to people's environmental consciousness. Apart from the obvious environmental impacts from excessive automobile use, there is a peculiar Swiss problem of destructive avalanches caused by forests dying from automotive air pollution. Young people were particularly targeted in marketing campaigns. Now 80 percent of trips made on Zurich's transit system are with presold tickets, and 25 percent of the population are classed as "committed" transit users (people who possess a pass of twenty-eight days' or longer duration) (Laube, 1995).

So effective was the coordinated transit campaign that the modal share of car trips in Zurich for the journey-to-work fell by nine percentage points between 1980 and 1990. Zurich offers a key to resolving the problem of automobile dependence: a city should always strive to provide something more appealing to its citizens than the options provided by decisions based around the automobile.

Copenhagen

Resistance to automobile dependence can be found in most European cities, but Copenhagen has shown that the dilemma of the automobile can be resolved using innovative social planning. Table 4.9 summarizes Copenhagen's strategies for overcoming automobile dependence.

Copenhagen has a transit-oriented urban form (a "finger plan" based on radial rail lines) that includes places such as Ballerup, at the end of one "S-tog" line (Copenhagen's local electric train service), where a shopping center, office complex, community facilities, and apartments have been built over and around the station. The station environment includes pedestrianized boulevards, a large bus feeder station, and extensive provision for bikes.

However, the transit-oriented urban form alone was not enough since the car was taking over and needed to be resisted. Professor Jan Gehl described the process by which Copenhagen began to win back its city over a twenty-year period:

> By the 60's American values had begun to catch on—separate isolated homes and everyone driving. The city was suffering, so how could we reverse these patterns? We decided to make the public realm so attractive it would drag people back into the streets, whilst making it simultaneously difficult to go there by car. (Gehl, 1992)

Each year Copenhagen reduced central area parking by 3 percent. Each year the city pedestrianized more streets, built or refurbished city housing, introduced into the streets all kinds of attractive landscaping, sculptures, and seating (including 3,000 seats along footpath cafes). And each year the city introduced more buskers (street performers), markets, and other street life and festivals that became more and more popular. As Jan Gehl said, "the city became like a good party" (Gehl, 1992).

The result has been not only a reduction in traffic, but growth in the vitality of the city area. Social and recreational activity has tripled in Copenhagen's major streets (Gehl and Gemzøe, 1996).

Danes are finding that the public realm of the city is so attractive that there is a declining market for single, detached homes on the urban fringe—they are

Photo 4.15. Nyhavn (Copenhagen). "We decided to make the public realm so attractive it would drag people back into the city whilst making it simultaneously difficult to go there by car," says Jan Gehl about Copenhagen's strategy of coping with automobiles.

Table 4.9. Copenhagen's Strategies for Overcoming Automobile
Dependence

Traffic Calming	Favoring Alternate Modes	Economic Penalties	Non-auto-dependent Land Uses
Regional traffic calming but extensively pedestrianized in city center.	Emphasis on bike lanes and pedestrianization	Usual European fuel tax and very high vehicle registration costs.	Corridors of growth. Urban villages around rail lines.
Extensive thirty-kilometer-per-hour zones.	No extra road capacity, and reduction of parking by 3 percent per year for fifteen years.	No congestion pricing. High parking fees.	Mixed use in centers.
Enforcement of car restraint.	Culture of respect for bicyclists.		

apparently "too far away" and "too private." Copenhagen is now building a light rail system in response to the increased demand for travel to the city and between its subcenters, and this is being paid for entirely out of the land development opportunities it is creating.

Copenhagen is also one of the world's best bicycle cities. One-third of the city goes to work by bike. Like many European cities, Copenhagen had a lot of bicycle use early this century, but unlike other cities, it has not abandoned bicycling as it has modernized and become wealthy. Car use grew and threatened the more humble bike, but in the 1960s, at the same time as the processes above were beginning to happen, Copenhagen decided to stay with its bikes.

The city's decision was reflected most of all in its rejection of a massive freeway system; such systems had been drawn up for implementation in most developed cities in the 1960s and 1970s. The public opposition in Copenhagen was very strong and creative. Researcher Michael Varming, one of the original activists, tells of campaigns in which they tied hot-air balloons to major buildings threatened by the road program and placed large, colorful buoys in a lake showing how much would be reclaimed for a motorway. Mass rallies of bicyclists demanded that the plans be scrapped. And they were.

In their place, and at a much reduced cost, the city began to invest in cycleways and traffic management. Although Copenhagen has only 300 kilometers of separated bikeways (much less than in Amsterdam and other Dutch cities), the city has created safety and priority for cyclists by much cheaper means: paint on the roads and a successful education program that generated a "culture of respect for cyclists." Thus at every intersection there are blue strips for cyclists to ride in, giving them priority over all turning vehicles.

The result is a city where cyclists have safe and easy access comparable to other modes. The data on transportation deaths summarized in chapter 3 show Copenhagen to have one of the lowest rates in the world (7.5 deaths per 100,000 people, compared to an average of 14.6 in U.S. cities and 8.8 overall in European cities). This low rate of transportation deaths probably has something to do with this "culture of respect," which was generated for cyclists but which extends to all other road users, especially pedestrians. Bicycles are now used by people of all backgrounds, ages, and incomes.

The latest innovation in Copenhagen is the City Bike program, in which colorful bikes are provided free, after a deposit is placed in the bike-holder as you would for an airport baggage cart. The bikes are paid for by commercial advertising and are maintained by the City of Copenhagen with assistance from the prison system, which collects and repairs damaged bikes overnight. It is hard to find a free bike from among the present 2,500 bikes available, but as the originator of the program, city administrator Soren Jensen, says: "When there are 10,000 bikes in a few years, it will be a normal thing for anyone downtown to just jump on a city bike to move around the inner city" (Jensen, personal communication, 1997).

There is, of course, a close link between the policies to reurbanize and revitalize the inner city of Copenhagen and the policies to not build major infrastructure for vehicle access and to favor alternative modes. This link shows that sustainability can be a meaningful policy, since the city has done very well economically, as well as having no growth in car use in the inner city for twenty years (Gehl and Gemzøe, 1996). This policy has been consistent with community

Photo 4.16. The new urban village of Skarpnäck in the outer suburbs of Stockholm is a classic example of planning to overcome automobile dependence in a wealthy city.

interests and political parties of all persuasions during the past thirty-five-year period.

Copenhagen has, of course, been subject to all the pressures of suburbanization and car use. It has developed some car-dependent areas and some that tend that way (further discussion of these areas is found in Chapter 5). But, overall, it has not allowed itself to be dominated by car-based thinking. For example, city engineer Jens Rorbech, who has overseen the infrastructure priorities for the past fifteen years, has responded to motorists who suggest that unless they get more parking or road access in the inner city they will go to the suburbs: "Please go, because the reduced traffic in the city will only make it a better environment, and we will get even more investment and people coming to the city" (Rorbech, personal communication, 1997).

Stockholm

Stockholm, which is also one of the richest cities in the world, was the only city in our global cities study cited in Chapter 3 to show an absolute decline in car use in the 1980s. It reduced car use by 229 kilometers per capita. This was associated with a growth in transit from 302 to 348 trips per person. Table 4.10 summarizes Stockholm's strategies for overcoming automobile dependence.

Stockholm in recent years has demonstrated how to put in place both reurbanization and transit-oriented development in new suburban locations. Our

Table 4.10. Stockholm's Strategies for Overcoming Automobile Dependence

Traffic Calming	Favoring Alternate Modes	Economic Penalties	Non-auto-dependent Land Uses
Regional traffic calming, but extensively pedestrian and bicycle-oriented around each rail station. Pedestrianized old center-city.	Strong commitment to transit since the 1950s. Rail system and feeder buses provide highly coordinated, effective system.	Usual European fuel tax and vehicle registration costs. No congestion pricing but tolls on new roads. High parking fees.	Corridors of transit-oriented development (TOD) around rail system and no other growth. Urban villages around new rail stops with high levels of walking and cycling within and between adjacent centers.
Extensive thirty-kilometer-per-hour zones.	Total segregation of pedestrians and bicyclists from road traffic in New Towns.		
Enforcement of car restraint.	Little extra road capacity and tolled.		Mixed use in centers.
	Transit culture.		

data on population between 1980 and 1990 show an increase in the density of Stockholm's central city, inner city, outer suburbs, and the municipality as a whole. No other city in our sample has shown that. Stockholm is therefore setting a standard to follow on land use sustainability.

This has been achieved chiefly by building urban villages around their rail system in the inner city (e.g., South Station) and in new outer suburbs (e.g., Skarpnäck). These new developments are all dense, mixed-use areas with a careful eye for the kind of design characteristics found in the old inner city of Stockholm (see also the discussion of its satellite centers). But most of all, they are built around a quality rail service that links the whole city. They are popular as places to live and work and have some of the highest transit levels found in the world.

Cervero (1995) analyzed the process that Stockholm has gone through in transforming itself from "a pre-war monocentric city to a planned post-war multicentered metropolis" using a development model similar to the kind of "Sustainable" City concept illustrated in Figure 4.3. He found that local self-sufficiency was not particularly high in each of the subcenters, but that the good rail system, excellent bus feeders to the rail stations, and compact land use pattern meant that people used the rail system for a large amount of their travel. Although many people did not live and work in the same center and cross-commuting between centers was common by train, residents of the new subcenters along the rail lines were not as automobile-dependent as those in UK New Towns. The towns, such as Milton Keynes, have high car use because they are so low in density and scattered in their land use. Promoting greater self-sufficiency is discussed in the next chapter, but it is useful to see that Stockholm shows the importance of having a good rail-based transit system and closely integrated land use patterns around stations to ensure that travel patterns are sustainable and not automobile-dependent.

The data on Stockholm show that it is a world leader in sustainable urban development in terms of reducing automobile dependence. Its current phase of development, called the Dennis Package, is designed to double the transit system with an orbital rail service and a downtown semi-rapid-transit bus service. Additional road infrastructure will also be built, but it will be heavily tolled and paid for from the money so raised.

Freiburg

Freiburg, Germany, is another city that has shown it is indeed possible to virtually stop the growth of car use, even when car ownership is growing. Table 4.11 summarizes Freiburg's strategies for overcoming automobile dependence.

Pucher and Clorer (1992) provide data that show how Freiburg's car ownership has risen from 113 cars per 1,000 people in 1960 to 422 per 1,000 in 1990, only a little under the average for the Zurich agglomeration and only 12 percent less than the national average for West Germany at that time (481 per 1,000). Table 4.12 shows how, despite this growth in availability of cars, daily auto use virtually remained constant between 1976 and 1991. Transit passengers increased 53 percent and bicycle trips rose 96 percent over the same period.

Freiburg's growth in car trips in fifteen years was only 1.3 percent, yet total

Table 4.11. Freiburg's Strategies for Overcoming Automobile Dependence

Traffic Calming	Favoring Alternate Modes	Economic Penalties	Non-auto-dependent Land Uses
Regional traffic calming but extensively pedestrianized in city center.	Strong commitment to light rail transit and bicycle infrastructure.	Usual European fuel tax and vehicle registration.	Corridors and nodes of transit-oriented development (TOD) and no other growth.
Extensive thirty-kilometer-per-hour zones.	Bus feeders strongly support the rail system.	No congestion pricing. High parking fees.	Urban villages around new rail stops.
All new streets in urban villages traffic calmed.	Little extra road capacity. Transit pass similar to Zurich's.		Most internal movement within villages on foot and bicycle.
Enforcement of car restraint.			Road penetration into urban village sites strictly limited.
			Mixed use in centers.

Table 4.12. Transportation Trends in Freiburg, Germany, 1976–1991

Transportation Factor	1976	1991	Percent Increase 1976–1991
Total daily trips	385,000	502,000	+30.4%
Total daily auto trips	231,000	234,000	+1.3%
Auto's share of nonpedestrian trips	60%	47%	n.a.
Bicycle's share of nonpedestrian trips	18%	27%	n.a.

Source: Pucher and Clorer (1992).

Photo 4.17. Freiburg's success story: "First, it has sharply restricted auto use in the city. Second, it has provided affordable, convenient, and safe alternatives to auto use. Finally, it has strictly regulated development to ensure a compact land use pattern." (Pucher and Clorer, 1992).

trips increased 30 percent. Freiburg's growth in mobility was supplied principally by increased transit and bicycling. In fact, the share of trips by car decreased over the fifteen years from 60 percent to 47 percent. Pucher and Clorer (1992) also show how the growth in car ownership has also begun to slow down.

Pucher and Clorer attribute Freiburg's success at "taming the automobile" to a combination of transportation and physical planning strategies:

> First, it has sharply restricted auto use in the city. Second, it has pro-
> vided affordable, convenient, and safe alternatives to auto use. Finally,
> it has strictly regulated development to ensure a compact land use pat-
> tern that is conducive to transit, bicycling and walking. (p. 386)

Restricted auto use has been achieved through mechanisms such as pedestri-anization of the city center, area-wide traffic-calming programs (a city-wide speed limit of thirty kilometers per hour in residential areas), and more difficult, expensive parking. Freiburg's improvements to transit have focused on extending and upgrading its light rail system as opposed to buses. Buses are used as feeders to the light rail system. Land use regulations are similar to those in many other parts of Europe and have involved limiting the overall amount of land available to devel-opment and strictly zoning land for agriculture, forests, wildlife reserves, or unde-veloped open space.

Pucher and Clorer stress the important automobile use reduction of the more compact urban patterns that have resulted from these latter policies. It is also worth noting that after the Second World War it was decided to rebuild Freiburg, totally destroyed by the war, on the old model, not on an Auto City model. Pucher and Clorer note that even in the post-1960s period, as Freiburg expanded on flatter land to the west, the resulting development "... is at a much higher density than outlying portions of American metropolitan areas," as well as being within easy reach of transit and well served by bikeways.

Overall, Freiburg shows how a coordinated, three-pronged approach to overcoming automobile dependence is effective—that is, traffic calming, better transit systems and priorities to pedestrians and cyclists, and compact, mixed land use patterns reinforce one another in providing a city with the conditions necessary to keep automobile dependence at bay and even to reverse it.

Case Study 4: Toronto and Vancouver— Canadian Success Stories

The ascendancy of the automobile and its reshaping of urban settlement patterns is most closely associated with North America, and the cities found there are often thought of as a more or less homogeneous group. However, data provided in Chapter 3 show the considerable distance between the automobile dependence of U.S. cities and that of Canadian cities. While U.S. cities such as Los Angeles, Detroit, and Houston face by far the largest dilemmas in resolving their automobile problems, Canadian cities have had a different history and evolution,

Photo 4.18. St. Lawrence Market (Toronto). "Good, efficient public transit and scarce, costly parking is a key to being a successful city... The other significant policy in Toronto was bringing people to live in the city centre and sub-centres," says Art Eggleton about Toronto's success in the 1980s creating a livable city without building freeways.

despite having similar cultural and economic development in the past fifty years (see Raad and Kenworthy, 1998).

Stories from Toronto (Greater Area population of 4,235,756 in 1991) and Vancouver (Greater Region population of 1,602,502 in 1991) below show how they have overcome, to varying degrees, the dominant paradigm of automobile-based planning. Central to both stories is how the community forced planners to think again about freeway proposals.

Toronto

Toronto's strategies for overcoming automobile dependence are summarized in Table 4.13.

Toronto has made a deliberate policy of transit-oriented development for a number of decades. While the policy is not always consistently applied, the city has been more successful than any other in North America in shaping a significant role for transit. Its success is seen most of all by comparison with its neighboring city, Detroit. Toronto and Detroit are only about 100 miles apart and are very similar in climate, but they have very different transportation patterns. In 1991, Greater Toronto (which includes the whole suburban region of Toronto) had 51 percent of the per capita car use in Detroit and is managing to control its growth in car use better (Greater Toronto grew by 873 kilometers per capita in annual car use between 1980 and 1990, while Detroit rose by 1,298 kilometers per capita). Detroit has only 1 percent of its passenger travel (total motorized passenger kilometers) by transit, while Metro Toronto (the core of the Toronto area, with more than half of the population) has 24 percent of travel on transit and Greater Toronto has 15 percent. Detroit's metropolitan density is also half that of Greater Toronto.

Toronto is far less dominated by cars and is the best North American example of transit-oriented development (Kenworthy and Newman, 1994). From 1960 to 1990 there was a large growth of 127 percent in Metro Toronto's transit use up to 350 trips per capita, which represents European levels of transit ridership, while Detroit's declined by 50 percent to a paltry 24 trips per capita. Even Greater Toronto, which includes the lower-density, more car-oriented suburbs of the region had 210 transit trips per capita in 1990, by far the highest in North America and some 35 percent higher than the next highest metropolitan region, New York.

The central city area (CBD) of Toronto has continued to grow in population over the past decades, adding some 20,000 new dwellings between 1975 and 1988 (Nowlan and Stewart, 1992), and Metro Toronto's density increased by 13 percent between 1960 and 1990 (particularly along its transit lines). On the other hand, Detroit's city center and inner area spiraled downward very rapidly, with inner-area density dropping from sixty-eight persons per hectare in 1960 to twenty-nine per hectare in 1990, and the overall density of the metropolitan region dropping by 32 percent over the same thirty-year period.

Two cities close in proximity—two very different urban histories. Why?

Art Eggleton, the mayor of Toronto from 1980 to 1991 (and councilor from 1969 to 1980), tells how it happened (Eggleton, 1992). The city was very influenced by the author Jane Jacobs, whose importance in the ethical underpinnings

Table 4.13. Toronto's Strategies for Overcoming Automobile
Dependence

Traffic Calming	Favoring Alternate Modes	Economic Penalties	Non-auto-dependent Land Uses
Some local traffic calming but no pedestrian core.	Historically strong commitment to effective subway system, plus some new construction.	Commercial concentration tax (through parking).	Strong corridors of transit-oriented development (TOD) within Metro Toronto along subway lines, though suburban development in outer areas is about twice the density of that in the United States and Australia. "Main street" program of densification along light rail/tram lines.
Efforts to make subcenters pedestrian-friendly.		Vehicle registration surcharge for air quality initiatives.	
Surface light rail lines act to calm traffic to a degree in inner areas.	Commuter rail diesel system to distant suburbs being extended and improved.	Feebate on large vehicles.	
	Some new light rail lines being added.		
	Some reasonably well-developed off-road bicycle networks.		Strong mixing of land uses along main streets and at rail station nodes.
	Strong integration between transit modes to provide good radial and cross-city coverage in Metro Toronto.		
	Generally low road availability compared to U.S. and Australian cities.		
	Limited parking in CBD and in subcenters.		

of sustainability and whose wonderful book *The Death and Life of Great American Cities* (1961) are discussed further in later chapters. Jacobs stressed the need for people to respect the integrity of their organic city, go back to a more urban character, rediscover their public spaces, and protect against auto-based planning. She moved to Toronto from the United States and was very influential there, along with other prominent figures, in a citizens' movement designed to stop the building of a major north-south freeway, called the Spadina Expressway, which would have carved its way southward through old suburbs into the central city (see, for example, David and Nadine Nowlan's 1970 book *The Bad Trip: The Untold Story of the Spadina Expressway*). The community eventually won the fight through a Provincial Cabinet decision that overturned Metro Toronto's decision to build the Spadina Expressway.[14]

The Spadina decision was a landmark victory for citizen action in Toronto and marked a fundamental reversal in government transportation policy, consolidating growing pressures from many quarters for a different kind of city.

Once the freeway issue had defined the city's direction, government policy more seriously emphasized transit-oriented development in its planning priorities. The Spadina subway line was built instead of the freeway, and existing subway lines dating back to the 1950s (plus some major extensions, such as the advanced LRT line to the Scarborough subcenter) became the sites of very intensive nodal development, especially along the Yonge line.[15]

Most station precinct areas have been developed with close cooperation between the Toronto Transit Commission (TTC) and land developers so that a mutual benefit has been obtained by the twenty-two transit-oriented subcenters that grew up around the subway like pearls on a string. The TTC has a land development arm devoted to trying to maximize development possibilities around its stations (e.g., through publication of a booklet showing land development opportunities throughout the system). It tries to ensure that joint development and value capture opportunities occur wherever possible and that there is some direct financial return to the community from the economic advantages reaped by the private sector in locating over and around subway stations (e.g., air rights and station connection fees).

Toronto changed in less than thirty years from a city that was becoming increasingly car-based to one that is now substantially based around a transit network, certainly in Metro Toronto, with its 2.3 million people. As a result, it has been able to revitalize the downtown area and develop a density in Metro Toronto (forty-one persons per hectare) that is closer to European levels than American. Even the Greater Toronto area has a density of twenty-six persons per hectare, which is almost double the average U.S. and Australian metropolitan densities.

In addition, Toronto has a strong "Main Street" program aimed at increasing inner-city population and revitalizing light rail/tram streets by incorporating a large quantity of new shop-top housing and other infill residential development. Infill development and redevelopment are indeed strongly emphasized on all available vacant and underutilized land throughout Metro Toronto, but especially around subway stations.

In most automobile-dependent cities it is found that catering to the car drains a city center of its life; jobs and residents are dispersed; and conditions for an effective transit system are undermined. Metro Toronto's twenty-two smaller subcities, together with a healthy downtown—which has even managed to reduce parking supply per 1,000 jobs by 11 percent between 1980 and 1990—provide the basis for a viable transit system. There are plenty of lower-density suburbs around these subcities, but they each have a local center providing many services nearby, and it is only a short distance for residents to a good transit service whenever longer trips are needed. The city center and the subcenters are complementary. In many other car-based cities, the city center has declined and new jobs have become increasingly accommodated in scattered employment centers across the region, or in larger "Edge Cities," almost exclusively accessed by car.

Toronto's new central city housing has reduced the morning peak by 100 cars for every 120 units built (Nowlan and Stewart, 1992). There are families living in the city center in the European tradition, which greatly enhances the vitality and safety of the city. Meanwhile, in Detroit's city center, as in so many other car-dominated cities, the downward spiral appears to continue, despite the efforts to bring people there to shop with the promise of free and easy car parking.

The overall process of becoming more transit-oriented and "centered" was something that the mayor said they were never confident about; they were not sure that they would be able to achieve a city that was moving away from the automobile. But they were surprised by how well it worked. Toronto is now a very vibrant city that, despite some recent problems (see below), is still a model for transit-oriented planning in North America.

The mayor, Art Eggleton, concluded his story in the following way: "Good, efficient public transit and scarce, costly parking is a key to being a successful city . . . The other significant policy in Toronto was bringing people to live in the city center and subcenters."

Recent political decisions in Toronto are threatening to take some of the gloss away from these gains for sustainability as large-scale cuts in the transit system have been implemented, causing reductions in patronage (Perl and Pucher, 1995). Some tragic and bizarre decisions have also been made, such as filling in the tunnel for the Eglinton subway extension to the west toward the airport, after several hundred million dollars had been spent building it (the filling in itself cost a large sum of money). This action was taken based on the present provincial government's belief that the extension was no longer affordable. Indeed, much of the future transit vision established for Toronto in the 1980s under a $5 billion investment program has not gone ahead.

A significant contributor to these problems is the change in urban governance being implemented in Toronto and other Canadian urban regions that is pushing toward a model of fragmentation in urban government, the politics of local self-interest, and harmful competition between municipalities. These changes are tending to favor auto-dependent land use and transportation planning (Raad and Kenworthy, 1998).

Toronto is not easily going to give away the gains it has made over the previous thirty years. For example, parallel with some losses, significant transit improvements are still occurring in places, such as the opening in August 1997 of the Spadina Avenue light rail line, which replaced a host of diesel buses, and the continued construction of the east-west Sheppard subway line, around which further integration of high-density development might occur. However, in the latter part of the decade it appears that the mantle of commitment to transit-oriented development in Canada may have shifted to Montreal and to Vancouver.

Vancouver

The City of Vancouver, the core of the Vancouver region with a 1991 population of some 460,000 people, still does not have an urban freeway. The vibrant downtown and the extensive inner suburbs with their relatively high densities (more than forty persons per hectare) and intensively mixed land uses are not marred by the alienated swaths of freeway land characteristic of U.S. inner cities that sever neighborhoods, decimate the potential for walking and cycling, and create a whole host of local environmental and social problems.

Instead, the main traffic arteries in the City of Vancouver are mostly dense, mixed-use strip developments, with wide sidewalks, pedestrian crossing points every few hundreds meters, and thousands of pedestrians who help to keep the public realm vital, safe, and interesting. Travel speeds are relatively slow, but this is compensated for by greater ease of accessibility to many activities over a small area. In a continent dominated by the automobile, Vancouver has thus retained significant resistance to the excesses of automobile dependence characteristic of so many other Auto Cities. How Vancouver has achieved this outcome is the subject of this case study, and a summary of Vancouver's strategies for attempting to overcome automobile dependence is presented in Table 4.14.

Like all North American cities, Vancouver had grand transportation studies done in the 1950s and 1960s in which prominent transportation consulting firms recommended generous networks of freeways throughout the inner city, focused particularly on the CBD. And just as in Toronto, the fight to keep freeways out of central and inner Vancouver was a community-based movement and occurred roughly around the same time.

Photo 4.19. The Vancouver Skytrain has helped to facilitate the development of dense nodes such as Patterson and Metrotown.

Table 4.14. Vancouver's Strategies for Overcoming Automobile Dependence

Traffic Calming	Favoring Alternate Modes	Economic Penalties	Non-auto-dependent Land Uses
Selected use in areas such as the West End to create pocket parks in the grid network through street closures.	City of Vancouver has no freeways and the greater region has had few road capacity increases in thirty years.	Gasoline surtax in Vancouver region for BC Transit.	Medium- to high-density development throughout much of the region, especially City of Vancouver.
City of Vancouver characterized by a very dense grid of roads with un-controlled inter-sections that form natural barriers to high speeds.	Extensive bus system (diesel and trolley) in City of Vancouver provides good radial and cross-city services well integrated with Skytrain.		Mixed-use, medium-density strips oriented to transit and pedestrians along main roads.
Frequent pedestrian crossings on all main-road com-mercial strips keep traffic at lower speeds.	New light rail sys-tem a priority in transportation infrastructure.		Transit-oriented, mixed-use subcenters around Skytrain stations with good provision for pedes-trians and cyclists.
No pedestrianized city center but bus transit mall on main street in CBD.	Commuter rail system for suburbs being progressively implemented.		
	Good-quality pedestrian and cycling environ-ment throughout much of the city and prioritized in physical planning, especially around subcenters.		

The watershed was the defeat of Vancouver's Strathcona Freeway and the election of an activist city council in the early 1970s to replace the previously pro-freeway one. This fight was centered in the Chinatown area of the City of Vancouver, where the Chinese community hired a young lawyer, Mike Harcourt, to argue their case. Harcourt went on to be part of a city council that fundamentally reoriented the vision for the future of Vancouver toward one based on transit and pedestrian-friendly neighborhoods. It actively facilitated high-density redevelopment, got the False Creek/Granville Island redevelopment off the ground (see earlier section on examples of urban villages), and was instrumental in making the West End of the city what it is today (see later discussion). Harcourt went on to become a Premier of British Columbia.

The absence of large freeways and auto-dominated environments is one claim that Vancouver can now justifiably suggest is a sign of progress—toward sustainability. Indeed, compared to most American cities, the transportation patterns and land use characteristics of the whole Vancouver region are consistent with this claim of significantly greater sustainability. For example, Greater Vancouver enjoys quite high levels of transit use (117 trips per person in 1991, compared to the average for thirteen large U.S. cities of 63 trips per person in 1990), and its car use and road infrastructure provision are both 25 percent below the U.S. city average.

Vancouver has achieved:

- Intensification of housing in the inner area through small- to medium-scale, compact, infill projects near good transit services (mostly electric trolley buses).
- Development of large-scale urban villages close to the city center with good transit service and opportunities for walking or riding safely on segregated cycle systems to many destinations.
- Very rapid integration of new residential and mixed-use development in strong nodes around stations on its driverless, elevated train service known as Skytrain, which opened in 1986.

The City of Vancouver (inner Vancouver) population rose by 40,000 people between 1986 and 1991 due to its strong commitment to reurbanization. But not only is the quantity of the reurbanization impressive, so is the quality of the development, as in the West End example discussed here and the False Creek example in an earlier section.

The historic West End around English Bay is an extremely dense, high-rise neighborhood (second only to Manhattan in North America) that continues to intensify and retain a strong transit orientation through a good trolley bus service linking both a ferry service to North Vancouver (sea bus) and the Skytrain. It is also strong in walking and cycling due to the intense mix of land uses along the main street (Robson Street) and the attractive public environment with its wide sidewalks, as well as magnificent Stanley Park at the foot of the West End.

The West End retains an endearing human quality reflected in the people strolling along the beautifully landscaped, tree-lined residential streets off Robson Street and other main roads, or simply walking, cycling, or using their electric carts to get to the shops or restaurants within a short walk of apartments. There are also small pocket parks formed by numerous, short street closures in which seats and gardens are provided and older people, in particular, congregate to talk. These parks have enhanced the pedestrian quality of the West End through traffic-calming its regular grid of streets, where previously drivers used to speed.

Transit-oriented Subcenters in Vancouver. Earlier a few examples were provided of urban villages that have sprung up around stations on Vancouver's Skytrain. These new subcenters, such as at Metrotown and New Westminster, and smaller developments at other stations, such as Joyce and Edmonds, are all good examples of the kind of dense, mixed-use, transit-oriented development that forms the basis of the future "Sustainable" City concept discussed in this chapter. It is thus important to understand these in more detail than that provided earlier in this chapter, and to appreciate some of the processes that have led to these developments. In some sense, Vancouver provides a living laboratory for understanding how one city has begun to actively reshape itself into a more transit-oriented urban form.

The pace of redevelopment around many Skytrain stations has been extraordinary, and the process is continuing, particularly near the central city. In providing funds to help build Skytrain, the provincial government also presented directions to the local authorities, such as the City of Vancouver, Burnaby, and New Westminster, about the need to actively support the investment in transit through appropriate rezoning of station precinct land for higher-density, mixed uses. However, other important factors have been at work, as described below.

Past population trends in Vancouver were contributing to a number of problems, including increasing distances that Vancouver residents were required to travel between home and work. Automobile dependence and urban sprawl were growing, and air quality and some of the region's valuable open spaces were under pressure (City of Vancouver, 1987b).

Given these problems, the Greater Vancouver Regional District (GVRD) in close collaboration with all the local municipalities, developed a "Liveable Region Strategy," which has contributed significantly to the current positive situation regarding land use intensification within rail station precincts. Plans were formulated for a number of factors in Vancouver, including the conservation of land resources (Greater Vancouver Regional District, 1990). In Vancouver, it has been recognized that the region is limited, especially by topography, in the quantity of land resources available for urban growth, and thus "'green zones" have been established in an "Urban Containment Policy." Under this policy, land beyond designated boundaries has been made unavailable for urban development (Greater Vancouver Regional District, 1990). The process of developing the green zones has been achieved in conjunction with each local authority in the region in order to develop strong ownership and commitment to the plan (Greater Vancouver Regional District, 1995).

Accompanying this was the realization that it was not sustainable in the long term to create residential areas that were primarily served by cars, and therefore appropriate transportation policies accompanied the urban containment policy. Most importantly, this included the encouragement of development at regional centers, based on Skytrain, that allow for walking and cycling within station precincts and easy access to fast, frequent rail travel for longer trips (Greater Vancouver Regional District, 1990).

Skytrain has had a significant effect on the development of station sites in Vancouver for a number of reasons:

1. The notion of regional town centers has been promoted since the first Liveable Region Strategy in the 1970s. The community prepared for change for a decade before Skytrain was built. This meant that regional development policy for the integration of development with Skytrain was basic common sense.

2. There has been a successful partnership between BC Transit and private developers whereby the location and development of stations in the first stage of the system was a joint exercise, including joint financing of station costs.

3. Land at strategic sites near Skytrain was in public ownership.

4. The land with the highest densities was rezoned from industrial land uses (both privately and publicly owned), which meant that surrounding neighborhoods were either accustomed to other uses or were buffered from them. It was unusual in Vancouver for single-family neighborhoods to rise up in opposition to a conversion from industrial to residential land uses, even if they had become accustomed to the industrial or derelict sites.

5. Despite severe criticism, BC Transit consciously decided not to provide any park-and-ride facilities north of the Fraser River—that is, along that major part of the system between the downtown and New Westminster. This prevented any negative effects of these facilities on patronage and avoided the loss of development potential around the stations in the already established communities.

6. The sprawling suburbs in Vancouver have not had the freeway infrastructure to support them. In the thirty years since the Trans-Canada Freeway opened up the Fraser Valley, the only increase in road capacity was the six-lane Alex Fraser Bridge. Over the same period, the regional population in the nineteen suburbs outside the City of Vancouver boundaries rose from 400,000 to 1.3 million people.

7. One of the most important factors in achieving a development form based partly around transit in Vancouver is the scarcity of land in the region. With high land prices, the development industry intensifies development, as there is a market acceptance of higher-density living.

It is realized that zoning does not, by itself, create development unless the market perceives opportunity. British Columbia municipalities intensify sites for higher zonings in their official community plan bylaws, and joint development is actively sought in Vancouver through a proactive government. In the case of the Joyce station area, development was preceded by an extensive station area planning process that dates back to the first announcement of Skytrain in 1981. A strategic industrial site in this area was provided by the City of Vancouver. This site constituted approximately 10 percent of the land that was used for the redevelopment and was an important jump-start to the process (personal communication, Joe Stott, 1996, Greater Vancouver Region District).

Generally, the zoning in Vancouver has resulted from a planning process that has a long tradition of community involvement. Redevelopment is a sensitive issue anywhere in the world, and particular efforts have been made by local authorities in Vancouver to consult with the mostly single-family housing areas to be affected by the changes.

For example, in the City of Vancouver, local area strategies were designed for residents and businesses located within a ten-minute, or 800-meter, walk of stations. This was done through public meetings and the establishment of local advisory committees (City of Vancouver, 1987b).

The plans for intensifying development were pursued with the following specific aims and were supported by a series of specific strategies. The aims were to (City of Vancouver, 1987a, 1987b, 1987c):

- Provide new housing within station precincts without compromising the quality of life for existing residents.
- Create subcenters with diversity and character.
- Encourage medium-density, residential development.
- Encourage commercial, mixed-use development.
- Increase train patronage.
- Reduce the impacts of rail-generated traffic and parking problems (e.g., by enhancing the pedestrian environment).
- Update facilities required to serve future population increases, such as parks and libraries.

An important aspect of these local area strategies was that general, widespread redevelopment within the station precincts was not undertaken. Rather, development was concentrated on publicly owned vacant sites, land severely impacted by the rail system and underutilized or derelict land (City of Vancouver, 1987a). Construction on only these land types helped to reduce community fears that the development was out of character for the local area and that redevelopment within the station precincts would compromise existing lifestyles.

The long-range planning in Vancouver is focused on strengthening its land use–transportation connection and containing urban sprawl by protecting the established green zone, building "complete" communities, concentrating development and increasing transportation choice by enhancing transit supply and service, controlling automobile use, and providing pedestrian and cyclist priority. Plans call for further rail development in the form of a surface light rail system and commuter rail to improve transit and to provide more opportunities for compact development.

The Liveable Region Strategy and Transportation 2021 enshrine this direction, though they have no legal backing to implement them. As in Toronto, it would be possible to undermine this direction if there were transit cutbacks, difficulties in securing funds for transit expansion, and tensions between suburban municipalities and the City of Vancouver (Raad and Kenworthy, 1998). However, in the late 1990s Vancouver has been able to secure a long-term funding package for its transit expansion.

The continued absence of freeways in many parts of the Vancouver region ensures the attractiveness of the inner city and neighborhoods around existing and future transit stations as sites for residential and commercial development.

It will take a lot of bad decisions over a long period to completely undo the positive moves toward enhanced sustainability that Vancouver has made over the last thirty years. As in Toronto, however, vigilance and commitment will be required to ensure that sustainability objectives based around reduced automobile dependence and increased transit orientation continue to be honored in implementation.

Case Study 5: Boulder, Portland, and Boston—U.S. Cities Turning the Tide

The use of cars in U.S. cities continues to grow, with little sign of slowing down. Our survey of global cities outlined in Chapter 3 does not show, however, that this is a universal phenomenon. There are encouraging signs in many European, Canadian, Australian, and Asian cities, but in many U.S. cities the processes of sprawl and highway building seem to be as out of control as ever. Nevertheless, Boulder (population of 88,650 in 1990), Portland (population of 1,412,344 in 1990) and Boston (population of 2,793,701 in 1990) seem to be reflecting a few signs of hope.

Boulder

Data on car usage in Boulder show that demand management efforts shifted 42 percent of former car users who traveled to downtown Boulder to other transportation options. Transit use to the downtown area between 1993 and 1997 rose from 10 percent to 21 percent. This modal shift from the car to alternative forms of transportation took place over a four-year period; it included downtown employees and others who made trips for shopping, eating, business transactions, recreation, or simply to watch other people, especially along the one-kilometer pedestrian Pearl Street Mall. The alternative modes used include bus, bicycle, walking, carpooling, and shuttle service from outlying parking areas (Havlick, 1997).

Boulder has had a policy to try to tame the automobile for the past ten years. It has done this through a range of strategies that are presented in Table 4.15.

In 1993 the Boulder City Council mandated that nearly 20 percent of the city's transportation department annual budget be reallocated away from car-related expenditures such as road widening, double turn lanes, more car parking, more stoplights, and better signalization to alternative mode functions. Over a fifteen-year period this 20 percent budget reallocation will be dedicated to non-car alternatives, such as smaller buses with bicycle racks, improved pedestrian crossings and footpaths, an expanded network of off-roadway bike paths for com-

Photo 4.20. Downtown Boulder has thrived under restricted auto access (*top*). The growth boundary in Boulder is firmly set in a publicly owned green belt (*bottom*).

muters, and user-friendly bus passes (the Ecopass) for university students, employees, and entire neighborhoods. A separate division called GO BOULDER was formed, with a twelve-person staff, within the Transportation Department. GO BOULDER staff members carry out marketing campaigns, coordinate alternate mode innovations, and work on regional traffic demand management schemes. Other cities throughout the Denver metropolitan area consult frequently with GO BOULDER staff in efforts to reduce single-occupancy vehicle (SOV) uses. Experiments are under way to implement peak pricing or congestion pricing of SOVs during rush hour. Programs are in place to reduce traffic and speeding in neighborhoods with roundabouts, speed bumps, photo radar, new small buses, and private shuttle services using main transit corridors.

Specific car disincentive programs have been implemented, such as doubling rates for car parking to more closely reflect parking-lot land values, doubling parking fines, creating neighborhood parking permits for residents only, and reducing the number of car spaces required in new residential and commercial development.

The encouragement of telecommuting, a city-wide bicycle network, 300 free bicycles in the central business district (Spokes for Folks), "Bike to Work" weeks, and bicycle-mounted police officers are part of the demand management strategy to encourage noncar mobility.

The impact of Boulder's initiatives are flowing on to the regional level. The

Table 4.15. Boulder's Strategy for Overcoming Automobile Dependence

Traffic Calming	Favoring Alternate Modes	Economic Penalties	Non-auto-dependent Land Uses
Extensive traffic calming, including pedestrianizing city center.	Strong commitment to bicycle infrastructure.	Congestion pricing for SOVs. Double parking fees and fines.	Growth management and green belt.
Slow zones (thirty kilometers per hour in most residential neighborhoods).	Hop, Skip, and Jump bus system, new rail link, telecommuting, shuttles for kids.	Preferential parking fees for HOVs.	Noise barriers and open land buffers. Urban villages with restricted car ownership.
	Little extra road capacity allowed, cap on parking with assistance to park on CBD edge.	Mixed use in centers.	
Enforcement including digital speed displays, double fines in slow areas.	Ecopass, free bikes, bus passes, computerized carpooling, flextime, four-day week.		

Denver Regional Transportation District (RTD) has installed bike racks on all 1,400 buses. Bike paths are being designed with regional intercity connections. Boulder is being included in plans for passenger rail connections because of the proven demand for alternative transportation modes. Other towns and cities in Boulder County and the Denver Regional Council of Government (DRCOG) jurisdiction are either duplicating Boulder's car-taming experiments or asking that they be considered.

The Hop, Skip, and Jump bus system is an example of metropolitan regional cooperation with the major mass transit provider in the Denver metro area. The large, diesel-burning Regional Transit District (RTD) bus service was very underused in Boulder. They were seen as "intruders" and out of place in the streets of Boulder. They were considered not only as noisy, polluting, and inefficient (most were empty), but also as antisocial. The staff of GO BOULDER and the Boulder City Council recognized this and began to work out an arrangement whereby the City of Boulder would help finance a colorful fleet of small (twenty-four-passenger) circulator buses called the "Hop" in cooperation with the RTD. It was a very successful eighteen-month experiment that carried 1.5 million passengers.

As a follow-up to the present Hop circulator buses, a major north-south RTD large-bus route was replaced (with city and University of Colorado student funding) by fifteen small buses called the Skip, complete with bike racks and circulating on a ten-minute interval. The Skip service began in August 1997. The third phase is called the Jump, which is planned to connect other nearby cities with direct express service to Boulder.

Boulder's land use strategies are a critical part of its overall strategy. Traffic calming or car elimination is an integral part of land use regulation and zoning in Boulder's comprehensive plan. Mixed-use development (work-live proximity), neighborhood market centers, and rezoning of commercial land to reduce jobs and car trips began in 1997. Building permits that show little or no need for SOV use are given priority under the 1 percent per annum growth management scheme for Boulder (Havlick, 1997).

Boulder's growth management program has been the focus of a great deal of attention. This program sets a very clear growth boundary with surrounding land being purchased for regional open space. According to Deputy Mayor Spence Havlick, "This sends a strong signal to the marketplace that low-quality, car-dependent urban sprawl is not what is being demanded in Boulder" (Havlick, personal communication, 1997). The result has been a strong and very popular green belt now in place, and far from scaring away development, Boulder has attracted higher-quality development that is building up the city in a less car-dependent way.

Boulder has shown how local government can begin the process of overcoming automobile dependence in a way that is better for the economy, a distinct improvement for the environment, and strongly supported by the community.

Portland

Portland's strategies for overcoming automobile dependence are presented in Table 4.16.

Photo 4.21. The Portland light rail system, MAX, moves quickly through a restored market area where the Mt. Hood Freeway was planned to be built (*top*). Pioneer Square replaced a downtown parking structure (*bottom*).

Portland went through a painful period of assessing its future during the 1970s when it planned to build the Mt. Hood Expressway through the city, a project that would have demolished 3,000 homes. When it was decided not to build it but instead to opt for a light rail system (MAX), the majority of transportation experts laughed. It was dubbed the "streetcar named expire," as expert transportation professionals anticipated that in a modern U.S. city it would be impossible to get people out of their cars. Their predictions were that the system would be a hopeless failure.

It is very hard to find any of those people today. The MAX light rail line is a transportation success story, with a doubling of the patronage over the bus system it replaced and a large off-peak usage by families, especially on weekends going into the city to the popular downtown market area through which MAX runs. The only political problem with the decision to opt for light rail instead of a freeway is that now so many other corridors want MAX. As a result, plans are being

Table 4.16. Portland's Strategies for Overcoming Automobile Dependence

Traffic Calming	Favoring Alternate Modes	Economic Penalties	Non-auto-dependent Land Uses
Extensive traffic calming and pedestrianization in city center, particularly traffic lane reduction to accommodate transit.	Historic cap on parking in the CBD.	Cap on parking in CBD.	Region-wide growth management strategy seeks to limit new urban land development and to focus all new growth in existing areas, especially around the light rail system (MAX).
	Scrapping of some freeways in favor of transit development, especially light rail.		
Reclaim Your Street program to institute traffic calming in local areas.	Priorities (to both buses and rail) in central city.		Significant new development appears around MAX stations.
			Revitalization of public spaces in CBD.
			Strong program to focus residential development in CBD, where pedestrians, cyclists, and transit are priority modes.

developed to extend the LRT in a number of directions, and the first of these, to the west toward Beaverton, has begun.

But there have been several other important side effects and changes that have occurred in downtown Portland in parallel with the introduction of MAX. One is that the city center has come alive through a constructive partnership between the business community and City of Portland planners working toward a more livable, human, and economically vital city. For example, some of the business community recognized the opportunity provided by MAX and took the initiative to help repave some of the city streets with cobblestones made of ballast from the old sailing ships that once plied the Willamette River. Together with strong support at the city level through visionary planning and progressive urban design, the downtown area of Portland has been gradually reinvented around the idea that it should be a human, livable environment in which people can walk, sit, dine alfresco, be entertained, and find residence in housing set in attractive public environments. Involvement of the wider community has been important in setting this trend, symbolically expressed in the thousands of individually inscribed bricks making up Pioneer Square in the heart of Portland.

Part of the downtown revitalization process was to introduce lots of trees, seats, flower planters, sculptures, period lighting, artwork, and many other elements of good urban design at the street level. A central city, multistorey parking garage was torn down and replaced with a public meeting place, and a downtown freeway was replaced with a riverfront park. In addition, lanes have been taken away from traffic on the two main streets along which MAX runs. The space has been used to provide an exclusive right-of-way for the trains and to widen footpaths, plant trees, and provide flower planters. Bus-priority streets running across MAX lines have also limited cars to one lane and have been significantly improved with generous tree plantings and high-quality bus shelters incorporating comprehensive transit system information.

On top of these factors, the City of Portland strongly supported, over many years, the residential revitalization of downtown Portland and a ceiling on parking provision that held parking spaces more or less constant, despite significant growth in jobs in the downtown area. Combined with transit priority measures, downtown jobs increased 50 percent with no increase in car commuting to the central area (Arrington, 1993). Residential projects have included the attractive River Place development, described earlier in this chapter in the section on examples of urban villages.

In combination with the introduction in 1986 of the completed MAX light rail line, central Portland has begun to take on the air of a European city, so unlike the average U.S. city. The city center is now probably the most attractive in the United States.

Through a combination of enhanced transit access, human attractions, and extra housing, rather than more road space and parking, the downtown improved its competitiveness in the local economy by increasing from 5 percent to 30 percent of the metropolitan area's total retail turnover.

The other spin-off has occurred in the suburbs, where citizens keyed up by their victory over the freeway have started to push for traffic calming. In response, city government has begun a "Reclaim Your Street" project whereby residents and local government together are planning how to slow down traffic and make it easier for pedestrians and cyclists.

Finally, the city has recognized that MAX provides the opportunity to develop an integrated approach to land development. It has now developed a plan to curtail outer area growth and direct it to urban redevelopment around transit stops; 85 percent of all new growth must now be within five minutes' walk of a designated transit stop. This is the highest commitment to growth management in the United States.

A whole metropolitan region cannot change overnight, and Portland's overall transit patronage is still low despite the good results in the MAX corridor, but this will grow as the LRT is extended. Portland has shown that it has a new direction based on reconnecting its city to good transit services and that it is not inevitable for the automobile to continue to dominate the city.

Boston

Boston's patterns of automobile dependence are beginning to show some signs of reversal. Though fewer than in the cities discussed above, Boston's strategies for overcoming automobile dependence are presented in Table 4.17.

Some of the data from our global cities study in Chapter 3 are summarized in Table 4.18, which highlights the position of Boston relative to the average U.S. city, as well as to Australian and Canadian cities, European cities, and Asian cities. It shows that although Boston is very much a U.S. city in its overall transportation patterns, it does appear to be restraining growth in car use and improving transit use. This case study examines some reasons behind these positive trends.

Photo 4.22. Boston, the U.S. city with the least growth in car use and the most evidence of reurbanization, has a vibrant inner city (North End) (*left*) and downtown (Quincy Market) (*right*).

Table 4.17. Boston's Strategies for Overcoming Automobile Dependence

Traffic Calming	Favoring Alternate Modes	Economic Penalties	Non-auto-dependent Land Uses
Large parts of Cambridge and the inner city have widened sidewalks and encouraged cycling and walking.	New rail lines as part of central area redevelopment. Ban on inner radial road expansion. Low transit fares.	Gasoline tax used for MBTA. Parking supply freezes for twenty years	Reurbanization of inner city facilitated (community policing). Park creation and improvement.

As discussed in Chapter 3, the data show U.S. cities not only using cars at a much higher rate than other cities, but the increase in the car use per capita in the 1980s is higher than in the previous two decades. The increase in car use per capita is an extraordinary 2,113 kilometers per capita, almost equal to the total use of cars in 1980 by residents in some European cities, such as London, Paris, and Amsterdam. And this increase occurred in a decade when many people were predicting that suburbanization of jobs would begin to slow down car use in U.S. cities (e.g., Gordon and Richardson, 1989).

Only Boston has shown a reduction in its car use growth rate—from an

Table 4.18. Transportation Patterns in Forty-six Global Cities, Highlighting Boston, 1990

	U.S. Cities	Boston	Australian and Canadian Cities	European Cities	Asian Cities
Car use per capita (kilometers)	11,155	10,280	6,560	4,519	1,727
Percent of total transportation (passenger kilometers) on transit	3.1%	3.5%	9.1%	22.6%	48.2%
Percent journey-to-work on public transit	9.0%	14.7%	17.3%	38.8%	45.0%
Percent journey-to-work on foot and bike	4.6%	7.4%	5.7%	18.4%	19.0%
Car use increase 1980–90 (kilometers per capita)	+2,113	1,428	+907	+993	+647
Transit use increase 1980–90 (trips per capita)	6	34	−5	+38	+37

increase of 55 percent in the 1960s, to 39 percent in the 1970s, to 16 percent in the 1980s. The latter was two-thirds of the average U.S. city increase in car use from 1980 to 1990. It is still, however, a lot more driving and has helped to create more traffic problems in Boston, but it is a small ray of light in an otherwise dark story for the larger U.S. metropolitan regions.

How did this hopeful change come about? First, there has been significant growth in the number of transit trips taken in Boston—from 80 to 114 per person per year. This is now nearly twice the U.S. average, but is still well below other cities in Europe or even those in Canada, where the seven largest urban regions average some 141 trips per capita per year. The increase in Boston occurred mostly in the rail system (as in most cities in our global survey). However, this cannot explain all the difference between Boston and other U.S. cities, as the increase in passenger kilometers on transit of 109 kilometers per annum from 1980 to 1990 is equivalent to a little more than the replacement of 64 kilometers of per capita car travel (if it is just a simple transfer of car use to transit use at the average overall car occupancy for Boston of 1.69). This reduction in car use is not enough, even considering the so-called transit leverage effect, which is the extra savings in car use when people start using transit—for example, some car travel is replaced as people tend to shop or incorporate other essential activities on the way to the train, or even manage without a second car if they decide to switch to transit. This factor is perhaps up to five times the direct travel replacement (see previous discussion on mixed land use).

We still need to explain why Bostonians had a lower increase in their use of cars of an additional 1,000 kilometers or so per year. It would appear that some other urban processes are at work in Boston that are reducing the need to travel. As noted many times in this book, the key to beginning the process of reducing car use is reurbanization.

Boston's data are similar to the trends found in Australian cities, where in the 1960s car use grew at 53 percent per capita per year, decreasing to 29 percent in the 1970s and to 14 percent in the 1980s. This has occurred without much change in transit and seems to be related to a large-scale revitalization of inner-city living. Inner-city residents have far lower car use—in Australia it is about two to three times less, but in New York it is more than four times less—than outer suburbs residents with their greater inherent automobile dependence (in 1990 it was 3,200 kilometers per capita car travel in Manhattan, compared to 13,000 kilometers per capita in outer suburbs).

A similar process appears to be happening in Boston. The inner city (roughly the City of Boston) increased in population by 14,000 and in jobs by 51,000 between 1980 and 1990. This is a major reversal, particularly in population, since in the 1970s inner Boston lost 85,000 residents, in common with big declines in most U.S. inner cities. Of the U.S. cities in this study, only in Boston, San Francisco, and Portland was there a reversal in these patterns of decline, and in these latter cases the proportion of reurbanization is smaller than in Boston. It is not unrelated that Boston has also had a dramatic reduction in its inner-city crime rate (pursued further in Chapter 7, "Churches and Sustainability").

The revitalization of Boston's inner city is a signal to the rest of the United States that suburban sprawl and decline of inner cities is not inevitable; it can be reversed. This is highly significant for achieving a more sustainable U.S. city.

The revival of older areas of Boston can go much further. Opportunities for infill and rehabilitation are obvious in many parts of the city. The city center itself has some wonderful development sites, especially the Seaport area and once the Central Arterial Tunnel is completed, offering a chance to build inner-city housing that should not be missed. Such development will be an obvious boost to the local economy, but it will have much better flow-ons to the wider Boston economy as well. As Boston continues to show U.S. cities how to reurbanize, it is predicted that it will do better economically than other U.S. cities, which continue to develop almost entirely on the basis of car-based development.

The above suggests that innovation in urban sustainability begins in the inner city. It can then spread to other parts of the city and suburbs. The design qualities and human scale of Newbury Street or some of the center of Cambridge can now be translated to suburban centers. This will be the next big challenge for Boston.

In comparison to patterns of change outlined in this book in Europe and Asia, the 1980s in U.S. cities were a lost decade—except for some small signs in cities such as Boulder, Boston, and Portland. Perhaps these three cities can build on this fledgling start as the innovative U.S. cities. Perhaps they can show that controlling car use growth is one of the keys to economic health in the next century. Perhaps they can show how revitalizing neighborhoods with traffic calming and mixed-use developments can become so attractive politically that it becomes normal practice. Perhaps they can start the trickle that becomes a flood as U.S. cities recognize that returning to a more urban way of life is not only the way to stop urban sprawl and develop more sustainable transportation, but that there are many more opportunities for livability that come with such a change.

There is much that any city can learn about sustainability from other cities; however, in the United States there has been a long-held belief that the kind of changes we have discussed in Europe or even Canada could not work there. The importance of cities such as Boulder, Portland, and Boston is that they are showing that U.S. cities can be reshaped to begin overcoming automobile dependence in ways that fit *their* culture and values.

Case Study 6: Perth, a Hesitant Start in Australia

The data on Perth (population of 1,142,646 in 1991) in Chapter 3 show a city almost completely in the automobile-dependent category. Some of the limits of this are being seen, and thus the beginning of a process to overcome automobile dependence is evident (Table 4.19).

For more than fifty years new suburbs have been built in Perth on the assumption that the majority of people will not need a high-profile transit service. Thus suburbs were built at uniformly low densities of ten to fifteen persons per hectare and without access to rail services. This left suburbs with a subsidized bus service that rarely came more than hourly at off-peak times. It is not surprising that the Perth suburban lifestyle rapidly became highly automobile-dependent.

Photo 4.23. Central Perth Station. Perth's restored, electrified, and extended rail system has shown that growth in automobile dependence is not inevitable.

Despite the high degree of automobile dependence in all Australian cities, recent trends indicate a slowing down in the use of cars in all and a turn-around in transit in some cities. This seems to be a reflection of a growing desire by many Australians to return to the city. The decline of the inner city has reversed, and now a major part of all new residential and commercial development is in established areas, with a strong demand for housing close to good urban facilities, particularly rail services. This trend toward more transit-oriented urban life is now beginning to occur in some very car-dependent suburbs.

One such corridor in Perth was the city's northern suburbs, which grew rapidly in the 1960s and 1970s on the low-density, car-dependent model. Two corridors set aside for rail systems from the original metropolitan plan of 1955 were removed in the 1960s as planners saw no future for rail transit and believed that all necessary transit services could be provided by buses.

By the 1980s, however, the freeway serving the corridor was clogged at peak hour and the community was dissatisfied with the bus service. A strong political push for rail service resulted in the Northern Suburbs Rapid Transit System (Newman, 1993). The new thirty-three-kilometer electric rail line has only seven stations, which permits a very rapid service reaching a maximum speed of 110 kilometers per hour. The service runs along the center of a freeway, which is far from ideal for land development, but it has been designed to link closely with bus services that interchange passengers directly onto the stations. This allows cross-suburban bus services to be provided because the station nodes have become the focus for bus routes rather than the CBD. Another benefit of the rail

Table 4.19. Perth's Strategies for Overcoming Automobile Dependence

Traffic Calming	Favoring Alternate Modes	Economic Penalties	Non-auto-dependent Land Uses
Central city area becoming progressively more traffic-calmed and pedestrianized, though much remains to be done.	High investment in upgraded and extended electric rail through the 1980s. Commitment to further extend rail system.	Fuel tax, but used entirely for roads.	Recent extensive new central city housing projects, including revitalization of old industrial land for resident/mixed-use development.
Traffic calming or local area traffic management practiced on ad hoc basis throughout the region.	New bus service initiatives to improve cross-city travel (circle route), plus upgraded bus stops and information systems.		Beginnings of urban-village-style development around rail stations through sinking of line at one station and large redevelopment project.
Some good examples in many local centers.	A good off-road network of cycleways, especially for recreation, and increasing attention to direct, on-road routes for commuting and other trips.		A focus on land use planning to discourage automobile dependence in regional centers.
Forty-kilometer-per-hour zones around schools.	Some favoring of pedestrian, cycle, and transit access at regional centers over last five years.		Development of community code to encourage urban villages in any new urban development.

service's fast freeway route is that motorists stuck in stalled traffic get a good look at the advantages of unimpeded urban rail travel.

The new service has been extremely successful, but it reveals, more than anything else, the problem of transportation planners not believing sufficiently in the ability of good transit to succeed in modern cities. Three predictions were made, which all proved to be wrong, as presented in Box 4.6.[16]

Perth has a long way to go before it overcomes its automobile dependence. There has, however, been a positive trend in land values near the transit stations that may enable development of transit-oriented urban villages. This process has

Box 4.6 The Northern Suburbs Rapid Transit System in Perth: Predictions, Results, and Conclusions

- *Prediction:* Rail will lose patronage over the already existing express buses, since people don't like transferring from bus to rail.
- *Result:* In the first year of operation there was a 40 percent *increase* with rail-bus use over bus-only use in the corridor. This had grown to a 56 percent increase a few years later.
- *Conclusion:* People will transfer if they can move to a superior, reliable form of service.

- *Prediction:* You will never get people out of their cars, since the freeway is so good and parking is so easy in Perth.
- *Result:* Twenty-five percent of the patrons on the new northern rail line gave up using their cars for the journey-to-work in the first year of operation.
- *Conclusion:* Even in an automobile-dependent city people can give up their cars.

- *Prediction:* The rail system will be a financial disaster.
- *Result:* The system was completed on budget and on time, winning many awards for engineering and architecture. It is almost breaking even in operating costs, though, unlike roads such as the freeway down which it runs, whose capital funds come from grants, it must still service a US$195 million capital debt.
- *Conclusion:* If people are given a good option, then rail infrastructure can be viable in modern, automobile-dependent cities and can do better than roads financially, given a level playing field in funding.

happened on some of the other three electric train lines, but will require some rather special design for the northern line because it is in freeway alignment. Plans are now being developed for extensions to the rail service to the south and for an orbital light rail line linking Perth's car-based shopping centers and universities. The potential success of such a line is highlighted by the overwhelming success of the first stages of a bus-based "circle route" introduced in 1998. The aim of such transit innovations is to try not only to provide the city with better transit, but to build many more transit-oriented urban villages, as discussed in this chapter.

The federal government in Australia established a US$638 million fund to build model transit-oriented urban villages in all major cities as a way of demonstrating this new and important way of coping with the automobile. The program, called "Better Cities," has several very successful demonstrations in Perth. Such developments have been shown to save Australian cities very large amounts of money from less expenditure on new infrastructure and transportation, compared to development at the urban fringe, as well as a much improved environment (Kenworthy and Newman, 1992; Diver, Newman, and Kenworthy, 1996; see also Appendix 4). The integration of the urban village model into the structure of Perth's planning system has now occurred (as a voluntary model) after the government recognized that its traditional approach was no longer providing an economically viable solution to city development in the Information Age (WA Planning Commission, 1997).

The kinds of concepts in many of these urban villages are also being built into the Sydney 2000 Olympic Village as a demonstration of Australian urban sustainability. These are small starts in an urban policy history that until recently was almost totally dominated by the inevitability of automobile dependence.

Conclusions

The sustainability agenda has pushed the world toward a reconsideration of how cities are built. The biggest threat to sustainability in cities is automobile dependence. The "Sustainable" City concept outlined here illustrates how the Auto City could change over time and be more sustainable. It brings together, among other things, the processes of reurbanization, traffic calming, state-of-the-art transit and bicycle planning, the New Urbanism design of streets for pedestrians, growth management, economic penalties on private transportation, and transit-oriented development planning in new and old suburbs, particularly the development of urban villages. These concepts are to a degree idealistic, but as has been shown, they are well under way in a number of innovative cities.

Singapore and Hong Kong are showing how some of these approaches can be implemented in spectacularly successful ways within booming economies susceptible to rapid motorization. There are some true success stories in Europe, particularly in Zurich, Copenhagen, Stockholm, and Freiburg. And in Canada there are clear success stories as well, with Toronto and Vancouver having some excellent sustainability characteristics.

Very heavy automobile dependence in American and Australian cities make success stories there harder to find. However, the case studies presented here on Boulder, Portland, and Boston in the United States and Perth in Australia show that there are signs of a commitment to tackling automobile dependence taking shape, and of course these selected studies are by no means exhaustive. There are innovative things happening in many cities. The case studies do offer some hope, although few U.S. and Australian cities have truly integrated, coherent plans to overcome automobile dependence, and most are relying too much on technological advances in the automobile to resolve more fundamental problems in the planning of their cities. Both countries are still heavily subsidizing the car and new suburb building. But the signs of change in the way communities and planners think about their cities are emerging in a number of ways through individual projects that, for example, improve transit, begin demonstrating alternative, compact land use patterns based around transit, and tame the automobile in selected centers and streets through traffic calming. What appears to be needed is a process whereby such approaches are coordinated better and become the mainstream professional praxis, developing their own sets of technical standards, manuals, and regulations to ensure their consistent application in the process of urban and transportation planning (see Chapter 6).

However, as discussed in Chapter 1, overcoming automobile dependence is not the only aspect of sustainability that needs to be considered. Chapter 5 shows how the other elements relating to the greening of a city can be simultaneously achieved while moving toward a city with reduced automobile dependence.

Notes

1. The data trends show that, in general, European cities were reducing in density but at a slower rate than U.S. cities. Now they are reversing; Stockholm, for example, grew in density in all city sectors in the 1980s and also grew in wealth.

2. See, for example, the many publications from the Center for Livable Communities that all appear to show this change in urban values.

3. An interesting variation on this occurs in Calgary, Canada, which is renowned for its frigid winters. Here the planners say that the reason Calgarians like their low-density, single-family homes so much is because the climate is so cold. How so? "Well, if you live in such an awful climate, you want to be able to rush outside as soon as the weather turns nice!" (Calgary City Planner, personal communication, 1995).

4. "It might just be that here, in the biggest State in the sparsest continent, we love space . . . It may be a faintly amusing concept to many of us to imagine Perth people crammed together in a transportation efficient city on the edge of the wheat-belt and outback, and next to the void of the Indian Ocean" (Director General of Transport, 1982, p. 65).

5. Indeed, as is shown in our latest data, Stockholm is the only city that actually lowered its per capita use of cars a little between 1980 and 1990; it grew in transit use from 302 to 348 trips per capita and, at the same time, grew in density in its central city, inner city, and outer area.

6. Snell and others (e.g., Holtz Kay, 1997) also highlight the role of the "National Highway Users Conference," pioneered by General Motors' Alfred Sloan, which, in 1932, brought together automobile, oil, and other highway interests to lobby for road funds and an end to mass transit funding. The result was the U.S. Highway Trust Fund, through which the U.S. government spent $1,845 million on highways between 1952 and 1970, while rail systems received only $232 million. The establishment of this fund and its massive spending on the U.S. Interstate Highway System initiated automobile-dependent trends that have continued to grow steadily to the present day. Between 1981 and 1995 the spending on federal highways in the United States grew from $9 billion to $19 billion while transit remained at $4 billion. It is not hard to see why U.S. cities continued their rapid car use growth in the 1980s.

7. Todd Litman's Victoria Transport Policy Institute has done considerable work on this concept and its cost implications; see www.islandnet.com/~litman.

8. For a more detailed discussion of traffic evaporation, see Phil Goodwin's work at www.ucl.ac.uk/~ucetwww/pbginau.htm.

9. Technological change is often seen to be rapid (in comparison to land use change), but as Mees (1999) points out the promise is rarely eventuated; for example, the fleet fuel efficiency of Australian cars has moved from 11.4 liters/100 km to 11.5

liters/100 km in 35 years. The promise of pricing seems even more illusory. Those cities without the political ability to force vehicle efficiencies or to increase the price of automobile use to account for its true costs will need to do even more in the planning area to minimize car use expansion.

10. More detail on this is provided in Appendix 6.

11. For a summary of car-free housing in Europe, based on car sharing, see Jan Scheurer's (1998a) "Car-free Housing in Europe: A New Approach to Sustainable Residential Development" on wwwistp@central.murdoch.edu.au in the "Sustainability Planning Network" section. Details on car-sharing programs can be found on www.mobility.ch/links.

12. Even though False Creek is not presently linked directly to rail service, its proximity to a variety of trolley bus routes and its walking/cycling distance to downtown ensure that it works well from a transportation perspective. There are, however, plans to link it to a light rail system via an old freight right-of-way that runs at the rear of the development.

13. The revival of supermarket home-delivery vans in the world's inner cities has shown that a car is not necessarily needed for shopping trips.

14. It should be noted, however, that a few kilometers of the northern end of the Spadina, known today as the Allen Expressway, were constructed and cause a number of problems for transit operation due to traffic it attracts and the impossibility of developing transit-oriented land use patterns.

15. The location of the northern end of the Spadina subway line in the middle of the Allen Expressway has, however, inhibited the strong nodal development characteristic of other parts of the subway system—development that is clearly visible from the air as clusters of high-rise development above and around many subway stations.

16. The Perth rail system has grown from 8 million passengers per year in 1991 to 30 million passengers per year in 1997; this extraordinary growth is due to the replacement of an old diesel rail system by a fast electric service. Adelaide and Auckland continued in the 1990s to use a slow diesel system and both have remained static and low in their patronage.

Chapter 5

Greening the Automobile-dependent City

Introduction

So far in this book, we have tried to show what sustainability means in the fundamental shape of the city, how transportation priorities have been such a force in this, and how planners and other urban managers can do much to create a more sustainable urban form. The major global and local environmental issues addressed by this approach include the need to reduce energy use, regional air pollution, and greenhouse gases; the need to reduce urban sprawl; and the need to minimize the local impact of traffic. Other livability issues are closely linked to this through the economics of efficient use of infrastructure and the importance of pedestrian-scale interactions for the development of community.

There are, however, other aspects of sustainability in cities we have not yet addressed. They mostly relate to how the urban system fits into its local ecosystem. These issues include the water supply, stormwater and sewage system, the material inputs and solid waste management system, and the greening issues of urban parks and urban agriculture. All these are linked by the need for a city to fit more closely into the natural cycles in the bioregion in which it is located. If a city does not address these issues, then it is not participating in the local sustainability agenda.

These matters have not been addressed in this book until now because we believe that the context for sustainability is to at least begin by addressing global greening issues. If a city were to begin by addressing its local greening issues, it is possible to end up not being able to address the larger issues that relate to automobile dependence.

Sustainability has come from a global political agenda, and those who neglect the global and say that only the local matters, are not doing justice to the concept or their responsibilities as global citizens. The city is not ultimately going to be able to continue to hide its head in the local and hope that the wider issues will go away—this is one of the fundamental problems, for example, of "gated communities." On the other hand, as will become evident below, it is difficult to do anything about the global unless the actions are simultaneously local. Sustainability requires us to be innovative on the local and global issues—together.

240

Having examined how an automobile-dependent city needs to address its problems, it is now feasible to see how we can also, simultaneously, be addressing local greening issues, and to see how the issues overlap. This chapter therefore examines:

- the urban water system and how the sustainability agenda is changing our approach to managing the total urban water cycle;
- how to resolve some underlying conflicts about the best way to green a city and, in particular, whether greening a city is in conflict with reducing automobile dependence; and
- local urban ecology, what it means, and how it raises questions about global approaches to sustainability, and in particular the urban ecology innovations occurring in Denmark.

Sustainability and the Urban Water System

In the same way that sustainability is forging a new paradigm for transportation planning, it is beginning to change the way that people manage the water cycle in cities. The same basic processes are causing the rethink:

- the need to take the environment seriously, and to integrate this with economic considerations;
- the importance of understanding how infrastructure changes land use;
- the need for more holistic approaches that see the city as an ecosystem; and
- the critical role of local community processes in future management.

The approach discussed below looks at the total water cycle and begins with an historical perspective on how cities have managed the water cycle. To do this requires a perspective on how transportation infrastructure and water infrastructure are linked to urban form.

The Walking, Transit, and Auto City Urban Forms and Water Management

Much of today's urban water management and technology was developed in the nineteenth century. In the walking-based pre-nineteenth century cities (as shown in Figure 2.1), water was managed with a localized supply and treatment—that is, local wells and small, household toilets that were either just a hole in the ground or a container that was collected and taken to nearby fields for agricultural use. Small Walking Cities were able to manage quite adequately without the need for more extensive water supply, sewage collection, or treatment. Rainwater was collected frequently and stored in cisterns, and drainage was a part of street and alley design.

When the Industrial Revolution came, however, and cities grew rapidly, it was no longer feasible to manage cities in this way. The much greater quantities of water needed and the associated increase in sewage, as well as the increased stormwater from the larger urban area, generated the need for new technology, new management processes, and new urban form. The Transit City (Figure 2.2)

Box 5.1. Nineteenth-century Solutions to Urban Water Management

Water Supply	Stormwater	Sewage
• Large-scale water and supply system from a few large water sources via long pipes.	• Collect and discharge to receiving waters, usually through pipes.	• Collect by pipes and discharged, after some treatment, to nearest receiving waters; based on dilution.
	• Engineer water courses and drains like "big pipes."	

not only provided a new way to solve the problem of where people lived and worked and moved around, but it provided a way to manage water as presented in Box 5.1. In addition to rail tracks to solve transportation problems, city engineers found other linear technologies to solve their water problems. They developed the "big pipes" engineering approach—both for bringing water in and for removing waste water. This technology was closely associated with the particular form of the Transit City—the dense linear corridors along which linear infrastructure could easily fit.

The highly centralized kind of city in urban form gave rise to a highly centralized water management approach. This "big pipes,"centralized approach, in which the engineer applies the same technique to every city and is not only the expert but the source of power, we now describe as "modernist." Even the watercourses of cities were straightened out and "disciplined" into pipelike drains.

With the twentieth century and the automobile, cities have increased considerably in population and have sprawled extensively in area and in every direction with low-density development (Figure 2.3). Along with the problems of automobile dependence outlined earlier in the book, there are now problems with water management in such Auto Cities. This is because the large, sprawling city is approaching new limits in the capacity of surrounding water supplies and receiving waters, there is new awareness of the ecological value of natural water systems, and there are new constraints on the economics of providing the infrastructure for the nineteenth century "big pipes"–oriented solutions (CEPA, 1993) (see Box 5.2).

Water and the Sustainable Future City

The Future City needs to provide not only a more sustainable transportation system, but also an integrated solution to the need for a more socially sensitive, economically efficient, and environmentally responsible urban water management system.

The processes for rebuilding the urban form of the Auto City are well under way in some cities and are based on reducing automobile dependence, as discussed in previous chapters.

> **Box 5.2. Environmental Problems with Nineteenth-century Urban Water Management Approaches in the Twentieth-century Auto Cities**
>
> - Receiving waters cannot sustain the organic loads, and especially nutrient loads, from sewage treatment outfalls.
> - Urban creeks and wetlands are now valued inherently (i.e., for their ecological and recreational qualities rather than their ability to channel or dilute wastes).
> - Stormwater from sprawling, asphalt-based cities is excessive in quantity and quality.
> - Water supply augmentation solutions (big dams and large aquifer drawdowns) are becoming economically and environmentally questionable.

The goals for sustainability as far as water management is concerned are presented in Box 5.3.

The fundamental goal is to restore the natural systems around and within a city so that they have more of their ecological integrity. Removing all "big pipe" ocean and river outfalls presupposes that another means of treatment and recycling is found (discussed further below). Ecological integrity also means that urban creeks can be restored to provide a more diverse habitat than when they were turned into concrete stormwater drains. The process can be undertaken in ways that improve flood control as the water flow is slowed down and a lot of water is able to recharge aquifers rather than being channeled away as quickly as possible (see Register, 1987; Hough, 1984).

It is also possible, and indeed it is necessary, to build more soft surfaces into the city so that stormwater is able to be absorbed rather than being forced into pipes. This means less asphalt, which in a city such as Los Angeles is about 30 to 40 percent, and in some places can be more than 60 percent of the land area due to the excessive parking and road area requirements of a highly automobile-

> **Box 5.3. Water-oriented Goals for a Sustainable City**
>
> - Ocean and river outfalls no longer necessary.
> - Recycling of water for various urban and peri-urban uses.
> - Recycling of nutrients and organics.
> - Creeks and wetlands an integral part of the city but managed for their ecological integrity.
> - Increased soft surfaces (and reduced urban sprawl) for stormwater retention.
> - Reduced requirement for large pipes.

dependent city. Berry et al. (1974) found that the more automobile-dependent, low-density cities in the United States had the largest stormwater pollution problems.

The goals listed in Box 5.3 go against much traditional civil and sanitary engineering practice, particularly making outfalls unnecessary. They also challenge most of the highly centralized water management systems that have grown up with the old modernist paradigm. It will require new technology and new urban management processes in order to create a more water-sustainable Future City.

New Urban Water Technologies and Management Systems

The kind of urban water technologies and management processes that are being developed with potential to solve the problems of the future "Sustainable" City, within the new ecological and economic constraints, are presented in Box 5.4.

New Urban Water Technologies

Revising technical approaches to water would entail a variety of interlinking technologies that mean less water is needed, less rain and stormwater are harvested, and less wastewater is recycled.

In recent years, particularly in dry regions such as many in Australia, there has been a concerted effort to develop a whole range of water-conserving technologies, mainly at the domestic level. For example, the low-flow tap fittings and the new ultra-low-flush dual-flush toilet make a contribution to sustainability. Similarly, outside the home and in public open space, modern irrigation technology now has electronic control systems and low-water approaches to private and public open space (Hill and Nicholson, 1989). All these technologies reflect the progress in reducing water supply demands. As with automobile dependence, however, the water issue is not just about more-efficient technology, but about creating an urban system that has inherently less requirement for water. This means land use patterns with less need for water and a greater reuse of stormwater and wastewater locally (Clark, 1990).

Box 5.4. Water and Sustainable Cities

New Urban Water Technologies	New Urban Water Management Processes
• Small-scale high-quality sewage treatment	• Water-sensitive design processes.
• Localized stormwater treatment and recycling	• Total water cycle planning
• Water harvesting for localized supply purposes management	• Urban integrated catchment
• Water-efficient appliances, fittings, and technologies	• Localized community processes in water management

At the same time, we must recognize that the continual flux of nutrients being transferred (through the water system) from land to natural water systems is not sustainable. For the sake of nutrient conservation, these cycles must be closed, and the production of useful biomass from these wastewater resources must be a minimum target. Similarly, the nondegradable toxic substances in these fluxes must be prevented from entering food chains.

With urban stormwater, the traditional emphasis has been focused on the "conveyance" approach, with the primary objective of flood protection. In recent years, as a result of the increasing recognition of the environmental impact of urban stormwater on receiving water bodies, there has been a marked shift toward the "storage approach," where retention, detention, and recharge are the design focus, along with other objectives, such as protection and enhancement of the social and ecological values of urban water environments. It has become increasingly apparent that a whole range of "best management practices" are available for stormwater quality enhancement through our urban catchments; these involve simple biological processes rather than "end of pipe" technologies. If incorporated into local greening projects, they can become a part of the rejuvenation of parts of a city. (See the case study on San Antonio's River Walk.)

The next step is to see whether this shift in attitude to retaining stormwater can be extended to seeing stormwater as a resource for various uses. Argue (1995) has demonstrated in Australia how to collect stormwater in simple gravel "pipes" that direct the water to a series of local aquifer recharge points. The water can then be used in summer for park watering. Rainwater tanks are gaining popularity with the public. Both the Melbourne Water Review and the Perth Water Future studies have revealed the public's perceived preference in this area, and most urban ecology projects in Denmark (see later in this chapter) involve

Photo 5.1. A "Better Cities" restored urban wetland in Adelaide.

them. Research is ongoing into developing household systems for both potable and nonpotable uses (see Waller, 1989). For uses that require bulk storage, however, it appears to be more economical to provide storage through urban wetlands or aquifers. The most notable example of water harvesting is in the investigations for the Multi Function Polis in Adelaide (a twenty-first-century ecotechnology city), where the potential to harvest up to 23,000 megaliters of runoff per year is being implemented. The water will be directed (along with treated effluent) to parks and gardens, local industry, household gardens, and toilet use.

The design and redesign process of our cities becomes one of truly integrating water into the urban design and land use allocation process, not just seeing it as an isolated engineering process. Some of the important elements of the new approach will therefore be development of local water-harvesting techniques and groundwater recharge and abstraction systems in combination with point-of-entry and point-of-use approaches to water quality treatment.

In the wastewater area, a whole range of technologies has emerged to manage wastewater at the local level. At the on-site scale these are:

- modified septic tank systems with soil amendment around a leach drain to neutralize nutrient contamination;
- aerobic treatment systems that treat to the tertiary level on a small scale; and
- composting toilets (the potential of this technology in cities should not be dismissed as urban agriculture, especially permaculture, grows in popularity).

At the community level, all of the traditional primary, secondary, and tertiary processes are available on a small scale; however, it is more likely that combinations of emerging high-tech and low-tech solutions will outcompete these older approaches. High-technology approaches using filtration systems (developed from kidney dialysis), biogas technologies, and ultraviolet disinfection seem to work best on a smaller scale. Low technology approaches that use wetland systems or solar aquatic systems (aquaculture, hydroponics, condensed greenhouses) are also all small scale (see Saldinger, 1992).

The technology is available; therefore the challenge is not simply a water engineering problem, but more a question of the integration of land and water planning under the new sustainability goals to create a new set of urban management processes.

New Urban Water Management Processes

The techniques for sustainable urban water management that have arisen in the Australian context have been labeled: "urban integrated catchment management," "total water cycle management," "water-sensitive design," and "localized community water management" processes. The first three of these are outlined below, and the fourth is discussed in more detail in the next section.

Urban Integrated Catchment Management The idea of land and water planning integration has its origins in natural resource management issues in rural areas to integrate agency programs and community aspirations. This process is well under way in most water management agencies around the world. In New Zealand, water catchment boundaries were used as the basis for reestablishing local government boundaries.

But integrated catchment management has not been extended much to urban areas until recent times, when urban communities have begun to demand more say in the way water management issues are resolved, particularly with creeks and rivers subject to pollution and drainage (Mouritz, 1997). The community desire to reestablish a sense of place with their local environment means that urban water features can no longer be regarded as places of low value or convenient discharge points for urban wastes.

There are now legally established urban catchment management districts operating in Adelaide with the ability to raise money via a local taxing scheme and the responsibility to integrate land and water planning along their urban watercourses. This involves local government and community representatives as well as state government water management professionals.

Total Water Cycle Management   This term has become increasingly used in water resource management and service provision circles. It aims to emphasize the integration of land use planning with the management of water supply; wastewater collection, treatment, and disposal; and stormwater drainage services. Total water cycle management therefore provides a framework for optimum management of the water use cycle while recognizing the environmental constraints and potential conflict with other aspects of water resource management. Many urban water agencies have adopted this framework in their assessments of options within environmentally sensitive urban expansion areas (e.g., Dodds et al. 1991). There is, however, a long way to go before truly integrated total water cycle options are commonplace.

Water-sensitive Design   The term *water-sensitive design* (WSD) was coined in Perth, Western Australia, where water is one of the key issues in city development. The aim was to devise and illustrate an approach to urban planning and design that incorporated water resource and related environmental management into the planning process at various scales and time horizons (Water Sensitive Urban Design Research Group, 1990). The term *sensitive* was selected to capture the elements of water management concern, water balance, water quality, and water consumption in one phrase. The WSD initiative has similar expressions in other cities, but in Perth it has produced a planning policy framework and comprehensive guidelines consisting of some eighty "Best Planning Practices and Best Management Practices." Some of these are presented in Table 5.1.

All of the new water technologies outlined above, and all of the other urban water management processes, require a largely decentralized water management system to be developed. The reasons for this are important for a more general discussion on sustainability and cities, and thus they are presented in some detail below.

Why Is Local Scale Best for Sustainability?

The reasons for local scale management options for sustainable water systems in cities appear to lie in the nature of new water technology, the nature of ecosys-

Table 5.1. Water-sensitive Urban Design Objectives
for Best Planning and Management Practices
_____

Water Balance Objectives
• Maintain appropriate aquifer levels and recharge and stream
flow characteristics in accordance with assigned beneficial uses.
• Prevent flood damage in developed areas.
• Prevent excessive erosion of waterways, slopes, and banks.

Water Conservation Objectives
• Minimize the import and use of public water.
• Promote the reuse of stormwater.
• Promote the reuse and recycling of effluent.
• Reduce irrigation requirements.
• Promote regulated self-supply.

Water Quality Objectives
• Minimize water-borne sediment loadings.
• Protect existing riparian or fringe vegetation.
• Minimize the export of pollutants to
surface or groundwater.
• Minimize the export and impact of pollution
from sewage.

Environmental/Social Objectives
• Maintain water-related environmental values.
• Maintain water related recreational and cultural values.
• Implement any necessary, site-specific water-sensitive objective
identified by the appropriate resource management authority.
_____

tems, the nature of water/land integration in cities, the economics of large
city forms, and the nature of postmodern management systems (Saldinger,
1992). These systems work better at the small-scale level because the new
technologies for sewage treatment are not very economic for individual households, nor for traditional large sewerage works, but are best for the 50 to 500
household scale. This is probably associated with the thermodynamics of removing nutrients at the tertiary level of treatment that is essential for all new wastewater systems.

The Nature of Ecosystems

Integrated stormwater management, water-sensitive design, and the recycling of
water all require detailed knowledge of local natural processes. This intimate
knowledge of local soils, slopes, creeks, and wetlands—as well as knowledge of
the urban aspects of nature, such as open space, community gardens, and street
trees—is ideally suited to the role of a local environmental scientist working in a
local authority or local community-based organization with responsibility for
local urban water management. The reality is that nature is diverse, and each
urban catchment would have different requirements within the broad goals of a
city's overall management strategy.

The Nature of Integrated Water Management

It is not possible to manage the total water system incorporating water supply, stormwater, sewage treatment, and recycling unless it is integrated at the point where water is needed (Waller, 1989). This requires a more localized management system as well as changes at the consumer end.

The Economics of Large City Forms

As discussed earlier, Auto Cities have grown outward rapidly into thinly spread suburbs rather than small, compact Walking Cities or corridor-shaped Transit Cities. Thus the nineteenth-century solution of "big pipes" now means a lot of big pipes. The efficiency of this approach changed once the form of the city changed. For a typical Australian Auto City, up to 85 percent of the capital investment is in the provision of the pipes and less than 15 to 20 percent is in water treatment (Thomas and McLeod, 1992). Thus, if ways can be found to save on the big pipes, there is theoretically a lot more money available to do advanced treatment to meet sustainability goals. In fact, if a total approach is taken, there should be plenty of scope for saving money. In a case study approach to more sustainable water development, Mouritz (1997) has found that this is indeed possible. The most savings will be found as infrastructure wears out and is slowly replaced by this new approach, or as new urban villages and subcenters are built in the reurbanization process described in Chapter 4.

Signs of Sustainable Water Systems

New technologies and management approaches are actively being examined by urban water authorities facing increasing pressure to be more economically efficient and environmentally effective (Niemczynowicz, 1992). This is particularly evident in Australia, the driest continent in the world (Australian Institute of Urban Studies, 1991; Clark, 1990; and Department of Technology, Industry, and Commerce, 1992).

Water management in Australia is rapidly moving in the direction of a more sustainable model. While it will be some time before fully integrated systems are widespread and the existing ocean outfalls are made unnecessary, there are plans under way in this direction. Outfalls will continue where cities have high groundwater tables. Otherwise there are countless ways of reusing water, some of which are outlined in the next section. The push for new approaches to urban water management is coming as much from the enormous difficulties in funding the "big pipes" as it is from the environmental problems due to water management in the city. Thus, like the problem of automobile dependence, the need for new approaches to urban water is a true challenge of sustainability.

The Australian government's Better Cities program has been able to include many innovative elements of water management in its demonstrations of sustainability across the country. Better Cities–funded projects involved the redevelopment of urban areas incorporating water conservation technology and water-sensitive design, small-scale water treatment to the tertiary level at a community-based greening center, several aquifer recharge programs for stormwater involving wetland systems, and a number of urban creek regeneration projects as part of dense, mixed-use reurbanization (Diver, Newman, and Kenworthy, 1996).

Thus it is possible to see the start of sustainability in urban water systems and to imagine how they could easily catch on in the Auto City and rapidly become an everyday part of urban management in the future "Sustainable" City.

Greening the City with Parks and Agriculture

The importance of green spaces in a city is almost universally recognized. Planning techniques to ensure that there is a proportion of local open space available in any new development are standard professional practice around the world in all city forms and types. This does not always ensure that the best kind of greening occurs, and in old parts of cities there is a need to find new ways to make open space available.

In the pages that follow are some examples of more creative processes in which cities have made nature a more significant part of the urban system.

Rehabilitation of Urban Waterways

The rehabilitation of urban wetlands and creeks has become an integral part of the greening of the city.

Register (1987) has shown how to rehabilitate a concrete drain in Berkeley, where one of the first city drains was converted back into an attractive piece of urban ecological landscape. This drain runs through a dense urban area. Two similar projects, in Zurich and San Antonio, are outlined below.

Zurich's Refurbished Creeks

A refurbished creek that was once a concrete drain in Zurich is part of the open space for a high-density housing complex with agricultural allotments adjacent to it. The creek once fed into the sewer system in order for the water to be cleaned up before entering the Lake of Zurich. This drain was exhumed by the developer of an urban village and now percolates through the area and assists in giving the development a more natural quality. The urban village, located on the junction of a light rail line and trolley bus line to reduce car use, is built on a disused quarry site near the center of Zurich. It contains a number of ecological features that contributed to the developer being granted some significant density bonuses. For example, all water that falls on the site is captured there, and the on-site compensation basin has become an attractive water feature of the development, with a boardwalk and seating area integrated with it. The developer also allowed land surrounding the water area to undergo a natural ecological succession by providing soil and hollow logs so that native plant species and local small mammals and frogs would reinhabit the area.

Zurich has other examples in which creeks, previously diverted to the sewer system, are being brought back to the surface in order to create havens for birds and many aquatic species. It is possible to do this now because pollution sources

Photo 5.2. This green corridor snaking into old Zurich was once a drain, but is now a significant component of urban open space—see also the allotments in the adjacent area.

have been cleaned up and the creek water no longer requires treatment before entering the lake. Another creek in Zurich has been brought back alongside a street. It is possible to identify these sites in Zurich through the serpentine green corridors that are created, providing important links between rural areas and open space across the city.

San Antonio's River Walk

The River Walk in San Antonio, Texas, the result of a central city revitalization scheme, is a successful early attempt in the United States to bring some ecological thinking and greater human sensitivity into urban planning and management practices as they relate to natural features.

San Antonio's River Walk is built along a narrow, meandering waterway in downtown San Antonio some twenty or so feet below street level, and bordered on both sides by a rich array of restaurants, hotels, richly landscaped garden walkways, amphitheaters and other activity centers, and Venetian-style bridges linking both sides at regular intervals. It is a cool, attractive, and quite unique urban oasis in the midst of a typically car-dominated and often ugly downtown environment.

The idea originated as a flood control program for the San Antonio River, which would periodically burst its banks, inundating the downtown area. The original plan was essentially to call in the U.S. Army Corps of Engineers to turn the river into a concrete ditch whose water level could be controlled through traditional engineering techniques—a very crude approach to controlling nature that would have added more ugliness to the city center. However, the city authority at the time believed that more creativity could be used to turn the flood control exercise into something that would contribute uniquely to the quality of downtown San Antonio by exploiting the water theme in conjunction with good urban design and aesthetics. The council at the time was strongly represented by women.

The resulting water course is more natural and meandering but still serves its function as a flood control device. The integration of a more human element as well as being more ecological is a true exercise in urban sustainability.

The very successful River Walk, which now runs some distance through downtown San Antonio, has been extended at least on one occasion to take in a wider area of the city. By adopting a more organic, ecological approach to the problem of flood control, and a creative use of engineering technology, San Antonio has been able to exploit the positive human aspects and beauty of urban design and landscape architecture based around a water theme.

Urban Agriculture

The expression of nature in cities is not restricted to the rehabilitation of watercourses, but extends to other features, such as agricultural or garden allotments throughout the city (a particularly strong tradition in European cities), extensive common garden areas around housing complexes, urban forests, and permaculture gardens. There are many good examples of these other forms of urban nature around the world.

Photo 5.3. River Walk in San Antonio, Texas. A flooding problem led to an important greening project for the central city.

Zurich is again a showpiece of a medium-density, transit-oriented European urban region (forty-seven persons per hectare) that has retained an exceptionally green character through its extensive use of garden allotments, its commitment to preserving large forested areas on the ridges all around the city, and its retention of extensive common garden areas around almost all apartments and other housing areas.

Garden allotments consist of sizeable pieces of land divided into a series of small parcels that are used by individuals and families as a place to grow a wide array of flowers, vegetables, and fruit. In Zurich, they are often found abutting or adjacent to forested areas, creating an urban landscape that in parts looks more like the country than the city. Each allotment usually features a small shed or miniature "house" that is used to store gardening equipment and other items, such as barbecues for summer recreation. They are not supposed to be used as residences, but in practice many people do use them in this way in summer for short periods. Composting of organic waste on these sites is standard practice, as it is in the common garden areas around virtually every apartment complex in Zurich.

An interesting aside to the very prevalent commitment to composting is the city's policy on garbage disposal. Garbage can only be disposed of in special bags purchased from local supermarkets at a very considerable price. Garbage left on the street in any other form of container is not collected. For economic reasons it is important for residents to utilize each bag to its maximum extent, so the disposal of green wastes in this way would be almost unthinkable. Interestingly, supermarkets in Zurich are also forbidden to supply plastic bags for shopping. Customers must bring their own bags or pay a significant sum to purchase strong paper bags at the checkouts.

The effect of the garden allotment approach to green space and productive land in the city is to consolidate, in quite large areas, a lot of the open space that in lower-density cities would be scattered across the landscape in the form of often underutilized front and back yards. These large allotment areas in Zurich appear in the most unlikely places, such as next to a large warehouse distribution center, virtually in the CBD of the city near the central railway station. Also, the common garden areas around apartment complexes in Zurich, which are often concealed from view from the road, boast extensive communal space. This land is frequently exploited in a creative way to produce colorful and diverse gardens, as well as very productive fruit and vegetable plots.

It would appear that in a city such as Zurich, despite lower standards of private open space, the access to nature and productive land is of a higher standard than in automobile cities where the demands on land for sprawling housing, roads, and car parks is so intense that it defeats the possibility of preserving significant pieces of nature in the midst of the city.

Permaculture, or "permanent agriculture" is an international movement started by Australian Bill Mollinson (see Mollinson, 1988) that has institutes and training programs now operating in most parts of the world. The approach to food production (and fiber, as well as the many other ecological services from growing plants) is based on an innovative integration of different ecosystem niches. Mollinson defines it as "the conscious design and maintenance of agriculturally productive ecosystems which have the diversity, stability and resilience of natural ecosystems." It closes the cycle on water and nutrient use by integrating aquaculture, a huge variety of plants (including vegetables, herbs, fruits, and grains), and small animal production.

Permaculture is seen as an ideal way of using private spaces around houses in low-density Auto Cities; however, some of the most successful permaculture experiments are in community gardens, often rehabilitating land in old inner-city areas (see Fremantle case study in Chapter 7). This is not unexpected, since the skills and labor needed to operate a permaculture garden invariably are more than is feasible for other than the most avid household gardener. They lend themselves to an urban (or rural) community that focuses its activity around a shared public space.

Urban agriculture has been very active in European cities through allotment programs for many decades and has become a tool for rehabilitating parts of U.S. inner cities through groups such as Denver Urban Gardens that facilitate the development of community gardens and urban farms. Urban farms provide a focal point for unemployed youths to learn practical skills as well as providing locally grown food (see case studies below).

However, the role of food growing in cities is far more important economically in many (or most) Third World cities (Smit, Ratta, and Nasr, 1996). The UN Development Program has estimated that 800 million people worldwide are engaged in urban agriculture. People engaged in urban agriculture for some part of the year vary between 15 and 70 percent of households in cities surveyed in Africa, Russia, and Eastern Europe. In Dar Es Salaam (Tanzania) urban agriculture is the largest land user (33 percent of the city region), with 34,000 hectares producing more than 100,000 tons of food in 1988 and employing 20 percent of the urban population (Mougeot, 1998). In Harare, Zimbabwe, the amount of urban open space in cultivation grew from 4,822 to 8,392 hectares between 1990 and 1994.

Cities developed through history around this extra advantage provided by the density of settlement and immediate markets (Jacobs, 1969). In the eighteenth and early nineteenth centuries Paris was an exporter of food (mostly vegetables) based on intensive allotments fed by the waste from horses (used for transportation) and human sewage (composted from carts that collected it each night—the origin of the phrase "night soil").

Many cities now recognize that they must plan to incorporate urban agriculture into their economies and urban management. Hong Kong and Singapore have elaborate systems to manage urban agriculture (Boyden et al., 1981). These extremely dense cities use their adjacent rural land very intensively.

Most Auto Cities, however, do not see urban agriculture as more than a hobby, and adjacent peri-urban market gardens and farms are often just regarded as future urban land that will inevitably be rezoned for suburbs. Growth management needs to incorporate a far more serious approach to the importance of urban agriculture, and the reurbanization process needs to have a simultaneous process of ecological renewal involving an integrated approach to water, waste, and urban agriculture.

Inner-area Open Space Projects

In some dense cities access to nature is at a premium, and in those cases radical approaches sometimes have to be taken to secure green space. One such case is central London, which, for the many residents who live there, seems replete with office buildings and other intense urban uses, and short on open space.

This shortage of open space and nature has been the inspiration for concerted and effective community action to create community gardens right in the heart of London's business center.

Perhaps one of the best examples of this is the Calthorpe Project in the Borough of Camden, opened in September 1984. This 1.2-acre site was originally earmarked for office development. Under intense community opposition, however, the site was eventually purchased by the Borough for the purpose of turning it over to the local community for establishment of a community garden. The sign at the entrance partly reads:

> The project is funded by the London Borough of Camden. Local people fought and won against office development and created these community gardens, play space and under fives' area. Enjoy your green belt in Kings' Cross.

The garden consists of a number of different sections designed for different needs. There are quiet sections with water features and seating, grassed areas surrounded by flower beds where many office workers and residents come to eat their lunch, greenhouses and other areas for germinating seeds and tending seedlings, an area expressly for those under five years old, tennis courts, a small pond area where children can catch tadpoles, a playground for older children, as well as an on-site office, information center, meeting area, and small restaurant. The building housing these latter uses is constructed of wood, and its roof consists entirely of a flat garden area. There is a special path running through part of the garden that is a tile mosaic created by the local community to celebrate life.

The garden is managed by members of the community with an annual budget provided by the Borough, a good deal of which is used to pay nominal salaries to a few local residents who act as official caretakers/managers. The green space provided by this project is quite different in character from a local park, and there is more of a feeling of community ownership and control. Sound management is important since it is in an intense inner-city area with problems such as homelessness and drug abuse. It is locked at night but still has to be regularly checked and cleaned up to guard against such dangers as used syringes.

Within walking distance of the Calthorpe Project are many other smaller community garden projects established by local residents that help to green the inner-city environment and make effective use of leftover spaces. For example, there is a small meadow area called the Harrison Street Wildflower Meadow, which has been created out of a sliver of leftover land between residential buildings. It is used to grow wildflowers common in the English countryside but no longer present in London. It is expressly designed to serve as a reminder of dis-

Photo 5.4. A community garden in Fremantle featuring permaculture and recycled "gray water" from surrounding houses.

appearing nature under the spread of urbanization in England and bears a sign reminding passersby of the natural heritage that is being lost.

Within 100 meters is another small garden called the Garden for Peace, built by the Cromer Street Garden Association on a corner abutting a local church and surrounded by shops and flats. It has murals painted on the adjoining stone walls of the church, small painted garden seats, an entry arch of climbing roses, and various other displays of flowers. Such small projects are as important for the care, involvement, and sense of security they express in the local area as they are for the amount of attractive public space they contribute.

A little farther away is another larger natural area called the Camley Street Natural Park, which has been etched out of waste industrial land surrounded by derelict reminders of the Industrial Revolution and set along a manmade canal. The park consists of different kinds of spaces, such as pond areas, trees, and shrub areas, in which young children in particular are treated to nature study classes right in the inner city, as well as quiet, secluded spots for reading and relaxing. At the entrance to the park is an office that provides information about wildlife and plants in the area and a formal classroom used by different primary school students brought to the park every day for nature study.

Another particularly good example of a community garden in this same area of London is the Phoenix Community Garden, which is made up of many of the same elements as the Calthorpe Project, but on a smaller scale. This, too, was to have been the site of an office building, but through organized civic action, a community garden has been created instead, with a variety of very attractive green spaces for people to bring children, relax, and do gardening.

The garden receives an annual budget from the local authority, as does the Calthorpe Project, and local people come mostly on weekends to participate in the planting and upkeep of the garden using tools kept on site. The garden is surrounded by new, high-density residential construction, which benefits from its location next to well-managed natural space in the heart of the city. A small playground/park area on the other side of a stone wall forming the community garden's boundary is punctuated with graffiti and signs of a lack of ownership, whereas the Phoenix Community Garden bears no such scars.

Is the Green City in Conflict with the Low-energy City?

When reviewing the form of cities required for achieving sustainability, Radberg (1995) described the rationale for a more compact city that can conserve energy, very much along the lines of our work presented in Chapters 2 through 4. He then proposed the form of a city for achieving green objectives that are "related to the ecological perspective" for "recycling and cultivation"; this city is "greener, more ruralised, more spread out." He therefore raises the question as to whether there is not a conflict between the need to have more urban land for the green city in order to accommodate local ecological processing, and a low-energy city with its need to minimize travel distances and thus have a frugal use of land.

This conflict is a genuine issue among ecologically oriented people trying to see what sustainability means for cities. Troy (1996) insists that the best way to improve the environment and livability in cities is to ensure that everyone has a large block for gardening, growing trees, and participating in the recreational activities they like. At the Second International Ecocity Conference in Adelaide in 1994, the conflict surfaced and became an emotional issue dividing the participants. We have found that there is a growing dichotomy between the two approaches. Thus we have tried to examine the basis for this conflict and to see how it can be resolved.

Two Models of Ecologically Sustainable Cities

The two approaches taken by those who are involved in assessing the problems of ecological sustainability in our cities can be seen to cover a spectrum of views, rather than being in two totally distinct categories. The approaches have in common the desire for reducing the use of resources, minimizing pollution, using land in a more biologically sensitive way, and having a more green and aesthetic urban environment. However, one is more oriented to rural values and the other is more oriented to urban values. We will attempt to outline the basis of these two approaches and show that unless their differences are resolved, the problems of the Auto City may never be overcome. But first we will try to expand on the common ground in the two approaches.

The "Commons" as Common Ground

The alternatives are characterized below as the "rural commons" view and the "urban commons" view to emphasize that they share a belief in the commons—that age-old concept of land that is held in common trust for the use and benefit of all (Hardin, 1968). Here, though, the concept is expanded to take in all those common elements of the environment—the air, the water, the natural terrain, the wildlife—that surround our settlements and on which these settlements depend. In cities, such commons include not only the parks and reserves but also the common areas associated with roads and streetscapes, neighborhoods, schools, shopping areas, playgrounds, public buildings, buses and trains, transit stations—the whole arena outside our own private domain that gives civility and human meaning to our cities.

The fundamental concept linking these two perspectives is that our cities are flawed because they over-emphasize the private, individualized world at the expense of the commons. Both approaches see that the late-twentieth-century Auto City is characterized by:

- private splendor in houses and backyards and in cars, but public squalor in air and water and common public areas of cities
- depletion of the rural environment at the urban fringe as it is continuously falling under the subdivision's bulldozer;
- enormous dependence on fossil fuels, particularly oil, and the associated deterioration of the global environment due to greenhouse gas emissions;
- diminished community in suburbs that have only feeble communal activity as people have extremely high levels of mobility; and
- the decline of transit, which has been allowed to deteriorate and become vandalized and unsafe.

The motivations of both approaches start by recognizing these problems. However, from here the two approaches diverge as set out below.

The Rural Commons View

This view says that cities are too big and need to be broken down into little pieces that should be substantially self-sufficient. Such areas are said to bring back into the city the rural values that have been lost. Thus, in these areas, the environmentally damaging and socially isolating city can become more in tune with nature through the development of local self-sufficiency. Most of the food, it is suggested, could be produced locally; most of the work could be available locally; most of the educational and recreational opportunities will be available locally; and most of the friendships and social meanings could be found locally.

The local environment orientation also is aimed at re-creating creeks from drains and creating more habitat for wildlife, as well as recycling solid waste and wastewater instead of sending them somewhere else.

In this context of a local self-sufficiency, it is suggested that a solution can be found to the heavy dependence on fossil fuels that characterizes our cities. The view is built on the assumption that a more cooperative social structure will emerge with the commons being managed for the good of all. For example, a permaculture kind of food production could occur, with backyard agriculture merging into shared management of local production. Cooperative ventures could be established to manage water and solar power, to establish and run urban forests, to develop artisan and light industry workshops, and so on.

The view is not necessarily antitechnology, and indeed it warmly embraces modern communications and home computers as ways of assisting such self-sufficiency in retaining contact with a wider world. However, little is ever said about transportation, apart from the importance of bicycles, because self-sufficiency is meant to do away with the need for larger transportation requirements. It is sometimes called the "low mobility" city, though it is only low because of radical lifestyle changes, not because of the form of the city. But its major thrust is to reduce densities and create more rural activities in the city.

Major proponents of this approach include Morehouse (1989), Gordon (1990), Todd and Tukel (1981), Coates (1981), Berg et al. (1990), Rogers (see Sustainable Human Habitat Consultants, 1996) and Troy (1996).

The Urban Commons View

This view is concerned mostly with the city as a system. It suggests that the city should become more urban not less, contained from its sprawl, and rebuilt from within. It suggests that there is far too much wasted space in cities given over to automobiles for parking and roadway space, and that there is excessive and often greatly under-utilized private space. It suggests that the public areas, public concerns, transit, and so on should become the focus of an urban renewal based on a redesign and recommitment to the city and its public values. Central to the urban commons approach is the need to overcome automobile dependence. More than any other technology the car is seen to be the source of so many of the problems of modern cities, as outlined above.[2]

In practical terms, the urban commons view suggests that auto-dependent cities should start to address their problems by reurbanization and reorientation of transportation priorities, but this can have significant overlap with rural commons goals concerning natural features of the city. Indeed, part of the urban commons view is to include innovative approaches to greening the city. For example, traffic calming should involve landscaping that can provide a wildlife habitat and serve as a link between parks and water systems, as well as being aesthetically important to the city. Urban villages should have trees and gardens for a quality environment and have urban agricultural production and urban forestry conducted in the public commons area. Indeed, it is believed that most greening issues will be better managed by the urban commons approach (see Box 5.5).

Thus local ecological goals can be met but the context is more global and urban. The city in this view does not need to be a replacement for the country, but it does need to be more in harmony with the environment, to use resources carefully, and to be closely designed to fit in with the local water regime, the local terrain, and the local habitat. But it is a city with all its specializations, diversity, and commerce.

Publications of the major proponents of this approach include Calthorpe (1993), Roseland (1992), Elkin et al. (1991), Walter, Arkin, and Crenshaw (1992), and Engwicht (1993), as well as our own work. The U.S. World Watch

Box 5.5. Local Environmental Problems Solved More Effectively by an Urban Commons Approach (in the "Sustainable" City Model)

- *Urban sprawl* is contained by new urbanization to focused subcenters rather than fringe development.
- *Direct impacts from automobile dependence* (air pollution, noise, traffic, highway severance, loss of public space to cars and parking, etc.) are reduced by shifting modes and minimizing the need to travel.
- *Energy use* (in buildings and transport) is reduced by density increases where the shared insulating effect means considerable reductions in space heating/cooling (far more than the small loss in embodied energy due to greater use of steel structures) and considerable transport energy reductions due to reduced automobile dependence.
- *Solid waste* is reduced by density increases in focused areas as there is less private garden waste and more recycling due to easier collection and management than in severed developments.
- *Water use* is reduced by density increases as there is less private open space/grass to water in focused centers and a greater opportunity to manage the complete water cycle in the local area due to more opportunities to create urban community.

Institute presented this urban commons perspective in their booklet "Livable Cities" (Lowe, 1990).

Resolving the Differences in the Two Alternatives?

Can the differences in these two alternatives be resolved? It is too easy to say that the two approaches are essentially the same because they share a desire for a better environment. This common feature will not be enough to make them the same; they have genuinely different motivations and in practice they clash over the central concepts of density, transportation, and the priorities for change in our cities.

The rural commons group abhors increasing density, they are fanatical about the need for large lots as well as plenty of public space. They are keen to use this space for informal economic uses (Stretton, 1975), especially permaculture. They are prepared to concede that this may mean more sprawl (but often say this is an "emotive" word, as sprawl can be good). They also recognize that this space can create more car dependence, but they often say telecommunications and bicycles will suffice and cars should just be taxed more heavily. They are more often than not, however, prepared to turn a blind eye to sprawl and car dependence as unwanted but necessary aspects of their rural approach to cities, while they stress the importance of getting down to work on local ecology.

The urban commons group is attracted to increased density because it provides more urban diversity and more pedestrian-based and transit-based environments (i.e., more urbanity). They see sprawl and car dependence as not only environmentally damaging but as draining the life out of the city through misplaced investment in high-capacity roads and suburban infrastructure when city areas are often languishing. They also see low-density suburbs as unattractive and unstimulating. Urban commons proponents appreciate the importance of urban greening and shared urban agriculture, but they are not keen to see that as the only force driving their approach to cities.

The difference between these two approaches to cities is becoming critical in urban policy debates. Environmentalists are at the center of most land use–oriented debates and are now in serious conflict in many cities on what should be done to make urban areas more ecologically sensitive and sustainable. The debates have become highly personalized and emotional, which highlights the basic worldview difference at stake.

The big problem in not resolving these two conflicting views of reality is that it gives the impression to politicians and developers that the environment in cities is just a matter of personal taste. Thus "green speak" is being adopted by developers to produce "environmentally sensitive" ranchettes and "gated communities" and other packaged land that is designed to be self-sufficient but in reality is just unserviced suburbia. The city just sprawls further and car dependence increases.

There are, however, two ways in which the alternatives can be resolved.

Rural Development

The rural commons approach is precisely what is needed to give life to rural areas. Throughout inland Australia and the United States (as well as on many other continents) there is a decline in rural population accompanied by land degradation due to large-scale monocultural agriculture. In such areas it is possible to imagine small country towns and rural villages facilitating a permaculture-based subdivision of land based on the rural commons ideals.

The approach being developed by the Global Eco Village Network (see Context Institute, 1992) is to create model eco-villages that can demonstrate how to make a more sustainable rural land use pattern.

The Crystal Waters Permaculture Village in Queensland seems to be a model of how such a community can work to bring greater diversity of rural products and jobs, and a more rehabilitating approach to the land (Lindegger and Tap, 1989; Young and Lindegger, 1990). Such a concept can not only help to make a more sustainable countryside but can also slow the growth of the city. It does not mean cities have to become like this but that rural areas need to be the focus. This perspective suggests that sustainability means cities should become more urban and the countryside more rural, but both need to incorporate a more sensitive approach to the natural systems on which they depend (Newman, 1992).

Thus the essential nature of this approach is to be rural where it matters most. It cannot be acceptable for people to have a small rural hideaway with uncommitted permaculture and unmanaged animals and either commute long distances to the city for work or live in the country only on weekends. This is not a sustainable alternative; it does not take the rural commons approach seriously enough. This will not provide the resolution that is required. It loses the essence of both rural and city sustainability. The countryside needs more rural commons experiments.

Urban Development

The urban commons approach is needed to give life to urban centers throughout a city. It is no longer necessary to have the CBD as the one focus of a city; it is possible to develop a multicentered city that is linked by rapid transit. Within these subcenters or small centers can be a dense array of diverse urban activity all within a walking-oriented environment. Many people would live in such highly urban settings and have no need for backyards—they are prepared to exchange the time and energy involved in food production (even food preparation) and certainly waste management for other urban services. Such is the nature of cities that exist because of their diversity of opportunities.

If cities put their resources into building these urban subcenters as well as the public transport links between them, then the pressure for the city to sprawl outward would be dramatically reduced. These pockets of urban commons development would be deliberately planned as the places where density should increase.

At the same time there are parts of the city where it is possible and easy to reduce density based around the rural commons model in order to better accommodate ecological processes. In these areas the land could become more oriented to shared production, urban forestry, and waste disposal and recycling for the local urban region (as large-scale sewerage systems with their "big pipes-in/big pipes-out" approach are phased out).

These parts of the city would therefore contribute to the adjacent urban area in terms of environmental and agricultural services. In return, people living in these areas would have access to urban services. Although having lower accessibility than those living in the adjacent urban centers, they would likely not be as car dependent as in present urban structures. This would depend on the extent to which a rural commons approach to community in the area was able to create a meaningful life for the people involved. No doubt bicycles and telecommunications would help as well. But a good transit system in a city will not be possible unless there are pockets of high-density activity in focused centers, as stressed so often here.

The rural commons and urban commons approaches to sustainable cities can be made compatible, but they are not the same and need to be recognized for their differences. Emphasis only on rural values in the city will exacerbate the problems of automobile dependence. As set out in Box 5.5, the urban commons approach can be the basis for revitalization of sprawling car-dependent cities in ways that use less energy, less land, and less water while producing less waste and having a greater sensitivity for the natural setting. This approach can also provide greater human opportunities in the city and facilitate the development of communities if dense, walking-based subcenters linked by transit are permitted.

If urban commons approaches are developed in partnership with rural commons approaches in those areas where ecological functions are best concentrated, then it will be possible to develop local water and waste management, local urban agriculture, and other ecological services that require more use of land. Thus, the conflict can be resolved: increase densities in subcenters and reduce them in areas away from the transit corridors to allow for ecological servicing. Register (1987) has developed this concept in a case study on Berkeley.

In the next section, examples are given of urban ecology innovations occurring at all levels of density, though there are difficulties in promulgating all aspects of sustainability in all areas of the city. Radberg (1995), who was quoted previously on this conflict over the two approaches to urban form, has resolved the issue by finding how different parts of the city need to be used for different parts of the sustainability agenda.

The key to the resolution of the alternatives is that the urban commons approach is allowed to be sufficiently urban. This is the most significant part of the process and needs to happen before an Auto City can begin to be seen as sustainable. At present, in Australian and U.S. cities, the pressure to prevent density increases from occurring *anywhere* are a substantial barrier to achieving a more sustainable city. Rural commons–oriented environmental groups, academics, and professionals often become extremely upset about any kind of density increases. For example, Troy (1996, p. 167) in *The Perils of Urban Consolidation* says that:

> the proponents of high density living and the kinds of urban lifestyle they yearn for, and which they claim results from it, simply express a variation of cultural cringe.

In other writing he describes urban villages as just "the new feudalism" (Troy, 1992).

The resolution of this impasse between urban commons and rural commons approaches in the city lies in an acceptance that density increases in city centers and subcenters are necessary for more pedestrian and human-scale processes, and density decreases in other areas are necessary to provide space for more ecological processes. However, the stance of rural commons groups and some academics is such that any attempts at density increases (or new rail systems) are treated with hostility, if not contempt, due to a worldview that cannot allow others to appreciate density. It is necessary, therefore, to try to emphasize that some density increases can indeed be a good thing and to begin to expose the basis for the emotional reaction that density evokes.

Urban Mythology and the Rural Ideal

A possible way to help resolve the issue over the urban commons ideals of density (and transit) is by examining the cultural origins of the rural commons reaction to density and urbanity in general and exposing some of the mythology that appears to be behind it.

Many of those writing in the eco-city literature who emphasize the ruralizing of the city tend to suggest that the city is inherently a bad influence on people (see Chapter 4). The anti-urban tradition in Anglo-Saxon culture is a powerful force based on the "pastoral" writers. It asserts that the countryside is the only way to find solitude, innocence, and happiness. Cities corrupt, the countryside purifies (Williams, 1985).

This pastoral tradition was taken up in Australia and in the United States and had a powerful effect on the populace and intellectual life (Davison, 1983 and 1993; White and White, 1962). The English industrial cities were probably a major cause of this reaction, but the popularity of this pastoral tradition has remained long after such cities had their filthy air and open sewers cleaned up.

The kind of environmental values that the pastoral tradition promotes are to be lauded, as they show people the importance of nature and rural ecosystems. Such values have helped to frame the modern environmental movement. But the problem comes when pastoralists suggest that all cities are inherently bad. Having pro-rural values does not mean you have to be anti-city. This sets up a dualism that has not been helpful for cities in this century.[3]

Urban Ecology Innovations

This section examines how the quest for urban sustainability can be brought into every building project, no matter how small or how large, no matter what the density or the location.

What Is Urban Ecology?

Ole Michael Jensen of the Danish Building Research Institute has made the most detailed attempt to define what "urban ecology" is and to distinguish it from more commonly accepted approaches he calls just "environmentally sound planning" or "environmental management" (Jensen, 1994). Urban ecology is primarily local and tries to experiment with ecologically sensitive building, achieving a number of tasks in the one locality; environmentally sound planning is more global and tries to carry out each environmental task with a general approach suitable for all localities. His distinctions are summarized in Table 5.2.

Jensen says the difference is one of doing many little stories as opposed to doing major global ones. Although the global approach has had center stage, he says that there is "a clear trend for the little stories to take the floor" (p. 365). The features that urban ecology would like to see in any new building or urban project are:

- energy efficiency (in buildings), with solar orientation, insulation, and heat pumps;
- renewable energy, such as wind, solar photovoltaics, and solar heating;
- reestablishment of green areas;
- planting of greenery along streets, in courtyards, on roofs, and on facades;
- promotion of pedestrian and bicycle transportation;
- introduction of water-saving measures, including recycling gray water and percolating rainwater to groundwater, lakes, and watercourses;
- minimizing and recycling of refuse, especially composting;
- use of materials that are environmentally positive and healthy for the indoor climate (e.g., nonallergenic);
- use of natural building materials, such as mud, straw bales, stone, and wood; and
- recycling of building materials.

Table 5.2 Overview of the Differences Between Urban Ecology and
Environmentally Sound Planning

	Urban Ecology	Environmental Planning
Task	All environmental tasks in one locality.	One environmental task in all localities.
Focus	Individual building or collection of buildings.	Individual task by subject and sector, e.g., automobile dependence.
Timing	Solutions are simultaneous.	Solutions are one at a time.
Character	Solutions are unique, imaginative, intuitive, visionary, and very local.	Solutions are general, rational, and based on scientific documentation and universal common sense.
Tradition	Architectural, utopian urban planning tradition, e.g., Ebenezer Howard's Garden Cities.	Engineering, technohygienic tradition, e.g., Haussman's Paris.
Philosophy	Efforts take place in a "life" world relating to the human moment in time. It is both premodern (non-intentional) and post-modern (intends to be nonintentional).	Efforts take place in a "system" world relating to a universal time. It is modern (intentional).
Approach	Uses design alone.	Uses implementing techniques, e.g., policy levers, economic instruments, audits, and life cycle analysis.
Scale Involvement	Small and local, grassroots (bottom up).	Large and global, civic involvement (top down).
Innovation	Practical experiments that are never completed; tinkering.	Demonstration project; research.
Influence	Contributes to cultural change.	Contributes to social change.

Source: Based on Jensen (1994).

Jensen (1994, p. 354) says that "In practice these efforts are based on combining a number of tested and untested techniques in new and frequently creative ways and adapting them to conditions in the locality."

Across Denmark there is a proliferation of these urban ecology projects, which Jensen describes as "a mixture of design and tinkering." They are part of Denmark's long history of architectural experimentation, and indeed the ecological motivation is easily traced to a series of events and squatter settlements in the early 1970s, especially the Christiania commune in Copenhagen (see case study in Chapter 7), which is still actively experimenting with urban ecology (and is now one of Denmark's top tourist attractions). The cohousing movement in Denmark is also one of the expressions of urban ecology (McKamant and Durrett, 1988) and is where a lot of the experimentation continues. These Danish experiments are discussed later in this chapter.

The distinction between urban ecology and environmentally sound planning, as described above, is a useful one. Jensen says this dispute is not new; urban planners have always been divided between two camps—one dominated by architects, with their insistence on addressing just the local and using only design as their tool, and the other by engineers, with their insistence on more global and scientific solutions. Troy (1996) suggests, in a deprecatory tone, that "scientific environmentalism" is the problem, with approaches that end up suggesting city form needs to be more compact.

However, the differences are not quite so watertight as suggested by Jensen. It is entirely possible to have global, urban systems changes, such as reducing automobile dependence or creating more water-sensitive cities, that also require visionary and imaginative solutions. These approaches can use all the large-scale policy levers and economic instruments, but they also can be integrated into the local ecological solutions of urban ecology.

Integrated Approaches to Urban Ecology and Environmentally Sound Planning

The sustainable city of the future outlined in this chapter, which integrates transportation and water management into land use management (i.e., environmentally sound planning), can also integrate all the other areas of urban ecology mentioned by Jensen above. To do this requires all the ingenuity of the urban ecologist and all the skills of the environmental engineer and planner.

Building Energy

The focus on energy efficiency and renewable energy in buildings has developed rapidly since the 1973 oil crisis. Urban ecologists around the world have found all kinds of ingenious ways to create better buildings that use less fossil fuels. One of the key findings is that if buildings are joined together they save a great deal more energy—that is, dense, compact buildings not only save transportation fuel but save building energy. Troy (1996) suggests that dense buildings use more energy because of the materials required, but embodied energy is only a small part of the ongoing energy used in buildings.

The ability to save energy by joining buildings is achieved through a shared insulating effect—the fact that waste heat from one house can help to heat its neighbors. It is in many ways a symbol of how communities can work in a city to create a better use of resources than if individuals are by themselves. It is also a message to urban ecologists that their inventions in individual dwellings can be extended in a more global fashion if a community is built around their ideas. Thus engineers and planners can take these ideas and find out how they can better be used to raise standards in all new development and thus encourage the more extensive community-wide processes of sustainability.

On the other hand, an individual urban ecologist could develop a low-energy house sitting by itself in all its ecological splendor but do nothing for the community; this house, too, would fall short of its ecological potential because it is not attached to others.

Recycling

Recycling of household and building waste requires things to happen in the individual household or in the design of buildings, but it also requires things to happen in the local community in order for processing to occur and markets to be created. Thus the urban ecologist is needed to show how we can separate waste and make compost, and how we can design buildings with low-waste and recycled materials. The environmental engineer is needed to collect these recycled materials and other waste and do something with them for the local community.

In the past, the technohygienic engineer mostly dug a big hole and buried solid waste, especially in Auto Cities, where it is very expensive to have to collect solid waste due to so much scattered land use. But in European and Asian cities, which are more compact, there has been a long tradition of recycling. Garbage has been burned for power and heat or turned into compost, and materials such as paper, metal, and glass have always been recycled at quite high rates. It is in the Auto City that it became standard for solid waste to just be collected and dumped.

In European cities recycling is heavily supported in high-density apartments, where everything required for recycling is just a short walk from each door. Troy (1996) argues that large residential blocks are needed for recycling in order to have space for composting. This is a very limited view since it assumes that people can only do composting as an individual household task. Collections of buildings can have neighborhood composting and can share in the tasks of managing it.

In order to facilitate more recycling in the Auto City, it will be necessary to conduct urban ecology experiments in all parts of the city and to be more ingenious with solid waste. But it also requires community-scale solutions to be worked out by engineers. This is a process that is well under way in Auto Cities due to the sheer pressure of ordinary householders wanting to do something for the environment (e.g., see the example of Sydney in Chapter 1). However, if OECD data can be relied on, Auto Cities in Australia and the United States have a long way to go to catch up to other parts of the world. The future "Sustainable" City would be of benefit for recycling.

Localized subcenters should be better able to organize solid waste management, particularly local composting systems, as part of a recycling system. Collection can be more efficient due to shorter travel distances in the compact center, and then recycling can be integrated into the ecological functions of the community operating in the less compact parts of the urban village. Urban ecologists and environmental engineers would have more opportunities to develop localized recycling systems in this kind of city. The advantages are multiplied many times when, as shown below, the other urban ecological issues are integrated into this approach.

Urban Agriculture

Within urban villages it is also possible to develop new community-based approaches to open space and urban agriculture, such as outlined by the United Nations Development Program (1996) and as expressed in community permaculture. This new food production system is based on a more diverse, ecological approach to agriculture that is more sustainable. Again, permaculture can be conducted in individual backyards, but it is not the only way, nor is it even the best way. It appears to work much better if it is based around the diverse skills and commitments of a local community, rather than an individualized approach in each household. Many European cities, with their extensive community gardens or allotments, are already models of this and have shown a lot of interest in permaculture.

As noted above, we have suggested that the permaculture approach should be an important orientation for improving the sustainability of small country towns (Lindegger and Tap, 1989; Newman, 1992). It will also be very important for big cities, particularly when urban water begins to be managed more locally, increasing the need to absorb nutrient-rich water in local situations. At present, the average environmental engineer cannot imagine how this can be done because he or she can only see how to solve sewerage problems by big pipes. Urban ecologists are going to be needed to experiment with localized sewerage linked to community permaculture before water engineers' perceptions will be changed. Then, when they see that it works, they will be able to take some of this "tinkering" at the building level and scale it up to be viable at the community scale. This is the skill of the engineer. Thus the visionary urban ecologist and the technohygienic environmental engineer can together help create the more sustainable city of the future.

Currently, there are very few examples of this "scaling up" process happening, but there are many examples of household-scale urban ecology experiments. In Fremantle (Australia), a community park has been refurbished as a model of permaculture and community art. The water supply for the new diverse ecosystem is coming from the three surrounding houses, whose gray water is filtered and then trickled through the different levels of the park. The King William Street Park is now a very attractive and productive piece of urban land in a dense inner-city location. It is managed by local volunteers (Stocker and Barnett, 1998).

This permaculture park has been an important community-building exercise, but most importantly, it has been a successful experiment in urban ecology, showing Australian environmental engineers that it is possible to recycle gray water. Up until this project it was not allowed, and this urban ecology experiment gained permission only under great pressure and with extreme suspicion being expressed. Now it needs to be scaled up to take a larger proportion of local wastewater, which can be used to upgrade a larger piece of open space with permaculture.

Photo 5.5. The Calthorpe Project community garden in the borough of Camden, in London.

Urban Nature

As noted above, in the future "Sustainable" City, development should increase densities around nodal centers to reduce automobile dependence and reduce densities in other sectors where natural ecological areas are important. Thus urban nature areas can be created and maintained by local communities. The most eco-sensitive areas are usually along watercourses, and therefore drains and concrete creeks can be given back some of their ecological integrity.

Local open space systems can also be designed to provide wildlife corridors through the city along such watercourses. The Zurich creek described earlier runs several kilometers through the city and is a haven for birds and many aquatic species. Other green wedges can be provided through extensive landscaping along roads. The landscaping of roads is not only useful for traffic calming, as explained in Chapter 4, but it is important for urban ecology.

Most of the examples of creatively bringing nature back into the city have come from small groups of private urban ecologists who lobbied city governments and often (as in Berkeley) even provided the labor to dig up the drains and create the new slow-flow conditions in the creek. But once demonstrated, it is up to municipal environmental engineers to further implement this in other parts of the city. Thus once again the partnership is needed.

New Suburbs

The future "Sustainable" City model tends to emphasize the importance of redeveloping our cities rather than any further fringe development. However, wherever they are necessary, those new suburbs can be designed with a community focus and small-scale technology that provide for local management. Such ecology-oriented urban villages are now a preferred development option for environmentally sensitive fringe locations in Perth and in other Australian cities (Landmarc, 1992). They are using urban ecology inventions and extending them through engineering and planning to a new community.

Most of these new communities are still not compact enough for them to have much transit or pedestrian quality, but they are better than traditional suburbs. Similar developments are found in the United States in some of the New Urbanism developments, such as Kentlands outside Washington, D.C., which are neotraditional in design but have no transit due to their location on the urban fringe. Even worse, in terms of transit, are gated communities (see Blakely, 1994), which often have many urban ecological features but are only for the very wealthy and so have deliberately ensured that there is no transit service. These communities do not wish to be joined to most other parts of their city because, in their perception, this enhances the possibility of crime. Thus they are "ecological" but are totally auto-dependent.

Local Community: The Integrating Force

The factor that unites the urban ecology approach and the environmental planning approach is the local community focus. Although it is possible to engage in environmentally sound planning that is highly removed and technocratic, we suggest that this will, in the end, be counterproductive. As shown in many ways throughout this chapter and the next, any environmental goal needs to be localized if it is to be sustainable.

But urban ecology is also not automatically going to be of use to local communities either. It is possible to have urban ecology projects that are highly individualistic and do nothing to help create a better local community. If urban ecology is elitist it will not be sustainable. It will serve only to create a better world for the few who, if they follow the trend to U.S. gated communities, will do nothing for transit or the inner city or any other part of the city. They will simply be hiding while others suffer the impacts of a deteriorating urban environment. The global (i.e., the sphere outside the individual) is important. Urban ecology, like all the visionary ideas of architects, will ultimately be tested by what it can do for the broader community in the city.

The key first steps in sustainable city planning are to provide the transit corridors and sites of urban villages and to begin to enable communities to enter into the local processes of sustainable urban management. The experiments and the visions are an essential part of the process. Demonstration transit-oriented urban villages, with all the ecological and water-sensitive aspects in their design, are an important part of 1990s and twenty-first-century sustainable city policy.[4]

Some of the most innovative urban ecology approaches are occurring in Europe, especially in Denmark, and there the best examples are a combination of urban ecology and more global environmentally sound planning.

Urban Ecology in Denmark

Denmark and some other Northern European countries are leading the world in terms of implementing urban ecology. Numerous projects and programs ranging from individual buildings to entire municipalities aim to transform settlements toward sustainability. This applies equally to inner city areas, suburbs, small towns, and rural villages.

The examples given here are from the inner city, middle suburbs, and urban fringe. Many more examples of Danish urban ecology can be found in the book *A Guide to Urban Ecology in Copenhagen* by Munkstrap and Lindberg (1996). It contains forty-five sites across the city, and to be included in the guide, each development needed to show most of the following characteristics:

- better insulation than the building regulations require;
- low-emissivity windows;
- energy-efficient major appliances;
- low-energy lighting in common areas;
- water-saving equipment in dwellings;
- rainwater recovery;
- local percolation of rainwater;
- the opportunity to sort waste into more categories than the three (paper, glass, and other waste) required by law;
- residents' gardens;
- existing natural features of the site being considered when the complex is constructed so that existing trees and lakes are preserved; and
- car-free common areas that ensure that pedestrians and cyclists can move around in the area safely.

There are obviously other characteristics found in particular developments. Some of them and the best overall approaches are summarized below.

Inner-area Urban Ecology

There are a number of projects in inner Copenhagen and other inner-city areas that are described as "ecological urban renewal." In these the process of renewing buildings, which is an ongoing process in a city, has involved some additional components.

- *Oster Faelled* is a private infill development of 500 apartments that includes large underground tanks for collecting rainwater for gardens, water-efficient taps and toilets, energy-efficient lighting, electronic meters for each apartment (these allow more individual responsibility for power), and district heating (i.e., community-based heating).
- *BO 90* is an inner-city ecological cohousing project in Norrebro, which, along with common laundry, freezer, and recreation facilities, has an electronic control room for water and energy, a roof-length solar air panel for supplementing space heating and water heating, double pipes for recycling gray water (not yet functioning due to regulations), stored rainwater for flushing toilets and for gardens, composting, and a common area of fruit trees.
- *Korsgade 20* is an infill building that is built entirely of recycled bricks, timber, and tiles with recycled concrete for the foundation, as part of a Danish EPA experiment.
- *Mariendalsvej 14-18* is a complex for the elderly in the downtown area that is spectacularly designed, incorporating a curved roof entirely made of solar pan-

eling, which is used to heat the building and the indoor swimming pool. Rainwater is collected and used for the common laundry, garden, and toilet flushing. The building is for retired economists.

- *Baldersgade 20-22* was occupied by squatters before a foundation purchased the building so that they could continue to live there on the condition that they helped to renovate it. This has happened, along with an innovative gray water recycling system that purifies the water in the cellar (through a biofilter, a charcoal filter, and UV disinfection) before pumping the water back to be used for flushing toilets.
- *Christiania* is a social experiment that is one of the best known examples of urban ecology. Unused military land in the center of Copenhagen was taken over in 1970 and has slowly been developing into a city inside the city. It is one of Denmark's top tourist attractions. The 800 or so residents pay a small sum to be part of the collective and share in the management (see Chapter 7 for a further discussion of Christiania).
- *Kolding*, a regional town, has perhaps the most spectacular of the Danish inner-city urban ecology projects. Here, a run-down inner-city block of some 145 apartments (in five-storey traditional buildings with an enclosed courtyard) was transformed by a process that not only renewed the buildings but created a beautiful water-recycling system based on a glass pyramid.

The wastewater from the complex is first treated by a small-scale primary and secondary waste treatment plant located underground; then the water that still contains some organic matter and most of its nutrients is pumped to the glass pyramid using photovoltaic cells and a battery. Once in the pyramid, water passes

Photo 5.6. Ecological kindergarten in Christiania, Copenhagen.

Photo 5.7. The glass pyramid sewerage system, centerpiece of the "ecological urban renewal" of an inner-city neighborhood in Kolding, Denmark.

into a series of ponds on the ground floor containing first algae, then plankton, and finally a fish pond complete with aquatic plants that absorb much of the remaining material; water is then pumped to the top of the pyramid, where it trickles down over trays containing 15,000 plants that, when grown, are sold to a local nursery. Inside, the pyramid is like an exotic greenhouse.

The water then passes out to a small wetland before it is allowed to run down a cascade to form a small creek through the common gardens and a children's water playground. This water is mixed with rainwater collected from the roofs and stored in an underground cistern. After it has been aerated through the cascade and creek, this water is used for toilets and washing machines in the buildings. Any excess water is percolated to the groundwater.

The complex also solarized its buildings and has a solid waste recycling center complete with a worm composting unit (that also takes sludge from the treatment process), and a community garden. The project was a partnership between the community and the local government, whose engineers and planners are eager to make Kolding a global leader in city sustainability.

Middle-suburbs Urban Ecology

The suburbs examined here were built in the 1960s and 1970s in the Danish dense-low tradition—that is, no high-rise, but little emphasis on isolated single-family homes; instead, houses of two and three storeys are clustered around common courtyards and open space. At a density of about 35 persons per hectare, this is lower than most European urban development, but is still a lot more compact than Auto City suburbs of about 10 per hectare.

The examples are all taken from the Municipality of Albertslund. This municipality of 30,000 people won the European Sustainable City award from the International Council on Local Environmental Initiatives for 1996. It has a range of projects, but five in particular are discussed here.

Hyldespjaeldet This neighborhood of 390 houses was built as a public housing project in the 1970s. In 1989 the community decided they wanted to do something to integrate urban ecology into their present suburb. They began small by building a shared chicken coop on public land, managed by ten families, that would take all their green waste and provide sufficient eggs for all. Although it took some time and agony for the Municipality to approve it, the idea of people working together on an ecological project was recognized as very worthwhile. The idea really caught on (particularly among the children), and now there are 400 similar cooperative chicken coops in the Municipality.

Next, a group of people set up a recycling depot that hand-sorts waste delivered by the community into forty-eight different categories. All organic waste goes into household composting bins or to chickens. There has been a 40 percent reduction in waste, and the profits from recycling have gone into the community center built at the recycling depot.

Then another group established a community vegetable garden on a rented 2.5-hectare site; other groups established children's nature playgrounds; and the local school was converted into a School of Culture and Ecology.

The result has not only been a better environment with reduced metabolic flows of resources and waste, the community is also much stronger. Most people are part of one of the different ecological groups. None of these activities have been done in backyards but are now part of what it means to live in Hyldespjaeldet. In the early days the suburb had a very high turnover in residents since it is a relatively poor area and there is nothing very special about the design or the buildings themselves, which are prefabricated. However, now it is a different story, and the annual turnover has decreased from 40 percent to 16 percent. The implications for reduced transportation were confirmed in an evaluation of Danish urban ecology projects that found Hyldespjaeldet to have 30 percent less car ownership than a similar "control" middle suburb, 50 percent lower vehicle kilometers traveled per year, and 15 percent fewer car trips; in fact 74 percent of the households in Hyldespjaeldet live in a "car-free" way—that is, they make less than 10 percent of their trips by car (Scheurer, 1998b).

Agenda 21 Center This local community center was established by the Municipality of Albertslund and the state to provide information to communities about sustainability. It employs five people who go into each of the sixty-five neighborhoods of Albertslund to help the community develop projects like those in Hyldespjaeldet or to develop a local traffic plan (traffic calming, cycle plans, carpools, and common cars for rent, as well as suggested transit improvements) or to speak at schools.

The center also runs an Ecological Cafe with only organic food. People come to this place for information and to talk about environmental issues. It is involved in advocacy for local communities and helps in the "green accounting" process (see below).

Green Accounting Each year since 1993 the Municipality has provided a set of green accounts for all of their sixty-five neighborhoods. These consist of the per household consumption of water, electricity, gas, heat, and the calculated carbon dioxide from all energy use. Some travel data are also provided. Each neighborhood then discusses the data in public meetings, which are run by the Agenda 21 Center. No legal or financial pressure is used by the Municipality, just moral pressure. And with the encouragement of the Agenda 21 Center and awareness of which neighborhood is doing best, the people themselves come up with all kinds of suggestions as to how the metabolic flows in their neighborhoods could be reduced.

Every year since 1993 there has been a reduction in the energy and water use by almost all neighborhoods, with some showing quite sharp reductions.

The green accounts are also done for all Municipality buildings and functions, and all industries with each of them being discussed internally. In addition, a list of all pesticides used within the borders of the Municipality is provided; no pesticides are used by the Municipality itself.

Green accounting is simultaneously addressing the global needs of sustainability and facilitating local urban ecology. Other local governments in Europe are now starting to copy this innovation from Albertslund.

Municipal Planning The Municipality is promoting several innovations to try and minimize the need to travel.

First, it has a strong transit-oriented subcenter at the Albertslund regional rail station. It is a bus interchange point with good bicycle access. The station precinct has a large shopping center, many local services (e.g., day-care centers), and a cultural center and library run by the Municipality. The subcenter is ideal for Walking City residential living, and some apartments above shops are provided, but the Municipality could assist by allowing more people to live near and in its subcenter.

Second, it has a strong growth management boundary, which prevents further sprawl into surrounding farm and forest. Any houses outside the boundary, such as old farm cottages no longer used by farmers, are destined to be destroyed when the present owners die (including the house owned by the mayor). Some have already been bulldozed.

Third, like all of Denmark, the Municipality takes cycling seriously and has sixty kilometers of bicycle paths.

Fourth, it offers houses from its public housing program (50 percent of the community) with a priority that favors anyone who has a job in the area, thus minimizing commuting.

Municipal Buying Program The Municipality has taken seriously its ability to help create markets for green products through its own purchasing program. Thus it purchases only goods and services that have at least received the ISO14,000 certification, whether it be paper, computers, graphic design services, or food.[5] The Danish government certification of organic food is quite strict, and most supermarket products now have an organic option. Often the products are a little more expensive. The proposal to purchase only organic food in Albertslund's day-care centers was opposed by teachers and parents, but after a trial period was found to be cheaper since they purchased less meat and had less waste.

The mayor of Albertslund, Finn Aaberg, who has overseen much of this move toward sustainability for the past twenty-two years, concluded that "A people is not a people without a project, and this is ours." They clearly are one of the global leaders in urban ecology and environmentally sound planning.

Outer-suburb Urban Ecology

Other examples of urban ecology in Copenhagen's outer suburbs were examined for this book—for example, in Ballerup and Hoje Taastrup. Although there is a lot of discussion in these suburbs, the actual projects on the ground are very thin. Suburbs built from the 1980s onward are often lower in density and poorly located in relation to transit access, with U.S.-style, car-dependent shopping malls. They thus have little evidence of community of the kind observed in Albertslund. It may be just a time factor, but it may also be that the areas are too scattered and car-dependent for them to function other than by car. This, in our experience, no matter what the culture, means there is little opportunity for community to flourish. Some urban ecology projects are happening with chicken coops and permaculture, but there are few signs of the dynamism evident in Albertslund.

The same pattern is found in the low-density parts of Australian and U.S. cities. Although the big lot offers more space for individuals to do urban ecology, the reality is that not much happens. Urban ecology needs commitment and help from others. It requires a community approach to make it anything more than superficial. We find that the best examples of urban ecology are occurring in inner-city locations, rather than as Troy (1996) would suggest, in the areas where people have big lots.

We find that public activity is minimized in the Auto City and in those parts of any city that have Auto City characteristics. It is just too hard to manage, other than for activities such as organized sports or church, which are based around individual households. More committed community development occurs only with enormous effort and is hard to sustain. Community support for activities such as urban ecology projects seems to grow out of organic urbanism, which appears to require a certain level of pedestrian contact or "accidental interaction."

The exceptions to this are where there is an "intentional community" that provides a moral commitment binding people to work together. These, like the various cohousing projects in Denmark (e.g., the rural organic farm co-op Svanholm), are obviously creating community, and generally it is around urban or rural ecology. One such intentional community, Torup, is on the urban fringe of Copenhagen.

Outer-fringe Urban Ecology

Torup is a small eco-village on the edge of Copenhagen. Like a lot of urban ecology experiments, the people who established Torup were driven by ecological and social ideals. They were therefore careful in choosing their site and were able to

Photo 5.8. Ecological cohousing in Torup, Denmark.

locate adjacent to a small regional rail line, thus making them less auto-dependent than many eco-villages.

The Torup village began in 1990 when the cooperative bought a thirteen-hectare farm. Ten hectares are still used for cooperative cultivation, and the rest of the site has thirty houses and a village center. Four houses are dome structures and one is earth-covered.

The village is supplied with electricity from a windmill; all houses are well insulated with solar orientation and active solar heating.

Water comes from wells and rainwater tanks. Wastewater is treated by filtering it through a large earth mound. The village aims to become self-sufficient in food and jobs but is not there yet. Torup has minimal car use since it functions in a largely self-sufficient communal way, and where travel is needed, people generally use the train (Scheurer, 1998b).

The community approach so critical to Torup, and to so many of the other successful urban ecology projects discussed, is not always present in Danish urban ecology. One project, Villa Vision, instead tries to demonstrate how eco-technology can enable people to lead completely isolated, self-sufficient lifestyles (see Box 5.5).

Urban Ecology in the United States

There are many urban ecology projects developing in U.S. cities (summarized in Walter, Arkin, and Crenshaw, 1992; Roelofs, 1996; in publications by the

Box 5.5. Villa Vision: Urban Ecology as "Disneyland"

This example of Danish urban ecology is not as positive as the others in this chapter. It is a development paid for by industry as a demonstration eco-house of the future. This commitment from industry is worthwhile and should be encouraged. The problem with Villa Vision lies in its design values.

Although its combined "tinkering" probably fits the criteria of urban ecology, Villa Vision does not represent the kind of development that we believe helps make a sustainable city. The development is a "Disneyland"-style showpiece only. It is presented here to show how we need to do more than just "tinker."

Villa Vision is a high-technology eco-house designed to be self-sufficient in heating and electricity, with minimal water consumption and an emphasis on waste recycling. It has solar cells, water taps that you program for the exact amount required (one cup, two cups, etc.), light sensors that turn off lights if there is no movement in a room, sensors that control outside shades (like petals around a flower) whenever the sun is too strong, and sensors that open and close windows for programmed climate control. Its wastewater system treats water through a root zone ecosystem.

Villa Vision was lived in by a family and is now an office. It is not a livable environment since its circular shape reflects all sound inward, and so it is disconcertingly noisy. The small den used as the "entertainment room" contains all the electronic forms of entertainment, including CD stereo, TV, and Internet-connected computer. Everything about the building suggests that these would be well used. The design is not oriented to community. It is designed for people to sit in isolation. It represents the ultimate in self-sufficiency.

Villa Vision is located in the Danish Institute of Technology and is surrounded by a large parking facility. It symbolizes that urban ecology can be expressed as high-tech "tinkering" with the goal of creating self-sufficiency more for an elitist "green" market than any broader sustainability goals. If you want to escape the city and not have to interact with anyone other than electronically, if you want to avoid any civic responsibility, even the need to participate in a local community's infrastructure, then Villa Vision is the answer. This is not a global contribution to sustainability.

The importance of Villa Vision is that it shows how all technology, even green technology, is subject to a set of values. It is not enough to say that urban ecology is postmodern and so is "nonintentional," as though this means that Villa Vision is as acceptable as the other developments described above. We need to have a more global understanding of what our technology is designed to do, and we need to understand what this means for professional praxis (Chapter 6) and for personal and city ethics (Chapter 7).

Photo 5.9. Arcosanti, Paolo Soleri's ecological settlement near Phoenix, Arizona.

Institute of Local Self-Reliance; by the U.S. EPA in its *Sustainability in Action* [Concern Inc., 1995]; in the *Sustainable Communities* task force report of the President's Council on Sustainable Development [1997]; and in the *Urban Ecology* quarterly newsletter). The examples here are meant to represent something of the flavor of what is occurring, emphasizing a few urban examples, since most of the effort so far has gone into small eco-villages.

Arcosanti

One of the oldest examples of U.S. urban ecology is Paolo Soleri's Arcosanti in Arizona. This unfinished dream involves converting a mesa in the desert near Pheonix into a twenty-first-century example of eco-technology, solar architecture, and artistic expression. It is a prototype of what Soleri calls "arcology" (architecture and ecology working together) for 5,000 people. It is a compact Walking City with large-scale solar greenhouses on 10 acres of a 4,000-acre preserve.

Eco-Village at Ithaca

The United States has a growing eco-city movement spearheaded by groups such as Urban Ecology, Inc., and Eco-City Builders. Some projects are attempting to put into practice the principles of ecological city design by constructing eco-villages within established urban areas.

One such project is Eco-Village at Ithaca. This project is located on an agricultural parcel of land on a ridge above the medium-size city of Ithaca in New

York State and has strong ties to Cornell University through the people involved in it. The aim is to develop a small urban settlement by building groups of tightly clustered houses and community facilities that occupy only about one-tenth of the site, thus preserving the rich agricultural land for productive uses (a key aim of the overall project was to buy agricultural land and protect it from traditional sprawling development). Remote work opportunities will exist through community-based electronic workstations included in the common facilities. Much of the construction is complete. The village will attempt to use a range of environmental technologies for energy, water, and waste treatment, though difficulties with city authorities and traditional urban development practices are considerable (e.g., opposition to the idea of not connecting to the main sewer system and established ideas about access road standards).

One of the sustainability problems facing the development (and others like it, such as Arcosanti) is its relative remoteness and lack of a transit service and therefore the need most residents will experience to use cars on a regular basis for a lot of trips.

The innovation in the project is as much social as physical, with some of the biggest problems being associated with joint decision making and negotiation about critical decisions facing the community. There has been an effort to change some of the patterns of typical urban life away from privatized ways of doing things and toward a communal approach. The communal facilities, for example, include a common kitchen area and a roster for preparing communal meals.

Such projects are a drop in the ocean compared to the massive urban sprawl that is occurring on the fringes of U.S. metropolitan areas. However, they are fledgling, pioneering exercises that will hopefully help to bring a more ecological approach to urban development into the mainstream and to integrate ecological settlements into the heart of urban areas and not just on the fringes of cities.

Jericho Hill Village

This development is being planned as an alternative, ecologically sustainable "Edge City" fifty kilometers from the center of Vancouver in British Columbia (Paterson and Connery, 1997). It is immediately adjacent to a highly auto-dependent Edge City called Walnut Grove and is designed to highlight the difference between it and this unsustainable model.

Walnut Grove is not only completely car-dependent, but more than 50 percent of its surface is impervious (roads, driveways, and roofs); thus drainage has irrevocably altered the local stream ecosystem, there are no links to the regional forest and ecosystem with open space, there are just a few ornamental developments unsuitable for local bird and animal species, and there is no link to the agricultural land it replaced.

By contrast, the 140-hectare Jericho Hill development for 5,500 people has the following design goals:

- Provide 80 percent of the community's heat energy from local sources (passive and active solar).

- Provide 60 percent of the community's food from local sources.
- Reduce overall electrical energy use by 50 percent (efficient appliances and photovoltaic cells).
- Reduce transportation energy use by at least 50 percent (mixed-use, compact village with no more than 500 meters to the village center and a transit stop to the city).
- Reduce community water use by a minimum of 60 percent (surface runoff into three streams that go into filtration beds and solar aquatic systems that treat gray water, water-efficient devices, xeriscaping, and groundwater recharge).
- Treat 100 percent of domestic wastewater locally (solar aquatic greenhouses in each neighborhood with final treatment in adjacent community aquaculture).
- Recycle and reuse a minimum of 80 percent of the community's solid waste (neighborhood collection, composting, and use in community gardens).
- Assume a zero net increase in stormwater loadings for the area's drainage basins (77 percent permeable and recharge beds).

In order to achieve this, Paterson and Connery (the designers) say:

> residents need to accept living in communities which are denser than those provided in current edge community developments; residents also need to reduce their dependency on the automobile. Such change, however, is seen as essential if our cities and towns are to become truly sustainable. (p. 344)

The land use comparison of Walnut Grove and Jericho Hill is given in Table 5.3.

The actual development has yet to begin. Like a lot of urban ecology in North America and Australia, this project remains in the literature (e.g., Downton, 1994), so there is a real need for demonstrations that can show people what it is all about. Jericho Hill aims to simultaneously resolve the environmental and community-building crises of North American Edge Cities. It needs to be built to ensure that some real lessons can be learned.

Conclusions

All cities have different problems to solve in the sustainability agenda. The major focus of this book is the Auto City, and here the resolution of an approach that makes the city simultaneously greener and less auto-dependent is very much in debate. The kind of city form that would enable sustainability solutions to be worked out (see the future "Sustainable" City presented in Figure 4.1) shows the establishment of localized urban management areas based around transit-oriented urban villages. The inherent reductions in transportation energy use in such a city are already being realized in cities that are adopting such a strategy (e.g., Toronto, Stockholm, Portland, and Zurich). These localized areas can also become the basis for water and waste management by using small-scale wastewater treatment systems, recycling locally, using various water harvesting possibilities, sorting and reusing solid waste, and creating permaculture gardens.

The space for these ecological processes may be on the edge of the urban vil-

Table 5.3. Land Use Comparisons of Walnut Grove and Jericho Hill Village

Feature	Walnut Grove	Jericho Hill
Residential	65.5% site coverage	28.5% site coverage
Low density (20 units per net ha)	38 ha (749 dwellings)	none
Medium density (20–44 units per net ha)	6.5 ha (295 dwellings)	none
High density (45–80 units per net ha)	none	16 ha (2185 dwellings)
Commercial	none*	1.0 ha (1.8% coverage)
Agricultural	none	12.5 ha (22.3% coverage)
Roads	14.5 ha (21% coverage)	3.5 ha (6.0% coverage)
Public open space	9.0 ha (13.2% coverage)	23 ha (41.4% coverage)
Total population	3,100	5,500
Total land	68 ha	56 ha
Gross density (people per ha)	46	98
Net density (people per ha)	70	230
On-site energy, water, and food production		
Energy production	0–10%	approximately 75%
Water supply	0%	approximately 65%
Waste recycling (solid and liquid)	0%	100%
Food production	0%	50%
Ratio roads to open space	1.0–0.62 m^2	1.0–6.5 m^2
Road allowance per person	47 m^2	6.4 m^2
Number of intersections (roads and pedestrian paths)	approximately 25	approximately 125
Farthest distance to services	1,300 m	350 m
Farthest distance to open space	650 m	100 m
Percentage of lots/buildings solar oriented	15%	80%

Source: Paterson and Connery (1997, p. 342).
*Typical of most "communities" in Walnut Grove, the community used for comparative purposes in this study does not have any commercial facilities. All commercial facilities in Walnut Grove are strip malls or shopping centers situated along the major thoroughfares.

lages, away from the intensively used transit-oriented land uses, though still part of the local community. But what the Danish urban ecology examples clearly illustrate is that even in the midst of all these intensive urban functions, the ecological can be present and can be used to help reduce local metabolic flows. Indeed the city must have sufficient density for urban ecology to be taken on by the community. Urban ecology is unlikely to thrive in an Auto City. Localized urban ecology experiments and global environmentally sound planning are not conflicting—they are the two sides of the one urban sustainability agenda.

Critical to all of the above changes that are envisaged for sustainability in cities is the role of professionals and the role of the local community. The next chapter thus draws together some of the key ideas about professional praxis and sustainability in cities and how the community can become the focus for managing the transition to a more sustainable city.

Notes

1. Niemczynowicz (1992) says: "The traditional approach to water related problems must change drastically; wastewater treatment technologies applied at present need to be complemented, and eventually replaced by novel, economically efficient and environmentally sound technologies" (p. 134). And later he suggests that the basis for a new approach must include all of the following key elements:
   • A systems approach, with both structural and nonstructural elements in contrast to narrow-minded technological approaches.
   • Multidisciplinary cooperation in order to solve complex problems.
   • Small scale in contrast to technological monumentalism.
   • Source control instead of "end of pipe" approaches.
   • Local disposal and reuse instead of exploitation and wastefulness.
   • Pollution prevention instead of reacting to damage.
   • Use of biological systems and ecological engineering in wastewater treatment.

2. The approach taken in this book is firmly in the urban commons camp. Many before "have shown the link between low urban density and a range of environmental and economic problems" (RERC, 1974; Berry et al., 1974).

3. The reality is that there is no evidence for better, happier, healthier people coming from rural areas than from cities (see Chapter 1).There are, of course, fewer opportunities in rural settings and hence cities have continued to grow around the world, though rural images are often used as the basis of residential development.

   The powerful mythology behind the anti-urban idea is still frequently used by real estate marketers who depict ideal rural living areas on the urban fringe in their brochures and TV ads with isolated homes in natural settings. However, such areas are soon engulfed by suburbia as it flows forever outward and people soon become trapped in automobile dependence. Meanwhile, opportunities for creating urban centers with a dense, walking-oriented environment are rejected as too urban.

4. "Top Down" demonstration projects can create a context in which urban ecology can flourish. In Australia the Better Cities program provided money for such demonstrations but did not involve a simultaneous "bottom up" component of innovations from the community. There is no reason why this could not have been tried, especially with design competitions and awards for experimental ecological

houses. Similarly, an innovative urban-village design project in Melbourne described in Chapter 4 (Energy Victoria et al., 1996) is not proceeding very well, perhaps because it is too top down; the only part to proceed (in Sandringham) has a much more local initiative behind it. And the Sydney 2000 Olympic Games Village, which has ecological principles set by Greenpeace, began to lose some of its urban ecology edge, probably because it lacked grassroots innovation pushing these changes (Greenpeace Australia, 1993).

5. ISO14,000 is a World Trade Organization standard for the production and labeling of "green" services and products; it is potentially a powerful tool in the sustainability agenda.

Chapter 6

Promoting Sustainable Urban Change

Urban Change

Urban change comes from a combination of the market, government, and civil society, as shown in Figure 6.1. Each has a legitimate role to play, and they overlap at many points. When the three are working together, urban areas have a real chance of being sustainable. How this can be facilitated is the focus of this chapter.

- *Market:* The market provides the resources of wealth needed to make any development happen, whether it is helpful to sustainability or not. But the market is only short term and cannot determine what the elements of the "common good" are in urban change since it can only optimize what is best for individuals.
- *Government:* The government regulates and sets policy in order to ensure that the "common good" in cities is achieved and that issues to do with the long term (such as sustainability) are being resolved. But government cannot ultimately make the ethical judgments that set the priorities in society; its power to create urban change is, in the end, no greater than the collective values expressed by the community. And government is frequently not oriented to the long term, but to political terms of office.
- *Civil society:* Civil society is the guardian of culture and thus of ethics. Governments do not create ethics; they create laws that are meant to reflect as much as possible the ethics of the community. Government and the market can sometimes influence ethics, but mostly they are dependent on civil society for their morality and culture. The media, educational bodies, churches, and loose associations and collections of communities that we call civil society, are a highly significant force in shaping the long-term direction of society, including the shape of cities and their priorities in land use and infrastructure.

Civil society is also a major source of the labor that maintains the social institutions of our cities through paid and unpaid work. In Chapter 7 the importance of civil society in personal and community ethics is examined to see how fundamental it is to urban change for sustainability. This chapter focuses on professional praxis (i.e., the collection of systems, approaches, practices, and principles used by professionals in managing cities).

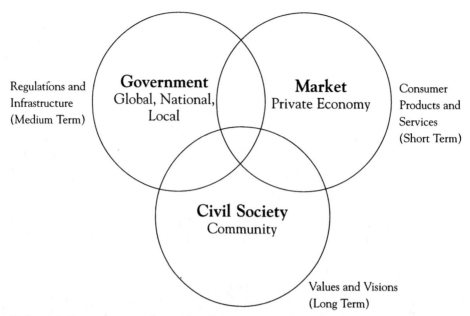

Figure 6.1. Government, market, and civil society components of urban change and their roles.

Professional praxis influences all three spheres of urban change: the market, government, and civil society. The paradigms and processes that professionals use to influence change, or sometimes to prevent it, work through government agencies, the private sector, and community groups. It is the urban "expert" who advises all three.

Urban management and the capacity to effect change are profoundly influenced by the combined ideas and techniques that come from engineers, economists, architects, designers, planners, environmental scientists, administrators, and political advisors. This chapter explores how professional praxis has influenced our cities in the past and how it can help to shape more sustainable cities for the future.

Modernist Professional Praxis

The modern city is an expression of the Industrial Revolution. The ideas that flowed from the Industrial Revolution, based on a mechanistic approach to life, have already been introduced in the discussions on transportation and on water. The railways, roads, and pipes of urban infrastructure bestowed order and control on the city that was not there before. These mechanisms became established in professional praxis manuals and were applied in every city as universal solutions. And to a large extent they were good solutions, especially when they were first developed.

The solutions being offered, as discussed below, were often essential for the health and livability of city dwellers everywhere. There is little room, however, for local variations and diversity in most modernist solutions; if cities want to be different, the power of the modernist professional manual to dictate the true and only way is a powerful force to overcome.

The mechanistic approach also became part of town planning. The profession was made into a kind of "science"—a science of codes, plot ratios, setbacks, percentages of open space, standardized road patterns and building forms, and endless other mechanisms for controlling land development by both government and developers.

Modernism in planning and architecture burst into our cities early this century with a radical agenda of rejecting the past and creating a new kind of mass-produced city. The Le Corbusier tower block set in a sea of open space, with no streets, was an expression of this movement, which is now in great disrepute. Today, however, the modernist ideals are just as mechanistic in our building of Auto Cities. Thus when modernism is in full flight, each new suburb is rolled out as though it came from a factory, no matter what the ecology of the area happens to be and with little consideration or concession to human creativity and community. Nature is kept to a bit of required open space and is usually a degraded piece of leftover land that soon needs cleaning up with lawns and disciplined trees. The human side of the city is left to the individual to create in private spaces, but this has little potential for any expression in the public spaces of our planned cities.

These identical, mechanical suburbs are becoming universal. Once you could find them only in the so-called English New World (i.e., North America, Australia, and New Zealand); now they appear in Europe, Asia, Latin America, and Africa.

Despite each new suburb claiming to offer "a unique lifestyle" or "fresh, country living," they all are absorbed into a monotonous megalopolis that sprawls in every direction, devouring natural areas and farmland and filling the air with automobile emissions.

There is a need to dissect the ideas that have led us to this form of city building if we are to find ways of overcoming their power to shape our cities. Such mechanistic thinking derives from applying technological thinking to all areas of life (Ellul, 1964). It is an approach that had great potency at the time, but it is no longer seen as having the ability to deliver on the "human" or "ecological" imperatives shaping the next century of city building. To say something is "modernist" in popular culture is to suggest that the life has been beaten out of it. The modernist, mechanistic era appears to be ending in most areas of human endeavor as postmodern critiques destroy the assumptions that it is built on:

- that all human beings are the same and can be programmed into lifestyles just as a machine can be driven or programmed;
- that nature is not important in itself but can be modified to suit our needs; and
- that efficiency is achieved through large-scale mass processes, whether they be industrial production, urban infrastructure, or governance (Cook, 1990).

The questioning of modernism began in the creative community (art, literature, architecture), but in the past twenty years it has been picked up by environmentalists, who have seen the impact of the industrial/mechanized mindset on forests, rivers, soils—anything natural and diverse. The creative and environmental objections to modernism are inseparable parts of the one critique of this force, as the human and the natural cannot be mechanized without both losing their core character. But what comes next? And what does it mean for cities?

Postmodernism

Modernism as a philosophy is dying, and its demise is impacting every aspect of life in the last years of the twentieth century. The death of modernism is due to a combination of factors:

- the artistic community can no longer accept modernism's denial of human diversity;
- the environmental community can no longer accept modernism's denial of biological diversity, and they are more aware now of the darker side to much modern technology;
- the women's movement and other "rights" movements can no longer accept the simple solutions of modernism that have shut them out;
- concerned people around the world can no longer accept that indigenous cultures should be absorbed into a single consumer capitalist culture; and
- everyone is made acutely aware through TV and the increasingly multicultural nature of cities in most Western industrial countries that the world is full of cultural differences.

The decline of modernism has led to the rise of postmodernism, a movement that is defined mostly by what it is not—it has no simple solutions. Postmodernism delights in uncertainty; it thrives on the lack of absolutes. It is a celebration of difference, but it is cynical about the future, it suggests that progress is unlikely (Cook, 1990).

Postmodernism is expressed in art, music, and literature, but what does it mean for professional praxis in cities, particularly in the context of sustainability?

Postmodernism and Cities

Many people now share the postmodern feeling of uncertainty about the future, and in urban matters they now see that:

- high-rise steel-and-glass towers are inhuman;
- low-density suburbs are monotonous sprawl with environmental, energy, and social problems;
- the car is the biggest polluter on the planet;
- the highway is symbol of monolithic modernism;
- regulations are stifling architecture and urban creativity; and
- infrastructure provision is shrouded in uncertainty, often being inappropriate, costly, and increasingly out of the question to even replace in old cities.

At the same time, we must live somewhere, use transportation and infrastructure, and try to improve the world, but the ease with which progress used to be defined is no longer there.

So what can be done? In many cities professionals are caught between those who are pushing for a "last gasp" in the old modernist paradigm and those trying to find their way to a different paradigm for doing things.

The challenge is to find a new basis for planning and managing cities that accepts the reasons for postmodern uncertainty but tries to find how we can go forward. As E. F. Schumacher said:

> progress ... is an essential feature of all life. The whole point is to
> determine what constitutes progress ... Hence the call for taking
> stock and finding a new orientation. The stock taking indicates that
> we are destroying our very basis of existence, and the reorientation is
> based on remembering what human life is really about. (Schumacher,
> 1974, p. 131)

In other words, we must try to redefine progress in the postmodern era, and
now it must be firmly embedded in the reality of sustainability. It will not be
enough just to accept postmodern uncertainty as a total approach to defining
urban life—little can be expected from that (e.g., Watson and Gibson, 1995). In
this chapter we try to identify some useful approaches that emerge out of postmodernism, particularly within the context of the need for sustainability.

We also want to try and build on another urban tradition that has existed
much longer than modernism and that many people are trying to rediscover as
the basis for some of the necessary approach to sustainability and professional
praxis. This movement we have called the "organic city movement" since it combines many aspects of the human and ecological that we discussed above.

The Organic City Movement

When any of us travel to Europe or the Middle East or anywhere there are premodern settlements, there are certain important qualities that become immediately obvious to us. These qualities are often summarized by the word *organic*,
which brings together not only the settlement's human and green texture, but
also the processes that allowed this to happen from within the community, rather
than through an imposed process. These qualities are:

- The buildings are nonuniform but part of a pattern; they appear to grow out of
  the landscape and in many places are hard to distinguish from it. Nature is not
  lost in this city. Water and trees can be central to its streets and public spaces.
  Waste is recycled. Resources are used frugally. And most of all, there are strong
  rural productive land uses immediately adjacent to the city that are integrated
  closely into the functioning of the city.
- The streets are filled with people walking, and all major local destinations are
  accessible by a short walk. The key to this is the kind of density and mixed
  land use that has grown from the need to have sufficient people living nearby
  and sufficient work, shops, schools, etc., within walking distance. Each combination of land use is organic to the city's peculiar history and culture, but all
  have the qualities of a "pedestrian" place. They are also often described as very
  "urban," and the two qualities are obviously linked. As Kostoff (1991) says:
  "Urbanism ... is precisely the science of relationships. And these relationships must be determined according to how much a person walking through
  the city can take in at a glance" (p. 83).

These are the "urban villages" of history, and although some characteristics
can be found in modern cities, mostly they have been obliterated. They can't just
be copied to replace our modern suburbs, but we can perhaps learn from the principles that lie behind their design and then maybe we can see how our technol-

ogy and urban processes could relate to this organic city tradition. This is the approach taken by the New Urbanism (Katz, 1994; Calthorpe, 1993; Duany and Plater-Zyberk, 1991) and many in the urban ecology movement.

The process that has substantially obliterated this "organic" form of city is largely due to the Industrial Revolution, as described in this chapter. It is an incorporation of the mechanistic, scientific approach to all aspects of life. It is the problem now recognized by ecological economists, who see how mechanistic economics destroys the human and the ecological (Daly and Cobb, 1989). However, the specific problems created in cities by the Industrial Revolution were also addressed by people who understood the ecological and human values that were under threat.

Greening the Industrial Revolution City

The Industrial Revolution brought about a rapid growth in cities as economics changed from rural production to industrial production. As more people and industrial processes filled the old Walking Cities of Europe they became impossible to live in. As discussed in Chapters 2 and 5, the wastes in the streets and the pressure for more and more housing in a confined walking diameter of about five kilometers created a major ecological and human crisis.

The cities did change. A new kind of city was invented: the Transit City. The new transportation technologies of trams and trains meant that urban villages could be linked together like pearls along a string. This solution meant that walking-scale areas could be retained within villages once a new form of linkage between them was created and natural areas could be retained in the corridors between development—that is, the city did change to become more sensitive to nature and to human community needs. As discussed in Chapter 2, North American and Australian cities were built in this form in the late nineteenth and early twentieth centuries, and many European cities such as Stockholm and Zurich have retained this basic urban form.

The process by which city governments came to build this type of city was quite chaotic and clearly involved a change in professional praxis. It involved technology, but it was propelled by major social movements associated with public health, social reform, ecology, and spirituality (see Hall, 1987, and Girouard, 1985). The town planning profession that emerged and the other associated urban management professions were not just technical but had a strong ethical framework that used ideas from the organic city tradition.

Thus the Transit City solution, although it was a part of early modernism, was also responding to more traditional values about the human and the ecological from this organic city tradition. The cities that emerged were forged as a combination of human/ecological values and a new kind of technology. Many cities benefited from this solution, but all had to battle through the painful changes associated with moving from one way of city building to another.

A new professional praxis was born that acted to manage the new kind of city, to provide and integrate the guiding ideas for a city in its layout and daily activities. Any history of these urban changes will show that the struggles to provide an answer to the challenge of building cities involved one group of reformers who stressed the need for organic values in the city. Now, as then, we find these ideas hard to locate as bureaucratic processes take over and squeeze out the organic life forces. We need to rediscover the origins and basic concepts of the organic city and recognize that modern-day environmentalists who are committed to winning back a more human and ecological city are not people who can't understand modern needs and wants. They are, in fact, part of a long and important tradition in city building that is neglected at the peril of the city.

The Organic City Family Tree

The lineage of those who have contributed to ideas on cities goes back to deep traditions of Greek philosophy and Judeo-Christian theology. The "polis" of the Greeks was a place for people to meet together and provide a community that would be more diverse and enriching than separated and self-sufficient individual families. The Jewish city had organic principles at its heart, as is discussed in Chapter 7.

But the lineage of importance to this chapter is the one that has fought for the organic city in modern times—that is, those who opposed mechanical values, who saw the human and ecological city as being squeezed out and replaced by dehumanized and artificial city values. This lineage can be traced through a number of writers and activists—for example, through John Ruskin (1819–1900), William Morris (1834–1896), Ebenezer Howard (1850–1928), Patrick Geddes (1854–1932), Lewis Mumford (1895–1990). There are many contributors in each generation. Our own includes Jane Jacobs (1961, 1969, 1986, 1996), Ian McHarg (1969), Ken Schneider (1979), Christopher Alexander (1979, 1987), Michael Hough (1984), and Roberta Gratz (1989). The writings of these people contain a common thread of organic thinking stressing diversity, human scale, heritage, nature, community, and artistic expression.

The Sustainable City Movement Today

Today, the organic city movement is alive again and has a new sense of vision. It is timely because, as we have shown, the Auto City has lost its organic values. Auto Cities continue to grow and sprawl, devouring farm and forest land, filling the sky with automobile emissions, and creating suburbs that engender considerable ambivalence.

The movement is also timely as the entire mechanical vision of how we should function is being questioned and torn down by popular culture. Without an alternative vision, however, the power of the mechanistic spirit to dominate and control our society will continue to fill the vacuum. The organic solutions are nevertheless being rediscovered. The urban sustainability movement is networked around the world and is struggling to:

- stop freeways and provide a new vision for transit-oriented urban villages, pedestrian-scale developments, traffic calming, and bicycle facilities (e.g., Surface Transportation Policy Project, 1994, and *Urban Ecology* newsletter);
- provide neotraditional planning that emphasizes real streets where people can

meet and children can play, which provide short distances to shops, schools, and other activities (e.g., the New Urbanism); and
- bring environmental thinking into city planning through water-sensitive design, waste recycling, community permaculture, and other green innovations, as well as a strong emphasis on community-scale technologies and processes (see Chapter 5).

But the battle for the city is just as fierce as it was in the 1890s, when an urban paradigm shift occurred that is similar in nature to the one we are facing now. Thus, at every level, these changes are opposed:

- There is a sudden freeway-building frenzy worldwide, almost as though engineers are initiating a last desperate push of the old paradigm before they have to admit defeat (Newman, 1994a).
- There is enormous cynicism among many town planners about neotraditionalists, urban ecology, and urban village concepts, and often "ecological" reasons are used to justify some of the worst low-density urban sprawl (see Chapter 5).
- There is constant bickering, if not war, between EPAs and planning authorities about who looks after the environment in cities—while the mechanical suburbs keep rolling out.
- Infrastructure agencies, such as water authorities, electricity commissions, and transportation agencies, are rarely able to let go of their central powers in favor of localized technologies and management; they seem ready to fight it to the end.

But small victories are also achieved, and they begin to form a pattern that gives heart to the new generation of organic city thinkers. Around the world, they are being expressed in sustainable city programs. The processes of change are gaining momentum at every level, but in the end they will mean nothing unless they are translated into the practical activity of urban professionals who build and manage our cities.

Professional Praxis at a Time of Paradigm Change

The kinds of problems described above—traffic engineers who want to continue building freeways, town planners who want to keep rolling out low-density, car-dependent suburbs, environmental scientists who keep doing de facto town planning through air-quality regulations, water engineers who want to keep building more big pipes–all these are part of the same problem: planning professionals were trained in particular techniques, and their manuals and codes still provide the same methods of doing things.

The world is changing, however. Cities are no longer responding to the old techniques, political reality is changing—in short, the paradigm is changing—but educational institutions and professional manuals take a lot longer to change.

So, what can professionals do in such a time of uncertainty?

Photo 6.1. The New Urbanist streetscape and design approach in Kentlands (on the outskirts of Washington, D.C.) builds on the best characteristics of the inner area in terms of walkability, density, and mix; but it lacks the transit.

First, professionals can try to understand the nature of the changes that are going on. This chapter tries to analyze some of these changes and suggest some principles that underlie the new paradigm.

Second, professionals can look at some new guidelines and codes that are emerging. Urban ecologists, New Urbanists, sustainable transportation reformers, etc., are pioneers who are experimenting with how the planning professions can now be expressed. Demonstration projects are being completed; urban ecology experiments are gradually working their way into new manuals; New Urbanists have a new set of codes available for professionals who want to create a Kentlands (see Photo 6.1) rather than a Levittown; and new ways of undertaking traffic calming and making quality transit systems are being professionalized too.

Appendices 2 to 6 present a number of guidelines and checklists that express something of the new sustainability paradigm in cities. These are: (a) growth management techniques, (b) a checklist for sustainable development in cities, (c) a guide for constructing an economic impact statement for urban development, (d) New Urbanism design guidelines, and (e) a guide to the provision of quality transit and land use integration in Auto Cities.

New Principles for Professional Praxis

In order to respond to the new postmodernist agenda and rediscover the principles of the organic city as we move into a new millennium, four important ideas seem necessary as an underlying basis for sustainable urban professional praxis: recognizing values, maximizing diversity, crossing boundaries, and facilitating organic processes. Each is discussed further to provide perspective on the future "Sustainable" City and the important role of professional praxis.

Recognizing Values

In any time of uncertainty it is necessary to seek out the core values that matter to a city. These are pursued further in Chapter 7 but would seem to include at least the following six values.

The Environment Matters

The environment still provides cities with sustenance even if we may not recognize it. And it has limits on how much it can be burdened with pollution and bulldozed to create new suburbs. No matter how much we may assert our postmodern individualism and lack of absolute values, the ozone hole will still allow our skin to burn if we stay outside in the spring and summer (especially in the Southern Hemisphere). Postmodernism can be no excuse for avoiding responsibility for the environment (Haughton and Hunter, 1994).

Social Justice Matters

Postmodernism cannot be a way of avoiding the need to consider the underprivileged, children, the elderly, and those with disabilities. A focus on social justice tends to remove a lot of uncertainty (Harvey, 1973).

Heritage Matters

The importance of heritage was discounted in modernism as it was so sure of its own way that it needed no sense of the past. Postmodern uncertainty makes us more aware of our links to the past in providing a more organic base for the future. We are building on a past that has significance because it involved people like us trying to resolve the complexities of their lives. This means we need an approach more like the "urban husbandry" of Roberta Gratz (1993) or Jane Jacobs (see Chapter 7).

The Public Realm Matters

Streets, parks, meeting areas, public transportation, and all other parts of the city not fenced off for private use are vital for us to value. When we do not value them and they begin to collapse as places for social interchange, then we really notice it. The Detroit and Los Angeles syndrome is not something we can afford. Postmodern uncertainty cannot be an excuse for abandoning the public realm to economic rationalists who see only individual consumption as what really counts (Vintila, Phillimore, and Newman, 1992).

The Urban Economy Matters

There is a growing awareness that the local urban economy must be the focus of how we develop in cities, particularly in the centers and subcenters of our cities. Writers such as Jacobs (1984) provide a theoretical framework for how to maintain the urban fabric with the local economy mixed in to where we live and recreate. Much job growth today is in small businesses based on information processing, and these businesses can be enhanced by being part of a cohesive local area with a lot of face-to-face contact, rather than being pushed into a CBD tower or a single-zoned, sterile commercial or industrial area.

Frost (1991) has also shown that we can drain our cities of their wealth by developing at too low a density, with the emphasis on greenfields development rather than reurbanization. It is important to direct limited capital into innovation rather than nonproductive suburban infrastructure.

Appendix 4 contains a guideline for conducting an economic impact statement on urban development, particularly how to compare the costs and benefits of reurbanization with those of fringe development.

The Community Matters

As broader certainties diminish, the need for local communities grows. Surveys of what people want for the future inevitably involve a greater role for the community—people want to live in "villages" again, even in cities (Community and Family Commission, 1992). Yet this sentiment is occurring just as we have created car-based communities with little that draws them together. Nevertheless, the desire for greater community involvement in the future of local areas is a strong part of the new agenda (Center for Livable Communities, 1997). There is also a much stronger sense of the need for a global community and the fact that we cannot survive without greater commitment to that (World Commission on Environment and Development, 1987).

These six values form the basis for urban professional praxis in our postmodern age of uncertainty. That they relate closely to the values of the organic city proponents is not a coincidence. The other key principles for professional praxis (see below) build on these values and provide a basis for sustainable urban policies and decision making.

Maximizing Diversity

Probably the most significant principle that comes out of postmodernism and is consistent with organic city insights, is the necessity to try to maximize diversity. Simplistic, mechanical solutions that provide "the one best way," as Ellul (1964) characterizes it, invariably erase diversity. This can be applied to many aspects of cities, but in terms of sustainability, we relate it to: housing types, transportation types, fuels, and even the provision of infrastructure, as well as cultural diversity.

Housing Diversity

Not only is there a wide diversity of tastes in different cultural groups, but there are very different requirements in the life cycle/demographic stage of households. All OECD countries have passed the baby boom and its echo and are now moving toward an absolute decline in the number of young couples seeking family housing, while there is a growing demand for housing suitable for the elderly. This is associated with an unprecedented increase in the number of single-person households.

The trade-off in housing types has always been with location: the lower the density, the poorer the location in terms of accessibility. This trade-off and the relative importance given to location is a very cultural matter. In non-Anglo-Saxon cultures, location tends to have a much higher priority than in Anglo-Saxon traditions. The growth in elderly and single-person households is now tending to increase the demand for location and therefore the importance of increased densities.

This is a challenge not fully accepted by all local governments yet, but clearly it has been put on the agenda of most national governments. It is part of the basis for our growing belief in the need for reurbanization and for urban villages in the suburbs as a central part of urban diversity. These options are just not available to more than a few wealthy people at present.

Urban development needs to find all kinds of creative ways to build more diversity into the housing stock. The New Urbanists are allowing very small pieces of land to remain that are normally added into other blocks, thus creating the chance to build affordable houses on the "slivers"; they are also deliberately creating "out buildings," such as small "granny flats" or "student homes" above garages. All these new suburbs have strict codes controlling their appearance, and thus the quality of the urban environment is improved by the diversity since it is within a broad context. The mix that results is better for the community and is a much better use of land. Some of the guidelines provided by the New Urbanists for creating a more diverse urban environment are presented in Appendix 5. They are often principles that are derived from the design of older inner city areas where organic values were expressed in the streetscape and infrastructure. A detailed design code is being developed by New Urbanists.

Opportunities for diversity in reurbanization abound, but are often thwarted by regulations designed for uniformity, not diversity. It is time for additional professional praxis changes to help build on the organic qualities of the inner city and not impose Auto City values everywhere.

Transportation and Urban Form Diversity

The uniformity of automobile dependence dominates our cities. The list of problems associated with auto dependence is substantial (see Chapter 2), and in Chapter 3 we showed how closely the land use patterns of cities follow their transportation priorities.

The need for greater diversity in our transportation and in the land use that follows it can be expressed in terms of the future "Sustainable" City. This city is not one that banishes cars, but one with much less car dependence. This is achieved by creating much greater diversity in how people can live without needing a car. All kinds of transit options meeting the need for crisscrossing the suburbs can be achieved when there is a range of subcenters of various types and sizes, all providing links in the transit chain. These dense, mixed-use subcenters would incorporate quality local services and links to global information networks. Unlike the modernist city with its single CBD, the future "Sustainable" City is likely to have a diversity of smaller CBDs throughout the city, each with its own specific emphasis and set of economic and social priorities.

The future "Sustainable" City provides for increased opportunities to walk, cycle, or use public transportation as well as use cars. Fundamental to this increased diversity is the transit infrastructure that is required to link its subcenters (with heavy or light rail), as well as transit to provide local services, such as demand-responsive bus services. This city provides far more options in travel and lifestyle than the monocultural car-dependent suburb of modernist cities.

The biggest force still driving the Auto City to build large freeways and accommodate the automobile rather than providing other options is the standard "black box" transportation/land use model for calculating benefit-cost ratios on road projects. These are based on how a new or widened road will save time, reduce fuel, and lower emissions and road accidents. As pointed out in Chapter 3 and elsewhere, these benefits are illusory due primarily to "induced traffic." Considerable research has now shown this to be an unequivocal reality—for example, the UK SACTRA report (Department of Environment, 1994), our own studies (Newman and Kenworthy, 1989a) and U.S. work by Hansen that shows that each new lane-mile of road capacity creates 1 percent more vehicle miles traveled (summarized in Surface Transportation Policy Project, 1998). Nevertheless, road planners continue to use these models, even when they are part of a wider approach to city planning as demanded by legislation such as TEA-21.

The alternative approach is to find a better methodology that can include all options and assess them on a sound economic basis that incorporates all the feedbacks, such as "induced traffic" and all external costs and benefits (e.g., transit systems can create external benefits to land owners nearby). Such a methodology does not seem to exist, though the LUTRAQ model from Portland seems to be beginning to show more realistic assessments. Given the lack of such a "sustainable transportation black box" it is necessary for transportation planning to be a more community-oriented process as the public in general have a good sense of overall priorities in this area. They certainly are acutely aware of how building big roads does not solve traffic problems and are looking for more diversity in the options presented to them. This is the basis of the U.S. TEA-21 legislation that has shifted infrastructure funding from a largely black-box approach to one that is far more community oriented.

Professional praxis must reflect the need for greater diversity in urban lifestyles based on the diversity of transportation options that are now available. A set of guidelines has been created to assist in achieving quality transit; it particularly emphasizes how to better integrate transit and land use (Appendix 6).

Fuel Diversity

One of the great certainties of our age is that we are reaching a critical point in the Golden Age of Oil. As discussed in Chapter 2, we are approaching the production peak of world oil.

Transportation in modernist cities is dominated by a dependence on oil. What happens as oil begins to decline? We believe this will mean that, whereas the Golden Age of Oil was represented by new suburbs increasingly scattered from the city and its centers due to cheap, easy car travel, the new age of increasingly difficult and more expensive oil will mean reurbanization of the city in the inner area and in new subcenters to minimize travel needs.

Not only will we need to ensure that there are many more options for reducing auto-dependent lifestyles, but that there is available a greater diversity of fuel sources. Electricity will be the important fuel of the future since renewable sources such as the sun, biomass, and the wind can be tapped in many different ways. But we will also need to convert in the early stages of the oil transition to the use of natural gas in vehicles and then eventually to liquid biofuels (grown differently for each region) and to hydrogen from solar electricity.

Professional praxis needs to ensure that cities can be assisted through this period. It is likely that there will be a number of further oil crises, but each one will just confirm the need for greater fuel diversity.

Infrastructure Diversity

The simple approach that came to us from nineteenth-century cities was that infrastructure was provided by experts in a centralized authority and was focused on big pipes, big rail, or big road systems that stepped down into smaller and smaller units.

As outlined in Chapter 5, an assessment of this approach is taking place at an institutional as well as at a technological level in most developed countries. The possibility of localization as the basis for infrastructure is gaining momentum and needs to be considered in the spectrum of options for infrastructure provision.

Localization is where the scale of the technology provides an infrastructure oriented to a local area. Such technology cannot stand alone, but its focus is nevertheless on a local solution rather than on a city-wide one. The momentum for this is coming from agencies that are looking at the enormous cost of rebuilding or expanding main sewers or building new dams or even just extending the big pipes out to new areas. Thus the old nineteenth-century approach is giving way to a new set of urban technologies and a new set of urban management processes that are local in their orientation and fundamentally more diverse.

The main step remaining before further advancement in localization is the development of professional praxis that ensures adequate standards and good networking, but that encourages, rather than discourages, local, community-scale solutions to infrastructure (see Box 6.1).

Cultural Diversity

Behind all of this desire for greater diversity is the recognition that there are different cultural values. The importance of multiculturalism in cities is that this diversity can be the basis of providing solutions that would not have been seen if monocultures existed. The importance of cultural diversity ought to be reflected in every aspect of urban professional praxis. Cities that can develop a policy to adequately facilitate cultural diversity will be more able to bridge the age of uncertainty in their planning. This is discussed later in the section on cultural boundaries.

Crossing Boundaries

The kind of diversity needed for our future requires urban professional praxis to become much more of a boundary-crossing exercise. This needs to occur in terms of physical boundaries, disciplinary boundaries, and cultural boundaries.

Box 6.1. Case Study: Malang, Indonesia

In Indonesian cities, as in many Third World cities, there is no real sewerage system. Septic tanks take wastes for a short period before they enter groundwater, surface drains, or rivers. Major studies by groups such as the World Bank are suggesting the standard "big pipes" solutions. These become impossibly expensive to contemplate and very difficult to implement since the very dense cities would need to be severely disrupted to put in the pipes.

Photo 6.2. A community-scale sewage treatment system is the only way that a squatter settlement like Embong Brantas in Malang (East Java) will be able to manage its domestic waste.

A research project in which we are involved is demonstrating a localization solution. It is providing several kampungs in Malang, a regional town, with small-scale treatment plants that do not need big pipes for them to work. The 500-household scale means that pipes (where needed) can be placed into the stormwater drains, thus not disturbing the kampung. Final effluent can pass through a banana tree garden. Furthermore, the management structure is already in place at this scale, so the system has some chance of succeeding on the cultural level.

Crossing Physical Boundaries

The new demands of sustainability require consideration of new physical boundaries to manage the environment, community needs, and infrastructure requirements.

Environmental Boundaries In New Zealand, local government boundaries have been redrawn to coincide with bioregions—that is, natural catchment boundaries that define the soil and water interactions and management needs of that area.

This is a good option for cities since there will be increasing pressures to focus on these environmental issues and the boundaries often shape responses to such matters.

It is not necessary to formally change boundaries if urban professionals (especially in local government) can group and regroup around particular environmental needs. In Australia, Landcare Groups have been established on catchment boundaries without these lines having any special legal status. In many places they have become de facto local governments for anything of an environmental nature.

Other environmental issues, such as air quality, require "whole of city" management, and hence local authorities need to join together to participate in the many transportation, industry, and land use inputs on this issue. In the United States, the Clean Air Act amendments of 1990 now require city-wide land use solutions to be developed that minimize vehicle use. This has meant that city regional plans must now be developed, forcing new boundaries to be created around the airshed of the city. Water pollution from stormwater is similarly pushing cities toward defining new catchment boundaries in their areas.

Of course, when dealing with the sustainability agenda it is important for professionals to see that the boundaries of significance include global boundaries.

Professional praxis needs to encourage people to move easily across a range of physical boundaries to find solutions for local, regional, and global sustainability issues.

Community Boundaries Communities are as real and important in their diversity as the bioregional natural diversity discussed above. The public realm of a neighborhood, precinct, or community may be hard to define too precisely, but if we are to provide ways of facilitating communities, then we must try to define some smaller-scale community boundaries.[1]

The readjustment of local government wards to more precisely represent particular types of communities could be an exercise with significance that goes beyond the obvious democratic benefits, as shown in the next section.

Infrastructure Boundaries The big-pipes approach to water infrastructure is beginning to be localized—that is, a new scale of community technology is being addressed. Water and sewerage are the first infrastructure areas to return to a more localized approach after it was lost in the "modern" era, but they are not the only ones. Power is already moving in this direction in many parts of the world, especially wherever cogeneration or renewable options exist, because by their nature, these options are small and dispersed. Transit and communication are also localizing to different degrees.

While the technology for infrastructure may be moving to a smaller-scale, localized system, it will still require a heavy degree of city-wide coordination. Localization does not mean cutting off from the city or region. Sustainability requires all levels to work closely together.

The question of how much a community or city can localize its infrastructure is a question of technology choice that depends on a city's values. There are technologies that work well at the local scale for most areas of urban professional praxis; however, they basically depend on what kind of city is being built and the basic values supporting it. The different kinds of infrastructure can be grouped into two levels:

- The first works best at a local scale because the city is oriented toward local communities; thus both technology and professional praxis will want to be oriented to them.
- The second works best at a large-scale level because the city is oriented only toward individual households and does not take seriously the community scale of operation.

Although the second level is only functional at the bigger scale, it means a significant orientation toward centralized bureaucracies and professional praxis; under this approach so many of today's Auto City problems will remain insoluble.[2]

The next stage of infrastructure management at the smaller community scale will require, as already stated, different management structures—in particular, new boundaries at the local level will be required. These could be associated with communities, as set out in the future "Sustainable" City vision. The benefits to local communities of becoming more involved in an integrated approach to local infrastructure management are multiple. Not only could the benefits be very tangible in terms of lower rates and taxes, but the responsibilities become key reasons for the community to work more as a community. It also creates local employment, not only in managing the technology, but in utilizing the resources—the water and waste, the community telecommuting center, the community bus services, etc.

The other aspect of physical boundaries, apart from the need for creating smaller local units and a regional whole-city boundary, is the need for local authorities to link into national and international sustainability goals. Local Agenda 21 plans, or Sustainability Plans, are becoming the basic strategic planning tool for local authorities. The need for national and international groups of local authorities to ensure that the global agenda is being covered becomes ever more obvious and apparent.

Crossing Disciplinary Boundaries

The new responsibilities for localization under the sustainability agenda will require new disciplines being brought into local government. The integrative, synthesizing abilities of local authorities will be extremely important. They will need to incorporate, at various times, environmental scientists, water and wastewater engineers, communications and power system engineers, public transportation planners, sociologists with community boundary expertise, heritage experts, local job creation experts, artists and grassroots community activists who can articulate local visions, and more. There are few disciplines that can be left out by the postmodern local authority with a commitment to sustainability.

Sustainability requires local-authority professional praxis to be characterized by openness, flexibility and self-confidence, with a low threshold for jargon and a sense of the genuinely local as well as the global.

Crossing Cultural Boundaries

In addition to crossing the artificial boundaries on maps and the artificial lines drawn up by universities to define professions, we need to cross the real boundaries between cultures. One of the great values of postmodernism is that it has allowed the importance of differences to be recognized. But this can be useful in our professional praxis only if we can learn to cross cultural boundaries.

Fremantle, Australia, has become famous for its cosmopolitan and pedestrian-friendly city center. One critical decision that was made in the early 1970s that helped it reverse decades of economic decline was simply to allow alfresco dining on the sidewalks. This response to Italian shop owners overturned a distinctly Anglo-Saxon regulation with its values of a far less "street-oriented" culture. Fremantle also changed regulations to favor markets, street entertainers and musicians, mixed land use, and higher density; all of these were challenges to Anglo-Saxon cultural values that tend to discourage the coming together of people in public places. But these changes were the key to the revival of Fremantle.

In recent trips to Canadian cities we have become increasingly aware of the reason they have more than half their new housing in the form of transit-oriented, high-density apartments and medium-density townhouses—it is a response to a more culturally sensitive urban marketplace. Planners and developers have listened to this demand from Asian immigrants (e.g., from Hong Kong), while also hearing the more obvious and strident demand from the Anglo-Saxon culture that this is not a "legitimate" demand. In the process of accepting the development of high-density housing around transit stops (an obvious way to make money for someone from Hong Kong), it has created a legitimacy for the whole culture to accept greater diversity in housing and lifestyle. Its positive implications for sustainability are now obvious.

This is the paradigm shift through which we are moving.

The concentration on cultural diversity as the basis of a new kind of professional praxis mentality is the approach being adopted by many cities that have had a lot of immigration in recent years. It is often difficult and always politically risky, but it is the social heart of the sustainability agenda.

Without culturally sensitive planning, cities find reurbanization of the inner city very difficult, and certainly in the United States, the sprawl of cities has been closely linked to the failure to overcome cultural prejudice (Shore, 1995; Massey and Denton, 1993).

Facilitating Organic Processes

This final idea is more related to process. First, we need to recognize more clearly the role of natural processes in the city, and second, we need to recognize how local community processes can be used to shape the city.

Natural processes—such as water systems, soil and air, as well as flora and fauna—are all part of the city. They provide all the free ecological services and when abused they impact our health and well-being. They also are seen to have their own ecological integrity, to be valued inherently themselves. To remedy this abuse, efforts are being made to turn drains back into creeks; to find ways to reuse nutrients and organic wastes in the urban system, rather than just allowing them to flow through it; to find out the limits to the air's natural assimilative and cleansing capacity, as well as the capacity of water bodies such as rivers, lakes, and estuaries, on which cities are built. With a better understanding of the local ecology and how the human ecology of the city interacts with it, a city can become more organic. Such processes are well under way, particularly when it comes to bringing water back into a city in a more natural way—for example, storm water management systems that are not completely functional but are also a celebration of water in the city.

Local community processes have always been seen as necessary for supporting local government functions, but not in any significant way for the important urban ecological functions of energy use, water supply, sewerage systems, recycling, and transit. As suggested earlier, the development of community-based technology in recent decades has meant that smaller-scale provision of these services is now feasible. Local government used to manage most of these services 100 years ago, when organic solutions in the Transit City were being created. But most of this century has seen them centralized into larger- and larger-scale citywide systems—usually justified by greater efficiency due to the scale and efficiency of large systems.

However, modern industry has discovered that such efficiencies are often lost because the creative human element is lost. Thus Post-Fordism is showing us how to break up large systems into more easily managed, locally responsive units that can enable the total system to work better. The business world now recognizes that quality of management is associated with greater autonomy in local decision making (Piore and Sabel, 1984; Mathews, 1994). This is echoed in the appropriate technology literature with the recognition that quality can be associated with small-scale, locally responsive technological systems rather than the gigantism fetish of our twentieth-century engineers.[3]

A localized, organic approach not only serves ecological purposes, but is also better for social and economic reasons (Gratz, 1989). In her many books on cities, Jane Jacobs says that grand economic schemes do little for cities but that the real vitality comes from the intricate, diverse relationships that flourish in urban communities where people meet casually in streets and social gatherings. She concludes that the "science of city planning and art of city design, in real life and in real cities, must become the science and art of catalysing and nourishing those close-grained working relationships" (Jacobs, 1961).

The first step in such an exercise is that all major decisions be made through community participation processes. Techniques for doing this are well advanced (Sarkissian and Walsh, 1996; Center for Livable Communities, 1997).

The second step is to facilitate local experiments or demonstrations of localization. There is much to gain from enlightened experiments in locally managed urban services that can help us to see whether such organic processes can work in the twenty-first century city. As with most aspects of the city and its future, the shift in power structures will not happen easily, but the process is certainly worth fighting for.

Having sung the praise of localization, it is also necessary to add that all local, organic processes can spiral into inward-looking reactions if they are not being fed by the more global agenda for change in our cities. Thus it is important for professionals to keep coming back to the overall goals of sustainability and the visions of what this can mean in our cities. As Brooks (1988, p. 246) suggests:

> The urban planning profession needs a new generation of visionaries, people who dream of a better world, and are capable of designing the means to attain it. That, after all, is the essence of planning: to visualize the ideal future community, and to work towards its realization.

Realizing this better world will be achieved only if the "designing" is a participative process, involving the community and all stakeholders in a way that allows them the time to become informed about the issues and opportunities to help suggest the solutions.

If we are to have sustainable cities, the organic qualities of local variability and local knowledge must be linked with what the global community is needing and dreaming. The ability of organic communities to network internationally means that this is not an impossible task. The global civil society is beginning to be a force for change in professional praxis as it collects information on the many successful experiments in city sustainability.

Conclusions

One of the key reasons for the postmodern age of uncertainty is the collapse of the Auto City as a paradigm for planning. Just as the Walking City began to collapse 100 years ago and the Transit City began to emerge as the solution to its demise, we are now entering a period in which the Auto City is perceived to be unsustainable. It is perhaps not too much of a leap to suggest that the profound problems that faced the Walking City in the Industrial Revolution are at least equaled by the plethora of factors that today challenge the viability of the Auto City.

The emerging city we are suggesting contains elements of all the three previous cities (with a greater emphasis on pedestrian and transit qualities) and a new emphasis on multinodal subcenters that are critical for transactions in the Information Age. A range of technologies that facilitate diverse communities and foster greater ecological sensitivity are also available for the "Sustainable" City.

The postmodern response to the Auto City is to question its underlying mechanical and simplistic values, but postmodernism does not offer solutions to the sustainability issues confronting us. On the other hand, it is suggested here that the organic urbanism tradition can provide principles to guide us, just as they helped cities through their ecological crises a century ago.

The key to all of this happening is the development of a new professional praxis that is able to reflect the new values of sustainability and organic urbanism in a world that has lost a lot of its old certainties. For this to occur, the role and importance of communities go beyond simple democracy, because their values are what professionals must use for guidance as they attempt to forge new ways of building sustainability into our cities.

Just as "progress" became more certain with the emergence of the Transit City but withered with the ascendancy of the Auto City, we believe we will again be able to revive our belief in progress as we perceive the benefits and authenticity of this new professional praxis. This is the great hope of those involved in the sustainability movement.

Urban professional praxis in an age of uncertainty and sustainability can be an exciting process. If in the future "Sustainable" City we can genuinely recognize community values, maximize diversity, establish new boundaries and move flexibly between them, incorporate a range of new disciplines, and facilitate organic processes, then we will probably recognize that the old Auto City model with its simple, modernist goals and regulations was not only inadequate, it wasn't nearly as interesting.

Notes

1. Many local governments have followed the example of North Sydney, Australia, the first local area to create precincts around which local transportation and land use issues are discussed. The process has been extremely successful so far. In Portland, Oregon, local areas are used to facilitate a "Reclaim Your Streets" program.

2. Any technology can be misdirected, because when small-scale, community-based technologies are used to create "gated communities," for example, it subverts the full meaning of community (see Chapter 7).

3. In order to have physical space for locally managed urban services, especially eco-services such as water and waste management, there will need to be a trade-off with density increases for pedestrian-village qualities, as outlined in Chapter 5. It is not hard to see that densities should increase around transit lines and in centers of activity, but adjacent to these locations there may be low-density areas of parkland combined with community permaculture/water recycling and waste management.

Chapter 7

Ethics, Spirituality, and Community in the Sustainable City

Introduction

Throughout this book there has been an implicit set of ethical assumptions or values expressed. It is not possible to write without values. These ethics have been developing out of the authors' personal lives, especially in our experiences being involved in urban actions where we sensed something was wrong, acted to try and show alternative approaches, and then upon reflection over the years developed an appreciation of the underlying value conflicts involved.

This chapter tries to trace some of the fundamentals of these ethical approaches and to find some of the sources that feed our culture in this area. Ethics are very personal; they help to define our individual lives. This book began with the global and has moved toward the local and then the professional; it concludes by seeing what defines the individual in relation to sustainability and cities.

Ethical Foundations for City Sustainability

In this chapter we will try to develop an ethical framework out of the work of three key people who have been pioneers in what sustainability means for cities. We will examine the lives and work of Gilbert White, E. F. Schumacher, and Jane Jacobs.

Movements associated with these individuals—that can be seen struggling with many of the urban environmental issues around the world—are called local ecology, human ecology, and urban ecology (though this definition is expanded from that used in Chapter 5 to include more of the organic city approach outlined in Chapter 6).

There is a guiding theme to these stories: that the inspiration for ethical action on urban environmental issues can be traced through the organic philosophers and activists mentioned in Chapter 6 back to more distant roots in what we have called the "Western spiritual tradition." In environmental ethics discussions there is little reference to this.[1]

Mostly environmental ethics discussions have little positive to say about

Western ethical traditions but suggest we must turn to Eastern and aboriginal sources for our environmental ethics (e.g., White, 1967; Beatley, 1994; Warren, 1997). Such an approach is not being analyzed in any way here to try and show its faults (or its value) but to affirm that the tools for sustainability are close at hand in our communities. We do not need to look to other ethical foundations to find the solutions to creating more sustainable cities—they lie in our stories and hymns and Sunday schools, and are embedded in our institutions. They must, however, be revived for each new challenge, and our Auto Cities are ready for such a revival.

The Western spiritual tradition, as outlined below, is the basis for much that we have talked about in this book as organic ethics. It is central to understanding the contributions of the three people whose lives and work are examined below. But our discussion is not just an academic exercise. For we, too, find the ancient narratives and organic approaches of the Western spiritual tradition, which we briefly summarize, to be full of meaning and relevance. They are not the kind of dualistic and remote philosophies that are often dismissed by eco-philosophers today.

We see that the ethical principles espoused in the organic traditions of the west have emerged through history from Western culture's struggle with its own environmental and social problems and that they coincide and cross again and again with the ancient narratives used to explain such struggles. Therefore, we are obviously seeking to find an enduring framework in our generalizations, but what fills out this framework is organic and grows from each new situation. Thus we look for case studies, and beneath them we find evidence that this Western spiritual tradition is still alive. But it could be better understood.

Gilbert White and Local Ecology

Gilbert White represents the best of Western spiritual tradition as it applies to nature. He was the originator of the natural history movement, or what we are calling local ecology. Throughout the world there are groups of scientists and local amateur botanists, ornithologists, and every other kind of biologist, who are collecting information on the local ecology of their areas. This is now a vital part of how our environment is protected, and many urban ecology projects described above are part of this tradition. It is local and community-based; it is organic in its approach to nature; and very few contributors to discussions on environmental ethics would do other than applaud it. But few who discuss environmental ethics seem to be aware of the crucial role of Gilbert White in pioneering this local ecology or natural history movement.

Gilbert White was an English country clergyman whose collected letters to the Royal Society were published in *The Natural History of Selborne*. This book, first published in 1788, is now the fourth most published book in the English language. The book's introduction, written by Richard Mabey, says:

> More than any other book it has shaped our everyday view of the relations between man and nature. I say "everyday" without in anyway meaning to belittle White's scientific contributions. These were con-

Photo 7.1. Gilbert White's church in the village of Selborne, Hampshire, England (*top*); the ancient yew tree White wrote about 200 years ago still stands in the churchyard (*bottom*).

siderable, particularly in the area of observational method. But their impact on scientific theory was small and they were soon overshadowed by the discoveries of giants like Darwin and Mendel. White's contribution was more personal, in both senses. He was perhaps the first writer to talk of animals—and particularly birds—as if they conceivably inhabited the same universe as human beings.[2]

White loved his local flora and fauna. He was totally fascinated by the way their patterns of life fitted together. He described other living things as though they had an inherent goodness, a life of their own with a richness and rhythm, to which we can respond.

The context of this is important. Not only was there great social upheaval in Europe during White's time, but it was the period of the Enlightenment, with a strong sense of progress from science. The Royal Society was building a huge model of how nature worked that was very mechanical. Every plant and animal was classified by Linnaeus with scientific names, and the explorers who went to the colonies were bringing back large collections of unusual plants and animals. Most naturalists were simply cataloguing dead species, as Mabey says, in "a desire to drill some order into the disarrayed ranks of Creation."

So in contrast to the grand scheme or system, White showed that there was an intensely interesting life in his local environment. For example, he talks with great affection about the giant yew in his churchyard, a tree that can still be seen. And this is the other great quality of the *Natural History of Selborne*: it tells a story that, as Maybey says, gives "an unbroken line of continuity in the life of the countryside."

White puts in perspective the debate about Genesis and what it has meant to people in the Western spiritual tradition. For several decades since the work of Lyn White (1967) and others in the 1960s, Genesis has been seen by many in the environmental movement as the rationale for how humans can exploit nature. It is very hard to glean a purely dualistic and exploitative meaning from these ancient words, though no doubt some may have. Many Western philosophers certainly do seem to have had this tendency. The main point we want to make, however, is that the Western quilt is far more complex than this and contains within it a more organic, spiritual tradition that Gilbert White was expressing. This tradition is at the heart of the sustainablility movement.

White's book and his life reflect three main ideas about the meaning of the human-nature relationship. First, White shows that the theology of Genesis in practice is to rejoice in the teeming life of creation. Rather than classifying dead nature into systems that can be used to show our dominance, we can indeed just appreciate the beauties of a living creation. It is interesting to speculate whether Gilbert White recognized consciously that his approach to go out and study the interconnections in his local ecology was, in fact, a direct attack on the Enlightenment philosophers of the day. They believed in the grand designs of human progress based on rational processes and science that would order nature to do human will. This led directly to the functionalism of the Industrial City, but now we are seeking a more organic philosophy or spirituality to guide our cities.

Second, White shows that by seeing nature as special, but not sacred, one can be scientific and can manage environmental matters better. White made detailed studies of earthworms and their importance to soil; but his great passion was to understand where birds went in winter, and he was the first to suggest that they migrated. He concluded this through much observation but also through ecological experimentation—he enlisted his parishioners to comb the winter forest, beating the bush to try and scare the birds out of hiding places that others said they occupied. As well as satisfying his curiosity about how the local ecology worked, White was able to use his knowledge for practical environmental management; he was known for his skills in landscaping and building "nature trails" that visitors can still use to appreciate the local environment.

The scientific information collected by the organic local ecology movement is basic input for the new discipline of environmental science and environmental impact assessment. Whenever new development is planned and its impact must be gauged and managed, scientists go to local natural historians to find out about an area. This applies to urban or rural developments. Environmental scientists add their own scientific data, but all the best studies build on the information that is known by locals. This information is the basis of local ecology and of our local communities in settlements of all kinds.

Third, White shows how the Western spiritual tradition is based on organic processes. His collection of local natural history provided a powerful sense of hope for ordinary people since any community can develop the story of their local ecology. He showed that they can, without being super-scientists, go out and observe and understand and appreciate their piece of countryside. And so it has been.

The natural history movement has spread worldwide, and in virtually every community you can find a small group with this interest. Many politically active conservation groups are based on knowledge gained from local ecology groups, including those attempting to stop freeways or undertaking urban ecology projects. Thus the movement has become part of how people in the Western spiritual tradition have provided an ethical approach to their cities.

E. F. Schumacher and Human Ecology

Cities necessarily focus on humans. Thus if we are to develop our environmental ethics beyond a simple rejection of cities, we must do more than can be gleaned from a local ecology approach alone. To develop our ethics further requires a perspective on the role of economics and technology and how they relate to nature. We have mentioned how, in the eighteenth and nineteenth centuries, the Enlightenment tended to deify science and technology as the basis of progress. In the twentieth century, progress was also seen as inextricably linked to the human science of economics. This system of managing the world was believed to solve our problems in ways that more primitive, organic, native peoples could never know.

Economics and technology have had a good record at creating wealth, but they have begun to come up against some significant constraints, not the least of which are in the environmental area. For many environmentalists in the 1970s and 1980s GNP became known as Gross National Pollution, and "technological progress" became dirty words. Global and local problems seemed to be out of control, and economics and technology were seen to be part of the problem, not the solution.

However, the economist E. F. (Fritz) Schumacher helped to reorient many people's thinking and give a more hopeful perspective: that it is indeed possible to develop a human ecology. His books are a culmination of years of struggle within the economics paradigm (Schumacher, 1974, 1980, 1985). Schumacher's approach was to remind us of the human values questions behind all our science, technology, and economics. He said: "Environmental deterioration does not stem from science or technology, or from a lack of information, trained people or money for research. It stems from the lifestyle of the modern world, which in turn arises from its basic beliefs" (Schumacher, 1974 p. 122).

Schumacher's transition to this understanding was not easy, but it is a story that illuminates our basic message about the Western spiritual tradition. After working as an economist on the UK Coal Board for many years (including a period when he was said to have provided Keynes with the basis of his theory), Schumacher became an advisor on economic development to a number of Asian countries. He became confused since his economic models did not seem to apply, and he recognized that many of the simple technology transfer solutions from the West had done more damage than good.

Instead of pushing them harder, he decided to reflect and went into a Burmese Buddhist monastery, where he rediscovered the importance of spiritual values. He was urged by a monk to rediscover the spiritual roots within his own tradition. He in fact rediscovered his Catholic faith, but in a more mystical way, and he slowly began to develop his concepts of appropriate technology and grassroots economics. He used the spiritual traditions of the West to illuminate how we should adapt our economics and technology.

Schumacher did not just theorize about this. He set up the Intermediate Technology Development Group and began showing that smaller-scale technologies that took more account of people and nature were indeed feasible. In essence, his values framework was to reassert the importance of communities. The key criterion in assessing whether a technology was appropriate was if it helped to build up a community or not. Much of Schumacher's work was helping rural women with their domestic and agricultural work in a way that enabled them to continue their community networking instead of isolating them in individualized work or leaving them with backbreaking drudgery. This work continues to develop through most grassroots development agencies.

Schumacher was taken seriously because he was able to show that different technologies and economics can emerge when you change your fundamental values. He thus provided a bridge for the increasingly warring parties of economists and environmentalists, since it was no longer possible to hide behind some inevitable, single solution that modern economics and technology had thrown up to every world problem. Different solutions can be found in different communities.

This insight, along with his ideas about the "economies of permanence," led directly to the forming of the Brundtland Commission and the concept of sustainable development as outlined in Chapter 1. Economics and environment can be joined. There is now a thriving discipline of ecological economics showing what this means in academic terms (e.g., Daly and Cobb, 1989), but more importantly the whole sustainability movement, which is now defining much of global and local politics, was given coherence by Schumacher's writing and work.

Schumacher was the father, therefore, of what we now call the human ecology movement, the movement that no longer accepts that humans with their technology and economics will inevitably harm the environment.

Schumacher's role in shaping environmentalism is well recognized, but it is not often accepted that he did this by using the Western spiritual tradition. He not only embraced this tradition, he used it to explain his concepts.[3]

The human ecology movement is now trying worldwide to create a more ecocentric approach to economics and technology. It began in rural parts of the Third World but has now embraced every activity that humans undertake in every part of the world, including the building of cities. Agenda 21, with its 500 pages of action statements, is a human ecology guidebook.

Schumacher was acutely aware of the problems of our natural environment and saw an inherent solution in the organic processes of communities. As he said: "The case for hope rests on the fact that ordinary people are often able to take a wider view, and a more 'humanistic' view, than is normally taken by experts" (Schumacher 1974 p. 132). And "Wisdom demands a new orientation of science and technology towards the organic, the gentle, the non-violent, the elegant and beautiful." (Schumacher, 1974, p. 27).

However, Schumacher did not apply his community-oriented human ecology approach as much to cities as he did to rural areas of the world. This struggle is now a part of the global sustainability agenda and is allied to the third element of the urban environmental ethics equation: urban ecology.

Jane Jacobs and Urban Ecology

Today there is a global movement to green cities, known variously as urban ecology, ecological cities, or, as we prefer it, sustainable cities movement. It is everywhere apparent, and it is seeking to find deeper answers to the urban issues of our day than can be provided by better technology or more efficient government (Stren, White, and Whitney, 1992; Haughton and Hunter, 1994; Roseland, 1998). As suggested by Jensen (1994) in Chapter 5, it challenges cultural assumptions, not just social systems. It is a paradigm shift, but it is not entirely new, since it builds on the same traditions of awareness of nature and of the organic processes of communities outlined in Chapter 6. These traditions come from our Western mosaic.

Jane Jacobs is perhaps the most influential person from this tradition. Although she clashed with Lewis Mumford on many issues, their common belief in the importance of urban community is stronger than their differences. She is the urban equivalent of an ecofeminist, who, without formal training in an urban profession, followed her instincts and developed her powers of observation on the workings of everyday city life until she knew why she was right and could publish books that are now classics (Jacobs, 1961, 1969, 1984, 1994). She was living and working in New York in the 1960s and became dismayed at the large-scale clear-

Photo 7.2. Jane Jacobs' beloved Greenwich Village, New York.

ance of urban areas in the name of urban renewal and freeway projects. Such developments threatened Greenwich Village, her home, and so she wrote a series of newspaper articles that grew into a book called *The Death and Life of Great American Cities*. This is now seen as probably the key book in the twentieth century on the organic approach to cities, with Jacobs' descriptions of the organic workings of street life and neighborhoods, such as in the North End of Boston, having reached almost legendary status.

Jacobs later moved to Toronto to enable her family to avoid the Vietnam War. There she spearheaded the movement that stopped the Spadina Expressway. This prophetic action was critical to how Toronto then changed its priorities and today is one of the most livable cities in North America. This story and many others in modern cities, as discussed in Chapter 4, show how communities were able to dramatize their urban environmental problems and begin struggles that eventually changed the priorities in their cities. They were, at their base, ethical struggles.

Jacobs had an intuitive insight into the nature of cities and urban environments that all the professionals and experts of her day did not seem to have. They had elevated their modernist assumptions to some unified view of the truth, but they had somehow left out nature (apart from a highly sentimentalized version) and even left out the people they were supposed to be helping. Jacobs could see this very clearly from her "nonprofessional" view of the world. She was then able to achieve some good sense in fighting things such as freeways because her moral outrage communicated to other ordinary people and eventually to politicians.

In her foreword to the 1992 edition of *Death and Life...*, Jacobs says that "at some point along the trail I realized I was engaged in studying the ecology of cities" (p. xvi). She explains how this is not a superficial ecology of how a few plants and animals may exist in a city but is a study of city ecosystems. She then outlines how natural ecosystems and city ecosystems have so much in common due to their complex interactions of diverse functions, and how diversity develops organically over time. She says that "to investigate either natural or city ecosystems demands the same kind of thinking" (p. xvii) and urges us to "understand as much as we can about city ecology . . . starting with the humble city street and neighborhood" (p. xviii).

In a personal letter she adds: "To my mind, economy is as basic to understanding cities as ecology is to understanding the rest of nature, both being at the core of the tradition of curiosity about how things work and respect for their own integrity" (personal communication, 1997). In a sentence she is able to help us see how her work on cities links with Schumacher's appropriate technology and Gilbert White's natural history: respect for the *integrity* of nature and of human community as well as *curiosity* about how they work. This seems to be the heart of the organic approach to ethics.

Christopher Alexander has tried to define this organic ethic in cities in his book *New Theory of Urban Design* by seeing every good urban development as somehow contributing to a healing of some part of the urban fabric. He says:

> Each new act of construction becomes related in a deep way to what has gone before. This can only be accomplished by a process of wholeness as its overiding purpose, and in which every increment of construction, no matter how small, is devoted to this purpose (Alexander, 1987, pp. 15–16).

Jacobs' organic approach to cities in *Death and Life . . .* was described by the *New York Times* thirty years after its first publication as "perhaps the most influential single work in the history of town planning" (quoted in preface to Jacobs, 1961, 1992 edition). This is rejected by Jacobs as she sees so many cities continuing to make the same mistakes. Nevertheless, she has been the inspiration to decades of urban activists and now to the urban ecology, or sustainable city, movement.

Jane Jacobs (and others in this movement) did not turn to other traditions to become enlightened. She simply acted out of the wisdom and assumptions of the Western spiritual tradition that she had inherited as part of her culture. She did not turn to other cultures for her inspiration, though in the organic tradition she has a profound respect for aboriginal cultures; in a recent book she edited and did commentary upon about her great aunt, an Alaskan schoolteacher with a deep personal faith, she discusses how the environmental ethical tradition is passed on and, in this case, how it intersects with aboriginal tradition (Jacobs, 1997).

Jacobs, like Schumacher, quotes biblical passages to illustrate her points. For example, she begins her introduction to *Death and Life . . .* by telling the story of some local clergymen in Chicago who felt that the destructive city rebuilding process in their neighborhood reminded them of the people castigated by Job in the Old Testament as they "shoulder the poor aside, conspire to oppress the friendless, reap the field that is none of theirs. . ." Like White and Schumacher, she does not reject her Western traditions but uses them in expressing the depth of her feelings about making good cities.[4]

These three people and their stories highlight the three facets of environmental ethics that appear to be currently active in our cities today:

- A local ecology approach, as developed in the Western tradition by Gilbert White into the natural history movement. This organic approach to local ecology is obvious in most aboriginal cultures around the world but had been largely lost by the West (Suzuki, 1997). It is one of the forces of the conservation movement in the West today.
- A human ecology approach, as developed by E. F. Schumacher, which is able to provide a spiritual understanding of economics and technology. This organic approach has helped to forge the basis of ecological economics and sustainability in the West today.
- An urban ecology approach, as developed by Jane Jacobs, which provides insight into the organic processes of cities and how we can create more human living environments that are more compatible with the earth. In the West, this is now expressed through the urban ecology, or sustainable city, movement.

All three worked from the Western spiritual tradition to enable us to better understand an environmental perspective on our world. They were not philosophers, but practitioners who forged their ethics in day-to-day responses to their environment. Present-day activists seeking to create sustainable cities are building on this tradition. In essence, this approach is prophetic in that it tries to depict what will happen if we continue to build our cities as we are doing, and at the same time it sets up an alternative vision of how the city could develop. In this way it builds on centuries of ethical tradition in our cities. City prophecy can be traced to the earliest parts of biblical history; the prospects of city death due to unsustainable practices are a feature of the Western spiritual tradition. Many cities have died, such as Ephesus (see Photo 7.3).

City prophecy in the Western spiritual tradition is based on the presentation of two contrasting visions for a city: the elements of city death are associated with greed and arrogant isolationism (these are usually called Babylon), and the elements of city life are associated with peace and community vitality (these are usually called Zion)—see Ellul (1970) and Newman (1997). Girouard (1985) devotes a whole chapter of his book *Cities and People* to how these conflicting images or visions of Babylon and Zion were used to heighten the moral dimension of cities in the Industrial Revolution as they struggled with pollution and poverty. He shows how the ethical vision of what a city should be helped to form town planning as a profession. In the next section, we apply these ethical approaches to our cities today.

City Planning and City Prophecy in the Late Twentieth Century

The twentieth century has not been without its city prophets. The kinds of ethical choices outlined above seem to have been a powerful inspiration to writers and commentators in the organic city tradition outlined in Chapter 6.

This book suggests there should be a renewed sense of an ethical basis for our city decisions. This is particularly necessary when an old paradigm is no longer working. Therefore, as shown in Chapter 6, we cannot fall back on our traditional professional praxis, but must feel our way through to the next paradigm. In such a context, community-based approaches are essential since we cannot rely on experts in the ways we could before.

City prophets are able to highlight the areas where we are failing and suggest new visions for change. They can tell us which characteristics bring life, hope, and sustainability to a city and which bring death, despair, and unsustainability. But to what extent can the urban issues of our day be linked to the processes of city life and city death as seen by urban prophets through history? Are there current urban ethical debates that can help us to focus on city life and city death?

Privatism and City Death

Modern civilization and modern cities are considered by most ethical commentators to be about new ways of individualistic consumption. Postmodernism begins to question many of the certainties of this era, but it does not question this fundamental value of individualistic consumption. And yet this value by itself can become most clearly akin to the city of death, the Babylon value of arrogance and self-orientation leading to frivolous consumption. Martin Pawley, in his book *The Private Future*, describes this value as privatism, or isolationism, and says that it is central to understanding our society and our cities:

> Western society is on the brink of collapse not into crime, violence, madness or redeeming revolution, as many would believe—but into withdrawal. Withdrawal from the whole system of values and obligations that has historically been the basis of public, community and family life. Western societies are collapsing not from an assault on their most cherished values, but from a voluntary, almost enthusiastic abandonment of them by people who are learning to live private lives of an unprecedented completeness with the aid of the momentum of a technology which is evolving more and more into a pattern of socially atomizing appliances. (Pawley, 1975, p. 75)

The automobile is the key appliance or technology for creating a private future, but it requires the city to be built around privatism for it to be seen in its fullest form. Thus in many cities it becomes difficult to do other than lead highly isolated or private lives, moving from a private, isolated, suburban home, complete with electronic entertainment (and now even electronic shopping and electronic work), to a private metal box for transportation to whatever other element of urban life one chooses. There need be no obligation to community and little to family, with certainly no obligation to the city. Thus the public realm of the city (the streets, parks, squares, public transportation, public buildings), its urban commons, can become neglected and begin to fall apart. Fear of public spaces then begins to dominate a city, particularly if inequity feeds crime in the streets.

In addition to public safety, the urban commons of air and water also begin to deteriorate as people go farther and farther out in the private quest to escape the city. This loss of the public realm then spreads like a cancer to invade the private realm—first in the house and then even the car, as evidenced by carjacking and freeway murders. Privatism allied with high levels of economic inequity can leave

Photo 7.3. The city of Ephesus was abandoned after its port silted up due to forest clearing in the Turkish mountains.

no secure place anymore. The collapse of the public realm is a sure sign of city death.[5]

The response to such loss of the public realm can be grounded in fear or in hope. Fearful responses can take a number of forms. One is to opt for ex-urban living, which tries to establish an isolation that can never be impacted by the city, with some people moving as far as 200 kilometers from the city and commuting three to four hours to ensure that their private lives are not interfered with.

A second response is that people move into "gated communities," highly guarded, fenced suburbs with everything that can be desired (golf courses, health clubs) and extremely high price tags (the most significant kind of boundary definition). There are 4 million people living in closed-off, gated communities in the United States, many with all the best solar and ecological designs (Egan, 1995). Both fear-based responses lead to sprawling metropolises with enormous automobile dependence and an obsession with private security.

Alternatively, a city can respond in hope to recreate community, to reclaim the urban ecological commons, and to break the back of privatism and its expression in technology and urban form. The choice appears to be just as relevant today as it has been over 3,000 years of urban choice.

Communitarianism and City Life

In addition to signs of city death there are also signs of city life in our era. Indeed, it is possible to point to a prophetic city-life tradition that is growing again and has a new sense of vision. It is, of course, very timely because cities continue to grow and sprawl, devouring rural land, filling the air with automobile emissions, and creating suburbs with little sign of community. It is also timely because the overall mechanistic vision of how we should function is being questioned and torn down by postmodern popular culture. Despite this, we should never underestimate the power of the mechanistic spirit to dominate and control our society, particularly when postmodernism only scoffs at it, but has no set of solutions to offer.

The prophetic city-life solutions are, however, being rediscovered. The urban sustainability movement, whether expressed through the urban ecology movement or the New Urbanism movement, networks around the world and is struggling to change priorities on transportation, on land use, and on the ecological base of all life, including city life. But the fundamental ethical inspiration is the need to rebuild community.

The movement that focuses on the importance of the community is called "communitarianism." The major philosophical foundation is set out by MacIntyre (1981), Bellah (1985, 1991), Sennett (1974), Lasch (1978), and Jordan (1989). Their approaches suggest that both the individual and the state find meaningful roles only when an adequate role is given to the community.[6]

There is growing support for communitarian approaches that suggest ethical frameworks are most meaningful when developed at the community scale, rather than from individual preference alone or on a national scale. The community-based approach to solving problems is developing a new coherence in today's political climate—for example, the UK Labour Party has been reorganized and based on this philosophy. The collapse of communism has shown that heavy-handed authoritarian states cannot be expected to deliver basic human needs, rights, and a good quality of life. At the same time, there is awareness that capitalism based on a market left to itself cannot deliver all this either, especially in social and environmental areas. Thus there is a quest to find an appropriate form of social democratic system that can fulfill economic, social, and environmental goals, particularly in our cities.

Communitarianism appears to be a "city life" form of ethics. Cunningham calls it the "altruistic surplus" of a city. He says:

> The role of altruism in sustaining the city is generally deprecated or ignored. Yet it is primarily the results of altruism that keep the city functioning as a healthy, quasi organic entity. Cunningham (1996)[7]

Communitarianism appears to be the city life process that most opposes individualistic consumption and arrogance toward the public realm. It is consistent with the ethical traditions described in this chapter and provides the kind of moral dimension to approaching the Auto City that is most akin to the urban prophets over millennia. Such prophets express what is wrong in images of everyday life. For example, Friedman says:

> I come from a city without streets. The dominant feature of Los Angeles is its freeways. And freeways are designed for rapid movement. We race in our private steel and glass capsules at 60 miles an hour. If someone cuts in ahead of me, I curse and yell, but the other driver, his windows rolled up, cannot hear me. No place is very far

away in Los Angeles. We go from somewhere to somewhere at a frantic speed, dipping under the city, now riding high above its roofs. The
buildings next to the freeway area are turned away from it, they are
shielded by noise barriers eighteen feet high. From the freeways the
city is invisible. Streets are meant to be places of encounter but the
streets of Los Angeles are empty. If you are caught walking the street,
you feel guilty: chances are a squad [police] car will pull up next to
you, demanding to know what you are doing there at that hour.
Friedman (1992)

Alternative images have been presented (Patsaoures, 1993; Walter, Arkin,
and Crenshaw, 1992) to try to show other paths. Such ethical visions are behind
decisions such as the new transit investment in Los Angeles. In the 1990s, bil-
lions of dollars have been spent on transit in the city that turned its back on transit sixty years ago and led the world into the Auto City age. But the question
remains whether it is possible to turn around a city so firmly dependent on the
automobile. The evidence of a ten-year decline in middle-class professionals living in Los Angeles (due to the smog and crime) may suggest that the city will rue
its missed opportunities in the 1980s (Gobor, 1993). Cities need to grasp the critical opportunities for change that present themselves. Reversing the process of
city death is always possible, but it begins by recognizing the nature of the underlying problem.

Can we make the link that the combination of heavy car use and sprawl in
the Auto City is the modern equivalent of a major city death process? Environmentally, there is little doubt that high auto dependence is the major cause of
high energy consumption, high air pollution, and high loss of natural and rural
landscape. Economically, there are now many who are pointing to the very
high costs of urban sprawl, as described in Chapters 2 and 3. Socially, it is a
more difficult task to link this process of automobile-based isolationism and community.

Most people can see that the kind of city Friedman discusses (above) is not
very conducive to community. It is hard to measure community, however. As discussed, we have found that crime rates correlate—that is, the highest car using,
lowest density cities have the highest crime rates. And we have found that there
is little happening on the urban ecology front in the Auto City, because urban
ecology projects require community for them to work.

We also found, during our visits to global cities for data collection, that the
vitality and attractiveness of urban life in a city's center seemed to be negatively
related to its automobile dependence, in particular the amount of parking and
road space provided (Newman and Kenworthy, 1989a). This is reflected in the
responses we received when talking to city officials, public servants, and community groups in these cities. In Auto Cities, the planners, politicians, and community groups were dispirited and despairing, often saying there was little that
could be done. By contrast, in cities where transit was good, with high levels of
cycling and walking, and where compact, community-oriented structures continued to be the norm in development, people exuded hope.

The questions then become: What can be done to reverse this process? How
can city life forces begin to move the Auto City toward sustainability?

The Role of Community Groups in City Sustainability

Quite simply, the task of the community is to be a community. This involves dramatizing the problems that prevent community so that the ethical issues involved in being a vital, alive, and sustainable city can be appreciated by government, the marketplace, and the many disparate parts of civil society. This means communities must be constantly finding antidotes to the isolationism or privatism that is so pervasive and so powerful in our cities.

Antidotes to Isolationism/Privatism

Three antidotes to auto-dependent privatism are summarized from the many discussions in other parts of this book that suggest what needs to occur in the Auto City. These are presented below.

- *Developing a "sense of place" in the public realm through a sense of history, a sense of social justice, and a sense of nature.*

This antidote is illustrated in the case study in our hometown of Fremantle (see Box 7.3). Most people can identify some part of their city where the above values could transform a public space with that special sense of place that can draw a community together for pure enjoyment. This was the guiding ethic behind the work of Jan Gehl and others in Copenhagen, as described in Chapter 4. They worked for years to transform their central city from a place dominated by cars to a place where people are drawn by the sheer attractiveness of the public spaces and the public life that occurs there. We discovered similar stories in the Copenhagen suburbs, in places such as Albertslund, where urban ecology projects have drawn people out of their homes, away from a lifestyle dominated by TV "soaps" and fantasy, into the reality of their community, their local ecology, and their city.

   The question remains as to whether such activity can begin to transform car-based suburbs, to bring community members together around their mutual problems of isolationism, car dependence, and all the implications of these interlocking forces. Can urban ecology be a focus for generating a new sense of local community? Can it provide a new sense of place that can lead to the development of a nodal center in the information-age "Sustainable" City? Can the community simultaneously increase the urban activity in its subcenter so that the center can provide local services and a quality transit service to the city, while creating ecological services in other, less urban parts of the suburbs? These are the challenges for sustainability in the suburbs.

- *Overcoming automobile dependence through (1) revealing the true character of automobile dependence, (2) fighting for public priorities in the provision of transportation infrastructure, and (3) being pro-urban.*

Automobiles are extremely isolating devices psychologically, and the most impacting technology on communities and the environment.

   Yet automobiles offer the most tangible form of freedom, power, and status.

To overcome this, a community needs to dramatize its awareness of how freeways damage them. This starts with the large issues of highways and transit debates, but it also comes down to a great many small issues at the local level.

One of the reasons for the success of New Urbanist developments is that they emphasize putting cars in garages around the back of dwellings, not allowing them to dominate a streetscape; they deliberately include narrow streets and follow natural contours, even putting in S-bends so that cars are not favored and pedestrians are; and they are unashamed of density and mix, which help to provide more diversity and shorter distances. Communities should demand these qualities from their local governments and the marketplace.

Communities should halt any further development of gated communities, exurban subdivisions, and other destructive symbols of automobile dependence. The Los Angelization of the earth cannot be allowed to proceed, and the communitarian movement is the key way it will be stopped. The sustainable city movements described in this book are alive and well, but they always need help, especially in the realm of creativity. These movements have a strong sense of their moral calling and generally are well able to articulate a coherent set of arguments to back them up. But they frequently lack an ability to tap into the deeper emotional issues. Thus the sections below stress how civil society can reach to the symbolic heart of car dependence and help to break this twentieth-century addiction.

- *Practicing hope rather than despair.*

One of the key characteristics of a lively city is the quality of hope. Hope is not blind optimism; it recognizes the depth of the problem and refuses to accept defeat. It is not a feeling—it is a choice (Moltman, 1967). Hope in the organic tradition described above is when people find their gem of local work and start to fashion it. Hope is also overcoming fear and replacing it with the expectation that you can really make a difference with your small gem. It is based on the quality of the relationships developing in the community as it seeks to overcome its problems.

Perhaps the best expression of what we mean by hope comes from Jim Wallis of the radical Christian community Sojourners, which is based in Washington, D.C., and works amongst the urban poor:

> Hope is not just a feeling or a mood, but the very dynamic of history. It is the energy of transformation and is the door from one reality to another. What seems impossible looking towards it (e.g., abolition of slavery in the U.S.) was inevitable with hindsight.
>
> Between the impossible and the inevitable, between the impossible and possible is a door, and that door is hope. The possibility of the transformation of history lies at that door. On one side of the door of hope there is nonsense. On the other side of the door is the best news ever heard. Hope not believed is always nonsense. Hope that is believed is transformation.
>
> Victories and transformations always seem impossible to begin with. They only become possible by stepping through the door of hope. To

walk through the door of hope you have first to see it and believe that
there is something on the other side. It is never easy. It is always hard!
This is particularly so for the first few to walk through. Others then
find it easier to follow. And that's how historical changes take place.

Hope is believing in spite of the others, and watching the others
change. Wallis (1994)

This hope process is generally started by creative elements of civil society such as
churches, artists, and community environmental groups.

Churches and City Sustainability

We are aware of many churches that take seriously the ethical challenges from
their organic traditions, as described above. But there are also many that do not,
that are so bound up in the culture of individualism that they can read no other
message in the Bible than that of individual salvation. There are also many
groups that are Christian in their focus and work but do not belong to any church
as such. These groups, like the Sojourners (quoted above), are generally working
on broader social issues, including issues of the city and sustainability. Their work
is on the front lines of civil society's efforts to create more just and sustainable
communities.

One such U.S. group is called Hope in the Cities (see Box 7.1), and it works
on the reconciliation of races as the primary issue behind urban crime and
poverty. Although not an explicit message of the sustainability movement, this is
one of the keys to sustainability in U.S. cities, because without this reconciliation process, there will continue to be inner-city decline, urban sprawl, and car
dependence (as discussed in Chapters 3, 4, and 6).

Stories of hope are essential for citizens if they are to make needed changes in
their cities. That they can do this with race issues suggests that U.S. cities can
reurbanize and reorient their priorities to more sustainable patterns of urban life.

Our sense is that this process is now well under way in U.S. cities. The evidence from Boston and other cities discussed in Chapter 4 shows that there is a
close link between the rapid decline of inner-city crime and the revival of the
inner city, and that this links clearly to a decline in growth of car use and sprawl.
In 1990 there were 152 teen murder victims in Boston while in 1995 there were
none. The turn-around was a program called Operation Night Light, a voluntary
program of probation and police officers who are trained to do social work by personally following up on every "at risk" teenager in their homes and offering
advice on how to keep away from crime, begin work training, and join sport
clubs. In addition, churches provide "big brother" partners to be there whenever
they are needed. Thus all the available arms of civil society are being used to provide some hope for children instead of only punishment.

In many other U.S. inner cities the teenage slaughter continues, though the
rate is also declining in most cities as these kinds of programs catch on. In
Philadelphia there has been a decline in the local crime rate and a parallel
growth in the central city as a place to live (Center City District, 1997).

The link between social cohesion and economic vitality in a community is

Box 7.1. Case Study: Hope in the Cities

Hope in the Cities works on a small-scale, quiet basis to bring people together so that racism can be exposed and healed (Henderson, 1996). It helped to organize a process of reconciliation in Richmond, Virginia, where the business of slavery had once been concentrated around the Manchester Docks. The process involved a Unity Walk in which city and community leaders of all races walked from one historic artifact of slavery to another and reflected on their meaning today. It also included the site of an Amerindian village. For most present it was a challenging experience, and it created the opportunity for reconciliation through a range of artistic performances, speeches, and symbolic acts.

The process has continued through many political changes and has a long way to go. But one issue that reflected the new mood of reconciliation was the question of how the city of Richmond should honor Arthur Ashe, the first black U.S. tennis player to win the U.S. Open and Wimbledon. Although a native of Richmond, Ashe had been banned from the city's tennis courts because, when he grew up there, they were still segregated. The suggestion had been made that a statue should be placed on Monument Avenue, where all the South's famous Civil War generals were honored. To whites this was a place of honor (for white heroes) and to blacks a place symbolizing enslavement. But if a figure like Ashe, who was mutually admired, could be memorialized there, it would be a symbol of reconciliation.

The city council debated the issue in public for six hours and then unanimously agreed to place the statue on Monument Avenue. Hope in the Cities suggested at the hearings that, for Arthur Ashe, the process they were going through was probably more important than the outcome. The mayor announced, "This is a city defining itself through its most public of symbols."

Urban ecologists and environmental activists in Richmond must build on these symbols of hope as they attempt to make their city more sustainable.

obvious. That this process is occurring in U.S. inner cities is extremely important for sustainability as it is critical to overcoming automobile dependence.

Artists and City Sustainability

In seeking to identify a particular role for artists in promoting a more sustainable city, we can only stress those things that apply to everyone in the city, but perhaps can be given a special edge by artists. This edge comes from artists' particular sensitivity to the cultural underpinnings of a city, to its soul. It is also a role of artists to try and dramatize the darker elements of the city that are sapping it of life, that are not sustainable, and to help provide an alternative vision of how it can be in the future. In other words, an artist can be, and probably should be, a prophet for a city.

Artists can help provide symbols and acts of beauty and truth that can flow through a city's public realm, breathing new soul and spirit into it, or this spirituality can be diverted into private consumption alone and be lost to the city.

Two case studies are presented below, one from Europe (see Box 7.2) and one from Australia (see Box 7.3), to illustrate the special role of artists in moving cities toward sustainability. A final case study on Liverpool (see Box 7.4) exam-

Box 7.2. Case Study: Christiania, the Pioneer of Danish Urban Ecology

The Christiania community in Copenhagen has been experimenting with urban ecology projects at their home on former defense land in the inner city for more than twenty-five years. They have fought constant battles with authorities over their right to be there. At each point that it seemed they would lose their battle and be removed from the land, they reversed the process by developing music, art exhibitions, and street festivals that by the sheer impact of their creativity have captivated the community and helped to spread their message.

One particularly difficult time was in 1982, when a smear campaign was started in Sweden by a group worried that the Christiania message would spread throughout Scandinavia. The community was accused of being the "drug center of the North and the root of all evil" (from the Christiania Guide, Anon, 1996).

The community's response was to "invade Sweden." Groups set out to "conquer" Stockholm, Goteborg, and Malmo with cabaret, exhibitions, and huge processions through the cities. Their message was that the new world restraining us should be about ecological limits, not personal limits and that the community was pioneering what this would mean. Christiania won the battle for Sweden and has been fighting other battles with the same community arts tools ever since.

The importance of Christiania in Europe cannot be easily gauged. However, Michael Jensen says:

> It was in Christiania that we first find buildings made of recycled materials, efforts to sort refuse, and the first primitive windmills and solar heating units at work in the midst of a metropolis. It was here too that we simultaneously find how ecological building is linked, for better or worse, with building aesthetics and creative self expression. Jensen (1994, p. 357)

Those who have followed in developing urban ecology projects in Denmark and in other parts of Europe have been given the moral space to experiment and suggest alternatives by the example of Christiania. Rational arguments by academics and others in the environmental movement have helped create the moral climate supporting the notion that sustainability is needed, but Christiania dramatized it and then demonstrated it. Others then began to have the courage to be a little different and move toward the new paradigm.

Box 7.3. Case Study: Fremantle and Its Renewal

Fremantle is a port city (about 25,000 people) associated with the larger metropolis of Perth (a city of 1.3 million). Like many old ports it was associated with an industrial base, but by the 1960s the port and the industrial base were in decline as sources of employment. Fremantle began losing its way economically as businesses started leaving and its population entered a sharp decline phase. Some predicted that Fremantle was finished, and that like all other modern cities, Perth should concentrate on its new suburbs and let the old city of Fremantle quietly deteriorate.

Fremantle had, however, three qualities that would not allow this to happen: (1) a strong commitment to social justice (based on a long history of waterfront unionism with a social vision); (2) multiculturalism (the city was 30 percent Italian, with many other migrant groups as well), with diverse groups integrated into a strong community; and (3) town planning and architectural heritage (its basic design had been set in the 1830s, and it remained an historic Georgian and Victorian town). All these elements were important in the processes that began to reclaim a future for the city in the late 1970s.

In this period the city council was becoming desperate for solutions to stop the economic hemorrhaging. It had begun to accept some of the modernist solutions being adopted in other parts of the world and that were well under way in the center of Perth, twenty kilometers upstream on the Swan River. These solutions were generally to knock down any old buildings and try to attract modern high-rises, and to provide easy access by car through freeways and easy parking.

The Fremantle community did not like this approach, and thus a community association was formed, the Fremantle Society, which presented an alternative vision for the city's future. It suggested that the city should try to build on its organic qualities: its historic building stock, its walkable streets, its mix of housing and businesses, its attractive (though rundown) public spaces, and its vibrant, though rather demoralized, community. It suggested that somehow, out of this attempt to heal the city based on its organic qualities, the economic base would rebuild.

The Fremantle Society was able to have some of its people elected to the city council and began to change the policies and culture of the local political scene.

As part of the suite of policies to regenerate the city, a policy was adopted of trying to facilitate artists in the city—both for the work they would bring and the qualities they would hopefully bring to the city's perspectives and plans for its future. A community-based planning process began, seeking an alternative future for the city other than that being sought in the rest of Perth, which had moved toward glass towers and a car-based suburbia. In the debates and decisions that followed, the city opted to retain its heritage qualities and develop a much greater commitment to transit and pedestrian qualities. After a long battle, the city won back its train service and had it upgraded and extended (Newman, 1992).

There was a lot of talk about making the human qualities of the city central to its ethos and economy. Multiculturalism was allowed to flourish, with rather non-Anglo-Saxon features, such as alfresco dining, being encouraged (see Chapter 6), as well as street festivals and other cultural activities.

(continues)

Box 7.3. Continued

The city began to look up as this process led to people wanting to live or work in Fremantle or at least visit there on weekends. Infill housing began to be built in the inner city, and a range of new businesses were attracted to the location due to its organic urbanism.

In 1986-87 the America's Cup was held in Fremantle, and a huge amount of money was poured into the city in the few years leading up to this major international event. The locals feared that the new money would swamp the city; fear changed from the problems of decline to the dangers of rapid growth. The event did not harm the city, however, since the community's values were strongly in place and had been firmly embedded in the city's town plan (predominantly a one-page set of goals for each area) and its planning process. Instead of modernist high-rise hotels and big roads, the city was restored and pedestrian/bicycle facilities were built, as well as cultural and artistic facilities and a heavy emphasis on public housing (Newman, 1988b).

But not everything was done during the Cup event, and as the city returned to less frantic planning, it had to rely more on local energy. One particular area was slated for rehabilitation at this time— a rundown piece of foreshore that was the original landing site of the first British settlers, a site that had significantly deteriorated as a public space.

Over a five-year period, a group of artists was able to work with the council to rebuild the foreshore area, creating a sense of place that embodies a sense of history (through public art displays), a sense of social justice (it is a space for all people to use), and a sense of nature (the foreshore was revegetated with native plants). This project is an excellent example of how artists, through their imagination and commitment, create a physical space that is now an important element in a community's life (Dawkins, 1990). Fremantle's renewal and community strength are reflected in its very low car use per capita compared to other parts of Perth (Newman, Kenworthy, and Lyons, 1985). It is also a symbol of the kind of community subcenter that can be built right across the Auto City as it begins to overcome automobile dependence.

Photo 7.4. The historic Fremantle foreshore, restored from a degraded dumping ground, has become a special site for ceremonies, such as the burning of an effigy representing the pain of aboriginal prisoners in the Fremantle jail who were eventually set free upon the jail's closure.

Box 7.4. Case Study: Liverpool, Back from the Brink?

In 1984 a British Council seminar on urban regeneration was held in Liverpool. One of us (PN) attended, keen to learn the latest European insights on how to revitalize a city. Each day, participants were given a different theory or approach. Then we were told: "But of course none of this seems to work in Liverpool!"

In the 1980s, Liverpool was teetering on the brink. It had been in decline since the 1960s and was losing population so fast that it had reached the level it was at in the 1920s in just twenty years. It was losing 1,000 jobs a week, so most young people left to search elsewhere for employment. The level of dependence in the city (adults on pensions or unemployment benefits, plus children below working age) had reached more than 70 percent.

Urban decline is not pretty. It's not good for people or for the urban environment. There's little spare cash for upgrading factories to stop pollution, create new parks, restore heritage buildings, or initiate traffic calming; little is there for new child-care centers or libraries or for schools. So the despair that can set in among those who remain can debilitate communities, spilling over into crime and violence and creating a deeper spiral of decline.

Among the racially mixed areas of Liverpool, centered around the inner-city area of Toxteth, the despair of poverty was exacerbated by a largely racist police force well known for picking on local Africans. In 1981 this explosive mixture was touched off in the now famous Toxteth race riots. After several nights of looting and burning, the city of Liverpool was left smoldering.

During the seminar, we were taken to whole neighborhoods that had been abandoned, high-rise buildings so vandalized they had to be destroyed before they had finished being paid for, public housing where there were so few people and so many apartments that if residents wanted to change units, all they did was set fire to their homes. We were taken to sites where beautiful Georgian and Victorian buildings could be bought for a song. We were told that the city council could not resolve how to proceed, but continued to blame everyone else, that capital investors had abandoned the city, and that everyone with any means (including all the university professors) had fled to live in the far-flung suburbs. The political, social, and economic divisions in the city seemed to be widening every year.

How can a city regenerate from such despair? Maybe it is not possible after such a process sets in and so the city will continue to slide ever downward to its death?

It will take another twenty years to know definitively, but from our perspective Liverpool seems to have come back from the brink and is regenerating. The signs are quite mixed, however, leaving no room for complacency:

- Population: there was a continuing loss of population through the 1980s, but the rate has slowed and the city is expecting stabilization in the 1990s. Nevertheless, the young and skilled are still leaving.
- Employment: jobs continue to decline, but this rate has slowed also. Unemployment in the late 1990s remains at twice the national average.

(continues)

Box 7.4. Continued

- Poverty: surveys show that in the late 1990s Liverpool has poverty at twice the national average, with 41 percent of households officially in poverty and 16 percent in intense poverty.

The numbers are not very encouraging, but the city has a new look about it that is no longer despairing. There has been a vast improvement in the buildings, streetscapes, parks, squares, and other public places—that is, there has been an environmental-quality-led regeneration. This has been closely associated with a return of investment in businesses, houses, and particularly tourism development.

Behind all this is a sense in the community that their divisions have been lessening, that the organic processes of community are beginning to win out. There are many stories of hope created by individuals and groups who have built bridges to heal divisions and forge political solutions. Two of these stories are briefly told below.

The Eldonian Community is an example of feisty local neighborhood residents who refused to be cleared from their inner-city location as so many others had been. Though their neighborhood stood in the way of a new traffic entrance, the people of Eldon Street decided they would not allow their community to be broken up and relocated to peripheral land. Instead, they formed a cooperative and began to design their own housing on a nearby abandoned industrial site. After many political setbacks and heartache they were able to start. Their leader, Tony McGann, was a forklift driver who had recently been laid off. Throwing themselves into the process, the community residents were able to design their own houses and streets so they could keep their neighbors and have a much better quality environment.

Now the residents have more than 300 houses and a community center. Tony McGann attributes their success to their "fighting Irish" qualities and points to many who helped, including the Catholic and Anglican archbishops who later co-wrote a book using the Eldonian motto as its title, *Better Together*.

The second example concerns major efforts to combat racism, including removing this cancer from the police force; providing special opportunities for those from the black community, such as a black enterprise agency; starting an

Photo 7.5. An "isolationist" gated community (*left*); Liverpool's Eldonian Community, made up of residents who rebuilt their neighborhood rather than allowing authorities to remove them, and whose motto is "Better Together" (*right*).

arts anti-racist program; and, perhaps of greatest spiritual and symbolic impact, opening the Museum of Slavery in the new Albert Dock tourism complex.

The award-winning museum shows how Liverpool was central to the slave trade, being the main port for slaves being transported from Africa to the Americas. The displays graphically depict the whole process of slavery, show that it was the biggest diaspora in human history (perhaps 50 million people), and name the many established Liverpool families who made their fortunes from slavery. There is no better way for a city to demonstrate its readiness to face up to its sad racist past and to build reconciliation with those who are a part of its legacy.

There is a long way for Liverpool to go, but a sense of hope ensures that regeneration is given a fair chance of taking hold. The message for other cities caught up in inner-city decline based on problems of race and dispirited neighborhoods is encouraging. The implications for sustainability are obvious.

ines how some important symbols of a city can be used to reverse the despair of decline and create a sense of hope for the future.

Community Environmental Groups and City Sustainability

Environmental groups in cities are central to the vision for change that a city needs. It is important for citizen groups to realize that the real visions for change rarely come from government or from the marketplace, but from civil society. Communities have the freedom to dream and the responsibility to continue the ethical traditions of organic urbanism. Communities have power because of their ethics and vision. They are not tied to the interests of capital but can help with the vision of how market forces are needed to help reshape our cities in a more sustainable way. They do not need to be tied to the institutions and processes that created the Auto City and that encapsulate the regulations of modernism; they can help to envision how government processes can be used to implement the sustainable city.

Urban environmental groups must provide a city with the outlines of a sustainability plan. It should show the dream of the future "Sustainable" City with its organic communities creating local urban ecology projects and at the same time creating more urban subcenters for community life. It should show where new transit lines could go and where streets could be traffic calmed and bicycle lanes provided. It should show how capital could be redirected to inner-city revitalization and transit-oriented development rather than further fringe development. It should show where stormwater drains could be turned back into creeks and where permaculture gardens could be built around waste recycling. It should dream a thousand urban ecological dreams.

Urban environmental groups must use every means available in civil society to communicate their vision: the Internet, the media, traditional public meetings, universities, churches and more.

As the dream catches on, the separate organic communities of the city can begin to implement their part of the dream. They can show others through their "tinkering" how to integrate ecological and reduced car use solutions into their community. The broader picture must be constantly advocated by a coalition of these smaller organic groups, linked through international networks to the global eco-city movement. Ideas and actions will flow from city to city around the world bringing change to our unsustainable urban spaces, converting them into lively communities no longer dominated by the automobile.

Conclusions

Ethical choices by communities are not often seen to be significant aspects of city management. However, as Kumar (1995) says, "We need to walk on two legs—we need to put the 'inner' and the 'outer' together to make our cities complete; to make them whole."

The ethics of city life and city death are processes that, over millennia, have been related to choices that lead to community building or community breaking. This involves choices concerning technology, priorities in infrastructure, the significance of social and community activity in the broad approach to life adopted by a city, and in everyday decisions by ordinary people. It is not hard to see the seeds of city death in many cities. But it is not necessary to see such processes as inevitable. The seeds of city life are evident everywhere in civil society and can become a source of hopeful change.

The challenge of sustainability is just another in the history of cities. It must not be underestimated or there will be many cities following the downward spiral associated with city death and unsustainability. But as we have shown throughout this book, there is hope, particularly if we look again at the ancient tension between alternative urban futures that is part of our spiritual tradition and then look to a future based on a renewed sense of hope and the power of organic communities to create more sustainability in our cities.

Notes

1. Apart from people like Mathew Fox, who edited a book in 1981 called *Western Spirituality* in which the contributors tried to trace some of these roots and relate them to environmental issues.

2. A quote about the swift from *The Natural History of Selborne* provides an example of his style and sense of values:

> It is a most alert bird, rising very early, and retiring to roost very late; and is on the wing in the height of summer at least sixteen hours. In the longest days it does not withdraw to rest till a quarter before nine in the evening, being the latest of all day birds. Just before they retire whole groups of them assemble high in the air, and squeak, and shoot about with wonderful rapidity. But this bird is never so

much alive as in sultry thundry weather, when it expresses great alacrity, and calls forth all its powers. In hot mornings several, getting together in little parties, dash round the steeples and churches, squeaking as they go in a very clamorous manner; these, by nice observers, are supposed to be males, serenading their sitting hens; and not without reason, since they seldom squeak till they come close to the walls or eaves, and since those within utter at the same time a little inward note of complacency.

3. For example, one famous passage from *Small Is Beautiful* says:

> Let us admit that the people of the forward stampede, like the devil, have all the best tunes or at least the most popular and familiar tunes . . . "More, further, quicker, richer," . . . There *are* no insoluble problems. The slogans of the people of the forward stampede burst into the newspaper headlines every day with the message, "a breakthrough a day keeps the crisis at bay."
>
> And what about the other side? This is made up of people who are deeply convinced that technological development has taken a wrong turn and needs to be redirected. The term "homecomer" has, of course, a religious connotation. . . . The genuine "home-comer" does not have the best tunes, but he has the most exalted text, nothing less than the Gospels. For him, there could not be a more concise statement of his situation, of *our* situation, than the parable of the prodigal son. Strange to say, the Sermon on the Mount gives pretty precise instructions on how to construct an outlook that could lead to an Economics of Survival.

> - How blessed are those who know that they are poor: the Kingdom of Heaven is theirs.
> - How blessed are the sorrowful; they shall find consolation.
> - How blessed are those of a gentle spirit; they shall have the earth for their possession.
> - How blessed are those who hunger and thirst to see right prevail; they shall be satisfied.
> - How blessed are the peacemakers;

> God shall call them his sons.
> It may seem daring to connect these beatitudes with matters of technology and economics. But may it not be that we are in trouble precisely because we have failed for so long to make this connection? It is not difficult to discern what these beatitudes may mean for us today:

> - We are poor, not demigods.
> - We have plenty to be sorrowful about, and are not emerging into a golden age.
> - We need a gentle approach, a non-violent spirit, and small is beautiful.
> - We must concern ourselves with justice and see right prevail.
> - And all this, only this, can enable us to become peacemakers.

4. Jacobs' book *Systems for Survival* (1994), subtitled "A Dialogue on the Moral Foundations of Commerce and Politics," is a broadranging perspective based on ethical sources from many backgrounds; however, it is primarily Western in its approach, using liberal democratic traditions.

5. Kumar (1995), from Schumacher College, puts it this way: "One of the greatest moral statements ever made is 'love they neighbour as thyself', but how can I love my neighbour if I have no neighbours, if I live in an apartment in an urban metropolis, cut off from my extended family, dominated by the cult of individualism and addicted to the druge of consumerism?" (p. 39).

6. In some places the collection of all communities is called "civil society" (in the UK tradition) or "social midfield" (in the European tradition). In the United States it is sometimes called "voluntarism" and there are strong exponents of the need for this focus in tackling the problems of U.S. cities. Friedman (1987) in his "Planning in the Public Domain" suggests planners need to "recenter political power in the civil society." Etzioni (1988, 1993) has founded a journal in the United States called *The Responsive Community* and suggests that we need to have an "I–We" paradigm in which we can express personal moral beliefs within a community framework. His training courses are designed to create community advocates and activists who can provide a "third way" in so many arguments between individual rights (including those of the market) and the rights of the state.

7. It also has growing support from other systems approaches, such as management theory and innovation theory, as discussed in Chapter 5. The social imperative in management systems today is to find the right scale at which to operate, and generally this means more localization of power. Only when a firm has adequate bottom-up processes that allow more humanly fulfilling participation and "flexible specialization," does it become truly productive. There is a growing awareness in studies on cities that the "local milieux" is what makes it function as a source of innovation rather than just government policies or the market. This "local milieux" is closely related to the environmental concept of bioregionalism and greater local autonomy. Both the management theory and innovation theory concepts fit neatly into the tradition of communitarianism, which suggests that the right scale for any change is the community scale. The demand for community-based solutions and participation is thus cutting across a range of disciplines.

Chapter 8

Summary and Conclusions

In the Preface to this book we presented a set of questions to guide the book's wide-ranging discussion and exploration of sustainability in cities and its relationship to automobile dependence. Here we would like to summarize the approaches we have made to answering these questions.

Chapter 1: The Concept of Sustainability and Its Relationship to Cities

- *What is sustainability?* Sustainability is a concept developed in the global political arena that attempts to achieve, simultaneously, the goals of an improved environment, a better economy, and a more just and participative society, rather than trading off any one of these against the others. While its primary context is global, sustainability is seen to be meaningful and achievable only when it is practiced through local initiatives with global significance.
- *How does sustainability apply to cities?* Sustainability can be applied to cities through extending the metabolism approach to human settlements so that a city can be defined as becoming more sustainable if it is reducing its resource inputs (land, energy, water, and materials) and waste outputs (air, liquid, and solid waste) while simultaneously improving its livability (health, employment, income, housing, leisure activities, accessibility, public spaces, and community).
- *What are sustainability goals and indicators for a city?* Sustainability goals and indicators are ways to incorporate the many overlapping areas of sustainability into a city's consciousness about what it values. They should cover the natural environment, resources, wastes, and human livability, the latter of which embraces the critical economic dimensions of a city. Each city needs a process to define a comprehensive list of important sustainability indicators and, in particular, ones that set it apart from others, such as Seattle's returning salmon, or The Hague's number of breeding storks, or Copenhagen's number of public seats. It then needs to build an awareness of a process that seeks to improve these indicators each year.
- *How does a city make a Sustainability Plan?* Sustainability Plans, or Local Agenda 21 Plans (as required in Agenda 21 and agreed to by all nations), are community-based processes that (1) create a set of objectives that fulfill the

sustainability agenda, (2) set out indicators that show how the progress toward sustainability can be measured, (3) assess how the city is performing on these criteria, and (4) provide policy options about how it can do better. The plans are updated annually.

- *How can Sustainability Plans help move a city forward?* A Sustainability Plan enables a city to focus on its global setting (increasingly required for its economic and social future), to create an integrated, community-centered approach to its future that is not usually possible within traditional professions, and to identify its local constraints and opportunities for innovation. The plan links a city into the global Agenda 21/sustainability networks and thus provides an opportunity to motivate creative, local contributions to a global audience.
- *How does city size relate to sustainability?* There are many ways that larger cities can contribute to sustainability through their economies of scale and density, which help to reduce per capita levels of resources and wastes and improve livability. However, they need to be constantly strengthening these advantages because local capacity limits on air, water, and land are frequently stretched in larger cities. Nevertheless, the idea that small cities are more sustainable than large ones is not supported by the findings in this book; thus it is important that all cities, regardless of size, tackle the sustainability agenda.

Chapter 2: The Problem of Automobile Dependence at the End of the Twentieth Century

- *How are cities shaped?* The urban form of cities is shaped primarily by transportation technology, but this works through economic and cultural priorities about infrastructure and where people like to live and work—the urban, suburban, and exurban choices.
- *What is automobile dependence?* Automobile dependence is when a city or area of a city assumes automobile use as the dominant imperative in its decisions on transportation, infrastructure, and land use. Other modes thus become increasingly peripheral, marginal, or nonexistent until there are no real options for passenger travel other than the automobile.
- *How does sustainability relate to automobile dependence?* Automobile dependence is the primary force driving cities to increase their use of land, energy, water, and other materials; their production of transportation-related air emissions (both greenhouse gases and local smog-related emissions), traffic noise, and stormwater pollution (due to the extent of asphalt in Auto Cities); and their economic problems due to the high capital costs of sprawl-related infrastructure, direct transportation costs, and indirect transportation costs (road accidents, pollution, etc.); along with the transportation-related loss of the public realm, safety, and community. It is not possible to solve sustainability in cities without addressing automobile dependence.
- *How has sustainability been addressed in other eras of city development?* The transition from the Walking City to the Transit City was due to the need to solve

the problems of pollution and overcrowding resulting from the Industrial Revolution. It was achieved through a combination of new technology, new urban design and management strategies, and new visions for social change. As the Auto City has reached its zenith and created new problems of sustainability, a similarly creative combination of solutions is required.

- *Can Auto City problems be solved by incremental changes (largely engineering), or do they require more fundamental urban system changes?* Addressing the problems in a short-term technological way is necessary, but if that is all that is done, it will ultimately only exacerbate these problems since automobile use will continue to rise. Therefore, more long-term urban system changes are needed that can also accommodate technological change in a positive way.

- *What are the new economic forces confronting the Auto City?* New studies show that significant economic problems are associated with Auto Cities due to their excessive automobile use (inefficiencies from direct and indirect costs) and the amount of land lost and opportunity costs that result from the diversion of capital into nonproductive suburban infrastructure.

- *Are globalization and information technology leading to greater or less automobile dependence?* The trend in global cities (information-based economies) is toward the need for face-to-face interactions for the creative aspects of economic functions, and these are best nurtured and developed in quality urban environments where the emphasis is on traffic-free space surrounded by a dense mix of different urban activities. Such environments are inherently much lower in automobile dependence. Thus automobile dependence can be reduced under these new economic parameters, which are tending to favor the social qualities of pedestrian- and transit-oriented land use.

- *What are the social views about automobile dependence and the continuing provision of Auto City infrastructure?* Despite the popularity of the automobile, most surveys show that people don't want priorities to emphasize Auto City infrastructure, such as freeways, but want greater development of transit systems, better conditions for walking and cycling, and a reduced need to travel in urban environments, which support the development of human community.

- *What kinds of scenarios face Auto Cities in an era of oil depletion?* It is possible to imagine scenarios in which oil dependence issues lead to fundamentally different choices that can mean Auto Cities either begin the process of reshaping themselves to be more sustainable or else enter a decline phase that is very hard to reverse.

Chapter 3: The Pattern of Automobile Dependence and Global Cities

- *What are the patterns of automobile dependence in global cities?* U.S. and Australian cities are the most extensive in their dependence on the automobile, as shown by their transportation patterns, infrastructure and land use. Canadian cities are less automobile-dependent, with better transit and greater integration of land use. European cities are three to four times less automobile-dependent than U.S. cities in terms of automobile use, infrastructure, and land use intensity. Wealthy Asian cities (Singapore, Hong Kong, and Tokyo) are eight times less automobile-dependent than U.S. cities. However, the newly industrializing Asian cities (Bangkok, Jakarta, etc.) are showing a marked and rapidly growing automobile orientation in their transportation patterns and infrastructure, and although fringe land uses are developing greater auto orientation, their overall land use patterns are still dense and strongly favor transit and nonmotorized modes. They are therefore classified as automobile-dominated rather than automobile-dependent.

- *How do transportation patterns relate to technology, infrastructure, economics, and urban form?* The fuel efficiency of motor vehicles cannot explain the large variation in gasoline use in the world's cities, but the extra efficiency and "transit leverage" of transit technology can explain it. The infrastructure variations in terms of road supply, parking, transit service, and the relative speed between traffic and transit, are all closely related to the level of gasoline and automobile use. The price of gasoline, incomes, and the level of wealth (GRP) in a city do not relate strongly to automobile use. Land use patterns, on the other hand, are closely correlated with automobile use and the levels of transit use, walking, and cycling, confirming the structural characteristics of automobile dependence and the inevitability of addressing urban form in the sustainability agenda.

- *What are the trends in automobile use, transit, and density?* Automobile use is increasing in all but a few cities (Stockholm and Zurich), but there are large differences in rates of growth. U.S. cities grew the most despite predictions that suburbanization of work would slow down car use. Australian cities grew much less, indicating that the reurbanization process may be influencing travel patterns. Transit use increased in all cities despite predictions of its demise globally. Spectacular increases in Europe continue to set the benchmark. Density patterns indicate an historic reversal is occurring globally, with increases or reversal of declines evident nearly everywhere. This may be related to the information-based economy. Inner city growth is much more evident than in previous periods except in U.S. cities, where density increases are mostly occurring in outer suburban "edge cities" that are heavily auto-dependent.

- *How do the direct and indirect economic costs of transportation vary in cities?* Automobile dependence as we have defined it is a combination of physical planning parameters. The new perspective that has emerged from the economic data presented in this book is that automobile dependence is not good for the economy of cities and that cities that are able to provide a balance of transportation options are more efficient on almost every economic indicator. This includes indicators covering external costs related to environmental and safety factors, but also the direct costs of transportation. The overall effect is that automobile-dependent Australian and U.S. cities use 12 to 13 percent of their city wealth on their passenger transportation systems; Canadian and European cities use 7 to 8 percent; wealthy Asian cities use 5 percent; and more-automobile-oriented, newly industrializing Asian cities use 15 percent of their city wealth on transportation. The implication for sustainability is that reducing automobile dependence is good for the economy of cities.

- *What does this suggest about the future of Auto Cities?* A case is made that there is no technological or economic inevitability underpinning automobile dependence. Indeed, it is suggested that the emerging processes of globalization and information-based employment could be highlighting the importance of face-to-face contact and therefore the need for reducing automobile dependence. The continuation of unsustainable automobile dependence is more than likely due to cultural factors, all of which can be overcome.

Chapter 4: A Vision of Reduced Automobile Dependence

- *What are the myths about the inevitability of the Auto City?* We have identified ten myths concerning the inevitability of automobile dependence due to wealth, climate, the spatial extent of some nations, the age of cities, the need for physical and mental health, the lure of rural living, the power of the road lobby and the land development lobby, and the lack of nonautomobile-based options provided by the traffic engineering and town planning professions. All are potential problems in particular cities, but are open to change through cultural and political processes.

- *How can cities reduce their automobile dependence?* Theoretical approaches and case studies are presented of cities from around the world that have (1) changed their transportation infrastructure priorities to favor new transit or nonmotorized modes and achieved reductions in automobile use, (2) traffic-calmed critical streets (and across broad urban regions), inducing reductions in traffic, as well as significantly improving the quality of the urban environment and hence all elements of urban sustainability, (3) integrated transportation and land use through urban villages that are more transit-oriented and pedestrian-friendly, (4) constrained urban sprawl through effective growth management programs such as green belts, and/or (5) introduced taxes on automobiles, thus better reflecting the true costs of this mode vis-à-vis nonauto modes, and enabling alternative infrastructure to be built.

- *Why is city planning so important to reducing automobile dependence?* Much of the attention of policy makers in the United States and Australia has been directed toward civilizing the automobile rather than reducing automobile dependence. However, greater efficiency can just lead to greater use, and this washes out much of the technological advance, as well as creating more traffic-related problems. Much of the academic literature has stressed the need to control automobile use through congestion pricing, but this has significant political and equity impacts unless it is part of an overall approach to reducing automobile dependence. Economic penalties will work if there are alternatives that are viable. Planning that shifts infrastructure priorities and addresses the underlying land use aspects of automobile dependence is thus seen to be more fundamental, while an isolated tough economic approach to automobiles remains largely in the realms of academic debate.

- *What is a future "Sustainable" City vision with reduced automobile dependence?* The future "Sustainable" City (replacing the Auto City) is envisioned as a multicentered city linked by good-quality transit on radial and orbital lines. Within the centers, walking-oriented characteristics would be favored, and such new nodes would be located to provide work, shops, and local services within bicycling distance or a short, demand-responsive local transit trip of all present suburban areas. Such a city is seen to be consistent with the emerging telecommunication/services city, which is showing evidence everywhere that face-to-face contact is still critical for an urban economy.

- *How can this future "Sustainable" City be achieved in stages?* The stages are considered to be (1) revitalizing the central and inner cities, (2) focusing development on transit-oriented locations that already exist and are underutilized, (3) discouraging urban sprawl by growth management strategies, and (4) extending transit systems, particularly rail systems, and building associated urban villages to provide a subcenter for all suburbs.

- *What cities are already showing reduced automobile dependence?* The best examples of reducing automobile dependence are to be found in European cities, especially Stockholm, Copenhagen, Zurich, and Freiburg, with continuing success being shown by the wealthy Asian cities Singapore, Hong Kong, and Tokyo, and selected poorer cities, such as Curitiba in Brazil. In Canada, Toronto and Vancouver have shown some good signs, which are reflected in significantly better land use and transportation characteristics than in U.S. or Australian cities. In the United States, Boulder, Portland and Boston are showing that tackling automobile dependence can begin even in the world's most automobile-oriented nation, with a range of positive results, such as more compact housing, a more vital public realm, revitalization of central and inner areas, and better transit systems. However, it will take longer for such changes to be reflected in the overall statistics characterizing these cities. Signs of reversal are also evident in Australian cities, where growth in automobile use has been declining for a number of years in parallel with active reurbanization of inner-city areas and new rail systems as in Perth.

Chapter 5: Greening the Automobile-Dependent City

- *How do other aspects of sustainability, such as management of the water cycle, solid waste, urban agriculture, and greening, fit into the future "Sustainable" City concept?* These approaches to sustainability are all necessary to reduce the inflow of resources and outflow of wastes in a city. They are also important in creating a more economically efficient city and a more attractive, quality urban environment, which is essential for a lively community and a vital economy.

- *Why are local, community-scale options proving to be more sustainable?* Water, waste, agriculture, and green space management require knowledge of particular local urban environments and thus require local involvement in management. The latest technology for making more efficient use of water and providing more complete treatment of waste is developing at a small scale suitable for community management. Renewable energy technology is also better applied at a small scale, and new light rail technologies provide strong focal points for galvanizing community involvement in reshaping urban form and streetscapes.

- *Is there a conflict between greener cities and lower-energy cities?* There is a conflict only if there is no flexibility provided in the planning system for the provision of more compact, higher-density development to foster the creation of a multicentered, mixed-use urban form. If no increases in density can be allowed, as some commentators (e.g., Troy, Stretton, Gordon, and Richardson) seem to be suggesting, then automobile dependence will continue. It is argued here that this will not only jeopardize low-energy goals, but will also undermine greener-city goals; local urban ecology goals seem to thrive where there is a symbiotic partnership with strong communities oriented to the sustainability agenda, and such communities rarely seem to form in automobile-dependent areas unless perhaps they are deliberate communities set up for that sole purpose.
- *Why is there conflict over density and transit in sustainability discussions and can this be resolved?* "Density" and "transit" seem to be mostly negative concepts in Anglo-Saxon traditions. This comes from industrial era cities where dense slums and transit were associated with poverty and pollution. The British Town and Country Planning Association adage "Nothing is gained by overcrowding" is associated with auto dependence. This approach, which has dominated English town planning for much of the twentieth century, is now being contested, though it is still a powerful part of the urban culture in English-speaking cities. It is a major barrier to city sustainability if allowed to be the dominant driving force in urban design, since it prevents the successful development of pedestrian-scale urban villages and transit systems. The resolution seems to be occurring with the creation of low-density eco-villages in rural but not urban areas and the simultaneous provision of higher-density urban villages to overcome automobile dependence and density reductions in areas of local ecological servicing (waste recycling, permaculture, etc.).
- *What is local urban ecology, where is it happening and how does it relate to global urban sustainability?* Local urban ecology is the process that tries to bring together all of the aspects of sustainability in a single development, whether it is a house or a group of buildings or an industrial estate. It is an innovative, design-based exercise with few rules or norms. Examples are now appearing everywhere as the need for integrated demonstrations of sustainability becomes more and more a local agenda. The best examples appear to be occurring in Denmark where there are forty-five documented demonstrations in Copenhagen alone. They relate to global sustainability when they fulfill the goals of reducing resources and waste while improving livability. However, there are also examples of an approach that just creates, for instance, a more self-sufficient building, which, while achieving some improvements in urban

ecology, actually increases automobile dependence and isolation, thus obliterating any claim to true sustainability. This shows the importance of community-based urban ecology (as in many rich examples of Danish ecological urban renewal).

Chapter 6: Promoting Urban Change

- *How has urban professional praxis been shaped by modernism and the Auto City?* The urban professionals who have shaped our cities for the past fifty years have been strongly influenced by modernism, with its "one best way" and its clear separation of disciplines. This has given rise to simplistic transportation models with their self-fulfilling prophecies of congestion, freeway building, more congestion, and more freeway building; to planning systems totally acquiescent to "unavoidable" increases in automobile dependence; to rigid separation of urban functions by zoning; to uniform low-density architecture in suburbs and high-rise towers in CBDs; to streets that serve no other function than the moving of vehicles; to "big pipes in and big pipes out" approaches to water management; and to various expressions of "straightening out" nature in cities.

- *How is urban professional praxis now being challenged by postmodernism and sustainability?* Sustainability is part of the postmodern phenomenon that recognizes that the assumptions of modernism are now inadequate for solving the ecological and human development issues of our age. However, the sustainability agenda goes beyond the deconstruction of our society and begins to reconstruct it around the goals of ecological sensitivity and local, organic processes in communities. Urban professional praxis that fails to respond to these new imperatives will become more and more irrelevant, a passenger on a rudderless, postmodern ship.

- *What is the organic city tradition?* The organic city tradition traces the values and approaches of ecological sensitivity and local organic processes in communities back through a number of nineteenth and twentieth century urban critics who could see the inherent failings of modernism, and links those views to fundamental values concerning community processes, natural processes, heritage, and artistic expression.

- *Can the organic city tradition be a guide for future professional praxis?* This approach does provide a guide for revamping professional praxis in line with sustainability through its (1) recognition of values associated with the environment, social justice, heritage, the public realm, the urban economy, and community; (2) delight in the diversity of expression of these values at a local level in terms of housing, transportation/urban form options, fuel types, an appropriate balance in infrastructure priorities, and cultural diversity; (3) crossing of boundaries in the physical and natural environment of cities, in disciplines, and in cultures; and (4) facilitation of organic community processes.

- *What are some detailed guidelines for sustainability in urban professional praxis?* Detailed guidelines are provided in such areas as sustainability in new development, the New Urbanism, economic impacts of urban options and better transit–land use integration. Collectively, these guidelines point to a need for a major rewriting of most of the technical planning manuals and regulations used so effectively for so many years to roll out the fabric of the Auto City. A new and diverse urban fabric, responsive to local and global needs for sustainability, will require new processes with the same stamp of authority afforded to their auto-oriented counterparts for more than half a century.

Chapter 7: Ethics, Spirituality, and Community in the City

- *What are the ethical foundations for city sustainability from traditions of local ecology, human ecology, and urban ecology?* Three traditions are traced through the life and work of three people: Gilbert White, E. F. Schumacher, and Jane Jacobs, who are shown to be in the organic, communitarian tradition that is sensitive to local ecological and community values. They are seen to have played critical roles in the development of sustainability as it applies to cities.
- *What spiritual tradition do they come from?* These pioneers in the application of organic, ecological values are all from within the Western spiritual tradition, rather than from Eastern views. This strong Western spiritual tradition of care, stewardship, and justice is not often recognized in discussions on environmental ethics. That such influential writers and thinkers come from our own spiritual tradition is seen as important for the West, because although the framework may be consistent with views from other traditions, the ethical base for sustainability in cities is not foreign to Western thinking. This is empowering to communities throughout the Western world that most need to tackle the sustainability agenda, but that may have come to accept a jaundiced view of their own spiritual capacity to be part of constructive change.
- *How can individuals and cities express these traditions today—in particular, how do they relate to the Auto City?* The fundamental value that drives automobile dependence and unsustainability in cities is privatism, or isolationism; this is the same ancient value that was viewed from the very foundations of the Western spiritual tradition as the destroyer of cities. This value discards all community or environmental obligations in the constant drive to find privacy, self-fulfillment, and consumption. Modernist technology makes such a quest easier than ever before. However, the values that can be used as antidotes to isolationism/privatism are also alive and well. It is suggested that these include (1) developing a "sense of place" through a sense of history, a sense of social justice, and a sense of nature in local communities; (2) revealing the true character of automobile dependence in activist fights over infrastructure priorities and other planning issues; (3) being pro-urban rather than trying to escape the city; and (4) practicing hope rather than despair over sustainability issues.
- *What is the role of the community, in groups such as churches and community artists?* The community needs to be a community and to dramatize its values in new and creative ways. Examples are given from the United States, Europe, and Australia of communities that have expressed their organic/ecological val-

ues in creative ways to claim some symbolic victories for sustainability in cities.

- *Is there hope for sustainability in our cities?* Yes! The opportunities for cities that are dominated by the automobile to overcome this dependence are always there. They need to be grasped or else unsustainable patterns will become entrenched. However, successful case studies are being shown globally and the ability of civil society to dramatize their visions and link to such successes has never been so good.

Appendix 1

Data and Methodology for the Thirty-seven-city Study for the World Bank

Methodology of Data Collection

The data set consists of ten indicators comprising twenty-one data items for the thirty-seven cities. This means there are 777 pieces of final data that we were seeking, of which we collected 747, or 96 percent, including data that we have confirmed as simply not available. The most significant missing parameter is road condition. Of the thirty missing data items, sixteen are road condition items. No city had reliable data on this, though some U.S. cities did give the percentage of roads classed poor. A few other cities made estimates of this parameter for us, while others could only give completely qualitative information such as "good" or "excellent." Road condition is thus not a satisfactory indicator to pursue, as it is just not practical to obtain; and where quantitative estimates do exist, they are certainly not comparable across cities (even on the same continent). Thus, no comments are made in the text on this parameter, though the data are given in Table A1.1. The fourteen other missing data items are ones that we feel exist but that we have been unable to locate in any authority, due mainly to lack of replies (e.g., Tokyo).

Method of Data Collection

This study required the collection of thousands of pieces of data. It was undertaken through a combination of methods, not the least of which was visits to many cities in the United States, Europe, Canada, and Asia, including a special visit to Beijing. These visits were undertaken by Felix Laube, Paul Barter, Chamlong Poboon, Benedicto Guia Jr., Tamim Raad and Hu Gang of ISTP's Sustainable Transport Research Group and coordinated through Jeff Kenworthy. Earlier visits were also made to many cities by Jeff Kenworthy.

What followed these visits was intensive analysis of the data collected and then followup via faxes, e-mail, and, especially, direct phone calls to all corners of the globe. Some information was ultimately tracked down using resources on the Internet. In numerous cases we had to purchase data, especially in Beijing.

Table A.1. Data from the Thirty-seven-city Study for the World Bank

Cities	JtW% Private	JtW% Public	JtW% NMM	MJ/Pass. km (cars)	MJ/Pass. km (bus)	MJ/Pass. km (all rail)	MJ/Pass. km (ferry)	JtW (km)	JtW (mins)	Transport deaths 100,000	% Transport Deaths of Total Deaths
AUSTRALIAN											
Perth	86.2	9.7	4.1	2.87	1.53	1.73	2.83	13.7	22.5	11.9	1.92
Adelaide	83.1	11.5	5.4	2.84	1.45	2.53	—			12.9	1.61
Brisbane-	80.4	14.5	5.1	2.80	1.91	0.56	—			12.5	1.91
Melbourne	79.4	15.9	4.7	3.43	2.40	0.50	—			11.6	1.67
Sydney	69.3	25.2	5.5	3.13	1.11	0.29	1.81	11.5	30.3	11.1	1.55
Average	79.7	15.4	5.0	3.02	1.68	1.12	2.32	12.6	26.4	12.0	1.73
AMERICAN											
Phoenix	93.7	2.1	4.2	3.76	2.43	—	—	17.4	23.0	20.2	2.69
Denver	91.3	4.4	4.3	4.15	2.99	—	—	13.8	22.3	14.1	2.22
Boston	77.8	14.7	7.4	2.91	2.86	1.19	9.99	10.1	24.5	10.4	1.21
Houston	93.3	4.1	2.6	3.36	2.32	—	—	19.1	26.2	20.8	3.34
Washington	80.6	15.0	4.4	3.06	2.71	0.76	—	14.2	29.2	11.6	1.80
San Francisco	80.0	14.5	5.5	3.60	2.12	0.71	4.41	15.4	26.6	13.0	1.60
Detroit	95.4	2.6	2.0	3.46	2.37	—	—	13.6	23.4	13.9	1.56
Chicago	80.6	14.9	4.5	3.30	2.53	1.10	—	15.1	28.5	13.7	1.61
Los Angeles	89.3	6.7	4.0	3.31	1.83	—	—	17.8	26.5	16.8	2.37
New York	66.7	26.6	6.7	4.20	2.31	0.72	2.25	13.6	30.6	11.8	1.27
Average	84.9	10.6	4.6	3.51	2.45	0.90	5.55	15.0	26.1	14.6	1.97
CANADIAN											
Toronto (Metro)	64.6	30.1	5.3	4.38	1.11	0.68	--	11.2	25.3	6.5	0.82

EUROPEAN										
Frankfurt	49.4	8.5	2.98	1.33	0.50	—	12.3	27.7	7.9	0.65
Amsterdam	40.0	35.0	2.13	1.50	0.50	—	9.2	27.9	5.7	0.53
Zürich	36.0	24.2	2.59	1.73	0.34	3.10	10.9	20.4	7.7	0.76
Brussels	45.5	19.1	3.10	1.89	0.81	—	5.6	22.1	11.7	0.98
Munich	38.0	16.0	2.40	0.69	0.54	—	9.6	25.0	11.7	1.13
Stockholm	31.0	14.0	2.93	1.34	0.48	—	8.6	32.2	7.3	0.75
Vienna	44.1	11.9	2.84	1.21	0.35	—	7.8	28.0	10.7	0.79
Hamburg	49.4	12.5	2.68	1.23	0.42	24.05	10.2	30.8	8.1	0.63
Copenhagen	43.0	32.0	1.89	1.64	0.74	—	13.9	28.8	7.5	0.60
London	46.0	14.0	2.28	1.12	0.36	—	9.2	32.0	8.1	0.79
Paris	48.9	14.9	2.95	0.88	0.35	—	12.2	35.0	10.6	1.45
Average	42.8	18.4	2.62	1.32	0.49	13.58	10.0	28.2	8.8	0.82
ASIAN										
Singapore	21.8	22.2	3.59	0.84	0.15	—	9.0	33.1	8.7	1.70
Tokyo	29.4	21.7	2.52	0.98	0.13	—			5.3	0.89
Hong Kong	9.1	16.9	2.96	0.71	0.19	3.74	10.9	44.0	5.7	1.12
Average	20.1	20.3	3.02	0.84	0.16	3.74	10.0	38.6	6.6	1.24
Kuala Lumpur	57.6	16.9	1.78	0.49	—	—	9.0	27.2	22.7	5.27
Surabaya	55.7	23.5	1.15	0.53	—	—	5.2	20.5	7.8	1.42
Jakarta	41.4	22.3	1.64	0.34	?	—	8.3	39.8	4.5	0.81
Bangkok	60.0	10.0	2.54	1.58	0.47	1.73	5.5	31.7	16.1	4.92
Seoul	20.6	19.8	2.15	0.81	0.18	—	11.2	41.2	24.9	5.98
Beijing	5.8	70.6	1.32	0.15	0.07	—	6.2	28.9	6.1	1.12
Manila	28.0	17.8	2.12	0.70	0.06	—	6.1	40.0	13.8	5.95
Average	38.4	25.8	1.81	0.66	0.20	1.73	7.4	32.8	13.7	3.64

Note: JtW is journey-to-work.

Table A.1. Continued

Cities	Total CO$_2$ per Capita (kg)	NO$_x$ per Capita (kg)	SO$_2$ per capita (kg)	CO per Capita (kg)	VHC per Capita (kg)	VP per Capita (particles) (kg)	Road Expenditure per Capita (U.S. dollars)	% GRP Spent on Commuting (%)	% Transit Cost Recovery
AUSTRALIAN									
Perth	2980.4	20.3	0.4	187.2	23.6	1.0	133	6.7%	28%
Adelaide	2561.3	18.2	0.4	168.1	21.2	0.9	133		40%
Brisbane	2898.7	29.4	1.1	187.3	24.7	2.2	167		54%
Melbourne	2915.8	18.0	0.5	179.2	22.7	1.3	89		24%
Sydney	2588.2	23.6	0.6	207.0	22.6	1.8	188	5.9%	55%
Average	2788.9	21.9	0.6	185.8	23.0	1.4	142	6.3%	40%
AMERICAN									
Phoenix	4654.3	21.5	1.7	166.0	23.6	1.0	399	7.4%	28%
Denver	4960.8	19.3	1.4	235.9	21.1	0.9	291	8.2%	19%
Boston	4238.1	25.5	1.8	222.7	22.1	1.1	284	5.5%	24%
Houston	5192.8	26.6	2.0	241.2	27.6	1.2	230	8.2%	28%
Washington	4403.0	22.0	1.6	184.0	20.5	1.0	262	6.9%	50%
San Francisco	5122.2	21.3	1.7	196.1	21.7	1.0	198	5.9%	45%
Detroit	4517.5	24.6	1.7	246.7	24.6	1.0	198	6.2%	23%
Chicago	4068.6	20.7	1.4	184.6	20.1	0.9	315	6.5%	46%
Los Angeles	4476.0	19.9	1.6	181.0	21.6	1.0	175	7.1%	43%
New York	3778.5	21.2	1.5	187.0	20.4	0.9	286	6.8%	47%
Average	4541.2	22.3	1.6	204.5	22.3	1.0	264	6.9%	35%
CANADIAN									
Toronto (Metro)	2434.3	27.0	2.3	160.6	21.7	3.9	150	5.2%	61%

346

City									
EUROPEAN									
Frankfurt	2813.0	20.1	0.9	68.2	12.1	0.9	8.8%	172	45%
Amsterdam	1474.8	12.8	N/A	34.2	5.7	N/A	3.8%		40%
Zürich	1762.0	12.1	0.4	32.4	8.6	0.1	4.7%	185	60%
Brussels	2113.8	16.7	1.2	65.9	10.3	0.1	4.3%	102	27%
Munich	1440.8	12.8	0.8	63.0	9.8	0.8	5.8%	100	54%
Stockholm	1993.8	17.8	1.0	207.6	26.7	N/A	5.8%	174	33%
Vienna	1537.7	4.2	3.2	50.0	5.2	N/A	4.4%	72	59%
Hamburg	2659.6	12.8	8.0	53.5	8.3	0.2	5.7%	97	62%
Copenhagen	1544.3	7.1	N/A	58.6	3.4	0.5	5.8%	166	66%
London	1704.2	16.4	0.9	97.0	17.0	2.8	5.2%	113	93%
Paris	1723.0	10.6	1.6	68.3	20.1	0.9	4.6%	166	61%
Average	1887.9	13.0	2.0	72.6	11.6	0.8	5.4%	135	54%
ASIAN									
Singapore	1317.4	N/A	N/A	N/A	N/A	N/A	6.6%	63	115%
Tokyo	1397.4	4.4	0.8	14.3	2.0	N/A		109	105%
Hong Kong	760.4	8.0	1.7	25.2	2.4	1.1	6.1%	94	136%
Average	1158.4	6.2	1.3	19.8	2.2	1.1	6.3%	88	119%
Kuala Lumpur	1424.0	11.2	1.0	90.0	22.8	1.0	6.3%	18	135%
Surabaya	404.0	3.1	0.9	42.0	11.7	4.3	10.0%	10	127%
Jakarta	653.2	16.2	0.9	57.7	9.3	3.4	7.5%	15	101%
Bangkok	1304.4	3.6	1.8	84.6	23.2	9.1	7.3%	71	93%
Seoul	704.7	8.9	1.5	28.8	3.6	1.4	5.0%	72	97%
Beijing	N/A	N/A	N/A	N/A	N/A	N/A	7.2%	61	20%
Manila	528.9	9.2	1.5	67.5	11.2	1.5	8.5%	23	122%
Average	836.5	8.7	1.3	61.8	13.6	3.4	7.4%	39	99%

It is our experience that without very close control, cross-checking, reality testing, and validation of data it is almost impossible to achieve useful international urban comparative data. By its very nature, this requires extreme patience and diligence on the part of those putting together the data. After intensive investigations into each city, involving innumerable agencies, libraries, and individuals, as well as a multitude of reports and studies, followed by scrutinizing of all the data obtained, we are convinced that the information provided here on the various transport indicators and broader background data is probably the best that is obtainable. We cannot claim, however, that in all cases the data will be without inadequacies or errors, as this depends on the quality of what was provided to us.

Modal Split for the Journey-to-work

Data on modal split for the journey-to-work were obtained either from population census data where a question on this is included (e.g., Australia, the United States and Canada), or from travel studies, surveys, and reports in individual cities where no centralized source was available. Where census data were not available, journey-to-work data can be difficult to track down; but in each case a source was found. One of the problems confronted was a lack of recognition of walking as a mode for getting to work. Modal split data from travel surveys often includes only motorized transport methods, so further searching was necessary. Although the method of obtaining these data where census data are not available varies in individual cities, the results appear to show reasonable patterns of variation between regional groupings of cities.

Energy Efficiency by Mode of Transportation

Energy efficiency by mode of transport is a deceptively difficult data item to obtain. Calculating this parameter on a consistent basis required the collection of many raw data items, rather than just simply locating energy-efficiency figures for each mode in already published sources. This necessitated collection of the following items in each city:

(a) vehicle kilometers of travel by cars
(b) average vehicle occupancy (twenty-four hour/seven days per week)
(c) calculation of car passenger kilometers from (a) and (b)
(d) energy use by private cars
(e) number of passenger trips by each mode of transit
(f) average distance of each passenger trip in each mode of transit
(g) calculation of transit passenger kilometers by mode from (e) and (f)
(h) energy use in each mode of transit

From these data, it was then possible to calculate the energy efficiency of each mode in terms of megajoules per passenger kilometer (MJ/passenger km).

In the case of vehicle kilometers and average occupancy, data were obtained from transportation agencies in each city. Generally these came from land use–transportation planning models or surveys. Energy use in cars came from a variety of published sources and was a very difficult item to trace in most cases. Transit data came mostly from transit operators and agencies, including, in the United States, from detailed American Public Transit Association (APTA) publications based on the Urban Mass Transit Administration's (UMTA now Federal Transit Agency: FTA) Section 15 reporting. Some data on transit in developing countries had to be obtained from large independent studies that were undertaken by the transportation agencies in various cities to make up for the sometimes poor record keeping by individual transit systems. This was also the case for deregulated, privatized transit systems throughout the First World.

Journey-to-work Trip Length

Surprisingly, these data are not readily available in most cities. In order to obtain them we had to make detailed inquiries with the relevant transportation agencies in each city and consult various transportation planning reports and other sources, especially in developing cities. For example, to develop the parameter in U.S. cities, we obtained a set of CD-ROMs called "1990 Census Transportation Planning Package" from the Bureau of Transportation Statistics, U.S. Department of Transportation. Using the actual raw data for tens of thousands of journeys-to-work, we were able to calculate average journey-to-work trip lengths for the correct spatial definitions used to specify each of the US cities in the sample.

One example of the problems encountered with this variable is found in Adelaide. Because of the way transportation modeling is set up and the way the model output is specified, Adelaide simply cannot supply a journey-to-work trip length, according to the best authorities in the city (despite concerted efforts to question this issue). Nevertheless, it was found that, with persistence, these data can usually be ferreted out, and when systematically compared they demonstrate a picture that is generally consistent with the other data in the study. The journey-to-work trip lengths are an average for all modes, including the much shorter walking and cycling trips.

Journey-to-work Trip Time

The journey-to-work trip time on the whole was a much easier data item to gather because most cities seem to consider this a key item in characterizing their transportation systems, despite a reasonably high degree of consistency in the factor across cities of very different types (see Chapter 3). Journey-to-work trip times are encountered in many transportation reports in cities, generally derived from a reasonably large survey sample. Overall, journey-to-work trip time data were obtained in a similar manner to that described for the journey-to-work distance. However, in the case of U.S. cities, the population census reports these trip times and from these detailed data we were able to calculate averages. The trip times in this study are curb-to-curb times, not door-to-door times, and cover all modes.

Traffic Deaths

It was thought initially that this item would be relatively easy to get, but again there were some important points that warranted consideration. If published data on traffic deaths are taken directly from various reports from the cities, it becomes clear very quickly that there are inconsistencies at work. One of the major problems seems to be that police data consistently under-report traffic deaths compared to official health statistics which use a system known as the International Classification of Diseases (ICD). Deaths from transportation-related causes (all modes) are recorded in a series of distinct categories (E810–E825). A key difference between these data and police data is that they record a death under a transportation cause if the death occurs up to thirty days after the accident, usually in the hospital. Police data only tend to pick up a death at the actual accident.

In each case, the data in this study sought to employ the ICD data. In most cases this could be tracked (e.g., in the U.S. cities the data were obtained through "Vital Statistics of the United States 1991: Volume II Mortality Part B" from the U.S. Department of Health and Human Services), though for some developing cities there remain some doubts about the integrity of the data supplied. For example, Jakarta's and Surabaya's numbers seem relatively low compared to other cities in the group. This relates to the poorer reporting of ICD in some developing countries as recognized by the World Health Organization, which administers this classification.

Transportation Emissions

Emissions of CO_2 were calculated directly from fuel use by public and private modes of transportation using standard rates of CO_2 emissions per megajoules of fuel burned. For electric transport, the rate of CO_2 emissions was adjusted according to detailed national data on how electricity is generated in each country (hydro, nuclear, coal, gas, etc.) and transmission losses from power stations. Energy use by all modes of transportation was carefully collected from the various transportation and transit administrations in each city as part of the modal energy-efficiency item discussed earlier.

For all other emissions, a transportation emissions inventory was sought and obtained in each city. Data for U.S. cities were obtained on a standardized basis from the U.S. EPA after some searching (all U.S. cities have prepared emissions inventories using the same method, and they are available from this agency). Apart from U.S. cities, and to a certain extent Australian cities, transport emissions inventories are for the most part elusive items and require persistent phone calls and other contacts to track them down. The data in this study appear to be the only information available from each city on this important subject.

Despite the inevitable differences in methodologies that will occur in such detailed pieces of work for each city, the data follow a reasonably sound pattern with some exceptions—such as Stockholm's CO emissions, which seem unduly high.

Road Expenditure

This was one of the hardest data items of all to gather. The trail of road expenditures in most cities is a tortuous path, whereas expenditures on transit tend to appear in a few easily identified publications. The split of responsibilities for roads between agencies, different types of expenditure, and different tiers of government make it a particularly difficult variable to trace.

The data given here represent a three-year average (generally 1989, 1990, and 1991 or 1990, 1991 and 1992, depending on the census year) of all expenditures on roads, including all construction and all maintenance by all levels of government in each city. For the most part, these data were obtained by phoning and writing to various authorities around the world and getting detailed data for each year. Sometimes the data were provided as a detailed project expenditure list encompassing literally hundreds of large and small projects in different areas that had to be included or excluded according to whether their exact location was inside or outside the city boundaries.

In the United States, a CD-ROM set titled "1992 Census of Governments: Finance Statistics, Individual Unit Records" was ultimately purchased from the U.S. Department of Commerce, Bureau of the Census, and the data were calculated by computer for each city. These data contained every expenditure on roads (and other categories of expenditure) by every authority for every city in the country. When checked against what we had already collected directly from each city, this source gave the same order of expenditures, though each city did have to be increased, suggesting that even the best attempts to extract road expenditure data are often incomplete.

Percentage of GRP Spent on the Journey-to-work

This was the most complicated item to calculate in this study and required the arduous collection of twelve pieces of separate data, as listed below:

- the total number of jobs in each city
- the modal split for the journey-to-work (from item 1 of the study)
- the car capital cost per kilometer
- the car variable cost per kilometer
- the average car work trip length
- the average car occupancy for the journey-to-work
- the transit fare per passenger kilometer
- the travel time cost per hour
- the capital cost of a bicycle
- the percentage of commuters by bike
- the per capita GRP for each city
- the number of working days per year

Needless to say, finding all these data for each city on a reliable basis was difficult. However, primarily through many phone calls, authorities and individuals within each city were contacted to access all the different items, and they were slowly pieced together. Some items, such as the car costs, had to be compiled from a plethora of other data on various cost components. Likewise, transit fares per passenger kilometer required fare revenue and passenger kilometer data for all systems and operators within the city in order to get a genuine, properly weighted transit fare cost. There were thus many chances of pitfalls in being able to complete this item due to a few bits of missing key data.

The parameter "percentage of GRP spent on commuting" in each city was derived by adding all costs of each main journey-to-work mode (car, transit, bike) and travel time costs and then dividing by metropolitan population and GRP per capita, as shown in the following formula:

$$\text{Expenditure} = \left(\frac{2D_w \left(\frac{JW_c(C_c + V_c)L_c}{O_c} + JW_tL_tC_t + JC_{tt}T \right) + JW_bC_b}{\text{Pop} \times \text{GDP}} \right) \times 100$$

Where:
J = number of jobs in the metro area
W_c = proportion of work trips in cars
C_c = car capital cost per kilometer
V_c = car variable cost per kilometer
L_c = average car work trip length
O_c = average work trip occupancy
W_t = proportion of work trips on transit
L_t = average transit work trip length

C_t = transit fare per passenger kilometer
C_{tt} = travel time cost per hour
T = average work trip time in hours
D_w = number of working days in a year
W_b = proportion of work trip by bikes
C_b = average capital cost of a bike per annum
Pop = metro population
GDP = GRP per capita

Transit Cost Recovery

Transit cost recovery was derived by obtaining all the financial pages from every relevant transit operator's annual report in each city. These generally contain the operating revenues and operating costs of each system. In the majority of cases, the item does not include interest payments on capital debts. However, the amalgamated accounts of the regional transit authorities in Germany and Switzerland had to be taken as given, although they quite possibly include some capital outlays. In these cases, the financial performance of their operations will be understated.

In some of the developing Asian cities, financial data on systems are not directly reported and thus require much more searching through independent studies and reports. In quite a few cases, separate requests had to be made to each operator to reveal these financial data. In nearly all cases, the final figures provided reflect every transit mode and operator in the system. The only missing data are for systems that contribute only very small amounts to transit operations in the city and thus would not impact the final figure. Surabaya and Jakarta data do exclude the common private microbuses due to lack of data. However, since these transit operators receive no public subsidy yet make a profit, it is to be expected that the cost recovery shown is a minimum (i.e., transit operations in these two cities are more profitable than indicated).

Metropolitan Area Definitions

The *metropolitan area* is defined as the functional urban area of a city. This wording keeps the definition from simply being the administrative boundaries of a particular territorial unit that carries the name of the city under whose name the area is generally known. For example, the City of Sydney, whose name is commonly used to describe a metropolitan area with a population of over 3 million, only contains the most central part of this area, home to only a fraction of those 3 million people. Most national statistical systems recognize this problem and have created criteria that define the outer boundary of functional urban areas. The most common among these relate to home and work locations of residents, where there is often a requirement that a certain percentage of workers have jobs inside the metropolitan area for a territorial unit at its fringe to be included. Likewise, the structure of the urbanized area can be used, whereby there is a maximum gap in the urbanization defined that is allowable for a marginal outlying settlement to be included. In practice, variations on such definitions are used, depending on data availability. Sometimes, for reasons of inadequate data, it is necessary to take an area that is less than the true functional urban region. Nevertheless, data can still be compared as long as the data remain internally consistent. Comparison of individual data items between cities can be done, with a full awareness of the exact areas being compared, using the metro area definitions provided below. In the case of the gross regional product, it is crucial to use a generous definition in all cases, as discussed below.

Overview of National Data

In *Australia,* all the studied metropolitan areas are well defined in the census statistical system and are known as capital city statistical divisions. In the *United States,* the census defines standard metropolitan statistical areas (SMSAs, now CMSAs and PMSAs) for every census according to its data on urbanized areas, which are based on one or several counties that are in part urbanized. In *Canada,* some metropolitan areas (Montreal, Toronto, Vancouver) have some form of regional government based on groups of municipalities working together, while in others the city boundary is constantly adapted to encompass most of the metropolitan area. *Europe* presents a mixed situation, with some metropolitan areas being roughly equal to a traditional city-state, others forming a province or region in the respective national administrative system, and still others very difficult to equate to administrative units. In *Asia,* the situation is even more difficult, with the exceptions of Hong Kong and Singapore, where national boundaries equate to the boundary of the functional region reasonably well.

Individual City Definitions

The following provides an alphabetical listing of the definitions of all the metropolitan areas in the study for the World Bank.

In *Adelaide*, the metropolitan area is defined as the Adelaide Statistical
Division, for which good data are available because it is the definition used by all
agencies across the board. It is also a good description of the functional region.

For *Amsterdam*, there are two definitions that were used. Most data relate to
a definition of the Amsterdam agglomeration, which includes the Gemeenten
(municipalities) of Amstelveen, Amsterdam, Diemen and Ouder-Amstel.
However, it was possible to retrieve some data only for Amsterdam, which contains 87 percent of the agglomeration's population but is actually a discontiguous
unit with Diemen sitting in between the two parts. Given the high proportion of
the population covered by the smaller definition, there are no major problems to
be expected from its use where no wider data could be found. This definition is a
tight one, but the data situation makes it difficult to expand it without taking in
the entire Randstad, a major multinuclear urban conglomeration that is home to
a good part of the Netherlands' population. Due to Amsterdam's very compact
character, its location on mostly reclaimed land, and the very planned and systematically developed layout of the city and its neighboring cities, it seems reasonable that the sample presented here gives a good impression of an even wider
area.

Bangkok features two definitions. The most commonly used one is the JICA
study area (JICA, 1990), whose boundary is defined according to the alignment
of a planned outer ring road around the Thai capital that encompasses most of
the region and thus gives a very valid definition covering most of Bangkok's urbanized area. As this definition doesn't follow administrative boundaries, it was
necessary to use data for the somewhat larger Greater Bangkok area, which contains the provinces of Bangkok Metropolitan Area, Nonthaburi, Pathum Thani,
and Samut Prakan for some data items.

Beijing is defined as the Official Metropolitan Area, which in China equates
to the actual urbanized area (7.362 million people in 1990).

In *Boston*, there are two definitions. Most data have been collected for the
Standard Metropolitan Statistical Area as defined by the U.S. Bureau of the
Census in 1980, comprising 103 towns. Some agencies, however, use a larger definition called the Greater Metropolitan Region of Boston, which consists of 164
towns; this definition was used where applicable. Both areas represent an acceptable definition.

In *Brisbane*, the metropolitan area is defined as the Brisbane Statistical
Division, for which good data are available. It is also a good description of the
functional region, despite covering a large territory that contains large genuinely
unpopulated areas. On some isolated occasions, data were only available for a
larger area called Southeast Queensland, which includes the Brisbane and
Moreton Statistical Divisions, thus expanding the covered area to the coastal
holiday resort strips of Gold Coast and Sunshine Coast to the north and south of
Brisbane, respectively, which are essentially urban in character.

Brussels is defined as the Brussels Capital Region, which is one of three regions in Belgium and for which good data are available. The functional region has somewhat outgrown this area, but the data situation outside this boundary is complicated because the former province of Brabant, which contains the hinterland of Brussels, has been divided into its Flemish and Wallonian parts and thus data, where available, would have to be assembled by individual municipalities. This is in stark contrast with the situation for the Capital Region alone, so it was seen as more valuable to present a high-quality set of data for this area alone.

The *Chicago* agglomeration extends well into the state of Indiana to the south, and into the state of Wisconsin to the north. To keep the data collection manageable, however, it was necessary to constrain the definition to six counties in the state of Illinois that contain the majority of the region. These counties are Cook, Du Page, Kane, Lake MacHenry, and Will and are also known as the Northeastern Illinois Planning Commission Area.

Good data for the *Copenhagen* functional region are available for a territory called Hovedstadsregionen, or the Danish Capital Region, containing the independent cities of København and Frederiksberg as well as the counties of København, Frederiksborg, and Roskilde.

In *Denver* there are two main definitions, namely the official Standard Metropolitan Statistical Area, including the counties of Adams, Arapahoe, Boulder, Clear Creek, Denver, Douglas, Gilpin, and Jefferson. For most data, however, the more marginal, much less-developed counties of Clear Creek, Gilpin, and Douglas have been eliminated from this definition. This area still contains significant genuinely rural areas, especially in the east end, and most modeled data applies to definitions that are independent of county boundaries. Where this was the case, the correct populations have been used in the standardization process.

For *Detroit* a somewhat reduced version of the Standard Metropolitan Statistical Area was used because the outer counties of Lapeer, Livingston, and St. Clair only have a very small population and are generally rural in character. The counties included are thus Macomb, Oakland, and Wayne.

Frankfurt is really part of a multinuclear agglomeration called the Rhein-Maingebiet. This area encompasses the cities of Mainz and Wiesbaden to the west, Darmstadt to the south, and Hanau to the east of Frankfurt. The administrative boundaries of this large area are exceedingly complicated and regional cooperation is in its early stages, meaning that consistent regional data are mostly unavailable. For this study, the Stadt (city of) Frankfurt am Main was used for most data, with some transit data relating to a larger region serviced by the Frankfurter Verkehrsverbund (FVV).

The traditional city-state of (Freie- und Hansestadt) Hamburg contains most of the *Hamburg* functional metropolis. As it is a state in its own right within the Federal Republic of Germany, there are excellent data available for this definition throughout. Only the transit data relate to the somewhat larger area serviced by the Hamburger Verkehrsverbund (HVV), and the appropriate population was used for them.

Hong Kong is very well represented by the area included in the British Crown Territory of Hong Kong, and good, well-published data are available throughout.

The *Houston* Standard Metropolitan Statistical Area includes the counties of Brazoria, Fort Bend, Harris, Liberty, Montgomery, and Waller. Galveston is excluded because it is considered to be a separate conurbation. This is a wide definition, but good data are available for this area.

The Indonesian National Capital District of Jakarta (Daerah Khusus Ibukota Jakarta) serves as a fair representation of the *Jakarta* metropolitan area. It is a little constrained because the city has somewhat outgrown this area. However, the definition is acceptable because it enables data collection of reasonable quality.

The *Kuala Lumpur* area is most commonly defined as the Klang Valley, which includes the Federal Territory of Kuala Lumpur as well as four districts (Klang, Petaling, Ulu Langat, and Gombak) in the surrounding state of Selangor. This is a very appropriate definition and was used for all but a few data that were available only for the entire state of Selangor and the Federal Territory of Kuala Lumpur.

London was defined as the area commonly referred to as Greater London. This area represents only the core of the much wider Southeast England metropolitan area. Greater London alone, however, produces consistent data over its territory.

Los Angeles is part of a larger conurbation covering a good part of Southern California. This complicated situation means that the Los Angeles Standard Metropolitan Statistical Area is considerably smaller than the Los Angeles Census Urbanized Area, two definitions that are usually only marginally different, with the latter generally being smaller. For the purpose of this study, all data collected refers to Los Angeles County only, thus leaving out the five other counties that could be included, namely Imperial, Orange, Riverside, San Bernardino, and Ventura. As this larger area is genuinely decentralized, it should be considered fair to look at this one county only. Also, a check on some key data items such as vehicle kilometers per capita reveals little variation between Los Angeles County and the wider area.

For *Manila*, the cooperative body of Metro Manila has reasonably good data for what covers most of the conurbation. Metro Manila includes the four cities of Caloocan, Manila, Pasay, and Quezon, as well as the municipalities of Las Piñas, Makati, Malabon, Mandulayong, Marikina, Muninlupa, Navotas, Parañaque, Pasig, Pateros, San Juan, Taguig, and Valenzuela, which are spread over two provinces.

In *Melbourne*, the metropolitan area is defined as the Melbourne Statistical Division, for which good data are available because it is a definition used by all agencies across the board. It is also a good description of the functional region.

Munich's peculiar urban form with a core and spokes along its radial S-Bahn suburban express rail system with rural areas in between the spokes means that what is known as Planungsregion 14 in Bavaria should really be used as a metropolitan definition. However, this area cuts across district (Landkreis) boundaries and data availability is poor. The solution was to report data on the Landeshauptstadt (city of) München only, which covers most of the central part of this agglomeration. Good data are available there, though for some data, such as transit, larger areas are used with appropriate adjustments to population.

The metropolitan area of *New York* extends into three states and data collection is therefore sometimes difficult, though some coordination on a regional level exists, which is helpful. This made it possible to use a comprehensive definition that includes the following territorial units: State of Connecticut planning regions of Central Naugatuck Valley, Greater Bridgeport, Housatonic Valley, South Central, Southwestern, and Valley; State of New Jersey counties of Bergen, Essex, Hudson, Middlesex, Monmouth, Morris, Passaic, Somerset, and Union; state of New York counties of Bronx, Dutchess, Kings, Nassau, New York, Orange, Putnam, Queens, Richmond, Rockland, Suffolk, and Westchester.

The Région d'Ile-de-France gives an excellent definition of the *Paris* metropolitan area, for which equally good data are consistently available.

In *Perth*, the metropolitan area is defined as the Perth Statistical Division, for which good data are available because it is a definition used by all agencies across the board. It is a good representation of the metropolitan area, although the fast-growing city of Mandurah to the south should probably be included.

Phoenix is defined as Maricopa County, which contains the metropolitan area but also includes large, mostly unpopulated desert areas to the west.

The *San Francisco* metropolitan area, also termed the Bay Area, has been defined as a five-county area including Alameda, Contra Costa, Marin, San Francisco, and San Mateo counties. Other counties in the vicinity that are often seen as part of that area are Napa, Santa Clara, Solano, and Sonoma. Apart from Santa Clara, these counties are truly marginal, and their inclusion would have significantly complicated the data collection task. Santa Clara has its own genuine core in San Jose, which the U.S. Census in fact considers a separate urbanized area.

Seoul presented some problems in that a lot of data were only available for the National Capital Region, which includes the independent cities of Seoul and Inch'on (Seoul-t'ukpyolsi and Inch'on-jikhalsi) and Kyonggi-do, the surrounding province. Wherever possible, data were collected only for Seoul and its satellite cities, a discontiguous but genuinely urban area. This definition includes the independent cities of Seoul and Inch'on, as well as the municipalities of Ansan, Anyang, Hanam, Koyang, Kunp'o, Kuri, Kwachon, Kwangmyong, Migum, Osan, Puch'on, P'yongt'aek, Shihung, Songt'an, Songnam, Suwon, Tongduch'on, Uijongbu, and Uiwang.

In *Singapore*, national boundaries provide a good definition, although there is some interaction mainly with Johor Bahru in adjacent Malaysia. The Republic of Singapore has been used for all data. Good information is available through national agencies.

Stockholm presented some more difficulties, with the true metropolitan area represented by Stockholms Län (County), although it contains vast, mainly forested areas. However, data availability for the county is low and it was necessary to resort to using Stockholms Staden (City) only on a consistent basis. It was possible to retrieve some data on a county level, however, especially on private transportation and transit, in which case appropriate population data were used.

The Kotamadya Surabaya covers a good part of the *Surabaya* functional region and was thus used as a metropolitan area definition.

In *Sydney*, the metropolitan area is defined as the Sydney Statistical Division, for which good data are available. It is a good representation of the metropolitan area, extending to Wyong to the north but excluding Wollongong to the south.

Tokyo is generally defined as Tokyo-to or Tokyo Metropolis. However, the functional region extends well beyond this narrow definition, which only contains one-third of the area's inhabitants. The Tokyo Metropolitan Region that was used wherever possible also includes the prefectures of Chiba-ken, Kanagawa-ken, and Saitama-ken.

The Municipality of Metropolitan Toronto has good data for *Toronto*, but has been significantly outgrown by urban development. A more appropriate definition would be the Greater Toronto Area, which includes the regional municipalities of Durham, Halton, Peel, and York. It was only possible to collect part of the data for the larger definition, so for this study the consistent data covering the Municipality of Metropolitan Toronto only was used.

Vienna is a city-state within the Republic of Austria that is equal to the Stadt Wien, for which excellent data are kept. The functional region extends somewhat outside those boundaries, but data availability deteriorates dramatically.

Washington's metropolitan area extends over the District of Columbia and into the two adjacent states of Maryland and Virginia. The definition that was used corresponds to the 1980 Standard Metropolitan Statistical Area and includes the District of Columbia; Montgomery and Prince Georges counties in the state of Maryland; and in the state of Virginia the counties of Arlington, Fairfax, Loudoun, and Prince William, as well as the independent cities of Alexandria, Fairfax, Falls Church, Manassas, and Manassas Park. Data collection for this tri-state area was complicated, but a comprehensive set of data was collected.

The agglomeration of *Zurich* is defined by the Swiss census according to a large number of Gemeinden (municipalities) that spread across two Kantone (states). Because data collection for this complicated definition would have been a very difficult task indeed, and taking in the entire Kanton Zürich would have included large rural areas to the north, a definition using Planungsregionen (planning districts) that correspond reasonably well with the census agglomeration was applied. The following Planungsregionen were included: Furttal, Glattal, Knonauer Amt, Limmattal, Pfannenstil, Zimmerberg and Zürich. It was possible to retrieve reasonable data for this definition.

Note: GRP and Area Definition

The gross regional product is available in most countries for functional economic regions and is made available through national statistical agencies. The boundary definitions of those areas are, for the purpose of standardization, highly sensitive to cross-border commuting, because the commuters take the wealth they create at their place of work to their place of residence. The functional economic regions are therefore bounded by a border where minimal cross-commuting occurs, or at least commuting in both inbound and outbound directions is of similar magnitude, such as the German "Arbeitsmarktregionen" (Statistisches Landesamt Baden-Württemberg, 1996).

These regions often don't totally match the metropolitan area definitions, but the per capita GRPs are representative as long as the correct populations are used in the denominator.

Appendix 2

Growth Management Approaches and Guidelines

The process of reurbanization whereby more residential and commercial development is focused within the existing urban area and especially in urban villages and subcenters can be greatly enhanced if some limits are placed on the potential for outward urban expansion. This is especially true in cities that see themselves as having almost unlimited potential to spread over vast expanses of cheap and non–topographically constrained land. The management of urban growth is also, of course, essential to protect productive farmland and natural landscapes around cities.

This appendix therefore first provides an overview of some greenbelt and growth management strategy options with comments on their potential to alter sprawling growth patterns and some insights into their possible limitations and other impacts. It then provides a review of some possible tools for establishing greenbelts around cities along with their potential and shortcomings.

Table A2.1. Greenbelt and Growth Management: Strategy Options

Strategy/Description	Potential	Comments
Limit population growth Use a greenbelt to impose an absolute limit on urban growth. Limit land available for development; do not provide for growth.	• Discourage migration; make relocation to the city difficult by limiting land and housing options. • Prevent further urban development in and around the city.	• Establishing a greenbelt without providing for growth somewhere is not a sustainable strategy. High land and housing prices would affect residents and be inequitable. Political commitment and public support is unlikely. • Would not change urban structure. • A greenbelt by itself is not a strategy for limiting population. Need to address other issues to stabilize population.
Decentralization Use a greenbelt to divert population/urban growth to areas beyond the metropolitan region. Limit land available for development and accommodate growth in other urban centers.	• Limit spatial expansion of the city. • Increasing population in other centers could have a positive social and economic impact on receiving areas and could reduce the dominance of larger cities.	• Would need to apply with regional development strategies to increase attractiveness and capacity of receiving areas. • Need to manage growth and consider carrying capacity and impact of growth in receiving areas. • Would not change the city's urban structure.
Limited fringe growth Use a greenbelt to set an urban growth boundary and encourage more intensive use of land allocated for urban growth at the fringe.	• Promote a more efficient pattern of urban development at the fringe; encourage compact and dense growth. • Shape growth to develop a compact urban form. • Limit spatial growth to protect rural areas.	• Could limit leap-frog development and promote denser and better integrated urban development. • Compact and contained urban form shaped by greenbelt. • Would allow limited expansion; would encroach on rural land and extend the urban area. • Pressure on greenbelt when fringe land is developed.

(continues)

Table A2.1. Continued

Strategy/Description	Potential	Comments
Managed expansion Use a moving greenbelt/growth boundary to influence the rate and location of urban expansion. No permanent limit on the spatial extent of the urban area. Similar to limited fringe growth, but the greenbelt is not permanent.	• Promote a more efficient pattern of urban development at the fringe. • Slow rate of urban expansion and avoid some nonurban areas.	• Responsive to growth, so would have a marginal influence on land supply. Would have a limited effect on growth patterns as it allows further expansion. • Rural land and habitat would continue to be lost as the urban area expanded. • Scope for arbitrary land release.
Reurbanization Use a greenbelt to set an urban growth boundary and focus growth inward, accommodating it through more intensive use of the established urban area.	• Promote denser, better integrated urban structure. Catalyst for consolidation, including development of urban villages. • Limit placed on expansion, protecting rural land from urbanization.	• Encourage restructuring of the existing urban area to develop a more sustainable development pattern. • Develop vacant and underutilized land and encourage redevelopment to create urban villages and denser housing in appropriate areas. Need strategies to facilitate such development and overcome political and regulatory barriers. • Could potentially accommodate growth without encroaching on rural environs. • May need time for reorientation of development from the fringe to established areas; without it a greenbelt could be undermined by land shortage. • Access to open space by residents of new development enhanced.

362

Urban concentration		
Use a greenbelt to set a growth boundary and concentrate development in centers in the established area. Accommodate growth through denser development. Similar to reurbanization but with more emphasis on concentrating development in nodes and reclamation of suburban areas to expand the greenbelt.	• Progressively shift urban activity and growth from a suburban pattern to denser, urban villages Develop contained, compact urban form. • Gradually reclaim low-density outer areas for other uses. No encroachment on rural land. Greenbelt area could be expanded inward as urban area contracts.	• Develop a more sustainable urban structure with denser urban land use in compact nodes. Use growth to establish this pattern of development. • Use former suburban areas for open space and farming; this would protect rural land. • Radical idea against current growth trends. However, it could be the long-term result of a reurbanization strategy.
Strategy mix		
Combination of strategies using a greenbelt to limit and focus growth: decentralization of some population growth to other centers, limited fringe growth and reurbanization. In long term, urban contraction and stable population may be possible.	• Divert some growth to smaller urban centers, promote opportunities and develop alternative growth areas in other parts. • Promote efficient fringe growth and compact, contained urban form. Encourage denser, better integrated urban structure, including urban villages. • Set a boundary to urban expansion and protect areas beyond it for rural use and conservation.	• In practice, a mix of strategies could provide the optimal and politically acceptable growth management model. • Suggested mix accommodates growth and provides a range of lifestyle and development opportunities. Allows for transition from sprawl to new development pattern. Protected, permanent green zone around the city. • Need to integrate with other strategies to manage land use.

Source: Adapted from Wake (1997).

Table A2.2. Tools for Establishing and Maintaining a Greenbelt: A Summary

Tool/Description	Potential
Maintain public land estate Maintain existing public land and manage appropriately. Public estate includes conservation reserves, state forest, vacant crown land, and water reserves. Develop management regime supportive of regional land use policies.	• Public land would form the essential core of a metropolitan greenbelt. Large areas may already be in public ownership around the urban area. • Provides security of tenure and use. • Should be kept intact and managed to protect landscape, conservation and natural resource values.
Land acquisition Acquire freehold land to protect conservation or productive values and hold from urban development or other inappropriate uses. Acquisition could include outright purchase by a public agency or land trust, land swap or ceding of land.	• Could not purchase all land that should be included in a greenbelt; however, land acquisition is important to secure critical areas. • Use acquisition to secure areas for public use and to protect areas threatened by development where no other means are available. • More resources needed for acquisition program. • Land needs to be managed by public agency or through lease for appropriate use.
Land stewardship Education, information, practical support, and community involvement initiatives to encourage and facilitate appropriate management of privately held land. Could cover habitat protection, water resource protection, maintaining viewsheds, and sustainable rural land use. Voluntary, participatory approach to manage land for public and private benefit.	• Some initiatives may already be applied to rural areas around cities and these should be extended. • Much greenbelt land would be in private hands, so it is important to extend and encourage land stewardship to protect values. • Promote community ownership and enhance support and understanding of greenbelt policy. • A greenbelt can provide a framework for government and community efforts to enhance conservation and sustainable land use in the rural area around the city.
Land covenants Landholders voluntarily enter into a binding agreement that is registered on land title and applies to future land purchasers. Covenants could involve protection of areas of remnant vegetation, maintenance of agricultural land, or retention of rural landscape. Support for appropriate land management is important to back up covenants. Public agency or community groups could promote covenants.	• Could not apply to all greenbelt land, because it is voluntary. • Legally binding, but enforceability uncertain, essentially relies on goodwill of landholders involved. • There is scope to promote covenant as part of a land stewardship program providing support to private landholders to manage land in keeping with regional policies.

Differential taxation

Rating or taxing land on the basis of preferred use to encourage maintenance of land use and reduce incentive for conversion. This can include current use or concessional rating or tax deferral. Use to protect farmland, rural use, or remnant vegetation retention.

- Maintains land in private ownership and use while recognizing public benefit and providing financial incentive to continue preferred land use.
- Not effective by itself; needs to be backed up by land use controls. May be a useful tool in greenbelt context.

Zoning controls

Land use regulated through zoning to permit appropriate activities and prohibit others. Apply zoning controls under regional and local planning schemes. Zone areas for specific uses and limit development and subdivision potential.

- Important tool to manage land use on private holdings.
- Current zones may be inadequate, may need additional zones to protect land of conservation value and landscape amenity and retain agricultural uses.
- Open to change, needs political commitment to be effective in holding greenbelt land.
- Zoning is the basic means of regulating land use. Support with other tools to enhance growth management.

Clustered rural development

Design approach for rural-residential development. Involves grouping residential uses together on part of a site snd retaining the remainder as open space or farmland.

- Rural-residential development affects agricultural use, habitat, and landscape values.
- Minimize impact by accommodating limited development in appropriate areas through clustering. Intensification of rural land use through rural-residential development is an important issue. Protect rural amenity by ensuring clustering of such development in greenbelt.

Urban growth boundary

Statutory boundary which defines the extent of urban growth. Urban development may occur within the boundary subject to zoning and planning approvals, not permitted beyond it. Boundary may be permanent or able to be expanded in long term according to growth management policy.

- The inside of a greenbelt would form an urban growth boundary. Critical tool for defining urban and rural areas; sets limit on urban expansion.
- Use to shape urban form and focus urban growth in appropriate areas. Need to manage land uses within the boundary to achieve compact development.
- Use interim growth boundaries to phase growth over time.

Purchase or transfer of development rights

Development rights attached to property could be purchased by a public agency or transferred between private interests. Purchase of rights maintains private land ownership but limits uses to which the land can be put, provides compensation for loss of development potential.

- May weaken the legitimacy of zoning controls.
- May be costly especially in urban fringe areas.
- Development rights are conditional so purchase or transfer may be of limited use. Needs further consideration under different planning systems.
- May be a means of protecting rural land in a greenbelt from development pressure.

(continues)

Table A2.2. *Continued*

Tool/Description	Potential
Statutory policy Statutory, legally enforceable policy can set planning framework and provide guidance for planning decisions. Scope for such policy under planning and environmental legislation. Applies to state and local government as well as private interests.	• Use to define the greenbelt area and establish land use policies for it. • Institute standing prohibition of urban development and guide local decisions for appropriate land use in keeping with overall principles. • Would give the greenbelt planning status and legal status. • To implement effectively it needs to be linked to other tools such as zoning.
Strategic planning and policies Strategic plans and policies are not legally enforceable but provide a basis for decision making and set goals and vision. State and local government can develop. Provides a way of defining preferred future and strategies to achieve it. Community involvement is important.	• Important to support statutory tools. • Provides vision and goals for land use and management initiatives and decisions. Could include a regional land use plan for rural policies and urban development policies, and conservation policies. • Use to identify issues, define aims, and address how to meet them. • Use to reinforce the greenbelt and support growth management. Use to guide decisions and link to implementation strategies.

Source: Adapted from Wake (1997).

Appendix 3

A Checklist for City Sustainability Using Economic Efficiency, Social Equity, Environmental Responsibility, and Human Livability Criteria

In every city, new urban development implies costs associated with the provision of physical and social infrastructure to allow the development to occur, as well as transportation costs associated with its ongoing functioning within the urban system. Depending on the characteristics of any particular development (e.g., density and mixing of land uses), its general location within the urban system, and any site specific features, these costs can vary considerably. Any new development will therefore fall somewhere within a wide range of infrastructure/service and transportation costs associated with creating and maintaining it, and it will either tend toward relatively poor economic efficiency or toward more efficient use of both private and public money.

Along with pure economic considerations, each new development will also tend to either increase or decrease the long-term sustainability of the urban region, either improve or detract from how equitably the city meets people's transportation needs, and either enhance or diminish the livability of the city. Rarely, however, is any serious or comprehensive attempt made to assess or rank a development according to all these criteria.

If new developments were to be subjected to a checklist of economic efficiency, equity, sustainability, and livability factors, then this would make the decision making process for new development more explicit and transparent. A decision to proceed with a development would be based on some more objective and open evaluation of its merits and its down sides and an "on balance" assessment that concludes that it is justified. Below is an example of a possible checklist that could become part of the urban development approval process.

Developing and Using the Checklist

Economic Efficiency

Obviously, economic efficiency is a relative matter such that the infrastructure, service, and transportation costs of a proposed inner city redevelopment might be compared to putting a similar development on the fringe to gauge whether there are any savings to be reaped. In practice, it may be necessary for each city to develop an accepted set of average infrastructure/service costs for each major item and various average costs for different components of the transportation picture. (A detailed set of costing procedures is set out in Appendix 4.) How far above or below these averages each urban development proposal falls would then determine its ranking on economic-efficiency criteria, perhaps on a scale of 1 to 5 above or below the average.

A similar approach could be used for the other factors of equity, environmental responsibility, and livability as outlined below.

Social Equity

Each city will need to determine its own criteria for assessing whether the new development improves or diminishes the access of those who are most vulnerable to transportation and location disadvantage. However, in our view, three of the most important keys to improving equity of access are to:

(1) Greatly enhance the quantity and diversity of services within a safe and easy walk of residences. This tends to reduce the access problems of all groups no matter the reason they may be transportation disadvantaged (e.g., lack of a car, personal circumstances such as dependent children or age, or low income, which makes car ownership and use more difficult);

(2) Improve the proximity of transit to housing as well as its frequency of service so that better connections can be made with activities that are not local in nature and;

(3) Locate new development, as much as possible, within existing areas that have established services—core and inner areas generally offer the best possibilities to reduce locational disadvantage.

Employing these methods should make it possible for cities to establish some objective physical measures of whether a new development is likely to be relatively equitable or inequitable in its access characteristics.

For example, each development could have a series of calculations to determine:

• Average distance from new residences to a standard set of urban services, such as shops, schools, entertainment/recreation facilities, and community services (health care, child care, library, etc). Ideally services should be less than 800 meters from homes (i.e., a maximum of a fifteen-minute walk or a five-minute bike ride).

• Average distance to a bus stop or rail station, average peak period and off-peak service frequency, and average Saturday and Sunday service frequency. Ideally, service frequencies should average ten minutes or less for peak periods and no more than twenty minutes for off-peak periods and weekends.

• Average transportation network distance of the development to the core of the city. This will usually be a strong indicator of the area's relative access advantage to most urban services, because access tends to systematically improve from fringe areas to the core of the city.

The scores of each development on these criteria would determine how it was ranked in the checklist of access and equity considerations.

Environmental Responsibility

Environmental responsibility criteria can be assessed using a range of quantitative, semi-quantitative, and qualitative methods.

Oil, Greenhouse Gases and Regional Air Pollutants

Vulnerability to oil, greenhouse gases, and major regional air pollutants are all linked most strongly to the amount of travel by car that each development brings by virtue of its location and other physical and social characteristics. The best method for determining how to score these factors is to make estimates of the annual per capita travel in cars and the annual per capita fuel use of residents; or if the development is primarily an employment site, the likely amount of travel that is going to be needed by different modes to access the jobs and/or other activities on the site should be estimated.

Every city has some detailed data on the travel patterns of residents in different zones of the city. These are usually obtained from detailed home interview surveys involving personal travel diaries. From this computerized data it is possible to calculate annual travel and fuel use of residents in all different areas of the city (e.g., by local government agency or by distance of a particular zone from the city center); and, by implication, the per capita emissions of major transportation pollutants can be calculated using data sets that provide the grams per kilometer of travel for each pollutant.

Thus, the annual travel for residents in each new development could be estimated from the transport data resources already existing in each city. The annual travel to access jobs and other activities in the development could also be estimated if necessary. From this it could easily be seen which types of development in which areas of the city are the best for reducing oil vulnerability, greenhouse gases, and regional air pollutants that either contribute to photochemical smog or are themselves a problem (e.g., lead).

Once this process became part of a city's standard procedures for urban development approval, it would not be an onerous task to complete for each proposal. As well, those associated with the assessment would soon develop a feeling for the magnitude of the travel, fuel, and pollution figures and hence would be able to rapidly distinguish those developments with a good ranking from those with a poor ranking. Calculations on annual travel per resident are outlined in Appendix 4.

Reduced Loss of Land on the Fringe

For each new development proposal it is a simple matter to determine how much new land, if any, must be developed. However, in the case of residential development, particularly in the outer and fringe areas, more than just the on-site land and roads must be considered. The contribution to the growth in urbanized area made by other activities associated with the development, such as schools, shopping centers, regional open spaces, commercial developments, community facilities, and so on, must be considered. This can be quantified in each city (as we have done for Australian cities—see Kenworthy and Newman, 1991).

Thus, each development proposal can be ranked according to the average amount of urban land that is required per new household, perhaps using zero as the yardstick where the development is an infill site whose population will be using already developed land and under-utilized facilities.

Reduced Traffic Impacts

This item is more difficult to assess but can be done on a case-by-case basis using the character and location of the development as a guide. In each parameter it is the likely urban systems impact of the development that is the major concern rather than the specific environmental qualities within the development; for example, it is possible to have a very quiet semirural subdivision with no shops or facilities but with each household having three or more cars that must be driven for every trip to other parts of the city, thus contributing to noise nuisance elsewhere. Similarly, such developments may have very low intrusion of roads or freeway infrastructure within them, but they may contribute strongly to the pressure for more freeways by virtue of their high auto travel demands.

Noise

How much and what type of extra traffic will the development generate and where will it affect urban noise levels? Some qualitative judgments would be necessary to decide the level of nuisance that the extra traffic would constitute, but there are also established scientific criteria to assist (e.g., Hothersall and Salter, 1977).

Visual Intrusion

What will the development imply in terms of new transportation infrastructure such as roads, car parks, and the sheer presence of cars in the urban system? A qualitative judgment would be needed concerning the type of structures and their prominence. Technical methods are also available to assist in the assessment of visual intrusion (e.g., Hothersall and Salter, 1977).

Severance of Neighborhoods

What new roads, freeways, or rail systems will be needed, and will they sever neighborhoods? As with noise, how much extra traffic of different types will the development generate, and where will this have a negative effect on the cohesiveness of neighborhoods?

Parking Problems in Local Neighborhoods

What extra demand for parking facilities will the development generate throughout the city? This can be estimated from a knowledge of the likely annual travel per resident and other data as detailed in the proposed economic impact statement.

Loss of Open Space to Cars

This can also be estimated in a quantitative way by knowing the likely demand for all types of roads and car parks (and other car-based facilities) that the development will generate.

Livability

The livability agenda should be assessed on the qualities being offered to future residents, workers, and general users of the development under consideration. These are based on a knowledge of the urban design of the development.

- Is the development designed to facilitate street interaction or are people always going to have to be in cars to go anywhere?
- Are there usable and sociable public areas apart from parks in the area (e.g., pedestrian pockets, traffic-calmed streets, children's play areas in the street)?
- Is the development designed with public security and safety in mind (e.g., good street lighting, landscaping that provides clear sight lines and few hiding places for intruders, good views from kitchen and living room windows into public areas)?
- Are parks and children's play areas separated from or integrated with residential areas, and does traffic pose a threat when accessing these facilities?
- How much mixed land use is there and at what distance is it from the homes? Is a car needed for many trips? What is the transit service like, in both frequency and proximity of service and in the quality of shelters and access to stops and stations?

A Final Note About the Checklist

Naturally, the simple completion of this checklist would need to be accompanied by some general agreement as to how to weight the importance of the various criteria. And, to carry any authority, the checklist would probably need to become part of the statutory planning process, in much the same way as all new subdivisions are accompanied by checklists of provisions such as water, sewerage, and drainage requirements that must be fulfilled before they can be approved.

Once weights are attached to each item and a scoring procedure established, perhaps the easiest way to use the checklist might be to set a score that a development must reach or exceed before approval. One important outcome of this process might be referral of proposals back to applicants with commentary noting the parameters in which the development is falling short of desirable features. This would provide the opportunity for the applicant to review certain features of the development, such as specific urban design elements, and thus improve its score.

Table A3.1. A Proposed Checklist for Improving Urban Development Practices

Economic Efficiency
Does the proposed urban development increase or decrease the economic efficiency of the city through:

	INCREASE	DECREASE
	1 2 3 4 5	1 2 3 4 5
(a) Economic savings from reduced infrastructure spending (e.g., water, sewerage drainage, education, etc.)?	☐ ☐ ☐ ☐ ☐	☐ ☐ ☐ ☐ ☐
(b) Economic savings from reduced car dependence over and above any necessary increases in transit expenditure (e.g., less fuel, fewer roads and less parking, lower external costs, etc)?	☐ ☐ ☐ ☐ ☐	☐ ☐ ☐ ☐ ☐

Social Equity
Does the proposed urban development increase or decrease social equity through its impact on access to urban services and employment opportunities:

	1 2 3 4 5	1 2 3 4 5
(a) For those without direct access to a car?	☐ ☐ ☐ ☐ ☐	☐ ☐ ☐ ☐ ☐
(b) For the most access disadvantaged household groups (i.e., older single people, single parents, couples with young children)?	☐ ☐ ☐ ☐ ☐	☐ ☐ ☐ ☐ ☐
(c) For women?	☐ ☐ ☐ ☐ ☐	☐ ☐ ☐ ☐ ☐
(d) For households in lower income brackets?	☐ ☐ ☐ ☐ ☐	☐ ☐ ☐ ☐ ☐
(e) For households in the public rental market?	☐ ☐ ☐ ☐ ☐	☐ ☐ ☐ ☐ ☐

Environmental Responsibility
Does the proposed urban development increase or decrease environmental responsibility through:

	1 2 3 4 5	1 2 3 4 5
(a) Reduced vulnerability to oil in transportation?	☐ ☐ ☐ ☐ ☐	☐ ☐ ☐ ☐ ☐
(b) Reduced greenhouse gas emissions from transportation?	☐ ☐ ☐ ☐ ☐	☐ ☐ ☐ ☐ ☐
(c) Reduced major regional urban air pollutants (in particular, lower photochemical smog)?	☐ ☐ ☐ ☐ ☐	☐ ☐ ☐ ☐ ☐
(d) Reduced loss of land on the urban fringe?	☐ ☐ ☐ ☐ ☐	☐ ☐ ☐ ☐ ☐
(e) Reduced local traffic impacts:	☐ ☐ ☐ ☐ ☐	☐ ☐ ☐ ☐ ☐
• Noise levels	☐ ☐ ☐ ☐ ☐	☐ ☐ ☐ ☐ ☐
• Visual intrusion	☐ ☐ ☐ ☐ ☐	☐ ☐ ☐ ☐ ☐

	1 2 3 4 5	1 2 3 4 5
• Severance of neighborhoods by roads, traffic, or other transportation infrastructure	☐ ☐ ☐ ☐ ☐	☐☐ ☐ ☐☐
• Parking problems in local neighborhoods	1 2 3 4 5 ☐ ☐ ☐ ☐ ☐	1 2 3 4 5 ☐☐ ☐ ☐☐
• Loss of open space to cars (e.g., road and parking requirements)	1 2 3 4 5 ☐ ☐ ☐ ☐ ☐	1 2 3 4 5 ☐☐ ☐ ☐☐

Human Livability
Is the proposed urban development
likely to increase or decrease human
livability through:

	1 2 3 4 5	1 2 3 4 5
(a) Community and neighborhood interactions based on accidental or unplanned interactions across front fences, in streets and public areas, and in increased use of transit?	☐ ☐ ☐ ☐ ☐	☐☐ ☐ ☐☐
(b) Urban vitality such that many different activities are facilitated and encouraged in public spaces that are not the sole precinct of vehicles?	1 2 3 4 5 ☐ ☐ ☐ ☐ ☐	1 2 3 4 5 ☐☐ ☐ ☐☐
(c) Public safety through the creation of more defensible urban public spaces, a greater sense of community coherence and identity, and more activity in the streets and other public areas for all types of households?	1 2 3 4 5 ☐ ☐ ☐ ☐ ☐	1 2 3 4 5 ☐☐ ☐ ☐☐
(d) Usable, safe, and interesting public green spaces accessible by children without the need to interact with traffic?	1 2 3 4 5 ☐ ☐ ☐ ☐ ☐	1 2 3 4 5 ☐☐ ☐ ☐☐
(e) The accessibility on foot, bicycle, and convenient transit of a wide range of urban services for those at home and without ready access to a car?	1 2 3 4 5 ☐ ☐ ☐ ☐ ☐	1 2 3 4 5 ☐☐ ☐ ☐☐

Appendix 4

An Economic Impact Statement for Urban Development

The cost of urban development is increasingly under the microscope. Most cities have now carried out major detailed studies to better quantify the true infrastructure and servicing costs of bringing new urban land into the marketplace. These costs are cumulatively very large, especially on the urban fringe, when the full range of physical and social infrastructure is considered. For example, a detailed study in Sydney, which only considered physical infrastructure, showed that the savings from consolidation compared to fringe development were significant. These savings showed a maximum of $A30,700 per dwelling when comparing 840-square-meter lots on the fringe with consolidated development at fifty dwellings per hectare in established areas. The minimum saving was $A17,000 per dwelling when comparing 450-square-meter lots on the fringe with eighteen dwellings per hectare consolidated development in an established area (Hughes Trueman Ludlow and Dwyer Leslie, 1991).

Although there is increasing documentation of these costs, urban development continues to proceed largely without any established way of building cost considerations into the urban development approval processes. Rather, the real costs of urban fringe development tend to remain hidden within the budgets of a number of public sector agencies, such as roads departments, energy authorities, and water and sewerage departments. For example, when a new parcel of land is rezoned from rural to urban, there is no requirement for submission of a statement of the cost implications of the rezoning. The costs are more or less accepted as part of the process of orderly planning and supply of new residential land to meet the needs of new population growth.

On the other hand, if a large new redevelopment is to occur in the inner city, requiring significant sums of money for new and upgraded infrastructure and services, then a clear statement and request must come before government with each component cost clearly laid out. Government approval is required for such decisions, which generally involve much less money than the annual sums spent on new greenfield sites that are not fully costed.

In order for better decision making to occur with regard to the location, timing, and size of new urban development, it can be argued that the economic cost implications need to be made more transparent in the decision-making process. This would not mean an end to fringe development simply because it is in many

374

cases more expensive in total than development in established areas. But it would mean that governments could see more clearly the actual costs of development in different areas and could make decisions that attempt to balance economic costs against other important considerations, such as the need to ensure that housing opportunities are available for everyone.

Infrastructure and servicing costs are also not the only economic cost implications of urban development, although they tend to be the items that draw most heavily on the public purse. Also important are the transportation cost implications of the development, including the capital and operating costs of private transportation and public transit systems.

The economic impact statement for urban development outlined below is an attempt to set forth an example of a form that could become part of the standard process for assessing urban development applications. It was developed in an Australian context but can be adapted.

Outline of the Economic Impact Statement

The economic impact statement is broken into three sections, as detailed in the following.

Infrastructure and Service Costs

The first section outlines the full costs of servicing any new development with all the necessary physical and social infrastructure. It considers both the residential and nonresidential components of any development, where applicable. The final part of this section sets out the total infrastructure and servicing costs broken down according to the party responsible for them (i.e. each level of government and the private sector).

Transportation Costs

The second section deals with all the detailed costs of transportation associated with any new development. It starts by specifying these costs on an annual basis for both the travel of residents of the new development and the travel that must be undertaken by people from all over the metropolitan region to access any work or other nonresidential opportunities on the site. For example, developments in core and inner regions will have more potential for residents to use transit than will fringe developments. Also, core and inner developments would be easier to access from outside using transit because of the convergence of transit routes on city centers. The last part of this section capitalizes the annual transportation costs according to public and private transportation so that transportation costs can be combined with the infrastructure and servicing costs.

Total Economic Costs

The final section of the statement combines the service and transportation costs into a total overall statement of economic costs split according to public and private sectors. Following this is a series of detailed notes, mainly on the transportation costs, suggesting how each item might be estimated. This section also outlines an example calculation for a fringe development in Perth compared to an inner city development.

Table A4.1. A Proposed Economic Impact Statement for Urban Development

Infrastructure and Servicing Costs

Per dwelling costs
Each new development proposal should be accompanied by
a statement that sets out the costs per dwelling for the following
items of infrastructure and service.

Cost item	Cost ($)
(1) Water	_____
(2) Sewerage	_____
(3) Drainage	_____
(4) Telephone	_____
(5) Mail service	_____
(6) Electricity	_____
(7) Gas	_____
(8) Transit[1]	_____
(9) Roads	_____
(10) Health[1]	_____
(11) Education[1]	_____
(12) Subsidy to local government	_____
(13) Land preparation	_____
(14) Town planning schemes	_____
(15) Professional fees	_____
(16) Any other costs	_____
TOTAL COSTS PER DWELLING	_____

TOTAL INFRASTRUCTURE COSTS
(costs per dwelling × number of dwellings)   _____

Costs of servicing nonresidential uses[2]   _____
In many developments there will also be a need to service nonresidential activities such as commercial and retail developments,
schools, service stations, and recreation facilities. The above costs,
where appropriate, need to be calculated for nonresidential uses
as well.[3]

TOTAL INFRASTRUCTURE AND SERVICE COSTS   _____
Once the costs of servicing residential and nonresidential
elements are known, a final statement of the total cost implications is required and should be split in the following way:

TOTAL SERVICE COSTS   _____

Public sector costs
  Federal   _____
  State   _____
  Local   _____

Private sector costs

TOTAL INFRASTRUCTURE AND SERVICE COSTS   _____

Transportation Costs

Annual transportation costs
Each new development proposal should be
accompanied by a statement that clearly sets
out the ongoing transportation costs for residents
and for accessing nonresidential uses from
outside the development.[4] These should be
calculated initially on an annual basis and
include the following:

Annual Costs of Transportation Items

Cost Item	Cost of Travel by Residents ($)	Cost of Access from Outside ($)
(1) Capital cost of cars[5]	_____	_____
(2) Fuel costs[6]	_____	_____
(3) Miscellaneous operating cost of cars [7]	_____	_____
(4) Time costs [8]	_____	_____
(a) Private transportation	_____	_____
(b) Transit	_____	_____
(c) Walking and cycling	_____	_____
(5) Road costs [9]	_____	_____
(6) Parking costs [10]	_____	na (see note 10)
(7) Externalities [11] (Total)	_____	_____
(a) Fatalities	_____	_____
(b) Injuries		
(c) Property damage	_____	_____
(d) Air pollution	_____	_____
(e) Noise pollution	_____	_____
(f) Other quantifiable external costs	_____	_____
(8) Transit costs (capital and operating) [12]	_____	_____
TOTAL ANNUAL TRANSPORTATION COSTS	_____	_____

Capitalizing annual transportation costs
Once the annual cost of each transportation
item has been calculated, it is possible to capitalize these costs to present values using an
appropriate discount rate and a period of fifteen years (the approximate life of an average
car). Transportation costs can then be included
with servicing costs on the same basis.

Capitalized Annual Transportation Costs

	Cost of Travel by Residents ($)	Cost of Access from Outside ($)
Private transport		
Transit	_____	_____
TOTAL CAPITALIZED TRANSPORTATION COSTS	_____	_____

Overall Economic Costs of the Development

	Public sector ($)	Private sector ($)
Infrastructure and servicing costs	_____	_____
Transportation costs	_____	_____
TOTAL ECONOMIC COSTS	_____	_____

DETAILED NOTES ON HOW TO CALCULATE THE ECONOMIC IMPACT STATEMENT

(1) Health, education, and transit costs should include capital items plus the capitalized annual operating expenses of each service using an appropriate discount rate and term of say fifteen years.

(2) Sometimes nonresidential services can be more expensive because they are more complex (e.g., telephones) or need to be of higher capacity (e.g., sewerage) than for dwellings. Also, depending on location, commercial and retail enterprises can be spread out over more land in fringe and outer locations, making servicing more expensive than in higher density developments in core or inner areas. On the other hand, core or inner areas can be expensive to service when major infrastructure upgrades are required. These factors have a bearing on servicing costs and need to be included in the economic picture.

(3) Where it is not feasible to calculate the servicing costs for nonresidential uses directly, it may be possible to derive an estimate by considering the amount of land these uses will occupy, extrapolating this area to the appropriate number of dwellings, and using the servicing costs per dwelling as a guide.

(4) Annual transportation costs are the full costs of the private and transit travel that would be undertaken by residents of the new area, as well as the travel to the new area by nonresidents wishing to gain access to employment and any other activities on the site. For example, the road costs are different from the on-site infrastructure costs in the previous section and are calculated on the basis of average road costs per kilometer driven all over the city (i.e., city-wide demand for roads).

(5) The capital cost of cars as well as transportation cost items 2 through 7 are calculated on an annual basis and rely on the ability to estimate with reasonable accuracy the likely level of car travel per capita (annual vehicle kilometers of travel, or VKT, per capita) for the residents of the proposed development, as well as the annual amount of travel necessary for people outside the development to access jobs or other services. (This last item is included only if it is relevant; in some cases the development may be purely residential in which case this would not be a factor.)

The general method for doing this in all cities would be to use the surveyed patterns of travel for households in the areas around the proposed development or for areas nearby and of a similar character. These data are obtained from computerized records of home interview surveys (HIS) in each city, which are based on personal travel diaries of all household members (generally over five years of age) for all trip purposes and modes including the origin and destination of each trip. Home interview surveys are carried out as part of major land use/transportation studies to assess future transportation network needs (e.g., the Road Reserves Review in Perth). These trip records, in combination with the modeled (or network) travel distance, can be used to calculate annual kilometers of travel (using appropriate annualization factors).

Once this has been established then the procedure to calculate annual capital costs of car travel for residents is: Annual VKT per capita × Average capital cost per kilometer for cars ($) × Estimated total number of residents = Total annual capital cost for residents' car travel ($).

For car travel to nonresidential uses within the development from the rest of the city, the method would principally be to estimate the total number of jobs to be located in the development and then to calculate an average journey-to-work trip length for work trips to the zone in which the development is located (or several nearby zones), as well as the private/transit modal split. The HIS in each city can be used to do this by looking at the origin, trip distance, and mode for all work trips to that zone or surrounding zones. Depending on the development, it may also be necessary to calculate trips to the site for shopping and other business activities. In this instance the same basic procedure as outlined above for work trips to the site can be repeated.

The method for calculating the annual capital cost of car access to nonresidential uses from outside then becomes: Number of daily two-way work (and other nonresidential) trips × Annualization factor (250 days) × Weighted average work (and other) trip length to the site (kilometer) × Average capital cost per kilometer for cars ($) = Total annual capital cost for car travel to the site for nonresidential uses ($). Capital costs of car operation are available on a per kilometer basis from sources such as McGlynn and Andrews (1991).

(6) Fuel costs for car travel also depend on the VKT calculations just outlined. However, it is also necessary to apply some fuel consumption per kilometer rates to each trip in order to calculate fuel use. The simplest way to do this is to use the fleet average fuel consumption rate for the particular city available from, for example, the U.S. Federal Highway Administration or the trienniel ABS Survey of Motor Vehicle Usage. There are, however, two possible refinements that can be made to this:

(a) Allowance for the type of vehicle: Sometimes the HIS includes details about the car used for the trip, in particular its number of cylinders. If these data are available then an average consumption rate can be applied to each cylinder category based on available information. Also, other modes such as motorcycles or vans are usually specified for each trip. Walking and cycling trips can be assigned zero fuel use.

(b) Allowance for congestion: Trips driven in congested conditions will have higher fuel use than those driven at higher speeds in free-flow conditions. Transportation model data allow network distance and average travel time for the trip to be used to estimate the likely average speed of trips driven between two zones. The average fuel consumption can then be adjusted using a well-established linear relationship between fuel use of a vehicle and average speed of urban driving [see, for example, Kenworthy and Newman (1982) for a typical graph of this on an "average" Australian car; and see Newman, Kenworthy, and Lyons (1985) for its application in fuel calculations].

Fuel cost calculations for residents of a development then become a matter of summing the following basic equation for all trips and all persons over a year: Trip distance (km) × 1/Fuel consumption rate (km/liter) × Cost of fuel per liter ($/liter) = Cost of fuel use for the trip ($). The fuel consumption rate in this equation will have been adjusted where possible for the type of vehicle and congestion.

The fuel cost calculations for access to nonresidential activities would be calculated on a similar basis knowing the total amount of travel (VKT) involved, the rate of fuel consumption, and the fuel price. That is: Number of daily two-way work (and other) trips to nonresidential uses × Annualization factor (250 days) × Weighted average work (or other) trip length to the site (kilometer) × Average fuel consumption rate per kilometer for cars × Cost of fuel per liter ($) = Total annual fuel cost for car travel to the site for nonresidential uses ($).

(7)   Miscellaneous operating costs of cars, such as repairs, insurance, and registration fees, are calculated directly from the per capita VKT data as in note 5 above using an average cost per kilometer. The calculation would be as follows: Annual VKT per capita × Average miscellaneous operating costs per kilometer for cars ($) × Estimated total number of residents = Total annual miscellaneous operating costs for residents' car travel ($). Average operating costs of cars can be obtained from sources in each city.

(8)   All travel involves time, and time spent in cars, on transit, walking or cycling has some economic cost for everyone, the value of which will depend on the type of travel involved. In 1992, for normal personal travel in Perth (the bulk of travel in any city) the value assigned to travel time was around $4.00 per hour, while for business-based travel in company cars the rate was $24.50 per hour (personal communication, MRD, Perth).

It is possible to make estimates of travel time in both private transportation and transit for residents and for travel to nonresidential uses in a new development.

PRIVATE TRANSPORTATION—RESIDENTS

Using the VKT calculations for each development outlined above, it is possible to estimate the total travel time involved by: (a) estimating the overall average speed of private transport based on average speed data for each trip (from HIS and model data as outlined above); and (b) deciding on an appropriate cost per hour of the travel (perhaps some weighted dollar rate per hour based on the relative proportions of different types of travel). Total private travel time cost for residents of a development then becomes a matter of estimating the following basic equation: Annual VKT per capita × 1/Average speed of private travel (km/h) × Cost of travel time ($/hour) × Number of residents = Total annual travel time cost for residents' private travel ($).

PRIVATE TRANSPORTATION—ACCESS FROM OUTSIDE TO NONRESIDENTIAL USES

The same basic method applies here and can be expressed as: Number of daily two-way work (and other) trips to nonresidential uses × Annualization factor (250 days) × Weighted average work (or other) trip length to the site (km) × 1/Average speed of private transportation travel (km/h) × Cost of travel time ($/hour) = Total annual time cost for private transportation travel to the site for nonresidential uses ($).

TRANSIT—RESIDENTS

Transit travel time can also be estimated by using the HIS information, which records the mode of travel of each trip. The average speed of different transit modes and an overall weighted average speed for transit in each city is readily derived from the transit agencies. Alternatively, direct average speed data from the transportation model associated with the HIS can also be used to estimate a transit travel time for each trip. The derivation in simple terms then becomes: Annual passenger kilometers per capita on transit × 1/Average speed of transit travel (km/h) × Cost of travel time ($/hour) × Number of residents = Total annual travel time cost for residents' transit travel ($).

TRANSIT—ACCESS FROM OUTSIDE TO NONRESIDENTIAL USES

The most important item to be calculated here is the rate of transit trip-making to the development to access work and other nonresidential activities. Generally this is very low in Auto Cities outside of core areas where transit routes are focused. Again, data from the HIS can provide this information as follows: Number of daily two-way work (and other trips to nonresidential uses) × Annualization factor (250 days) × Weighted average work (or other) trip length to the site (km) × 1/Average speed of transit travel (km/h) × cost of travel time ($/hour) = Total annual time cost for transit travel to the site for nonresidential uses ($).

WALKING AND CYCLING TIMES

Walking and cycling will often be only a minor component of travel times except in core and inner areas where these modes are very prevalent. It is generally rather more difficult to estimate walking and cycling times because these trips are often intrazonal trips thus the trip distances that are generated in transportation models in the HIS are frequently poorly specified. However, some estimates can be made of walking and cycling distances for both residents living in the new development and for any walking and cycling access to jobs and other activities. These, combined with average walking speeds of five kilometers per hour and average cycling speeds of fifteen kilometers per hour can be used to estimate the total travel time costs for these modes according to the methods outlined above.

(9)   Annual road costs are those associated with the total extra road travel implied by the development on roads throughout the city. For urban travel, road costs in Perth in the early 1990s in terms of capital outlay were on average around ten cents per kilometer. The calculations of road costs for travel by residents is then as follows: Annual VKT per capita × Average road cost per kilometer ($) × Estimated total number of residents = Total annual road cost for residents' car travel ($).

The calculation of road costs for access from outside to nonresidential uses is as follows: Number of daily two-way work (and other) trips to nonresidential uses × Annualization factor (250 days) × Weighted average work (or other) trip length to the site (km) × cost of roads per kilometer ($) = Total annual road costs for car travel to the site for nonresidential uses ($).

(10) The provision of parking in metropolitan areas is a major cost of car dependence, both in the land that is taken up and in the costs of construction and maintenance of parking facilities. In a study from the United States, Hart (1990) has calculated the total number of parking spaces that must be created per car across U.S. metropolitan areas to adequately provide for car-based access. His results show that the average U.S. city provides a total of eight parking spaces per car to allow for parking requirements in the central city; at shopping centers; sporting, entertainment and cultural facilities; educational institutions; suburban employment centers, such as business and office parks; industrial areas; at home; and so on. This study shows how parking provision is a major cost of automobile dependence that is rarely ever brought into the cost equation to its full extent.

This magnitude of parking provision naturally implies a certain level of car use, since a greater number and diversity of car trips will cause parking requirements to become larger. Our data comparing international cities, including ten U.S. cities, allows us to peg this level of parking provision to a corresponding average per capita car use and then make some estimates of the parking requirements for different levels of car dependence. Table A4.2 presents the comparison for U.S. cities, Australian cities, and some areas within Perth.

Using the data in Table A4.2 in combination with known levels of car ownership in various parts

TABLE A4.2. ESTIMATED METROPOLITAN-WIDE PARKING REQUIREMENTS PER CAR FOR VARIOUS LEVELS OF ANNUAL PER CAPITA CAR USE

Area	Annual per Capita Car Kilometers	Metropolitan-wide Parking Requirements per Car
U.S. cities	8,770	8
Australian cities	5,800	5
Perth inner areas	4,600	4
Perth outer areas	9,800	9
Perth fringe	11,325	10

of the city and the average cost of providing parking spaces in cities, it is possible to make some estimates of the parking costs that would result from different types of new urban development in different locations. The BTCE (1990, p. 60) estimates the average cost of providing a CBD parking space in an Australian city at $A15,000 with a life of fifteen years, giving an annualized cost of $A1,000 per bay. A non-CBD space is estimated to be one-third the annualized cost of a CBD space ($A333).

In any new development in Australia it is possible to estimate the car ownership level based on data for similar nearby areas from the ABS. From this the total number of cars can be calculated. Using data from Table A4.2 above, together with the estimated VKT per capita for the new development, the total number of metropolitan parking bays implied by the development can be calculated.

The only remaining estimate to be made so that costs can be calculated is how many of the parking bays will be CBD and how many non-CBD. A guide to this can be attained from our data on the supply of CBD spaces in cities relative to the population of cars (Newman and Kenworthy, 1989). For example, in Perth in 1981 there was one CBD bay for every 8.3 cars in the metropolitan region at an average car usage of 6,250 car kilometers per person. Thus, the demand for CBD parking spaces for new development could be apportioned according to the per capita car kilometers involved (e.g., a development with 10,000 car kilometers per capita is estimated to have a demand of one CBD parking bay for every 5.2 cars). Remaining parking spaces would all be non-CBD.

After these deductions have been made, the calculation to estimate the annual cost of parking of the new development then becomes: Total estimated number of CBD spaces × Annual cost of $A1,000 per CBD space + Total estimated number of non-CBD spaces × Annual cost of $A333 per non-CBD space = Total estimated annual cost of metropolitan parking requirements ($).

It should be noted that all metropolitan parking costs are addressed by this calculation for residential development because it covers all types of parking for all purposes. Thus, there is no need to repeat the exercise for the nonresidential uses in the development.

(11) The cost of the external impacts of transportation, such as noise, accidents, and air pollution, are more difficult to estimate because of the difficulties in quantifying their impacts in dollar terms (e.g., what is the magnitude of the medical bill attached to the increased incidence of asthma in children due to photochemical smog in Sydney's western suburbs, or what is the cost of damage to materials and plants from air pollution?). Nevertheless, estimates are available in the literature on the basis of a cost per kilometer of travel for all these externalities, although they are often very conservative and should be used with caution.

The external costs calculation for travel by residents of the new development then becomes: Annual VKT per capita × Average cost per kilometer for all externalities ($) × Estimated total number of residents = Total annual external costs for residents' car travel ($).

And for access to nonresidential uses from outside it is as follows: Number of daily two-way work (and other) trips to nonresidential uses × Annualization factor (250 days) × Weighted average work (or other) trip length to the site (km) × Cost of all externalities per kilometer ($) = Total annual external costs for car travel to the site for nonresidential uses ($).

(12) The cost of servicing the transit demands of new development needs to be considered. This is particularly true where new extensions to fixed rail systems are required or where a significant new number of buses and other facilities are required. There are different ways to calculate this, the best of which is probably on a case-by-case basis where the likely costs to the transit system may be known in more detail. For example, a development may be essentially cost neutral for transit where no new services are planned and any extra patronage would be using spare capacity that already exists in the bus or train system (in this instance there may actually be a net benefit in improved fare revenue).

However, the HIS data and associated transportation model can be used to calculate the likely number and purpose of transit trips by residents within a particular development and the annual passenger kilometers involved. A similar exercise can be done for the likely use of transit in accessing work and other activities in the development.

Once the annual passenger kilometers are known in each case, it is then possible to apply some average cost per passenger kilometer to cover the capital, operating, and external costs of transit [e.g., McGlynn and Andrews (1991) estimate an average for Australian cities for buses and trains of approximately twenty-five cents per passenger kilometer].

Table A4.3. An Example of an Economic Impact Statement Based on Fringe Development in Perth (1000 dwellings)

Infrastructure and Servicing Costs

Per dwelling costs
Each new development should be accompanied by a
statement that presents the costs per dwelling for the
following items of infrastructure and service.

Cost Item	Cost ($)
(1) Water	5,921
(2) Sewerage	6,598
(3) Drainage	2,881
(4) Telephone	705
(5) Mail Service	51
(6) Electricity	6,200
(7) Gas	901
(8) Transit[1]	4,515
(9) Roads	6,539
(10) Health[1]	13,195
(11) Education[1]	19,051
(12) Subsidy to local government	1,206
(13) Land preparation	2,950
(14) Town planning schemes	1,200
(15) Professional fees	1,200
(16) Any other costs	—
TOTAL COSTS PER DWELLING	73,113
TOTAL INFRASTRUCTURE COSTS	73,113,000
(costs per dwelling × 1000 dwellings)	

Once the costs of servicing are known, a final
statement of the total cost implications is required
and should be split in the following way: (percentage
splits are based on typical outer development in
Perth according to Western Australian Water
Authority data)

Total Service Costs

Public sector costs:	46,792,320
Federal (6.7%)	4,898,571
State (53.8%)	39,334,794
Local (3.5%)	2,558,955
Private sector costs (36.0%)	26,320,680
TOTAL INFRASTRUCTURE AND SERVICE COSTS	73,113,000

Note: Footnote numbers in this table refer to the numbered notes presented on pages 378–381.

Table A4.4. An Economic Impact Statement Comparing Fringe and Inner City Development (Fremantle)

Transportation Costs

Annual transportation costs
Each new development should be accompanied by a statement that clearly presents the ongoing transportation costs. These should be calculated initially on an annual basis and include the following:

Annual Costs of Transportation Items

Cost Item	Cost of Travel by Fringe Residents ($)	Cost of Travel by Inner City Residents ($)
(1) Capital cost of cars[5]	5,447,000	1,888,000
(2) Fuel costs [6]	2,055,000	760,000
(3) Other operating cost of cars [7]	2,689,000	932,000
(4) Time costs [8]		
(a) private transportation	5,183,000	1,967,545
(b) transit	na	1,920,028
(c) walking and cycling	na	na
(5) Road costs [9]	2,215,000	768,000
(6) Parking costs [10]	4,867,000	1,379,000
(7) Externalities [11] (Total)	443,940	153,860
(a) Fatalities	133,635	46,315
(b) Injuries	43,035	14,915
(c) Property damage	70,215	24,335
(d) Air pollution	165,345	57,305
(e) Noise pollution	31,710	10,990
(f) Other quantifiable external costs	—	—
(8) Transit costs (capital and operating) [12]	297,000	1,980,000
TOTAL ANNUAL TRANSPORTATION COSTS	23,196,940	11,748,433

Capitalizing annual transportation costs
Once the annual cost of each transportation item has been calculated, it is then possible to capitalize these costs to present values using an appropriate discount rate and a period of fifteen years (which is approximately the life of an average car). Transportation costs can then be included with servicing costs on the same basis.

Capitalized Annual Transportation Costs	Cost of Travel by Fringe Residents ($)	Cost of Travel by Inner City Residents ($)
Private transportation	174,180,000	74,300,000
Transit	2,259,000	15,060,000
TOTAL CAPITALIZED TRANSPORTATION COSTS	176,439,000	89,360,000

(continues)

Table A4.4. *Continued*

Overall Economic Costs of the
Development (per dwelling over 15 years)

	Fringe	Inner City
Infrastructure and servicing costs	$73,100	$20,000
Transportation costs	$176,400	$89,400
TOTAL ECONOMIC COSTS	$249,500	$109,400

Note: Footnote numbers in this table refer to the numbered notes presented on pages 378–381.

BASIS OF THE EXAMPLE

(a) The above example is based on developing 1,000 new dwellings on the urban fringe compared to 1,000 new dwellings in Fremantle as representative of the inner city. The infrastructure and servicing costs in the inner city will vary with each development. The $20,000 chosen here is based on the average cost of inner city infrastructure requirements estimated by Voran Consultants (1991) minus the health and education infrastructure costs that are more than adequate in the Perth inner area for considerably more population. Also, a new development proposed by Homeswest in the Fremantle area with 1,000 dwellings estimated $20,000 per dwelling for infrastructure.

(b) Individual service costs are based primarily on Water Authority of Western Australia estimates from August 1990. However, for health, education, and transit (which involve capitalized operating costs over fifteen years), as well as the items of subsidy to local government, land preparation, town planning schemes, and professional fees, average costs from a detailed study in Perth by Voran Consultants (1991) have been used.

(c) The overall split of service costs between the three tiers of government and the private sector is based on the WA Water Authority estimates.

(d) Employment development costs can be estimated as well as residential development costs using the guidelines provided, by assuming a certain equivalence between dwellings and commercial activity. See notes 2 and 3.

(e) Transportation costs are derived using the methodologies described in the notes to the general Economic Impact Statement (see also Newman, Kenworthy, and Lyons, 1985). Similar costs can be calculated for employment development. See notes 4 through 9.

(f) Annual transportation costs have been capitalized over fifteen years at a discount rate of 10 percent.

(g) The split of capitalized transportation costs between public and private sectors is quite difficult to evaluate. For the example here the cost of roads, transit, and externalities have been assigned to the public sector. In practice, some road costs of new subdivisions are paid for by the private sector. However, the road costs in the transportation section are based on an average cost per vehicle kilometer driven on the total road network of the city; so the impact is most heavily on main roads, which are mostly government's responsibility.

Appendix 5

Guidelines for New Urbanism Development (The Ahwahnee Principles)

The Ahwahnee Principles

The Ahwahnee Principles were first introduced in 1991 at a Local Government Commission conference for elected officials at the Ahwahnee Hotel in Yosemite National Park. Since then, they have become a nationally recognized set of land use principles, adopted by many local governments to guide their local planning. They were authored by Peter Calthorpe, Michael Corbett, Andres Duany, Elizabeth Moule, Elizabeth Plater-Zyberk, and Stefanos Polyzoides, and edited by Judy Corbett, Peter Katz, and Steve Weissman.

Preamble

Existing patterns of urban and suburban development seriously impair our quality of life. The symptoms are: more congestion and air pollution, resulting from our increased dependence on automobiles; the loss of precious open space; the need for costly improvements to roads and public services; the inequitable distribution of economic resources; and the loss of a sense of community. By drawing on the best from the past and present, we can plan communities that will more successfully serve the needs of those who live and work within them. Such planning should adhere to certain fundamental principles.

Community Principles

1. All planning should be in the form of complete and integrated communities containing housing, shops, workplaces, schools, parks, and civic facilities essential to the daily life of the residents.
2. Community size should be designed so that housing, jobs, daily needs, and other activities are within walking distance of one another.
3. As many activities as possible should be located within easy walking distance of transit stops.

4. A community should contain a diversity of housing types to enable citizens from a wide range of economic levels and age groups to live within its boundaries.
5. Businesses within the community should provide a range of jobs types for the community's residents.
6. The location and character of the community should be consistent with a larger transit network.
7. The community should have a center focus that combines commercial, civic, cultural, and recreational uses.
8. The community should contain an ample supply of specialized open space in the form of squares, greens, and parks whose frequent use is encouraged through placement and design.
9. Public spaces should be designed to encourage the attention and presence of people at all hours of the day and night.
10. Each community or cluster of communities should have a well-defined edge, such as agricultural greenbelts or wildlife corridors, permanently protected from development.
11. Streets, pedestrian paths, and bike paths should contribute to a system of fully connected and interesting routes to all destinations. Their design should encourage pedestrian and bicycle use by being small and spatially defined by buildings, trees, and lighting and by discouraging high-speed traffic.
12. Wherever possible, the natural terrain, drainage, and vegetation of the community should be preserved with superior examples contained within parks or greenbelts.
13. The community design should help conserve resources and minimize waste.
14. Communities should provide for the efficient use of water through the use of natural drainage, drought-tolerant landscaping, and recycling.
15. The street orientation, the placement of buildings, and the use of shading should contribute to the energy efficiency of the community.

Regional Principles

1. The regional land use planning structure should be integrated with a larger transportation network built around transit rather than freeways.
2. Regions should be bounded by and provide a continuous system of greenbelt/wildlife corridors to be determined by natural conditions.
3. Regional institutions and services (government, stadiums, museums, etc.), should be located in the urban core.
4. Materials and methods of construction should be specific to the region, exhibiting continuity of history and culture and compatibility with the climate to encourage the development of local character and community identity.

Implementation Strategy

1. The general plan should be updated to incorporate the above principles.
2. Rather than allowing piecemeal development, local governments should take charge of the planning process. General plans should designate where new growth, infill, or redevelopment will be allowed to occur.
3. Prior to any development, a specific plan should be prepared based on the planning principles. With the adoption of specific plans, complying projects could proceed with minimal delay.
4. Plans should be developed through an open process and participants in the process should be provided visual models of all planning proposals.

For detailed professional guidance on New Urbanist design see: "The Technique of Town Planning: Operating System of the New Urbanism," available from:

Andres Duany
Duany Plater-Zyberk and Company
1023 SW 25th Avenue
Miami, FL 33135

or contact:

Congress for the New Urbanism
The Hearst Building
5 Third St., Suite 500A
San Francisco, CA 94103
phone: (415) 495-2255

Appendix 6

A Guide to the Provision of Better Transit and Land Use Integration in Auto Cities

Introduction

Transit can play a key role in providing better accessibility in Auto Cities and meeting the requirements for greater sustainability, equity, efficiency and human livability. At present, urban transit is beset with many problems that seriously detract from the potentially important role it can play in improving access for all in Auto Cities. The generally low status of transit in Auto Cities compared to cars is one of the reasons why many people do not rank it highly in their choice of housing and location and why there seems to be a built-in assumption of car use in a large proportion of housing decisions.

This is not the case in many European cities where the status and level of service provided by transit is very good and highly valued by the population. A similar situation exists in many Canadian cities, such as Toronto, Vancouver, Ottawa, and Calgary, where transit plays an important role in access for all socioeconomic groups within the population and higher density residential and commercial development is concentrated around the transit system (e.g., see Cervero, 1986b). Transit is by no means a marginalized aspect of these cities.

Transit Issues in Auto Cities

The following points summarize the general issues that need to be addressed in developing better transit in Auto Cities (Table A6.1). These are derived from very detailed community and local council surveys in inner Melbourne where transit could be said to be comparatively better than almost anywhere else in Australia. Thus, most of the inadequacies would be generally amplified in other Auto Cities.

Strategies to Improve Transit

The major issues and shortcomings affecting transit in Auto Cities outlined in Table A6.1 can be used as a basis for developing a checklist of options for improving transit in local areas. The checklist is provided after the list of problems. The aim of the checklist is to help focus the attention of the various decision

Table A6.1. Major Transit and Land Use Integration Issues in Auto Cities

Operational and Service Delivery Issues
- Inadequate service frequencies
- Insufficient service in the off-peak, particularly nights and weekends
- Special events not provided with extra services
- Some stations without enough stopping trains
- Poor reliability of services
- Speed of all modes too slow
- Poor coordination of timetables between all modes
- Lack of proper modal interchange points for transfer passengers
- Insufficient direct cross-city connections
- Problems with transit staff and union outlooks
- Shortcomings in transit administration and management

Station, Bus (and Tram) Stop Environs
- Poor quality of waiting environments in terms of cleanliness, lighting, furniture, shelters, safety, toilets, phones, trash receptacles, and lack of commercial or service opportunities
- Lack of bicycle facilities at stations
- Insufficient attention to accessibility of the aged, disabled, and people with prams
- Inadequate provision of passenger information
- Poor location of stops in some instances
- Inadequate safety for users between trams and footpaths and at stops (Melbourne)

Transit Vehicles
- Train maintenance in terms of cleanliness and vandalism
- Access problems for elderly, infirmed, disabled, people with prams
- Provision for the carriage of prams, parcels, wheelchairs, and bikes

Transit Priority and Traffic Management
- Inadequate tram and bus priority at intersections
- Insufficient dedicated tram and bus lanes
- Too much traffic and priority for private transportation
- Lack of area-wide traffic calming and facilities for pedestrians and cyclists
- Traffic impacts destroying environment and livability

Passenger Information, Marketing and Education
- Inadequate passenger information systems
- Insufficient marketing and awareness of transit services
- Poor level of business involvement in "selling" transit
- Poor understanding about broad issues of car dependence and urban options

Land Use Integration
- Lack of vision about the possibilities of land use integrated with transit
- Absence of target population and employment increases for established areas to help justify better transit
- Inadequate support through town planning schemes and planning controls for building up land use around transit and minimizing parking requirements where there is good transit.
- Insufficient support and consistency by state government in integrating development with transit
- Resistance by local communities towards higher density environments
- Lack of appreciation by the business sector about the benefits of integrating development around transit
- Lack of good demonstration projects of land use/transit integration

makers on the importance of considering transit in development decisions. This should help in reducing the degree to which assumptions about universal car ownership and use are built into the design of land use developments and make it more convenient and viable to use transit for more trips. It could also provide the basis for a whole local authority to review its approach to transit and commence a program of upgrading in conjunction with other authorities where applicable.

Not all of the items listed will be relevant in every situation and the power to act on a particular item will reside to differing degrees with state and local governments and possible involvement of the federal government. Where an option for improving transit is more clearly a state responsibility, it is still within the scope of the local authority to lobby state governments and perhaps offer to contribute in some way to a particular improvement. Some of the options are relatively low-cost items and easily implemented or started in the short term. Other options would take a longer period to come to fruition but could be commenced now (e.g., demonstration transit-based urban villages).

Conclusion to Transit Guidelines

Transit has a key role to play in improving access in Auto Cities for all sectors of the population, but until it begins to be woven more into the basic fabric of urban life and achieves a status, coherence, and identity central to peoples' perception of the way the city functions, then it will remain largely marginalized for the majority of trips. The major thrust of the suggestions in the checklist is thus to progressively draw transit back into the mainstream of community thinking and decision making processes at a household, corporate, and government level, particularly its total integration into the land use planning system.

Table A6.2. A Checklist for Improving Transit Access and Quality of Service in Existing and Future Land Development

Operations and Service Delivery
Aim: To provide a transit service that is frequent, attractive, reliable, and convenient to all potential users.

Frequencies

	Yes	Act	No	Exists	N.A.
• Is it viable to introduce some "frequent flyer" bus/tram/train services of twelve minutes or less (i.e., nontimetable)?	☐	☐	☐	☐	☐

Night services

	Yes	Act	No	Exists	N.A.
• Has the possibility of "night rider" services been investigated to provide a basic round-the-clock transit service?	☐	☐	☐	☐	☐

Special events

	Yes	Act	No	Exists	N.A.
• Are "special events" such as large concerts and sporting events provided with sufficient extra services?	☐	☐	☐	☐	☐

Coordination of timetables and modal interchanges

- Have timetables been reviewed to ensure interconnections are under 5 minutes?

☐ Yes	☐ Act	☐ No	☐ Exists	☐ N.A.

- Has the possibility of "rhythmic timetables" been investigated where transit operates each hour at the same time?

☐ Yes	☐ Act	☐ No	☐ Exists	☐ N.A.

- Has good physical integration between modes been provided at transit interchange points?

☐ Yes	☐ Act	☐ No	☐ Exists	☐ N.A.

Minimum walk distance between services
Adequate weather protection
Facilities for elderly, prams, disabled persons, etc.

☐	☐	☐	☐	☐
☐	☐	☐	☐	☐
☐	☐	☐	☐	☐
Yes	Act	No	Exists	N.A.

Urban focal points at transit interchange points

- Are there moves underway to make transit interchanges into focal points of urban vitality by building up mixed land uses and services and making the transit user's environment convenient and useful in daily activities?

☐ Yes	☐ Act	☐ No	☐ Exists	☐ N.A.

Cross-city connections

- Do good cross-city connections exist so that travel through the CBD is not always necessary?

☐ Yes	☐ Act	☐ No	☐ Exists	☐ N.A.

- Has the possibility of a "timed-pulse" system (i.e., a multi-centered, timed transfer system of bus operation as developed for Edmonton, Alberta, and Austin, Texas) been investigated to improve connectivity across the city? (See note 1.)

☐ Yes	☐ Act	☐ No	☐ Exists	☐ N.A.

Station, Bus (and Tram) Stop Environs

Aim: To provide safe, attractive, clean, and well-maintained stations and stops that include a range of other urban activities and services and are easily accessible to all groups of users.

More local responsibility for transit

- Has more local responsibility and "ownership" (including maintenance, cleanliness, general appearance, and control of vandalism and graffiti), by councils and community groups of stations and stops been considered.

☐ Yes	☐ Act	☐ No	☐ Exists	☐ N.A.

Quality and identity of stations and stops

- Is there a program to give transit a strong, coherent identity for stations and stops through such things as high quality, highly visible, brightly colored signs and attractive shelters to mark every stop?

☐ Yes	☐ Act	☐ No	☐ Exists	☐ N.A.

- Do rail stations have:

Clear, properly maintained passenger information systems?

☐ Yes	☐ Act	☐ No	☐ Exists	☐ N.A.

Secure, weather-proof bicycle storage at most stations?

☐ Yes	☐ Act	☐ No	☐ Exists	☐ N.A.

(continues)

Table A6.2. *Continued*

	Yes	Act	No	Exists	N.A.
Weather-proof, heated, comfortable waiting areas?	☐	☐	☐	☐	☐
Weather-protected ramps and station access ways?	☐	☐	☐	☐	☐
Adequate lighting?	☐	☐	☐	☐	☐
Security systems?	☐	☐	☐	☐	☐
Properly maintained public telephones?	☐	☐	☐	☐	☐
Toilets that are clean and well-maintained?	☐	☐	☐	☐	☐
Adequate trash receptacles that are regularly emptied?	☐	☐	☐	☐	☐
Access ways that are negotiable by all groups?	☐	☐	☐	☐	☐
Locally maintained gardens/flower pots wherever possible?	☐	☐	☐	☐	☐

- Do bus and tram stops have:

	Yes	Act	No	Exists	N.A.
Weather shelters at all stops where there are no verandahs?	☐	☐	☐	☐	☐
Trash receptacles at or near to all stops?	☐	☐	☐	☐	☐
Close proximity for ease of transfer at relevant points?					
Telephone booths within a short distance of all stops?	☐	☐	☐	☐	☐
Proper passenger information/timetable systems?	☐	☐	☐	☐	☐
A coherent, high-profile identity through use of large, colorful and well-maintained signs and information systems?	☐	☐	☐	☐	☐

Naming bus and tram stops

- Has consideration been given to naming all bus and tram stops based on local landmarks or identities? (Naming of all stops in Europe is standard practice to improve passenger understanding of the system and to anchor land uses more closely to transit.)

	Yes	Act	No	Exists	N.A.
	☐	☐	☐	☐	☐

Major changes to the total environs of stations and stops

- Is there a program to improve the quality, productivity, and security (especially for women) of passenger waiting time through a variety of commercial and other service facilities either on or in very close proximity to as many stations and stops as possible, as well as new residential development? In essence, are transit stations/stops places where people want to go or stay away from?

	Yes	Act	No	Exists	N.A.
	☐	☐	☐	☐	☐

Transit Priority and Traffic Management

Aim: To provide a transit system which has optimum speed and priority as well as safe access and egress with minimum interference from cars.

Traffic priority for buses and trams

- Is there a program to provide absolute priority for buses and trams in the traffic system?

	Yes	Act	No	Exists	N.A.
	☐	☐	☐	☐	☐

Bus and tram lanes
- Are exclusive bus and tram lanes being actively pursued?

☐ Yes	☐ Act	☐ No	☐ Exists	☐ N.A.

Longer pedestrian phases
- Are longer pedestrian phases on traffic signals being provided to assist access to transit?

☐ Yes	☐ Act	☐ No	☐ Exists	☐ N.A.

Transit only streets
- Is there a program to provide a network of transit-only streets (e.g., transit malls along strip developments)?

☐ Yes	☐ Act	☐ No	☐ Exists	☐ N.A.

Review of car parking policies
- Is there a review of car parking policies underway to reduce parking requirements where transit is good or being improved? (Reduced parking will tend to favor development close to good transit and will assist its priority.)

☐ Yes	☐ Act	☐ No	☐ Exists	☐ N.A.

Business promotion and sponsorship of non-auto access
Is there a policy to promote and actively assist local businesses of various sizes to establish such things as :

(a) More effective delivery services to reduce the need for parking and car use on shopping trips?

☐ Yes	☐ Act	☐ No	☐ Exists	☐ N.A.

(b) Facilities for shopping by nonauto modes, such as bicycle racks and pram and shopping trolley access on all street corners?

☐ Yes	☐ Act	☐ No	☐ Exists	☐ N.A.

(c) Coordinated retail activities such as promotion of large, non-throw-away carry bags for shopping with advertising such as " I'm a Car-Free Shopper" and other slogans?

☐ Yes	☐ Act	☐ No	☐ Exists	☐ N.A.

(d) Financial incentives such as discounts on purchases to shoppers showing proof of transit use for the trip?

☐ Yes	☐ Act	☐ No	☐ Exists	☐ N.A.

Company car policies
- Is there potential for a review of company car policies in favor of promoting transit?

☐ Yes	☐ Act	☐ No	☐ Exists	☐ N.A.

Improving access through traffic calming schemes
- Is there a program of demonstration traffic calming schemes to provide better access and priority for transit, walking and cycling, including on main roads?

☐ Yes	☐ Act	☐ No	☐ Exists	☐ N.A.

- Are there any strategies or moves toward reducing the use of cars through effective economic and pricing mechanisms that penalize car traffic and reward the use of transit and nonmotorized modes?

☐ Yes	☐ Act	☐ No	☐ Exists	☐ N.A.

(continues)

Table A6.2. *Continued*

Passenger Information, Marketing and Education

Aim: To provide the broader community with specific, clear information on transit services and general information on the benefits of transit and the problems of high car dependence, and to expand the marketing outlets and opportunities for transit.

Passenger information options

	Yes	Act	No	Exists	N.A.
• Is passenger information being effectively distributed through:	☐	☐	☐	☐	☐
Distribution of kits of all relevant timetables to all households and businesses in each local area?	☐	☐	☐	☐	☐
Making all local timetables more readily available through news agents or other common local outlets?	☐	☐	☐	☐	☐
Having more timetable displays in shop and business windows that are less able to be defaced or destroyed?	☐	☐	☐	☐	☐
Ensuring that timetable displays at train stations and bus and tram stops are always clearly legible through regular replacement or more effective durable displays?	☐	☐	☐	☐	☐
Making timetable maintenance a local responsibility involving community groups and schools and a clearly established and easy mechanism for reporting damaged or vandalized timetables and getting them replaced quickly?	☐	☐	☐	☐	☐
Negotiating with private firms involving advertising rights for high-standard, weather-proof displays as part of new tram and bus stops?	☐	☐	☐	☐	☐

Electronic passenger information systems

	Yes	Act	No	Exists	N.A.
• Are there plans for some electronic passenger information systems which give more information about time of arrival of services and have some interrogation capabilities for the user?	☐	☐	☐	☐	☐

Better information about each route

	Yes	Act	No	Exists	N.A.
• Do services have informative destination names and details about major destinations?	☐	☐	☐	☐	☐

Marketing

	Yes	Act	No	Exists	N.A.
• Are transit authorities, local councils, and the business community combining their efforts to more effectively market and support the transit system through a series of initiatives which might include:	☐	☐	☐	☐	☐
Incorporating a transit ticket component in the price of all admission tickets to major sport, cultural, and entertainment events?	☐	☐	☐	☐	☐
Linking a range of transit fare bonuses to retail purchases?	☐	☐	☐	☐	☐

	Yes	Act	No	Exists	N.A.
Providing free "sample" transit tickets and other publicity information about the transit system in annual rate notices to households and businesses?	☐	☐	☐	☐	☐
High-profile marketing strategies for transit?	☐	☐	☐	☐	☐

Selected fare initiatives

	Yes	Act	No	Exists	N.A.
• Are special fares available, such as weekend family passes, that are linked to selected discounts at venues such as restaurants?	☐	☐	☐	☐	☐

Structure of transit boards

	Yes	Act	No	Exists	N.A.
• Do transit boards include user and community representation at a sufficient level?	☐	☐	☐	☐	☐

Regional transit directories

	Yes	Act	No	Exists	N.A.
• Are transit authorities together with local councils and businesses planning regional transit directories? (See note 2.)	☐	☐	☐	☐	☐

Community education programs

	Yes	Act	No	Exists	N.A.
• Are there programs to develop jointly sponsored, community education exercises about car dependence, transit, urban sprawl, urban lifestyles and the future of cities? (See note 3.)	☐	☐	☐	☐	☐

Land Use Integration

Aim: To provide compact, higher density residential, commercial, and community facilities in mixed-use, traffic-calmed settings that favor transit access and use for many trips and provide strong focal points for the transit system.

Town Planning Schemes and planning controls

	Yes	Act	No	Exists	N.A.
• Are local councils reviewing and amending their town planning schemes to create consistent provisions and incentives for the effective integration of land use development with transit through the following mechanisms:	☐	☐	☐	☐	☐
Residential and commercial density provisions?	☐	☐	☐	☐	☐
Joint development and value capture for increased private funding?	☐	☐	☐	☐	☐
Parking supply regulations and parking fees?	☐	☐	☐	☐	☐
Incentives to developers to integrate with transit?	☐	☐	☐	☐	☐
Urban design and physical linkages to transit?	☐	☐	☐	☐	☐
• Are state authorities:					
Being consistent in their urban consolidation and centers policies?	☐	☐	☐	☐	☐
Reorientating transportation priorities from freeways to transit?	☐	☐	☐	☐	☐
Cooperating with local councils in transit-integrated developments?	☐	☐	☐	☐	☐

(continues)

Table A6.2. *Continued*

Key development sites and development criteria

	Yes	Act	No	Exists	N.A.
• Is a directory available of the key high-density development sites for nodal development around transit, including planning details and development preferences for each?	☐	☐	☐	☐	☐

Population and employment targets

	Yes	Act	No	Exists	N.A.
• Are population and employment targets set for key development sites to maximize transit integration?	☐	☐	☐	☐	☐

Shop-top housing

	Yes	Act	No	Exists	N.A.
• Is there a program to encourage and facilitate housing above shops along major transit routes (e.g., as in Toronto's Main Street program)?	☐	☐	☐	☐	☐

Responsibility for transit at the local level

	Yes	Act	No	Exists	N.A.
• Do local councils have transit responsibilities built into the job briefs of the key traffic and planning positions?	☐	☐	☐	☐	☐

Community education programs

	Yes	Act	No	Exists	N.A.
• Are there efforts being made to educate local communities about the potential of higher-density, compact development and its positive environmental and social features (e.g., booklets, slide presentations)?	☐	☐	☐	☐	☐

Developer education programs

	Yes	Act	No	Exists	N.A.
• Are there efforts being made to educate the development community about the potential financial and urban design benefits of transit integration?	☐	☐	☐	☐	☐

Demonstration projects

	Yes	Act	No	Exists	N.A.
• Is planning occurring to implement demonstration projects of land use/transit integration in the form of:	☐	☐	☐	☐	☐
Central city urban villages around rail facilities?	☐	☐	☐	☐	☐
Inner area urban villages at rail stations?	☐	☐	☐	☐	☐
Urban villages around selected rail stations throughout the metropolitan area?	☐	☐	☐	☐	☐
Urban villages along bus/tram corridors at selected locations?	☐	☐	☐	☐	☐
Shop-top housing to improve access and diversity of housing choice?	☐	☐	☐	☐	☐

Notes:
1. Major regional shopping centers, large institutions such as hospitals and universities, other centers, and rail stations are the basis of the multicentered, timed-transfer system. This timed-pulse service consists of a series of equal travel time bus routes focused on the one center from numerous other centers. Buses all arrive within a few minutes of one another at a bus interchange (or bus/rail interchange), people change buses and new passengers enter the system from that center and then the buses all pulse out simultaneously in all directions to other centers. Transfers are reliable and people are able to go in all directions on transit, particularly across the city without the need to enter the CBD and go out again (see Bakker, Calkin, and Sylvester 1988).
2. Regional transit directories would contain maps and timetables of all relevant transit services, including location of all stops, with easy cross-references to the location of all businesses, institutions, and services. The directories could be totally funded through advertising fees and could be free. They could become as everyday and important as a road directory or telephone book.

3. Community education programs would be directed at greatly increasing general awareness about the environmental, resource, and economic implications of land use and transportation patterns and could be sponsored by different levels of government, business, and environmental organizations. The programs could involve:

    - the media;
    - non-English as well as English speaking groups;
    - production of highly illustrative color booklets;
    - educational material for various levels within schools;
    - public talks and seminars;
    - adult education courses;
    - other avenues of dissemination.

    People could be put through a short course that entitles them to be given a certificate as a *transit advocate*, qualifying them to speak to schools and other groups about the transit system and its advantages.

References

Alexander, C. (1979). *The timeless way of building*. Oxford University Press, New York.

Alexander, C. (1987). *New theory of urban design*. Oxford University Press, New York.

Algers, S., Hansen, S., and Tegner, G. (1975). Role of waiting time, comfort and convenience in modal choice for work trip. *Transportation Research Record*, No. 534. Transportation Research Board, Washington, D.C.

Allen, I. (1980) The ideology of dense neighborhood redevelopment: Cultural diversity and transcendent community experience. *Urban Affairs Quarterly* 15(4): 409–428.

Altshuler, A., Pucher, J. R. and Womack, J. (1979). *The urban transportation problem: Politics and policy innovation*. MIT Press, Cambridge, Massachusetts.

Altshuler, A., Anderson, M., Jones, D., Roos, D., and Womack, J. (1984). *The future of the automobile*, MIT Press, Cambridge, Massachusetts.

Anders, R. (1991). *The sustainable cities movement*. Working Paper No. 2, Institute for Resource and Security Studies, Cambridge, Massachusetts.

Anderson, G. (1996). *A smart growth bibliography*. U.S. Environmental Protection Agency, Washington, D.C.

Anderson R. (1998). *Sustainability report*. Interface, New York.

Anonymous (1996). *Christiana Guide*. Community of Christiana, Copenhagen.

Appleyard, D. (1981). *Livable streets*. University of California Press, Berkeley.

Archibald, R., and Gillingham, R. (1981). Decomposition of the price and income elasticities of the consumer demand for gasoline. *Southern Economic Journal* 47(4): 1021–1031.

Argue, J. (1995). *Stormwater source control*. Proceedings of Water Sensitive Design Seminar, Perth Institute of Engineers, Australia, September.

Arief, A. (1998). *A sustainability assessment of squatter redevelopment in Jakarta*. Master of Philosophy thesis, Institute for Science and Technology Policy, Murdoch University, Perth, Western Australia.

Arrington, G. B. (1993). Transportation and land use—A shared vision. *Passenger Transport* 2(3): 4–14.

Aschauer, D. A. (1989). Is public expenditure productive? *Journal of Monetary Economics* 23(2): 177–200.

Aschauer, D. A., and Campbell, E. J. (1991). Transportation spending and economic growth. Bates College, September [reported in *Earthword: The Journal of Environmental and Social Responsibility* 4(38)].

Ashworth, G. (1992). *The role of local government in environmental protection: First line defence*. Longman, London.

Austin Department of Planning and Growth Management (1986). *Stimulating development at transit stations*. Working Paper, Austin Department of Planning and Growth Management, Austin, Texas, June 11.

Australian Bureau of Statistics (ABS) (1981). *Housing survey 1978, Sydney, Newcastle and Wollongong Pt. 3: Anticipated residential movement and satisfaction with current housing conditions.* No. 87131 ABS, New South Wales, Sydney.

Australian Institute of Urban Studies (1991). *Water sensitive urban design.* Australian Institute of Urban Studies, WA Division, WA Water Resources Council, Perth.

Ayers, R. U., and Simons, U. E. (1994). *Industrial metabolism.* UN University Press, Tokyo.

Badcock, B. (1984). *Unfairly structured cities.* Blackwell, London.

Bakker, J. J., Calkin, J., and Sylvester, S. (1988). *A multi-centred timed transfer system for Capital Metro, Austin, Texas.* Paper presented to Transportation Research Board Annual Meeting, Session 38, January.

Baldassare, M. (1979). *Residential crowding in urban America.* University of California Press, Berkeley, California.

Bank of America (1994). *Beyond sprawl: New patterns of growth to fit the new California.* Bank of America, California Resources Agency, Greenbelt Alliance, Low Income Housing Fund, San Francisco, California.

Barter, P. A., and Kenworthy, J. R. (1997). Pacific Asian cities in a global review of urban transport and land use patterns: Problems in accommodating the automobile. Submitted to *Third World Planning Review.*

Bayliss, D. (1989). What's new in European and other international light rail transit projects? In *Light rail transit: New system successes at affordable prices,* Special Report 221, Transportation Research Board, Washington, D.C.

Beatley, T. (1994). *Ethical land use: Principles of policy and planning.* Johns Hopkins University Press, Baltimore.

Beatley, T. (1995). Planning and sustainability: The elements of a new (improved?) paradigm. *Journal of Planning Literature* 9(4): 381–395

Beder, S. (1993). *The nature of sustainable development.* Scribe Publications, Newham, Victoria, Australia.

Beimborn, E. et al. (1991). *Guidelines for transit sensitive suburban land use design.* U.S. Department of Transportation, Report No. DOT-T-91-13.

Bell, K. et al. (1995). *Environmental guidelines for Sydney 2000,* Sydney Organising Committee for Olympic Games, Sydney, Australia.

Bellah, R. (1991). *The good society.* Knopf, New York.

Bellah, R. N. et al. (1985). *Habits of the heart: Individualism and commitment in American life.* University of California Press, Berkeley.

Berg, P. et al. (1990). *A green city program for the San Francisco Bay area and beyond.* Planet Drum, San Francisco.

Bernick, M., and Cervero, R. (1997). *Transit villages in the 21st century.* McGraw-Hill, New York.

Berry, B. et al. (1974). *Land use, urban form and environmental quality,* Research Paper 155. University of Chicago Press, Chicago.

Birch, R. D. (1994). *Municipal reporting on sustainable development: A status review.* National Round Table on the Environment and Economy, Working Paper 24. NRTEE, Ottawa.

Blakely, E. (1994). Fortress America. *Planning,* January, p. 46.

Blanco, H. (1995). Community and the four jewels of planning. In Hendler, S. (ed.) *Planning ethics.* Rutgers University Press, New Brunswick, New Jersey.

Borja, J., and Castells, M. (1997). *Local and global: The management of cities in the information age*. Garthsaen, London.

Boyden, S. et al. (1981). *The ecology of a city and its people*. ANU Press, Canberra.

Boyer, M. C. (1983). *Dreaming the rational city: The myth of American city planning*. MIT Press, Cambridge, Massachusetts.

Boyer, P. (1978). *Urban masses and moral order in America*. Harvard University Press, Boston.

Briggs, A. (1963). *Victorian cities*. Othams, London.

Brindle, R. E. (1994). Lies, damned lies and "automobile dependence" —some hyperbolic reflections. *Proceedings of the1994 Australian Transport Research Forum*, Melbourne, pp. 117–131.

Brooks, M. P. (1988). Four critical junctures in the history of the urban planning profession: An excercise in hindsight. *Journal of American Planning Association* 54(2): 241–248.

Brotchie, J. et al. (1995). *Cities in competition*. Cheshire, Melbourne.

Brugmann, J. (1994). Sustainability indicators: Do we need them? *Initiatives*, ICLEI, Toronto, October 8, pp. 1–12.

Brugmann, J., and Hersh, R. (1991). *Cities as ecosystems: Opportunities for local government*. ICLEI, Toronto.

Burchell, R. W., and Listolein, D. (1997). *Land, infrastructure, housing costs and fiscal impacts associated with growth*. Centre for Urban Policy Research, Rutgers University Press, New Brunswick, New Jersey.

Bureau of Transport and Communication Economics (1990). *Urban rail 2001–02. The assessment of economic and social imports of urban rail scenarios*. A report prepared for the Railway Industry Council, BTCE, Canberra.

Buzacott, S. (1997). Inner city resurgence. *Australian Financial Review*, August 26.

Calthorpe Associates (1990). *Transit-oriented development design guidelines*. Calthorpe Associates, Sacramento County Planning and Community Development Department, November.

Calthorpe, P. (1993). *The next American metropolis: Ecology and urban form*. Princeton Architectural Press, Princeton, New Jersey.

Campbell, C. J. (1991). *The golden century of oil, 1950–2050: The depletion of a resource*. Kluwer Academic Publishers, Dordrecht, The Netherlands.

Campbell, C. J., and Laherrère, J. H. (1995). *The world's oil supply, 1930–2050*, 3 volumes, Petroconsultants, Geneva.

Campbell, R. M., and Newman, P. W. G. (1989). Local government and transport energy conservation. *Planning and Administration* 1: 68–75.

Canadian Urban Transit Association (CUTA) (1997). *Monthly summary of trends*. Canadian Urban Public Transport, Ottawa, August.

Castells, M. (1989). *The informational city: Information technology, economic restructuring and the urban regional process*. Blackwell, Oxford.

Castells, M., and Hall, P. (1994). *Technopoles of the world*. Routledge, London.

Center City District (1997). *Population trends*. Center City District, Philadelphia.

Center for Livable Communities (1996). *Participation tools for better land use planning: Techniques and case studies*. Local Government Commission, Sacramento, California.

Center for Livable Communities (1997). Emerging trends in community planning and design: Ahwahnee awards program uncovers a movement. *Livable Places Update*, November.

Center for Livable Communities (1998). Benefits of traffic calming realised across the country. *Livable Places Update*, March.

Cervero, R. (1986a). *Suburban gridlock*. Rutgers Center for Urban Policy Research, New Brunswick, New Jersey.

Cervero, R. (1986b). Urban transit in Canada: Integration and innovation at its best. *Transportation Quarterly* 40(3): 293–316.

Cervero, R. (1988). Land use mixing and suburban mobility. *Transportation Quarterly* 42(3): 429–446.

Cervero, R. (1992a). Transportation shapes the city, in *Perth beyond 2000*, Proceedings of City Challenge Conference, Challenge Bank, Perth.

Cervero, R. (1992b). Futuristic transit and futuristic cities. *Transportation Quarterly* 40(3): 293–315.

Cervero, R. (1995). Sustainable new towns: Stockholm's rail served satellites. *Cities* 12(1): 41–51.

Cervero, R. (1996). Mixed land uses and commuting: Evidence from the American housing survey. *Transportation Research* A 30(5): 361–377

Cervero, R., Hall, P., and Landis, J. D. (1992). *Transit-linked joint development: A national study*. National Transit Access Center, Monograph 42.

Chandler, W. U. (1985). Energy productivity: Key to environmental protection and economic progress. *Worldwatch Paper 63*. Worldwatch Institute, Washington, D.C.

City of Adelaide (1997). *Sustainability indicators for the City of Adelide*. City of Adelaide.

City of Frankfurt (1990). *Tempo 30—Leitfaden: 50 Seiten für Tempo 30*. Stadt Frankfurt am Main, April.

City of the Hague (1995). *Local agenda 21: Sustainable development in the Hague*. City of the Hague.

City of Seattle (1993). *Indicators of sustainable community*. Sustainable Seattle, Seattle.

City of Stockholm (1997). *An environmental program for Hommarby Sjortad*. City of Stockholm.

City of Vancouver (1987a). *Broadway Station area plan: Summary*. City of Vancouver Planning Department, Vancouver.

City of Vancouver (1987b). *Joyce Station area plan: Summary*. City of Vancouver Planning Department, Vancouver.

City of Vancouver (1987c). *Nanaimo/29th Avenue Station areas plan: Summary*. City of Vancouver Planning Department, Vancouver.

Clark, C. (1982). *Regional and urban location*. University of Queensland Press, St Lucia, Brisbane, Australia.

Clark, R. D. S. (1990). Asset replacement: Can we get it right? *Water: Journal of the Australian Water and Wastewater Association*, February, pp. 22–24.

Coates, G. (1981). *Resettling America: Energy, ecology and community*. Brick House, Andover.

Cock, P., ed. (1990). *Social structures for sustainability*. Centre for Resource and Environmental Studies, Fundamental Questions Paper No. 11.

Commonwealth Environment Protection Agency (CEPA) (1993). *Urban stormwater—A resource too valuable to waste*. CEPA, Canberra.

Community and Family Commission (1992). *Speaking out, taking part*. Final Report of Community and Family Commission. WA Government, Perth.

Concern Inc. (1995). *Sustainability in action: Profiles of community initiatives across the United States*. For U.S. Environmental Protection Agency, Washington, D.C.

Conservation Law Foundation (1994). *The costs of transportation*. Apogee Research, Boston.

Context Institute (1992). *Eco villages and sustainable communities*. A report for Gaia Trust, Context Institute, Bainsbridge Island, Seattle, Washington.

Conway, J., and Adams, B. (1977). The social effects of living off the ground. *Habitat International* 2(5) and (6): 595–614.

Cook, P. (1990). *Back to the future: Modernity, postmodernity and locality*. Unwin Hyman Ltd, London.

Cox, E. (ed.) (1978). *Urbanization and conflict in market societies*. Mathuen, London.

Cunningham, C. (1996). A philosophical framework for urban planning: The concept of altruistic surplus. In Van der Meulen, G., and Erkelens, P. A. (eds.) *Urban habitat: The environment of tomorrow*. Eindhoven University of Technology, Einhoven, The Netherlands.

Curry, J. A. (1995). *Institutional barriers to sustainability: A case study of transportation planning in Vancouver, BC*. Ph.D. thesis, School of Community and Regional Planning, University of British Columbia, Vancouver.

Dahl, C. A. (1982). Do gasoline demand elasticities vary? *Land Economics* 58(3): 373–382.

Daly, H. E., and Cobb, J. B. Jr. (1989). *For the common good: Redirecting the economy toward community, the environment and a sustainable future*. Beacon Press, Boston.

Danish Energy Agency (1995). *Denmark's energy futures*. Ministry of Environment and DEA, Copenhagen.

Danish Road Data Laboratory (1987). *Consequence evaluation of environmentally adapted through road in Vinderup*. Report 52, Danish Road Data Laboratory, Danish Roads Directorate, Herlev, Copenhagen.

Danish Road Data Laboratory (1988). *Consequence evaluation of environmentally adapted through road in Skærbæk*. Report 63, Danish Road Data Laboratory, Danish Roads Directorate, Herlev, Copenhagen.

Davidson, O., and Karekezi, S. (1993). *Energy options: A new environmentally sound energy strategy for the development of sub-Saharan Africa*. World Resources Institute, Washington, D.C.

Davis, M. (1990). *City of quartz: Excavating the future in Los Angeles*. Vintage, London.

Davison, G. (1978). *The rise and fall of marvelous Melbourne*. University of Melbourne Press, Melbourne.

Davison, G. (1983). The city bred child and urban reform in Melbourne, 1900–1940. In Williams, P. (ed.) *Social process and the city*, Urban Studies Yearbook 1. George Allen and Unwin, Sydney.

Davison, G. (1993). The past and future of the Australian suburb. *Australian Planner* 31(2): 63–69.

Dawkins, J. (1990). Fremantle's heartland: Understanding and designing a special place. *Continuum* 3(1): 168–187.

Department of Environment (1994). *Planning policy guidance 13: Transport*. Department of Environment and Department of Transport, Whitehall, London.

Department of Environment (1996). *Greening the city: A guide to good practice*. Department of Environment, London.

Department of Planning, Housing, and Environment (1995). *The right business in the right place*. VROM, The Hague, The Netherlands.

DeVilliers, P. (1997). New urbanism. *Australian Planner* 34(1): 30–34.

Devine, M. D. et al. (1987). *Cogeneration and decentralized electricity production*. Westview Press, Boulder, Colorado.

Director General of Transport (1982). *Transportation 2000: A Perth study*. DGT, Perth, June.

DITAC (1992). *Managing stormwater: The untapped resource*. Workshop Proceedings, Environmental Technology Committee, Department of Technology, Industry & Commerce, Canberra.

Diver, G., Newman, P., and Kenworthy, J. (1996). *An evaluation of Better Cities: Environmental component*. Department of Environment, Sport and Territories, Canberra.

Dodds, A. A. et al. (1991). Developing an appropriate wastewater management strategy for Sydney's future urban development. In Ho, G., and Mathew, K. (eds.) *Proceedings of Appropriate Waste Management Technologies*. Murdoch University, Perth, Western Australia.

Donald, W. R. (1993). Letter from Mass Transit Railway Corporation. June 8, 1994. Data in letter based on 1993 survey of users.

Downton, P. (1994). The Halifax Ecocity Project. *Proceedings of Ecocity 2 conference*, Adelaide.

Duany, A., and Plater-Zyberk, E. (1991). *Towns and town-making principles*. Rizzoli, New York.

Dunphy, R., and Fisher, K. (1996). Transportation, congestion and density: New insights. *Transportation Research Record*, No. 1552. Transportation Research Board, Washington, D.C.

Economist (1997). Jam today, road pricing tomorrow. *The Economist*. December 6, pp. 13–22.

Egan, T. (1995). The serene fortress: Many seek security in private communities. *The New York Times*, September 3, pp. 1–22.

Eggleton, A. (1992). The Toronto experience. In *Perth beyond 2000: A challenge for a city*. Proceedings of City Challenge Conference, Perth, September.

Ehrlich, P. R., and Ehrlich, A. H. (1977). *Population, Resources and Environment*. W. H. Freeman, San Francisco.

Elkin, T. et al. (1991). *Reviving the city: towards sustainable urban development*. Friends of the Earth, London.

Ellul, J. (1964). *The technological society*. Random House of Canada Limited, Toronto.

Ellul, J. (1970). *The meaning of the city*. Eerdmans, San Francisco.

Elms, C. P. (1989). Issues and requirements of real estate developers. In *Light rail transit: New system successes at affordable prices*. Transportation Research Board, Special Report 221, Washington, D.C.

Energy Victoria et al. (1996). *Urban villages project: Encouraging sustainable urban form*. Summary Report. Government of Victoria, August.

Engwicht, D. (1992). Canberra—Towards a healthy city. *Australian Urban Studies* 19(4): 1–4, 13–15.

Engwicht, D. (1993). *Towards an ecocity: Calming the traffic*. Envirobook, Sydney.

Etzioni, A. (1988). *The moral dimension*. Free Press, New York.

Etzioni, A. (1993). *The spirit of community: The reinvention of the American society*. Touchstone, New York.

Evill, B. (1995) Population, urban density and fuel use: Eliminating the spurious correlation. *Urban Policy and Research* 13(1): 29–36.

Federal Office of Road Safety (1993). *Towards traffic calming: A practitioners manual of implemented local area traffic management and black spot devices*. Federal Office of Road Safety, Canberra.

Fischer, C. S. (1976). *The urban experience*. Harcourt, Brace, Jovanovich, New York.

Fleay, B. J. (1995). *The decline of the age of oil*. Pluto Press, Sydney.

Fleay, B. J. (1998). Climaxing oil: How will transport adapt? Presented to Chartered Institute of Transport in Australia National Symposium: Beyond Oil—Transport and Fuel for the Future. November 6–7.

Fox, M. (ed.) (1981). *Western spirituality: Historical roots, ecumenical routes*. Bear & Co, Santa Fe.

Franz, J. D. (1989). *Views of Bay Area residents on traffic and growth issues*. Metropolitan Transit Commission, San Francisco, July.

Freedman, J. (1975). *Crowding and behaviour*. Viking, New York.

Freeman, C. (ed.) (1996). *The longwave in the world economy*. International Library of Critical Writings in Economics, Aldershot, Elgar.

Freeman, C., and Perez, C. (1988). Structural crises of adjustment, business cycles and investment behaviour. In Dosi, G., Freeman, C., Nelson, R., Silverburg, G., and Soete, L. (eds.) *Technical change and economic theory*. Pinter, London.

Freeman, C., and Soete, L. (1997). *The economics of industrial innovation*, 3rd ed. Pinter, London.

Friedman, J. (1987). *Planning in the public domain: From knowledge to action*. Princeton University Press, Princeton, New Jersey.

Friedman, J. (1992). The right to the city. In Morse, R., and Hardoy, J. (eds.) *Rethinking the Latin American city*. John Hopkins University Press, Baltimore.

Friends of the Earth (1997). *Less traffic, more jobs: Direct employment impacts of developing a sustainable transport system in the United Kingdom*. Friends of the Earth, London.

Frost, L. (1991). *The new urban frontier: Urbanisation and city building in Australasia and the American West*. University of N.S.W. Press, Sydney.

Gallin, N. (1996). *Land use-transit integration: An international overview and case study of Perth*. Honours dissertation, Social Ecology Programme, Murdoch University, Perth, Western Australia.

Garreau, J. (1991). *Edge city: Life on the new frontier*. Doubleday, New York.

Gehl, J. (1987). *Life between buildings*. Van Nostrand Reinhold, New York.

Gehl, J. (1992). The challenge of making a human quality in the city. In *Perth beyond 2000: A challenge for a city*. Proceedings of the City Challenge Conference, Perth, September.

Gehl, J. (1994). *Public spaces and public life in Perth*. Department of Planning and Urban Development, Perth.

Gehl, J., and Gemzøe, L. (1996). *Public spaces, public life*. City of Copenhagen.

Girardet, H. (1992). *The Gaia atlas of cities*. Gaia Books, London.

Girouard, M. (1985). *Cities and people*. Yale University Press, New Haven and London.

Gobor, P. (1993). Americans on the Move. *Population Bulletin* 48(3): 1–40.

Gomez-Ibañez, J. A. (1991). A global view of automobile dependence. *Journal of the American Planning Association* 57(3): 376–379.

Goodwin, P. B. (1991). *Transport: The new realism*. Transport Studies Unit, Oxford University, Oxford.

Goodwin, P. B. (1994). Traffic reduction. *Transport Policy* 1(2): 83–84.

Goodwin, P. B. (1997). Solving congestion (when we must not build roads, increase spending, lose votes, damage the economy or harm the environment, and will never find equilibrium). Inaugural Lecture for the Professorship of Transport Policy, University College, London, October 23.

Gordon, D. (ed.) (1990). *Green cities*. Black Rose, Montreal.

Gordon, P., and Richardson, H. W. (1989). Gasoline consumption and cities: A reply. *Journal of the American Planning Association* 55(3): 342–345.

Gordon, P., Kumar, A., and Richardson, H. W. (1989). The influence of metropolitan spatial structure on commuting times. *Journal of Urban Economics* 26: 138–149.

Gordon, P., Richardson, H. W., and Jun, M. (1991). The commuting paradox-evidence from the top twenty. *Journal of the American Planning Association* 57: 416–420.

Gottman, J. (1976). Urban geography and the human condition. In Harrison, G. A., and Gibson, J. B. (eds.) *Man in urban environments*. Oxford University Press, Oxford.

Gratz, R. B. (1989). *The living city*. Simon & Schuster, New York.

Greater Vancouver Regional District (1990). *Creating our future: Steps to a more liveable urban region*. GVRD, Burnaby, British Columbia, Canada.

Greater Vancouver Regional District (1995). *Liveable region strategy plan*. GVRD, Strategic Planning, January.

Greenpeace Australia (1993). *Green Olympics*. Greenpeace, Sydney.

Greyson, J. (1995). *The Natural Step 1995—A collection of articles*. The Natural Step, Sausalito, California.

Guskaynak, M. R., and LeCompte W. A. (1977). *Human consequences of crowding*. Plenum, New York.

Hajdu, J. G. (1988). Pedestrian malls in West Germany: Perceptions of their role and stages in their development. *Journal of the American Planning Association*, Summer, pp. 325–335.

Hall, P. (1988). *Cities of tomorrow: An intellectual history of urban planning and design in the twentieth century*. Basil Blackwell, Oxford and New York.

Hall, P. (1994). The innovative city. *Proceedings of OECD Conference*, Melbourne.

Hall, P. (1995). The European city: Past and future. *Proceedings of The European City—Sustaining Urban Quality*. Conference for Danish Government, Copenhagen, April.

Hall, P. (1997). Reflections past and future in planning cities. *Australian Planner* 34(2): 83–89.

Hall, P., Cleveland, C. J., and Kaufman, R. (1986). *Energy and resource quality: The ecology of the economic process*. John Wiley, Chichester, England.

Hamer, M. (1987). *Wheels within wheels: A study of the road lobby*. Routledge and Kegan Paul, London.

Hamer, M. (1997). Fighting for air. *New Scientist*, 19 April.

Hamer, M. (1998). Road blocks ahead. *New Scientist*, 24 January.

Hardin, G. (1968). The Tragedy of the commons. *Science* 162(3): 1243–1248.

Hart, S. (1990). The real cost of operating an automobile in America. *The Oregonian*, November 9.

Hart, S., and Spivak, A. L. (1993). *The elephant in the bedroom: Automobile dependence and denial.* New Paradigm, Pasadena, California.

Harvey, D. (1973). *Social justice and the city.* Edward Arnold, London.

Hass-Klau, C. (ed.) (1986). New ways of managing traffic. *Built Environment* 12(1 and 2).

Hass-Klau, C. (1990a). *The theory and practice of traffic calming: Can Britain learn from the German experience?* Discussion Paper 10, Rees Jeffreys Road Fund, Transportation Studies Unit, Oxford University, Oxford, England.

Hass-Klau, C. (1990b). *The pedestrian and city traffic.* Belhaven Press, London.

Hass-Klau, C. (1990c). *An illustrated guide to traffic calming: The future way of managing traffic.* Friends of the Earth, London.

Hass-Klau, C. (1993). Impact of pedestrianization and traffic calming on retailing: A review of the evidence from Germany and the UK. *Transportation Policy* 1(1): 21–31.

Hauerwas, S. (1981). *A community of character.* University of Notre Dame Press, Notre Dame, Indiana.

Haughton, G., and Hunter, C. (1994). *Sustainable cities.* Taylor and Francis, Bristol and Philadelphia.

Havlick, S. (1997). Great cities for the 21st century. *UNEP Regional Workshop for Asia Pacific,* Symposium, Murdoch University, Perth, Western Australia.

Hempel, D. J., and Tucker, L. R. (1979). Citizen preferences for housing as community social indicators. *Environment and Behaviour* 11(3): 399–428.

Henderson, M. (1996). *The forgiveness factor: Stories of hope in a world of conflict.* Grosvenor Books, Salem, Massachusetts.

Henry, L. (1989). Ridership forecasting considerations in comparisons of light rail and motor bus modes. In *Light Rail Transit: New system successes at affordable prices,* Transportation Research Board, Special Report 221, Washington, D.C., pp. 163–189.

Herbert, D. (1982). *The geography of urban crime.* Longman, London.

Hill, A., and Nicholson, C. (1989). Water conservancy designs for gardens and open space. Water Authority of Western Australia, Perth, Report No. WP89, December.

Hoch, I. (1976). City size effects: Trends and policies. *Science* 193: 856–863.

Hoch, I. (1979). Settlement size, real income and the rural turnaround. *American Journal of Agricultural Economics* 61(5): 953–959.

Holtz Kay, J. (1997). *Asphalt nation: How the automobile took over America and how we can take it back.* Crown, New York.

Holtzclaw, J. (1990). *Explaining urban density and transit impacts on auto use.* Report to Natural Resources Defense Council, Sierra Club, San Francisco.

Holtzclaw, J. (1994). *Using residential patterns and transit to decrease auto dependence and costs.* Natural Resources Defense Council.

Hothersall, D. C., and Salter, R. J. (1977). *Transport and the environment.* Granada Publishing Ltd, Great Britain.

Hough, M. (1984). *City form and natural process.* Routledge, London.

Howarth, C. I. (1976). The psychology of urban life. In Harrison, G. A., and Gibson, J. B. (eds.) *Man in urban environments.* Oxford University Press, Oxford.

Hu, G., and Kenworthy, J. (1996). A preliminary study of land use and transportation patterns in Chinese cities: Caging the automobile dragon. Paper presented to the Asia Research Centre, Murdoch University, Western Australia.

Hubbert, M. K. (1965). Energy resources. In Resources and Man. National Academy of Sciences, Freeman, San Francisco.

Hughes, T. L., and Dwyer, L. (1991). Where to now? Public sector cost savings of urban consolidation. Urban Futures 1(2): April.

Hughes Trueman Ludlow and Dwyer Leslie Pty Ltd. (1991). Public sector cost savings of urban consolidation: Final report. New South Wales Department of Planning, Sydney Water Board and Department of Planning, Technology and Commerce, Canberra, February.

Husler, W. (1990). Zurich—ein verdichtingstraun schafft sich luft, in Verkehr, Mensch, Umwelt, Zatu, E. V., Nurnberg.

Ife, J. (1995). Community development. Longman, Melbourne.

INRA Europe (1991). European attitudes to urban traffic problems and public transport. Survey for ECE and UITP, INRA Brussels, July.

Institut National de Recherche sur les Transports et leur Sécurité (1995). Budgets Energie Environnement des Déplacements (BEED) et Ile-de-France: Analyse de la Dépense Energétique at des Emissions Polluantes Liées à la Mobilité des Franciliens. Rapport de Convention ADEME-INRETS No. 690-9306-RB. INRETS, Arceuil, Paris.

International Council on Local Environmental Initiatives (ICLEI) (1996). The local agenda 21 planning guide: An introduction to sustainable development planning. ICLEI, UNEP, Toronto, Canada.

———. (1997). Cities to report success at COP 3. Initiatives, ICLEI, November.

Jacobs, J. (1961). The death and life of great American cities. Vintage Press, New York.

Jacobs, J. (1969). The economy of cities. Random House, New York.

Jacobs, J. (1984). Cities and the wealth of nations. Penguin, Harmondsworth.

Jacobs, J. (1994). Systems for survival: A dialogue on the moral foundations of commerce and politics. Vintage Books, New York.

Jacobs, J. (ed.) (1997). A schoolteacher in old Alaska: The story of Hannah Breece. Vintage, New York.

Jensen, O. M. (1994). Ecological building or just environmentally sound planning, Arkitektur DK 7: 353–367.

Jessiman, W. A., and Kocur, G. A. (1975). Light rail transit ridership attraction. Paper for the National Conference on Light Rail Transit, Philadelphia.

Johnson, E. (1994). Avoiding the collision of cities and cars: Urban transportation policy for the twenty-first century. American Academy of Arts and Sciences, Chicago.

Jordan, B. (1989). The common good: Citizenship, morality and self interest. Blackwell, Oxford.

Kageson, P. (1993). Getting the Prices right—A European scheme for making transport pay its true cost. European Federation for Transport and Environment, Stockholm and Brussels.

Kam, C. Y. (1993). Traffic management: Strategies, processes, techniques and assessment. In Wang, L. H., and Yeh, G. (eds.) Keep a city moving: Urban transportation management in Hong Kong. Asian Productivity Organisation, Tokyo.

Katz, P. (1994). The new urbanism: Toward an architecture of community. McGraw-Hill, New York.

Kaufmann, G. (1991). Current trends in planned unit developments (PUDs). In *The developer*, Proceedings of the 20th Naitonal Congress on the Urban Development Institute of Australia, Perth, March, pp. 19–27.

Keating, M. (1993). *The Earth Summit's agenda for change: A plain language version of Agenda 21 and the other Rio agreements*. Center for Our Common Future, Geneva.

Keefer, L. E. (1985). Joint development at transit stations in the United States. *Transportation* 12: 333–342.

Kemp, D. C. (1997). *Facilitating employment growth*. Western Australian Planning Commission, Perth.

Kemp, R. L. (1998). *America's cities: Problems and prospects*. Aldershot, Avebury.

Kenworthy, J. (1990). Don't shoot me I'm only the transport planner (apologies to Elton John). In Newman, P., Kenworthy, J., and Lyons, T. (eds.) *Transport energy conservation policies for Australian cities: Strategies for reducing automobile dependence*. ISTP, Murdoch University, Perth, Western Australia.

Kenworthy, J. R. (1991). The land use/transit connection in Toronto: Some lessons for Australian cities. *Australian Planner* 29(3): 149–154.

Kenworthy, J. (1995). Automobile dependence in Bangkok: An international comparison with implications for planning policies. *World Transport Policy and Practice* 1(3): 31–41.

Kenworthy, J. R. (1996). Bicycling the world: A global perspective on bicycles in cities and their role in reducing automobile dependence. Keynote paper to *Velo Australis*, *International Bicycle Conference*, October 27–November 1, 1996, Fremantle, Western Australia.

Kenworthy, J., and Newman, P. (1982). A driving cycle for Perth: Methodology and preliminary results. Presented to Joint SAE/ARRB Second Conference on Traffic, Energy and Emissions, Melbourne, May 19–21 (SAE Paper No. 82149).

Kenworthy, J., and Newman, P. (1991). *Moving Melbourne: A public transport strategy for inner Melbourne*. Inner Metropolitan Regional Association, Victoria and ISTP, Murdoch University, Western Australia.

Kenworthy, J., and Newman, P. (1992). *The economic and wider community benefits of the proposed East Perth redevelopment*. A commissioned report to the East Perth Redevelopment Authority, ISTP, Murdoch University.

Kenworthy, J. R., and Newman, P. W. G. (1993). *Automobile dependence: The irresistible force?* ISTP, Murdoch University, Western Australia.

Kenworthy, J., and Newman, P. (1994). Toronto—Paradigm regained. *Australian Planner* 31(3): 137–147.

Kenworthy, J. R., Newman, P. W. G., and Lyons, T. J. (1989). Urban planning and traffic congestion. *Urban Policy and Research* 7(2): 67–80.

Kenworthy, J. R., Newman, P. W. G., and Lyons, T. J. (1992). The ecology of urban driving—I: Methodology. *Transportation Research* 26A(3): 263–272.

Kenworthy, J. et al. (1994). Resisting automobile dependence in booming economies: A case study of Singapore, Tokyo and Hong Kong within a global sample of cities. Asian Studies Association of Australia Conference, *Environment, State and Society in Asia: The Legacy of the Twentieth Century*. Asia Research Centre, Murdoch University, July.

Kenworthy, J. R. et al. (1995). Is increasing automobile dependence inevitable in booming economies?: Asian cities in an international context. *IATSS Research* 19(2): 58–67.

Kenworthy, J. et al. (1997). *Indicators of transport efficiency in 37 cities*. Report to World Bank, ISTP, Murdoch University, Western Australia.

Kenworthy, J. et al (1999). *An international sourcebook of automobile dependence in cities, 1960–1990*. University Press of Colorado, Boulder (forthcoming).

King, A. D. (1978). Exporting planning: the colonial and neo-colonial experience. *Urbanism, Past and Present* 5: 12–22.

Kingsley, T. (1993). *Managing Urban Environmental Quality in Asia*, World Bank Technical Paper 220, Washington, D.C.

Kirwan, R. (1992). Urban form, energy and transport—A note on the Newman-Kenworthy thesis. *Urban Policy and Research* 10(1): 6–23.

Klein, J., and Olson, M. (1996). *Taken for a ride* (video). New Day Films, Yellow Springs, Ohio (55 minutes).

Knox, P. (1982). *Urban social geography: An introduction*. Longman, New York.

Korte, C. (1976). The impact of urbanization on social behaviour: A comparison of the United States and the Netherlands. *Urban Affairs Quarterly* 12(1): 21–36.

Kostoff, F. (1991). *The city shaped: Urban patterns and meanings through history*. Thames and Hudson, London.

Kreimer, A. et al. (1993). *Towards a sustainable urban environment: The Rio de Janeiro study*. World Bank Discussion Paper 195, Washington, D.C.

Kumar, S. (1995). From cities of greed to cities of God. *Resurgence* 167: 38–40.

Kunstler, J. H. (1993). *The geography of nowhere*. Touchstone, New York.

LaBelle, S. J., and Moses, D. O. (1982). *Technology assessment of productive conservation in urban transportation (ANL/ES130)*. Energy and Environmental Systems Division, Argonne National Laboratory.

Landmarc (1992). *Rural strategy report*. Shire of Serpentine-Jarrahdale, Perth, Western Australia.

Laquian, A. A. (1993). *Planning and development of metropolitan regions*. Proceedings of Conference, Bangkok, June/July, Asian Urban Research Network, Centre for Human Settlements, School of Community & Regional Planning, UBC, Canada.

Lasch, C. (1978). *The culture of narcissism*. Norton, New York.

Lasch, C. (1985). *The minimal self: Psychic survival in troubled times*. Pan Books, London.

Laube, F. B. (1995). *Fully integrated transport networks: An international perspective on applied solutions*, Ticketing Technologies Conference, Park Royal, Darling Harbour, Sydney.

Laube, F. B. (1997). *Optimising urban passenger transport: Developing a least-cost model based on international comparison of urban transport cost, transport patterns, land use, infrastructure, environmental and best practice in public transport*. Ph.D. thesis, Murdoch University, Perth, Western Australia.

Lave, C. (1992). Cars and demographics. *Access* 1: 4–11.

Lawton, R. (ed.) (1989). *The rise and fall of great cities*. Belhaven, London.

Lindegger, M., and Tap, R. (1989). *Conceptual permaculture report: Crystal Waters permaculture village*. Nascimanere Pty Ltd, Nambour, Queensland, Australia.

Linneman, P., and Gyourko, J. (1997). *The influence of city parks in local firm and neighbourhood development*. Report to the Farimount Park Commission, Wharton Real Estate Center, University of Pennsylvania, Philadelphia.

Linstone, H. A., and Mitroff, J. (1994). *The challenge of the 21st century: Managing technology and ourselves in a shrinking world.* State University of New York, New York.

Litman, T. (1998). *Generated traffic: Implications for transport planning.* Presentation to World Bank, Victoria Transport Policy Institute, Canada, January.

Lowe, M. D. (1990). Alternatives to the automobile: Transport for livable cities. *Worldwatch Paper 98,* October.

Lowe, M. D. (1994). Re-inventing transport. In Brown, L. R. et al. (eds.) *State of the world 1994,* Earthscan, London.

Lucy, W., and Phillips, D. (1995). Why some suburbs thrive. *Planning,* June, pp. 20–21.

Luymes, D. (1997). The fortification of suburbia; investigating the rise of enclave communites. *Landscape and Urban Planning* 39: 187–203.

MacGill, G., and Dawkins, J. (1988). Fremantle: An urban conservation success story. In Newman, P., Neville, S., and Duxbury, L. (1988). *Case studies in environmental hope.* Environmental Protection Authority for the Western Australian State Conservation Strategy, Perth.

MacIntyre, A. C. (1981). *After virtue: A study in moral theory.* Duckworth, London.

MacKenzie, J. J. (1994). *The keys to the car: Electric and hydrogen vehicles for the 21st century.* World Resources Institute, Baltimore.

Macklin, R. J. (1977). *Public open space in sub-divisions.* City of Wangaratta, Australia.

MacNeill, J., Cox, J. E., and Jackson, I. (1991). Sustainable development —The urban challenge. *Ekistics* 348: 195–198.

Manning, I. (1978). *The journey-to-work.* George Allen and Unwin, Sydney.

Marsh, G. (1864). *Man and nature: Or physical geography as modified by human action.* Lowenthal, D. (ed.) (1965). Harvard University Press, Cambridge, Massachusetts.

Marshall, P. (1992). *Nature's web: An exploration of ecological thinking.* Simon and Schuster, London.

Massey, D., and Denton, N. (1993). *American apartheid: Segregation of the making of the underclass.* Harvard University Press, Cambridge, Massachusetts.

Mathews, J. (1989). *The age of democracy: The politics of postfordism.* Oxford University Press, Melbourne.

Mathews, J. (1994). *Catching the wave: Workplace reform in Australia.* Allen and Unwin, Sydney.

McDonough, W. (1993). *Design, ecology, ethics and the making of things.* Sermon, Cathedral of St. John the Divine, New York. School of Architecture, University of Virginia, Charlottesville.

McGlynn, G., and Andrews, J. (1991). *The economic cost-benefits of urban scenarios that support ecologically sustainable development.* ESD Transport Working Group Paper, September.

McGlynn, G., Newman, P., and Kenworthy, J. (1991). *Towards better cities: Reurbanisation and transportation energy scenarios.* Australian Commission for the Future, October.

McHarg, I. (1969). *Design with nature.* Natural History Press, Garden City, New York, reprinted in 1992 by John Wiley.

McKamant, K., and Durrett, C. (1988). *Co-housing: A contemproary approach to housing ourselves.* Ten Speed Press, Berkeley, California.

McKenzie, J. J., and Walsh, M. P. (1990). *Driving forces: Motor vehicle trends and their im-*

plications for global warming, energy strategies and transportation planning. World Resources Institute, Washington, D.C.

Mees, P. (1999). *A very public solution.* University of Melbourne Press, Melbourne (forthcoming).

Metcalfe, S. (1990). Evolution and economic change. In Silburton, A. (ed.) *Technology and economic progress.* MacMillan, London.

Mills, J. R. (1989). Keynote address to: *Light rail transit: New system successes at affordable prices.* Transportation Research Board, Special Report 221, Washington, D.C.

Minister of Transport (1963). *Traffic in towns.* London, HMSO.

Ministry of Housing, Ministry of Transport and Public Works, Ministry of Economic Affairs (1991). *The right business in the right place: Towards a location policy for business and services in the interests of accessibility and the environment.* Netherlands Government, The Hague.

Ministry of Transport and Public Works (1982). *From local traffic to pleasurable living.* Ministry of Transport and Public Works, The Netherlands.

Mitlin, D. and Satterthwaite, D. (1994). *Cities and sustainable development.* Discussion paper for UN Global Forum, 1994, Manchester. IIED, London.

Moffet, J. (1991). *The price of mobility.* Draft, Natural Resources Defense Council, San Francisco.

Mollinson, W. (1988). *Permaculture: A designer's manual.* Tagari, NSW.

Moltman, J. (1967). *The theology of hope.* SCM Press, London.

Monheim, R. (1988). Pedestrian zones in West Germany—The dynamic development of an effective instrument to enliven the city centre. In Hass-Klau, C. (ed.) *New life for city centres.* Anglo German Foundation, London.

Moran, T., Evangelisti, M., McAulliffe, T., Mouritz, M., and Palmer, P. (1993). *Water sensitive urban residential design guidelines,* EPA, DPUD & WAWA, Western Australian Government, Perth.

Morehouse, W. (ed.) (1989). *Building sustainable communities: Tools and concepts for self reliant economic change.* Bootstrap, New York.

Morris, D. (1982). *Self reliant cities: Energy and the transformation of urban America.* Sierra Club Books, San Francisco.

Morris, W., and Kaufman, C. (1996). *Mixed use development: New designs for new livelihoods.* Department of Tourism, Small Business and Industry, Canberra.

Mougeot, L. J. A. (1998). Farming inside and around cities. *Urban Age* 5(3): 18–23.

Mouritz, M. (1997). *Sustainable urban water systems.* Ph.D. thesis, ISTP, Murdoch University, Perth, Western Australia.

Mumford, L. (1938). *The culture of cities.* Harcourt, New York.

Mumford, L. (1961). *The city in history.* Penguin, Harmondsworth, England.

Munkstrap, N., and Lindberg, J. (1996). *Urban ecology guide to Greater Copenhagen.* Danish Town Planning Institute, Copenhagen.

Naess, P. (1993a). *Energy use for transport in 22 Nordic towns.* NIBR Report No 2, Norwegian Institute for Urban and Regional Research, Oslo.

Naess, P. (1993b). Transportation energy in swedish towns and regions. *Scandinavian Housing and Planning Research* 10: 187–206.

Naess, P. (1995). *Urban form and energy use for transport: A Nordic experience.* Ph.D. thesis, Norwegian Institute of Technology.

Naisbett, J. (1994). *Global paradox: The bigger the world economy, the more powerful its smaller players*. Allen & Unwin, Sydney.

National Commission on the Environment (1993). *Choosing a sustainable future*. Island Press, Washington, D.C.

NCPA (1990). *MFP: An urban development concept*. A Report to the Department of Industry, Technology and Commerce, NCPA, July.

Neale, A. (1995). How green are congestion charges? Economic instruments and sustainable development. *International Journal of Urban and Regional Research* 3 (September): 447–455.

Neff, J. W. (1996). *Substitution rates between transit and automobile travel*. Paper presented at the Association of American Geographers' Annual Meeting, Charlotte, North Carolina, April.

Neutze, G. M. (1967). *Economic policy and the size of cities*. Augustus Kelley, New York.

Neutze, M. (1977). *Urban development in Australia*. George Allen and Unwin, Sydney.

Neutze, M. (1978). *Australian urban policy*. George Allen and Unwin, Sydney.

Newman, O. (1972). *Defensible space: Crime prevention through urban design*. MacMillan, New York.

Newman, P. (1974). Environmental Impact Part I and Part II. *Journal of Environmental Systems* 4(2): 97–108 and 109–117.

Newman, P. (1975). An ecological model for city structure and development. *Ekistics* 40(239): 258–265.

Newman, P. (1986). Lessons from Liverpool. *Planning and Administration* 1, 32–42.

Newman, P. (1988a). Australian Cities at the Crossroads. *Current Affairs Bulletin* 65(7): 4–15.

Newman, P. (1988b). Fremantle and the America's Cup. *Architecture Australia* 77(2): 72–76.

Newman, P. (1990). Sustainable development. *Environmental Education and Information* 8(4): 250–261.

Newman, P. (1991a). *The noxious industry transition*. ISTP Occasional Paper No. 3, Murdoch University, Perth.

Newman, P. (1991b). Social organisation for ecological sustainability: Towards a more sustainable settlement pattern. In Cock, P. (ed.) *Fundamental Questions Paper No. 11*, Centre for Resource and Environmental Studies, ANU, Canberra.

Newman, P. W. G. (1992). The rebirth of the Perth suburban railways. In Hedgcock, D., and Yiftachel, O. (eds.) *Urban and regional planning in WA: Historical and critical perspectives*. Paradigm Press, Perth.

Newman, P. (1993). Sustainable development and urban planning. *Sustainable development* 1(1): 25–40.

Newman, P. W. G. (1994a). The transport dilemma in developing nation cities. In Jayasuriya, L., and Lee, M. (ed.) *Social dimensions of development*, Paradigm Books, Perth.

Newman, P. (1994b). Urban environmental quality and economic competitiveness: An Australian perspective. *OECD Conference*, Melbourne, November.

Newman, P. (1994c). The end of the urban freeway. *World Transport Policy and Practice* 1(1): 12–19.

Newman, P. W. G. (1996a). Transport. In UNCHS *An urbanising world: Global report on human settlements*. UNCHS, Habitat and UNEP, Nairobi.

Newman, P. W. G. (1996b). Greening the city: The ecological and human dimensions of the city can be part of town planning. *Alternatives* 22(2): 10–17.

Newman, P. W. G. (1997). Environmental ethics and cities. Presented to EcoPolitics Conference, University of Melbourne, Melbourne.

Newman, P. W. G., and Hogan, T. L. F. (1981). A review of urban density models: Towards a resolution of the conflict between populace and planner. *Human Ecology* 9(3): 269–303.

Newman, P. and Hogan, T. (1987). Urban density and transport: A single model based on three city types. *Transport Research Paper 1/87*, Environmental Science, Murdoch University, Perth, Western Australia.

Newman, P. W. G., and Kenworthy, J. R. (1984). The use and abuse of driving cycle research: Clarifying the relationship between traffic congestion, energy and emissions. *Transportation Quarterly* 38(4): 615–635.

Newman, P. W. G., and Kenworthy, J. R. (1988). The transport energy trade-off: Fuel-efficient traffic versus fuel-efficient cities. *Transportation Research* 22A(3): 163–174.

Newman, P., and Kenworthy, J. (1989a). *Cities and automobile dependence: An international sourcebook*. Gower, Aldershot, England.

Newman, P., and Kenworthy, J. (1989b). Gasoline consumption and cities: A comparison of US cities with a global survey and its implications. *Journal of American Planning Association* 55(1): 24–37.

Newman, P. W. G., and Kenworthy, J. R. (1990). *Transport energy conservation policies for Australian cities: Strategies for reducing automobile dependence*. ISTP, Murdoch University, Perth, Western Australia.

Newman, P., and Kenworthy, J. (1991). *Towards a more sustainable Canberra: An assessment of Canberra's transport, energy and land use*. Institute for Science and Technology Policy, Murdoch University.

Newman, P. and Kenworthy, J. (1992a). Is there a role for physical planning? Counterpoint. *Journal of American Planning Association*, Summer, pp. 353–362.

Newman, P. W. G., and Kenworthy, J. R. (1992b). Transit oriented urban villages: Design solutions for the 90's. *Urban Futures* 2(1): 50–56.

Newman, P., and Kenworthy, J., with Robinson, L. (1992). *Winning back the cities*. Australian Consumers Association and Pluto Press, Sydney.

Newman, P. W. G., Kenworthy, J. R., and Laube, F. (1997). The global city and sustainability. *Fifth International Workshop on Technological Change and Urban Form*, Jakarta, June.

Newman, P. W. G., Kenworthy, J. R., and Lyons, T. J. (1985). Transport energy use in the Perth Metropolitan Region: Some urban policy implications. *Urban Policy and Research* 3(2): 4–15.

Newman, P. W. G., Kenworthy, J. R. and Lyons, T. J. (1988). Does free flowing traffic save energy and lower emissions in cities? *Search* 19(5/6): 267–272.

Newman, P. W. G., Kenworthy, J. R. and Lyons, T. J. (1992). The ecology of urban driving—II: Driving cycles across a city, their validation and implications. *Transportation Research* 26A(3): 273–290.

Newman, P., Kenworthy, J., and Vintila, P. (1992). *Housing transport and urban form*.

National Housing Strategy, Background Paper 15, Commonwealth of Australia, Canberra.

Newman, P. W. G., Kenworthy, J. R., and Vintila, P. (1995). Can we overcome automobile dependence?: Physical planning in an age of urban cynicism. *Cities* 12(1): 53–65.

Newman, P. W. G. et al. (1996). Human settlements. In *Australian state of the environment report*, Department of Environment, Sport and Territories, Australian Government Publishing Service, Canberra.

Newman, P. W. G. et al. (1997). *Car-free Copenhagen: Perspectives and ideas for reducing car-dependence in Copenhagen*. Royal Danish Academy of Fine Arts, Copenhagen.

Niemczynowicz, J. (1992). Water management and urban development: a call for realistic alternatives for the future. *Impact of Science on Society* 42(2): 133–147.

Noorman, K. J., and Uiterkamp, T. S. (1998). *Green households? Domestic consumers, environment and sustainability*. Earthscan, London.

Nowlan, D., and Nowlan, N. (1970). *The bad trip: The untold story of the Spadina Expressway*. Toronto New Press, House of Anansi, Toronto.

Nowlan, D. M., and Stewart, G. (1992). The effect of downtown population growth on commuting trips: Some recent Toronto experience. *Journal of the American Planning Association* 57(2): 165–182.

OECD (1988). *Cities and transportation*. OECD, Paris.

OECD (1996). *Innovative policies for sustainable development: The ecological city*. Project Group on the Ecological City, OECD.

OECD/ECMT (1995). *Urban travel and sustainable development*. OECD, Paris.

Ohmae, K. (1990). *The borderless world*. Fontana, London.

1000 Friends of Oregon (1993). *The pedestrian environment*. LUTRAQ Report, Portland.

1000 Friends of Oregon (1997a). *Making the connections: Technical report*. 1000 Friends of Oregon, Portland.

1000 Friends of Oregon (1997b). *Making the connections: Summary of LUTRAQ*. Thousand Friends of Oregon, Portland.

Osborne, F. (1948). *Our plundered planet*. Little Brown, Boston.

Paaswell, R. E. and Berechman, J. (1982). Light rail and development: Constraints and conditions. In TRB Special Report 195, *Light rail transit: Planning, design and implementation*. Transportation Research Board, National Research Council, Washington, D.C.

Parenteau, R. (1994). Local action plans for sustainable communities. *Environment and Urbanisation* 6(2): 183–199.

Passmore, J. (1974). *Man's responsibility for nature*. Duckworth, London.

Paterson, D., and Connery, K. (1997). Reconfiguring the edge city: The use of ecological design parameters in defining the form of community. *Landscape and Urban Planning* 36(4): 327–346.

Patsaoures, N. (1993). *A shared vision: A new Los Angeles TR as a catalyst for remaking our city*. City of Los Angeles.

Pathways to Sustainability Conference (1997). *UN Conference*, City of Newcastle, NSW, Australia.

Pawley, M. (1975). *The private future*. Pan, London.

Pearce, F. (1997). Devil in the diesel. *New Scientist*, October 25.

Pederson, E. O. (1980). *Transportation in cities*. Pergamon, New York.

Peirce, N. (1998). Curbing sprawl: Tennessee's surprise breakthrough. *Washington Post*, October 11.

Perl, A., and Pucher, J. (1995). Transit in trouble? The policy challenge posed by Canada's changing urban mobility. *Canadian Public Policy* 21(3): 261–283.

Pezzoli, K. (1996). *Sustainable development: A transdisciplinary overview of the literature*. Paper at joint international congress of Collegiate Schools of Planning and the Association of the European Schools of Planning, Toronto, July.

Pharoah, T. M. (1990). *Traffic calming: A pictorial overview*. Department of Planning, Housing and Development, South Bank Polytechnic, London.

Pharoah, T., and Apel, D. (1995). *Transport concepts in European cities*. Aldershot, Avebury.

Pharoah, T. and Russell, J. (1989). *Traffic calming: Policy evaluation in three European countries*. Occasional Paper 2/89, Department of Planning, Housing and Development, South Bank Polytechnic, London.

Pickrell, D. H. (1990). *Urban rail transit projects: Forecasts versus actual ridership costs*. U.S. Department of Transportation, Cambridge, Massachusetts.

Pindyck, R. S. (1979). *The structure of world energy demand*. MIT Press, Cambridge, Massachusetts.

Piore, M. J., and Sabel C. F. (1984). *The second industrial divide: Possibilities for prosperity*. Basic Books, New York.

Poboon, C. (1997). *Anatomy of a traffic disaster: Towards sustainable solutions to Bangkok's transportation problems*. Ph.D. dissertation, ISTP, Murdoch University, Perth, Western Australia.

Poboon, C., and Kenworthy, J. R. (1995). *Bangkok: Towards a sustainable traffic solution*. Paper presented to Urban Habitat Conference, Delft, The Netherlands, February.

Poboon, C., and Kenworthy, J. R. (1997). Bangkok's traffic disaster: An international comparative assessment of transportation and land use in Bangkok with its implications for air quality. Presented to *Pathways to Sustainability Conference*, Newcastle, NSW, Australia, June.

President's Council on Sustainable Development (1997). *Sustainable communities*. Taskforce Report, Washington, D.C.

Pucher, J. and Clorer, S. (1992). Taming the automobile in Germany. *Transportation Quarterly* 46(3): 383–395.

Pucher, J., and Lefévere, C. (1995). *The urban transport crisis in Europe and North America*. MacMillan, London.

Pun, K. S. (1980). Urban planning principles in Hong Kong—Concepts and approaches. *Asian Architect and Builder*, December, pp. 48–56.

Pushkarev, B. S., and Zupan, J. M. (1977). *Public transportation and land use policy*. Indiana University Press, Bloomington and London.

Putnam, R. (1993). *Making democracy work: Civic tradition in modern Italy*. Princeton University Press, Princeton, New Jersey.

Raad, T., and Kenworthy, J. (1998). The US and us. *Alternatives Journal* 24(1): 14–22.

Rabinovitch, J. (1992). Curitiba: Towards sustainable development. *Environment and Urbanisation* 4(2): 62–73.

Rabinowitz, H. et al. (1991). *The new suburb*. U.S. Department of Transportation, Report No. DOT-T-91-12.

Radberg, J. (1995). Termite's heap or rural villages? The problems of urban density and sustainability. In *The European city—Sustaining urban quality,* Proceedings of Conference, Copenhagen, Ministry of Environment and Energy, Copenhagen, April.

Rainbow, R., and Tan, H. (1993). Meeting the demand for mobility. *Selected papers*. Shell International, London.

Real Estate Research Corporation (1974). *The costs of sprawl*. RERC and Council of Environmental Quality, Washington, D.C.

Register, R. (1987). *Ecocity Berkeley*. North Atlantic Books, Berkeley, California.

Register, R. (ed.) (1990). *Proceedings of first international ecocity conference*. Urban Ecology, Berkeley, California.

Register, R., and Peeks, B. (1997). *Village wisdom: Future cities*. Ecocity Builders, Oakland, California.

Richardson, B. M. (1973). *The economics of city size*. Saxon House, London.

Richmond, H. R. (1994). The prospects for land use reform in America: Storm clouds or silver lining? Address to Greenspace Alliance, Philadelphia, September 29.

Roberts J. (1988). Where's downtown? 'It went three years ago.' *Town and Country Planning*, May, pp. 139–141.

Roberts, J. (1989a). *User-friendly cities: What Britain can learn from mainland Europe*. TEST, London.

Roberts, J. (1989b). *Quality streets: How traditional urban centres benefit from traffic calming*. TEST, London.

Roberts, J. (1991). *Wrong side of the tracks*. TEST, London.

Roelofs, J. (1996). *Greening cities*. Keene State College, Keene, New Hampshire.

Roseland, M. (1998). *Towards sustainable communities*, 2nd ed. Canadian National Round Table on the Environment and the Economy, Ottawa.

Rosenbaum, D. P. (ed.) (1986). *Community crime prevention: Does it work?* Sage, Beverley Hills.

Royal Commission on Environmental Pollution (1994). *Transport and the environment*. HMSO, London.

Saldinger, M. (1992). *Small scale wastewater treatment technologies—A guide*. Institute for Science and Technology Policy, Murdoch University, Perth, Western Australia.

Sale, K. (1980). *Human scale*. Basic Books, New York.

Sale, K. (1985). *Dwellers in the land*. Sierra Club Books, San Francisco.

Sandercock, L. (1975). *Cities for sale*. University of Melbourne Press, Melbourne.

Sarkissian, W., and Walsh, K. (1996). *Community participation in practice series*, 3 books and a video. ISTP, Murdoch University, Perth, Western Australia.

Sassen, S. (1994). *Cities and the world economy*. Pineforge Press, Thousand Oaks, California.

Schafer, A., and Victor, D. (1997). *Scientific American*. Special edition on transportation, October.

Scheurer, J. (1998a). *Car-free housing in Europe: A new approach to sustainable residential development*. Discussion Paper, ISTP web site, www.istp.murdoch.edu.au.

Scheurer, J. (1998b). *Evaluation of Danish ecological housing and planning*. ISTP, Murdoch

University, Perth and Danish Forest and Landscape Research Institute, Copenhagen.

Schmitt, R. C. (1963). Implications of density in Hong Kong. *Journal of American Planning Association* 29: 210–211.

Schmitt, R. C. (1966). Density health and social disorganisation. *Journal of American Planning Association* 32: 38–40.

Schmitt, R. C., Zane, L. Y. S., and Nishi, S. (1978). Density health and social disorganisation revisited. *Journal of American Planning Association* 44 (2): 209–211

Schneider, K. (1979). *On the nature of cities: Towards creative and enduring human environments*. Jossey-Bass, San Francisco.

Schoup, D. (1994). Commuting, congestion and air pollution: The free parking connection. UCLA Conference, *The transportation, land use, air quality connection*, UCLA Extension, California.

Schumacher, E. F. (1974). *Small is beautiful: Economics as if people mattered*. Abacus, London.

Schumacher, E. F. (1980). *Good work*. Abacus, London.

Schumacher, E. F. (1985). *A guide to the perplexed*. Abacus, London.

Schumann, J. W. (1989). What's new in North American light rail transit projects? In *Light rail transit: New system successes at affordable prices*, Transportation Research Board, Special Report 221, Washington, D.C.

Selman, P. (1996). *Local sustainability: Managing and planning ecologically sound places*. Paul Chapman Publishing, London.

Sennett, R. (1974). *The fall of public man*. Cambridge University Press, Cambridge.

Serageldin, I., and Barrett, R. (1993). *Environmentally sustainable urban transport: Defining a global policy*. World Bank, Washington, D.C.

Sherlock, H. (1991). *Cities be good for us: The case for close knit communities, local shops and public transport*. Paladin, London.

Shore, W. B. (1995). Recentralisation: The simple answer to more than a dozen United States problems and a major answer to poverty. *Journal of American Planning Association* 61(4): 446–503.

Silas, J. (1993). *Surabaya 1293–1993: A city of partnership*. Municipal Government of Surabaya.

Sirolli, E. (1995). *Ripples in the Zambesi: Passion, unpredictability and economic development*. ISTP, Murdoch University, Perth, Western Australia.

Sitarz, D. (ed.) (1994). *Agenda 21*. Earthpress, Boulder, Colorado.

Slocombe, D. S. (1993). Environmental planning, ecosystem science and ecosystem approaches for integrating environment and development. *Environmental Management* 17(3): 289–303.

Smit, J., Ratta, A., and Nasr, J. (1996). *Urban agriculture: Food, jobs and sustainable cities*. UNDP, New York.

Smith, M. A. F., Whitelegg, J., and Williams, N. (1998). *Greening the built environment*. Earthscan Publications, London.

Smith, R. (1997). Creative destruction: Capitalist development and China's environment. *New Left Review* 222: 3–42

Snell, B. (1974). *American ground transport: A proposal for restructuring the automobile, bus and rail industries*. U.S. Government Printing Office, Washington, D.C.

Spearitt, P. (1978). *Sydney since the 20's*. Hale and Ironmonger, Sydney.

Sperling, D. (1995). *Future drive: Electric vehicles and sustainable transportation.* Island Press, Washington, D.C.

Standing Advisory Committee on Trunk Road Assessment (SACTRA) (1994). *Trunk roads and the generation of traffic.* Department of Transport, United Kingdom.

Statistische Berichte des Kantons Zürich (1991). *Verkehrsverhalten im Kanton Zürich 1989.* Statistisches Amt des Kantons Zürich, Heft 4/1991, pp. 18–37.

Sternlieb, G. (1973). *Housing development and municipal costs.* Centre for Urban Policy Research, Rutgers University Press, New Brunswick, New Jersey.

Stocker, L., and Barnett, K. (1998). The significance and praxis of community based sustainability projects: Community gardens in Western Australia. *Local Environment* 3(2): 179–189.

Stocker, L. and Pollard, L. (1992). *In my backyard: Community based sustainable development.* ISTP, Murdoch University, Perth, Western Australia.

Stockholms Stadsbyggnadskontor (1972). *Stockholm urban environment.* Stockholm.

Stren R., White R., and Whitney J. (eds.) (1992). *Sustainable cities.* Westview Press, Boulder, Colorado.

Stretton, H. (1975). *Ideas for Australian cities,* 2nd ed. Georgian House, Melbourne.

Sucher, D. (1995). *City comforts: How to build an urban village.* City Comforts Press, Seattle.

Surface Transportation Policy Project (1994). *A citizens guide to transportation planning and livable communities.* STTP, New York.

———. (1998a). Smart growth and the market. *Progress* 8(1): 1–11.

———. (1998b). TEA-21—More than a free refill. *Progress* 8(4): 1–11.

Sustainable Human Habitat Consultants (1994). *Sustainable urban development in the Jerrabomberra Valley 1994 to 2020.* Winning Entry for National Ideas Competition for ESUD, University of Melbourne.

Suzuki, D. (1997). *The sacred balance: Rediscovering our place in nature.* Allen and Unwin, Vancouver.

Tennyson, E. L. (1985). Value of light rail transit as a major capital investment. In *Light rail transit: System design for cost-effectiveness.* State-of-the-art Report 2, Transportation Research Board, National Research Council, Washington, D.C.

Thomas, J. F., and McLeod, P. B. (1992). *Australian research priorities in the urban water services and utilities area.* Division of Water Resources Paper No. 7, CSIRO.

Tibbs, H. B. C. (1992). Industial ecology: An agenda for environmental management. *Whole Earth Review* (Winter)77: 4–19.

Tickell, O. (1993). Driven by dogma. *Geographical,* October, pp. 20–24.

Tjallingii, S. P. (1993). *The responsible city.* International Federation for Housing and Planning. International Conference, Berlin.

Tjallingii, S. P. (1995). *Ecopolis: Strategies for ecologically sound urban development.* Backhuys Publishers, Leiden.

Todd, J., and Tukel, G. (1981). *Rehabilitating cities and towns: Designing for sustainability.* Planet Drum, San Francisco.

Tolley, R. (1990). *Calming traffic in residential areas.* Brefi Press, Wales, UK.

Topp, H. H. (1990). *Traffic safety, usability and streetscape effects of new design principles for urban arterial roads.* Presented to the International Congress on Living and Moving in Cities, Paris, France, January 29–31.

Toynbee, A. (1978). *Mankind and mother earth.* Book Club Association, London.

Toyota Motor Corporation (1990). *Roads for people and cars: Considerations for residential areas*. The Wheel Extended 73, International Public Affairs Division, Tokyo.

Trainer, T. (1985). *Abandon affluence*. Zed Books, London.

Trainer, T. (1995). *The conserver society: Alternatives for sustainability*. Zed Books, London.

Trancik, R. (1986). *Finding lost space: Theories of urban design*. Van Nostrand, New York.

Transit Coooperative Research Program (TCRP) (1995). *Regional transit corridors: The land use connection*. Parsons, Brinkherhoff, Quade and Douglas, Inc., Robert Cervero, Howard/Stein Hudson Associates and Jefferey Zupan, Transportation Research Board, Washington, D.C.

Transport and Environment Studies (TEST) (1989). *Quality streets—How traditional urban centres benefit from traffic calming*. TEST, London.

Transportation Research Board (1995). *Expanding metropolitan highways: Implications for air quality and energy use*. TRB, Washington, D.C.

Tranter, P. (1993). *Children's mobility in Canberra: Confinement or independence*. University College, The University of NSW, Australian Defence Force Academy, Monograph Series No. 7.

Troy, P. N. (1992). Lets look at that again. *Urban Policy and Research* 10(1): 41–49

Troy, P. N. (1996). *The perils of urban consolidation*. The Federation Press, Leichardt, Sydney.

UN Centre for Human Settlements (1996). *An urbanising world: Global review of human settlements 1996*. Habitat, Nairobi.

UN Centre for Human Settlements (1997). *Changing consumption patterns in human settlements*. A Dicussion Paper, UN Centre for Human Settlements, Nairobi.

UN Development Program (1996). *Human development report 1996*. UNDP, New York.

United Nations (1987). Fertility behaviour in the context of development. United Nations Population Division, New York

Urban Redevelopment Authority (1991). *Living the next lap: Towards a tropical city of excellence*. URA, Singapore.

Van der Ryn, S., and Calthorpe, P. (1986). *Sustainable communities: A new design synthesis for cities, suburbs and towns*. Sierra Club Books, San Francisco.

Vintila, P. (1996). Planning for accessible public transport: Recent Australian experience and its lessons for New Zealand. *New Zealand Journal of Disabilities* 2: 93–114.

Vintila, P., Phillimore, J., and Newman, P. (1992). *Markets, morals and manifestos: Fightback! and the politics of economic rationalism in the 1990's*. ISTP, Murdoch University, Perth, Western Australia.

Voran Consultants (1991). *A comparison of urban consolidation and fringe development—Housing costs and benefits*. For Homeswest and Department of Health, Housing and Community Services, Perth.

Vuchic, V. R. (1981). *Urban transit: Systems and technology*. Prentice-Hall, Englewood Cliffs, New Jersey.

Vuchic, V. R. (1989). The great debate: Potential roles of different transit modes. In *Light rail transit: New system successes at affordable prices*. Transportation Research Board, Special Report 221, Washington, D.C., pp. 62–65.

WA Planning Commission (1997). *Livable neighbourhoods community design code*. WA Planning Commission, Perth.

Wachs, M., and Crawford, M. (1991). *The car and the city: The automobile, the built environment and daily urban life*. University of Michigan Press, Ann Arbor.

Wackernagel, M., and Rees, W. (1996). *Our ecological footprint: Reducing human impact on the earth.* New Society Publishers, Philadelphia.

Wagner, C. (1997). *Car sharing: More mobility, preservation of the environment and savings in your pocket.* http://members.aol.com/carsharing/links.html.

Wake, D. (1997). *A green belt for Perth.* Honours thesis, ISTP, Murdoch University, Petth, Western Australia.

Walker, R. A. (1978). The transformation of urban structure in the nineteenth century and the beginnings of suburbanisation. In Cox, E. (ed.) *Urbanisation and conflict in market societies.* Methuen, London.

Walker, L., and Kanaki, T. (1988). The reality of world oil production, demand and future prices. *Chemical Engineering in Australia* 14(4): 6–9.

Waller, D. H. (1989). Rain water—An alternative source in developing and developed countries. *Water International* 14: 27–36.

Wallis, J. (1994). Alive to God. *Journal of Sojourners,* Washington, D.C.

Walter, R., Arkin, L., and Crenshaw, R. (eds.) (1992). *Sustainable cities: Concepts and strategies for eco-city development.* Eco-Home Media, Los Angeles.

Wang, L. H., and Yeh, A. G .O. (eds.) (1993). *Keep a city moving: Urban transportation management in Hong Kong.* Asian Productivity Organisation, Tokyo.

Ward, P. (1988). The great Australian sprawl. *The Weekend Australian,* November 12–13.

Wardlaw, H. (1998). The United Nations Urban Renewal and Development Project, Singapore, 1967–1971. In *The twentieth century urban planning experience,* Proceedings of the 8th International Planning Society Conference and 4th Australian Planning/Urban History Conference, University of New South Wales, July 15–18. Faculty of the Built Environment, The University of NSW, Sydney, pp. 941–946.

Warner, S. B. (1968). *The private city.* University of Pennsylvania Press, Philadelphia.

Warren, K. (ed.) (1997). *Ecological feminism.* Routledge, London.

Water Sensitive Urban Design Research Group (1990). *Water sensitive residential design: An investigation into its purpose and potential in the Perth Metropolitan Region.* WAWRC, Perth.

Watson, S., and Gibson, K. (eds.) (1995). *Postmodern cities and spaces.* Blackwell, Oxford.

Watt, K. D. F. (1982). *Understanding the environment.* Allyn and Bacon, Boston.

Webber, M. (1963). Order in diversity: Community without Propinquity. In Wingo, L. (ed.) *Cities and space: The future use of urban land,* John Hopkins University Press, Baltimore.

Webber, M. (1964). The urban place and the non-place urban realm. In *Explorations in urban structures.* University of Pennsylvania Press, Philadelphia.

Webber, M. (1968). The post city age. *Daedalus* 97(4): 1093–1099

Weyrich, J., and Lind, F. (1996). *Conservatives and mass transit.* Free Congress Foundation, Washington, D.C.

Wheaton, W. C. (1982). The long-run structure of transportation and gasoline demand. *Bell Journal of Economics* 13(2): 439–454.

White, G. (1990). *The natural history of Selborne.* Penguin, Harmondsworth.

White, L. (1967). The historical roots of the ecological crisis. *Science* 155: 1203–1207

White, M., and White, L. (1962). *The intellectual versus the city: From Thomas Jefferson to Frank Lloyd Wright.* Harvard University Press, Cambridge, Massachusetts.

Whitelegg, J. (1993). *Transport for a sustainable future: The case for Europe*. Belhaven Press, London.

Wickham, E. D. (1987). Social malaise in urban areas and the concept of the city. In Milward, S. (ed.) *Urban Harvest*. Geographical Publications, London.

Williams, D. (1997). 'Pay as you drive' is the only solution say road experts. *London Evening Standard*, October 20.

Williams, R. (1985). *The country and the city*. Hogarth Press, London.

Willoughby, K. (1994). The 'local milieux' of knowledge based industries. In Brotchie, J. et al. (eds.) *Cities in competition*. Cheshire, Melbourne.

Wilson, P. (1976). *Public housing for Australia*. University of Queensland Press, Brisbane.

Winger, A. R. (1997). Finally: A withering aways of cities? *Futures* 29(3): 251–256.

Wolman, A. (1965). The metabolism of the city. *Scientific American* 213: 179

Wood, B. (1984). *E. F. Schumacher: His life and thought*. Harper and Row, New York.

Woodroffe, A. (1994). *Optimal urban population density: A case study in minimising energy use in transport and buildings*. ISTP Occasional Paper 1/94, Murdoch University, Perth, Western Australia.

World Bank (1994). *World development report 1994*. Oxford University Press, New York.

World Bank (1996). *Sustainable transport: Priorities for policy reform*. Development in Practice, The World Bank, Washington, D.C.

World Bank (1997). *Advancing sustainable development: The World Bank and Agenda 21*. The World Bank, Washington, D.C.

World Commission on Environment and Development (1989). *Our common future*. Oxford University Press, Oxford.

World Resources Institute (1996). *The urban environment*. WRI, UNEP, UNDP, World Bank, Oxford University Press, New York.

Wyse, J. (1990). Karlsruhe: Transit showpiece. In Ridley, T. M. (1990). *Light rail review 1*. Light Rail Transit Association, London.

Yanarella, E. J., and Levine, R. S. (1992). Does sustainable development lead to sustainability? *Futures* 24(8): 759–774.

Yeung, Y. M. (1977). High-rise, high density housing: myths and realities. *Habitat International* 2(5/6): 587–594.

Yoder, J. (1984). *The priestly kingdom*. University of Notre Dame Press, Notre Dame, Indiana.

Young, G., and Lindegger, M. (1990). *Cedar Lakes: Proposed group title development*. Permaculture Services, Crystal Waters, Queensland, Australia.

Zahavi, Y., and Ryan, J. M. (1980). Stability of travel components over time. *Transportation Research Record* 750: 19–26.

Zuckerman, W. (1992). *End of the road: The world car crisis and how to solve it*. Chelsea Green, Post Mills, Vermont.

Index

423